Gero Erdmann · Marianne Kneuer (Eds.)

Regression of Democracy?

Zeitschrift für Vergleichende Politikwissenschaft
Comparative Governance and Politics

Special Issue 1 | 2011

Gero Erdmann
Marianne Kneuer (Eds.)

Regression of Democracy?

Zeitschrift für Vergleichende
Politikwissenschaft
Comparative Governance and Politics

Special Issue 1 | 2011

VS VERLAG

Zeitschrift für Vergleichende Politikwissenschaft. Comparative Governance and Politics (ZfVP)
www.zfvp.de 2007 gegründet von Hans-Joachim Lauth

Herausgeber: Arbeitskreis „Demokratieforschung" der Deutschen Vereinigung für Politische Wissenschaft (DVPW), vertreten durch Prof. Dr. Hans-Joachim Lauth, Prof. Dr. Marianne Kneuer, Dr. Gero Erdmann und Prof. Dr. Gert Pickel.

Beirat: Heidrun Abromeit (Darmstadt), Arthur Benz (Hagen), Dirk Berg-Schlosser (Marburg), Klaus von Beyme (Heidelberg), Hans Blomkvist (Uppsala), Peter Burnell (Warwick), Consuelo Cruz (Tufts University, Medford, MA), Jan van Deth (Mannheim), Danica Fink-Hafner (Ljubljana), Adrienne Héritier (EUI Florenz), Kenji Hirashima (Tokio), Hans Keman (Amsterdam), Todd Landman (Essex), Steven Levitsky (Harvard University, Cambridge, MA), Zdenka Mansfeldova (Prag), Renate Mayntz (MPIfG Köln), Wolfgang Merkel (WZB Berlin), Ferdinand Müller-Rommel (Lüneburg), Guillermo O'Donnell (Notre Dame), Yannis Papadopoulos (Lausanne), Anton Pelinka (CEU Budapest), Andreas Schedler (CIDE, Mexiko-Stadt), Suzanne Schüttemeyer (Halle/Saale), Lars Svåsand (Bergen), Máté Szabó (Budapest).

Redaktion: Prof. Dr. Hans-Joachim Lauth (Universität Würzburg), Prof. Dr. Matthijs Bogaards (Jacobs University Bremen), PD Dr. Stephan Bröchler (Universität Gießen), Dr. Gero Erdmann (GIGA Hamburg), Prof. Dr. Marianne Kneuer (Universität Hildesheim), Prof. Dr. Gert Pickel (Universität Leipzig), Prof. Dr. Susanne Pickel (Universität Duisburg-Essen).

Kontaktadresse der Redaktion: Christoph Mohamad, M.A., Zeitschrift für Vergleichende Politikwissenschaft, Universität Würzburg, Institut für Politikwissenschaft und Sozialforschung, Wittelsbacher Platz 1, 97074 Würzburg. E-Mail: zfvp@uni-wuerzburg.de; Tel.: (0931) 31-80095, Fax: (0931) 31-84893.

VS Verlag für Sozialwissenschaften I Springer Fachmedien Wiesbaden GmbH
Abraham-Lincoln-Straße 46 I 65189 Wiesbaden
www.zfvp.de
Amtsgericht Wiesbaden, HRB 9754, USt-IdNr. DE811148419

Geschäftsführer: Dr. Ralf Birkelbach (Vors.), Armin Gross, Albrecht F. Schirmacher
Verlagsleitung: Dr. Reinald Klockenbusch
Gesamtleitung Anzeigen und Märkte: Armin Gross
Gesamtleitung Marketing: Rolf-Günther Hobbeling
Gesamtleitung Produktion: Christian Staral
Gesamtleitung Vertrieb: Gabriel Göttlinger

Abonnentenverwaltung
Springer Customer Service Center GmbH
Service VS Verlag, Haberstr. 7, D-69126 Heidelberg
Tel.: (06221) 345-4303; Fax: (06221) 345-4229; Montag-Freitag 8.00 Uhr bis 18.00 Uhr
E-Mail: vsverlag-service@springer.com

Marketing
Ronald Schmidt-Serrière, M.A., Telefon (06 11) 78 78-2 80; Telefax (06 11) 78 78-4 40;
E-Mail: Ronald.Schmidt-Serriere@vs-verlag.de

Anzeigenleitung: Yvonne Guderjahn, Telefon (06 11) 78 78-155; Telefax (06 11) 78 78-4 30;
E-Mail: Yvonne.Guderjahn@springer.com

Anzeigendisposition: Monika Dannenberger, Telefon (06 11) 78 78-148; Telefax (06 11) 78 78-4 43;
E-Mail: Monika.Dannenberger@springer.com

Es gelten die Mediadaten ab 01.01.2011

Produktion: Marina Litterer, Tel.: (06221) 48 78-755;
E-Mail: marina.litterer@springer.com

Bezugsmöglichkeiten 2011: Jährlich erscheinen 2 Hefte. Jahresabonnement / privat (print+online) Euro 128,–; Jahresabonnement / privat (nur online) Euro 108,–; Mitglieder der Deutschen Vereinigung für Politische Wissenschaft (DVPW) erhalten 25% Rabatt auf den Abonnement-Preis privat; Jahresabonnement / Bibliotheken Euro 348,–; Jahresabonnement Firma/Institutionen Euro 268,–; Jahresabonnement Studenten (bei Vorlage einer Studienbescheinigung) / Emeriti (print+online) Euro 79,–. Alle Print-Preise zuzüglich Versandkosten.
Alle Preise und Versandkosten unterliegen der Preisbindung. Die Bezugspreise enthalten die gültige Mehrwertsteuer. Kündigungen des Abonnements müssen spätestens 6 Wochen vor Ablauf des Bezugszeitraumes schriftlich mit Nennung der Kundennummer erfolgen.
Jährlich können Sonderhefte erscheinen, die nach Umfang berechnet und den Abonnenten des laufenden Jahrgangs mit einem Nachlass von 25 % des jeweiligen Ladenpreises geliefert werden. Bei Nichtgefallen können die Sonderhefte innerhalb einer Frist von 3 Wochen zurückgegeben werden.

© VS Verlag für Sozialwissenschaften ist eine Marke von Springer Fachmedien
Springer Fachmedien ist Teil der Fachverlagsgruppe Springer Science+Business Media

Alle Rechte vorbehalten. Kein Teil dieser Zeitschrift darf ohne schriftliche Genehmigung des Verlages vervielfältigt oder verbreitet werden. Unter dieses Verbot fällt insbesondere die gewerbliche Vervielfältigung per Kopie, die Aufnahme in elektronische Datenbanken und die Vervielfältigung auf CD-ROM und alle anderen elektronischen Datenträgern.

Gedruckt auf säurefreiem und chlorfrei gebleichtem Papier
Printed in the Netherlands
ISBN 978-3-531-18216-2

Zeitschrift für Vergleichende Politikwissenschaft Sonderheft 1 / 2011

Foreword	7
Introduction Gero Erdmann and Marianne Kneuer	9
Decline of Democracy: Loss of Quality, Hybridisation and Breakdown of Democracy Gero Erdmann	21
Quality Criteria for Democracy. Why Responsiveness is not the Key Hans-Joachim Lauth	59
Is the international environment becoming less benign for democratisation? Peter Burnell	81
The United States of America – a Deficient Democracy Josef Braml and Hans-Joachim Lauth	103
Deficits in Democratic Quality? The Effects of Party-System Institutionalisation on the Quality of Democracy in Central Eastern Europe Marianne Kneuer	133
Do Party Systems Make Democracy Work? A Comparative Test of Party-system Characteristics and Democratization in Francophone Africa Matthias Basedau and Alexander Stroh	173
Elections, Democratic Regression and Transitions to Autocracy: Lessons from Russia and Venezuela Rolf Frankenberger and Patricia Graf	201
Wilted Roses and Tulips: The Regression of Democratic Rule in Kyrgyzstan and Georgia Christoph H. Stefes and Jennifer Sehring	221
Democratic Survival or Autocratic Revival in Interwar Europe. A Comparative Examination of Structural Explanations Svend-Erik Skaaning	247

Foreword

This Special Issue is the first of its kind from the Zeitschrift für Vergleichende Politikwissenschaft/Journal of Comparative Governance. This German-language journal was founded in 2007 as the first German-speaking publication for Comparative Politics, which also includes English articles. As the idea was to build not only a platform for German-speaking scholars, the journal also regularly provides English online editions – such as the Supplement Volume of 2010 (see the archives of http://www.zfvp.de). This first Special Issue is exclusively and fully published in English. Special Issues allow us the opportunity to treat and address topics in a more comprehensive and in-depth way.

This first Special Issue addresses a topical theme – the decline of democracy – that has not been at the forefront of the academic and political agenda for two decades. The contributions to this Special Issue originate from a workshop with the title 'Demokratische Regression: Qualitätsverlust, Hybridisierung und Zusammenbruch von Demokratien/Democratic Regression: Loss of Quality, Hybridisation and the Breakdown of Democracy' organised by the Working Group 'Democracy Studies' of the German Political Science Association (DVPW), between 16 to 18 October 2008, at the German Institute of Global and Area Studies (GIGA) in Hamburg. Only those papers presented at the conference and submitted to the editors that triumphed in a first double-blind review process were included in this issue; in those cases where a paper received a contentious review, a third reviewer was then consulted. Among the reviewers were political scientists from Germany, other European countries as well as the United States.

We wish to take this opportunity to also extend an invitation to come forward to those scholars in Comparative Politics who are interested in assuming in future the editorship of such a Special Issue of Journal of Comparative Governance themselves. The next such Special Issues will be about 'The Use of Indices in Comparative Politics' and 'The (Dys-) Functionality of Corruption'.

Finally, we would like to thank the publishing house, VS Verlag für Sozialwissenschaften, especially its Reader, Frank Schindler. They were always open to the ideas of the editorial team, as well as to the idea of Special Issues, thus making possible what we present to you now.

The Editors

Introduction

Gero Erdmann and Marianne Kneuer

For a quarter of a century the transition from authoritarian rule figured very prominently on the Political Science research agenda. The reverse process – the transition *from* democracy – was largely ignored. This issue attempts to redress the balance, a choice for which there are a number of good reasons. It will address the regression of democracy – which might be a loss of democratic quality, a decline into a hybrid regime or a breakdown into an outright dictatorship.

Twenty years after the implosion of the Communist Bloc the euphoria in democratisation studies has come to an end. A more pessimistic or realistic view is spreading among scholars of democracy. This goes hand-in-hand with a significant expansion and differentiation in the research agenda of democratisation studies. While, since the 1980s, the transition towards democracy took the front seat, scholars began to concentrate on consolidation, its problems and its perils from the mid-1990s. This is due to the fact that, since then, democratisation has begun to display a mixed balance. It became evident that the linear and quite unproblematic evolution of democracies in Southern Europe did not become the role-model for everyone everywhere. The results of democratisation differed: while the neo-democracies in Central and Eastern Europe can be seen as largely consolidated and recipients of the democratic hallmark from the European Union in 2004, many other processes of democratisation, in other parts of the world – such as Africa, Asia and Latin America –, did not reach the same state of consolidation. Rather, they became stuck as unconsolidated or defective democracies, some 'regressed' into hybrid regimes and some even turned into autocracies. Axel Hadenius and Jan Teorell (2007) calculated that less than a quarter of the changes from authoritarian regimes between 1972 and 2003 effectively resulted in democratic governance.

Although transitions did not slip from scholarly attention, the relevance of democratic consolidation – especially of the persistence and the deepening of democracy – became the new focus, along with the varying results of democratisation – including defective, unconsolidated democracies and hybrid regimes. The empirical variety in democratisation results gave way to the conceptual creation of the multitude of 'adjective democracies' (Collier and Levitsky 1997). The innovative approach of creating subtypes helped not only to capture the existing variety but also to diversify the concept of democracy. However, not all proposed subtypes were convincing, so that different concepts of subtypes came to coexist, sometimes creating more confusion than clarity.

Although some concepts became prevalent – such as 'delegative' (O'Donnell 1994), 'electoral' (Diamond 1999), 'illiberal' (Zakaria 1997), 'defective democracy' (Merkel 2004; Merkel et al. 2003) or 'hybrid regimes' (Karl 1995; Diamond 2002) –, there is still no overall consensus about definitions. This is also true when it comes to measuring the variations. As several scholars have pointed out (Müller and Pickel 2007; Munck 2009; Burnell and Youngs 2010), there is a kind of 'babble' regarding methods of measuring and classifications, and thus it is essential to be cautious when using, presenting and interpreting these data. For example, the *Bertelsmann Transformations Index* uses the categorisations of 'highly advanced', 'advanced', 'limited', 'very limited' and 'failed or blocked' for assessing the status of political and economic transformation[1]; *Nations in Transit* differentiates between 'consolidated' and 'semi-consolidated democracy', 'transitional government or hybrid regimes', 'semi-consolidated' and 'consolidated authoritarian regimes'.[2]

At the same time, there is an ongoing debate about how to evaluate the trends in democratisation. Three different types of interpretation can be identified: Firstly, there is a pessimistic faction that sees an overall rollback of democracy and a reverse wave (Diamond 2008; Puddington 2008; 2010). A second view confirms the pessimistic reading of democracy's international prospects, and, in finding nuances within the rollback interpretation, suggests not to see it as a crisis but as a challenge for democratisation (Burnell and Youngs 2010). Thirdly, there are also scholars who refute this claim about a re-autocratisation, or the negative prospects of democracy on the global scale. Thomas Carothers (2009: 1) calls for a 'stepping back from democratic pessimism' and states that 'although democracy is certainly troubled in many places, when viewed relative to where it was at the start of this decade, democracy has not lost ground in the world overall'. Similarly, Wolfgang Merkel (2010) argues that 'there is no hard empirical evidence' for a reverse wave of autocratisation – while acknowledging that the democratic optimism of the early 1990s was indeed caused by inappropriate theoretical concepts of an irresistible trend towards worldwide democracy. Therefore, the system competition between democracy and autocracy should be considered as 'frozen'.[3]

Simultaneously, comparative authoritarian studies experienced a renaissance. The increasing literature on dictatorships deals with the persistence and change in, as well as different types of, these regimes, and one of the major findings of this research agenda is how autocracies increasingly employ democratic institutions for their non-democratic survival (for example, Brownlee 2007; Hadenius and Teorell 2007; Gandhi and Przeworski 2007; Schedler 2006; Köllner 2008). This research program, however, does not provide conceptual assistance to the issue of the regression of democracy. The two research fields – on the one side defective and unconsolidated democracies and on the other authoritarian regimes, authoritarian rollback and the possible 'reverse wave' (Huntington) coupled with the re-emergence of authoritarian great powers – remain largely isolated from each other.

---

1 http://www.bertelsmann-transformation-index.de/en/bti/ranking/status-index/
2 http://www.freedomhouse.org/images/File/nit/2010/NIT-2010-Methodology.pdf
3 See also Croissant and Thiery (2009: 70).

While transitology dealt with the transition from authoritarian rule, the reverse process – the transition *from* democratic rule – remained almost completely outside of scholarly consideration. One reason for why the reverse process was not addressed might have been that the reverse transitions simply did not happen or only during the last couple of years when the 'retreat of freedom' was discovered. Another reason could be that transitology by nature has as a starting point the emergence of democracy and its further development and thus looks at cases which can be subsumed as young or neo-democracies. Examining the loss of democratic quality or the breakdown of democracies is, then, a different research program. Hence, the starting point is, rather, a more comprehensive process of regression which possibly ends with the emergence of an authoritarian regime. Research has to deal with explanations for such processes in both young as well as established democracies. In fact, during the third wave of democratisation there were not only democratic transitions, which failed, but also a number of young and not-so-young democracies that regressed after a democratic period – not only into defective democracies and hybrid regimes, but even into authoritarian regimes.[4]

This special issue will address the problems of the regression of democracy and the aim is to close the gap between research on democracy and democratisation on the one side and the emergence of authoritarian regimes on the other. The topic of the regression of democracy raises one basic question: should the investigation be confined to young democracies or should old and/or established democracies be included in the research agenda? As regards the first part of the question, there is nothing new about the insight that transitions are open-ended and that other outcomes than fully fledged democracies are possible. This has been pointed out from the beginning of this research topic – although sometimes the non-democratic results might have been forgotten during the democratisation euphoria. 'Transitions are delimited [...] by the installation of some form of democracy, the return to some form of authoritarian rule or the emergence of a revolutionary alternative' (Schmitter and O'Donnell 1986: 6). It is quite safe to assume that there is a consensus among those scholars theorising and analysing transitions and democratic consolidations that either not fully consolidated or fragile democracies are the most vulnerable and prone to erosion. The spectrum of regression might encompass transitions into the so-called 'grey zone' between stable democracies and stable autocracies (namely, defective democracies, hybrid regimes, competitive autocracies), hence a decline not only into a subtype of democracy, but also into new authoritarian regimes.

The second part of the question addresses the issue of 'democratic survival' that takes us back to the contentious debate about the meaning of democratic consolidation (Schedler 1998). It is the question about the stage or level of democratic development that secures a democracy against authoritarian regression; in other words, which is the state of a democracy that leads us to believe or claim that the democratic rules are institutionalized in such a way that the regime is immune against authoritarian threats and that it will continue to persist in the future as a democracy? Since the issue of this state of 'irreversibility' of democracy, as it is sometimes called, is unresolved, a better under-

---

4 For a detailed overview of the cases of decline and the literature, see Erdmann in this volume.

standing of the democratic survival issue requires us to also include older, well-established democracies into the research agenda. Closely interlinked with this problem is the question and need for research about the quality or level of democracy, for two reasons. First, a particular quality or lack of quality might be the cause for endangering democratic rule that is not inherent in young democracies; second, changes in the quality of democracy[5] – for better and worse – can even be observed for some of the very old democracies of industrialized societies. An increase in research on the differences among, and ongoing changes within, established democracies is reflective of this issue.

The regression of democracy fans out into different phenomena: the loss of quality, which means a silent regression; the backslide into hybrid regimes (hybridisation); the breakdown of democracy. Essentially, there are two routes to decline: the 'rapid death', which insinuates a sudden breakdown of a democratic regime by such means as civil war, coup d'etat etc., thereby relapsing into authoritarian rule, and the 'slow death', displaying an incremental decay through 'the gradual erosion of freedoms, guarantees and processes that are vital to democracy' (O'Donnell 1995: 27; 1988). When Guillermo O'Donnell exposed these main routes to the perishing of democracy he also sketched the tasks for research on that field. One desideratum – more refined typologies – has been intensively elaborated, although there is still a way to go. The other tasks – like describing the risks and their evolution, as well as thinking about the necessary efforts at the domestic and international levels to reverse such trends of democratic erosion – remain to be fulfilled. Andreas Schedler emphasised that the description of democratic evolution or decay and their assessment are very much perspective dependent (Schedler 1998: 94f). That means that it is extremely important to make clear what the viewpoint and the direction of the view is. On the basis of Schedler's four-fold classification – authoritarianism, electoral democracy, liberal democracy and advanced democracy – he shows two scenarios: preventing democratic breakdown from a liberal or electoral democracy and democratic erosion from a liberal to an electoral democracy. Obviously, he assumed that advanced democracies would not experience democratic erosion.

This special issue goes beyond these scenarios. The empirical examinations are not limited to breakdown and erosion cases, but also include cases of the loss of democratic quality in advanced democracies. The contributions embrace conceptual considerations (Erdmann, Lauth, Burnell), as well as empirical analyses of the regression of democracy (Braml/Lauth, Kneuer, Basedau/Stroh, Frankenberger/Graf, Stefes/Sehring, and Skaaning). The focus is on gathering approaches that might open up fresh perspectives on how to capture conceptually and analytically this phenomenon that disquiets the democratisation community. The empirical cases cover the loss of democratic quality in old democracies such as the United States, in young democracies of Central Europe – considered to be consolidated – and of two liberal democracies in Africa – Benin and Mali. Also included are cases of hybridisation, such as Georgia and Venezuela, as well as the erosion of hybrid into authoritarian regimes, such as Russia. Further to these, a complete

---

5 See Beetham (1994); Altmann and Pérez-Liñan (2001); Beetham et al. (2002); Beetham (2004); O'Donnell et al. (2004); Diamond and Morlino (2005); Lauth (2004); Bühlmann et al. (2008).

survey of the instances of political breakdown and survival during the interwar period in twentieth-century Europe is also undertaken.

Since there is hardly any substantive research to date on the authoritarian reversals for the third wave of democratisation, in the first contribution *Gero Erdmann* sets out to sketch the research challenges faced in addressing the decline of democracy. His stocktaking of decline cases – which include changes in the democratic quality and changes from liberal democracy to hybrid and authoritarian regimes – provides basic data for the period from 1974 to 2008. The survey illustrates that most of the cases of decline refer to the change in and from young democracies that were established during the third wave. The predominant pattern of change is the loss of democratic quality and hybridisation. Not very surprisingly, middle-income countries seem to be the most vulnerable to the loss of democratic quality and hybridisation. The data analysis also confirms the institutionalist argument that the longer a democracy endures the more likely it will survive – although there are substantial exceptions. This points to crucial research areas, namely, to the analysis of the *gradual erosion* of democracy and the transition to a hybrid regime, while the phenomenon of the 'rapid death' of democracy seems to be a past pattern. After highlighting the richness of the 'eclectical approach' of transitology, the article concludes with a number of critical issues for the future research agenda. Among them is the volatility of middle-income countries, which points to the need for refined comparative research strategies that, to name a few only, might focus not only on the *process* of decline in reaction to and combination with economic crisis, but also, for example, on structural conditions such as the degree of social inequality and heterogeneity, as well as historical sequencing.

One crucial issue for the research on the regression of democracy, as conceived here, is the conceptual challenge of the quality of democracy. Any analysis of changes in quality and of the regressions of democracy obviously requires clear-cut criteria. *Hans-Joachim Lauth's* essay takes up the fundamental challenge and joins in with the ongoing debate about how to define and measure different qualities of democracy. After having suggested five 'pragmatic' rules for conceptualising the quality of democracy, he characterises democracy as a 'boundary concept' encompassing three dimensions: namely, freedom, equality and control; the three dimensions are competing and, simultaneously, complementary. Building on the tensions between these dimensions, he argues that 'complete responsiveness', although being a core criteria in many conceptualisations of democracy (for example, Dahl, Diamond and Morlino), should not be used for assessing and measuring the quality of democracy. This is not to eliminate responsiveness from the basic definition, but full responsiveness cannot exist for a number of methodological and empirical reasons, which are related to the tensions between the different dimensions of democracy. His analysis underlines that the definition and measurement of democratic quality is a daunting work-in-progress, and that we have still not reached consensus about the abstract content of the concept – not to mention the institutional domain and its indicators for empirical measurement. As just one example, it would be misleading to equate an increase of dissatisfaction with a quality regression of democracy without further qualification or contextualisation.

One of the major shortcomings in the early transitology research was the neglect of the international factors, whose relevance became acknowledged only at a later stage – although they have even now still not yet been fully integrated into a theory of democratisation. *Peter Burnell's* contribution opens up the issue right from the beginning of the research on the regression of democracy, and helps us to avoid repeating the same mistake with the question: 'Is the international environment becoming less benign for democratisation?' He reminds us that the 'international dimension' is not only an external politics factor and also is much more than internal democracy promotion and assistance. It further includes such components as diffusion, contagion, control, conditionality and consent (Whitehead), or snowballing effects (Huntington), which partly have a very indirect impact on domestic political processes, which might be either the transition from or to democracy. Based on the research experience of the international dimension of democratisation, he illuminates the methodological challenges that lie ahead for those assessing how more or less benign the international environment has become for democracy or dictatorships. His major point is that we need to modernise the framework of analysis for the external dimension, in order to establish whether there is such a trend or not; his own tentative answer to the question is a qualified yes. The subsequent problem, however, is: if the international environment has become less benign, does that mean it has also become more favourable for the international diffusion of anti-democratic values and the promotion of dictatorships? There is obviously no easy answer; simply to equate the international effects of the two different regime types seems to be questionable, as pointed out by Burnell. An answer requires thoroughly designed comparative studies, ones that include both types of regimes.

The first empirical case study of the decline of democracy in this special issue takes up the challenge of analysing the regression of democratic quality in an established – in fact the oldest – democracy, the United States of America. To assess the quality of the US' democracy, *Josef Braml* and *Hans-Joachim Lauth* apply the latter's 'democracy matrix', which builds on a three-dimensional concept of democracy – including political freedom, political equality and political and legal control (horizontal accountability). They argue that the US under George W. Bush has become a 'deficient democracy' since the terrorist attacks of 9/11 and the subsequent War on Terror. They see the democratic regression as a paradoxical result of the US' attempt to promote democracy even by military means, while sacrificing civil liberties at home. In effect, the power of the Executive was expanded whereas the rule of law, the effective control of the Executive by the Legislative and the Supreme Court deteriorated. However, they conclude with an optimistic view. First, the democratic regression under Bush was not a singular one, but historically a more frequent phenomenon caused by external threats – a regression from which US democracy usually recovered because of its inherent liberal tradition. Second, the election of Barack Obama and his commitment to the liberal ideals of the US constitution might be an indication that the decline of democratic quality will only be a temporary phenomenon.

The 'centrality of institutionalised party competition' (Lipset 2000) for a flourishing and consolidated democracy is common wisdom among scholars of democracy. However, there is little empirical research about the degree to which party systems affect the quality of democracy. The general assumption is that a highly fragmented, highly polarised and lowly institutionalised party system will have a negative impact on the democratic regime and might contribute its breakdown. Two contributions, those of *Marianne Kneuer* analysing the young democracies of Central and Eastern Europe and *Matthias Basedau* together with *Alexander Stroh* examining party systems in West Africa, address this issue and come up with different conclusions, which challenge some assumptions in the conventional wisdom about the role of party systems.

On the basis of the concept of party system institutionalisation – but introducing new indicators – Marianne Kneuer reveals, first, that most of the party systems of the eight young democracies of Central and Eastern Europe cannot be regarded as institutionalised. In a second step, she examines the effect of the unstable party systems on the quality of democracy by looking at three dimensions of democracy: the freedom and control dimension, the procedural dimension and the output dimension. Herein she discovers that the weak party systems had little influence in the first post-autocratic decade, but much in the second, especially in the freedom and control and the procedural dimensions. Government effectiveness, in contrast, seems less affected by instable party systems as deficits are compensated for by an executive concentration. Taking into account the four-level model of consolidation, Kneuer's analysis shows that while the Central and Eastern European countries dispose of stable and functioning institutions (constitutional consolidation), consolidation is not accomplished on the representative level, especially as regards the parties and party systems. Such non-simultaneous consolidation processes can interfere with the further deepening of democracy or the enhancement of its quality. An open question for further research is whether the weak intermediary actors and low citizen participation – correlated with a low degree of input agency and input capacity – could in the long run cause a debilitation of the input legitimacy.

In this respect, at least, the investigation of the West African party systems reveals similar results, as far as the apparently clear-cut relationship between the type of party system and democracy is concerned. In their analysis Matthias Basedau and Alexander Stroh add to the usual indicators (fragmentation, institutionalisation and ideological polarisation) a new indicator – namely, behavioural polarisation. On the basis of four cases, they reject the conventional hypothesis that moderate fragmentation, high institutionalisation and low polarisation are supportive of a high level of democracy. The reason is very simple: most of the indicators show no, and a few even a negative, impact. This might lead to the conclusion that the classical party-system characteristics do not matter at all for democracy – a suggestion, however, that the authors reject. Instead, they argue that the relevance of the party system might not be as strong as the functionalist wisdom maintains and that other causal mechanisms might be at work. At the very least, high fragmentation and low institutionalisation seem to be no major cause for high democratic volatility. Nevertheless, the authors concede that further research is required, especially to test their findings with a larger sample than the small-n comparison. Apart from the latter provision, which also applies to Kneuer's results, the results of both studies point to some shortcomings in the functionalist understanding of the relationship between the political party system and the quality of democracy, which seems to be more complex than conventionally envisaged. The introduction of new indicators obviously helps us to understand better the correlation between party system institutionalisation and quality problems. Interestingly, both behavioural polarisation (Basedau/Stroh) as well as the indicators Kneuer used (for example, fractional migration) point to the same problem: namely, elite behaviour.

The cases of Russia and Venezuela have been of central interest and focus in recent years, both being important players not only in their regions but also beyond, and both also experiencing a regression of democratic status: Russia degraded from a hybrid regime to an autocracy and Venezuela from a liberal democracy to a hybrid regime. The closing of the political systems has been achieved by the political leaders through the centralisation of power, the restructuring of federalism, the devaluation of political parties and the rise of informal institutions in the form of neo-patrimonial or clientelistic structures. *Rolf Frankenberger* and *Patricia Graf* focus on elections, assuming that they are a crucial means by which to gradually steer and even to smooth transition to autocracy, as they are the 'Archimedian Point' for changing political systems. Applying a functionalist–structuralist approach the authors identify several functions of elections such as legitimisation, structuring, integration and so on. The interesting finding is that, in both cases, functions of competitive, semi- and non-competitive elections coexist, although to a different degree. It is this mixture of different electoral functions that enables a smooth – even hidden – process of de-democratisation. In both cases, elections are neither a democratic technique nor do they constitute a democratic threshold against authoritarian developments. Thus, Frankenberger and Graf consider elections in both countries as a means to implement and/or stabilise authoritarian rule.

Christoph Stefes and *Jennifer Sehring* also analyse two cases that drew international attention: Georgia and Kyrgyzstan. Their coloured revolutions symbolised the hope for democratisation to sweep away semi-authoritarian regimes. Both cases show, however, that the new democratically elected leaders use similar techniques to their authoritarian predecessors, by which the democratic progress has been halted and reversed. Based on Steven M. Fish's work (2001), the authors find three explanations for this development: the moving from presidentialism to super-presidentialism, the weakly organised and fragmented opposition and the adverse impact of authoritarian states in the neighbourhood. In a way very similar to the Russian case, the main trait of the democratic decline is the centralisation of executive power – namely to the head of the state – through constitutional changes, repression of the opposition and the stifling of civil society. Stefes and Sehring identify, as a further important variable, the international dimension and the role of foreign actors. The authors argue that Western support was diminishing, while Russia was pulling the strings in the neighbourhood. Testing the international dimension, the authors conclude that both countries display low international linkages, which consequently means that the leverage of external actors is likewise low. As a result, the ability of foreign actors to deter authoritarian setbacks is also low.

While most of the contributions concentrate on cases of the third wave of democratisation, *Svend-Erik Skaaning's* analysis takes us back to the cases of the interwar period in Europe. These constitute an interesting sample as they were initially based on democratic euphoria, yet in the end more than half had collapsed into autocratic and totalitarian regimes. His study includes all 29 European countries in the period and uses a configurational comparative method: a crisp-set qualitative comparative analysis (csQCA). Skaaning follows a structural approach integrating novel factors besides wealth – namely, stateness combined with weak landlords, the subordination of religious interests to political authority and the existence of a pre-war liberal hegemony. The analysis shows that the dominant pathways to authoritarian reversal emerged through a mixture of a lack of a liberal tradition, strong landlords, and either a 'weak' state (late state-building) or a strong religious leadership. In order to draw lessons from these historic cases, Skaaning points out that a low degree of stateness was not just a problem in interwar Europe, but that, together with the presence of autonomous and undemocratic elite groups, the weak stateness might also be the cause for today's instability and the decline of democracies.

Our short overview of the contributions to this volume indicates how it was possible to touch upon only some of the themes and research challenges involved in the decline of democracy. Although it is a rather novel topic, it is obvious that future research on the transition from democracy can learn and build on the experience and the knowledge – including failures – accumulated in 20 years of research on the transition from authoritarian rule. What can be learned from transitology is, first, that no monocausal explanation can sufficiently help us to understand the decline of democracy. Second, no single methodological approach will be suitable either; only the application of multiple approaches will be fruitful. Third, a selection bias that favours negative cases only should be avoided; fourth, as already mentioned above, the international dimension ought to be included from the beginning. These are only a few very general points that need to be considered. Further questions will be: Can we distinguish special risks for vulnerable groups of regimes such as young democracies? Or, can we identify critical junctures where the decline has its origins? Of course, this volume cannot present a complete picture of the research challenges ahead and thus may also leave some open questions or provoke different viewpoints. If this is so, we have accomplished our goal; our intention is to provide inspiration for the ongoing scholarly debate.

Future studies will need to deepen the understanding of relevant factors – and the potential relationship or causalities between and from them that nurture democratic decline – in order to form a more solid basis for further prognosis on the prospects of democracy around the globe. This is an important aspect not only for students of democracy but also for practitioners of democracy building and development assistance. We know little about the effects of authoritarian powers on fledgling democracies or transitional regimes in their neighbourhoods. We also need to know about the reasons for regression before possible concepts for democracy promotion can be modified and tailored in a targeted way.

* * *

We are grateful for the collaboration and patience of all the authors and reviewers. Moreover, we wish to thank the Fritz Thyssen Foundation, which provided the financial support for the workshop that formed the basis underlying the planning of this volume. We also wish to thank the German Institute for Global Area Studies (GIGA) for providing us with the ideal setting for the workshop, namely the GIGA headquarters in Hamburg, Germany.

Bibliography

Altmann, David/Pérez-Liñan, Aníbal (2001), 'Assessing the Quality of Democracy: Freedom, Competitiveness and Participation in 18 Latin American Countries', Kellogg Institute Working Paper, Notre Dame.
Beetham, David (2004), 'Towards a Universal Framework for Democracy Assessment' in *Democratization*, 11, 2: 1-17.
Beetham, David (ed.) (1994), *Defining and Measuring Democracy*, London/Thousand Oaks/New Delhi.
Beetham, David/Bracking, Sarah/Kearton, Iain/Weir, Stuart (2002), *International IDEA Handbook of Democracy Assessment*, The Hague et al.
Brownlee, Jason (2007), Authoritarianism in an Age of Democratization, Cambridge.
Bühlmann, Marc/Merkel, Wolfgang/Wessels, Bernhard (2008), 'The Quality of Democracy. Democracy Barometer for Established Democracies', NCCR Democracy 21, Working Paper No.10a. National Center of Competence in Research: Challenges to Democracy in the 21st Century.
Burnell, Peter/Youngs, Richard (eds.), *New Challenges to Democratization*, London.
Carothers, Thomas (2009), *Stepping back from Democratic Pessimism*, Carnegie Papers No.99.
Collier, David/Levitsky, Steven (1997), 'Research Note: Democracy with Adjectives: Conceptual Innovation in Comparative Research' in *World Politics*, 49, 3: 430-451.
Diamond, Larry (1999), *Developing Democracy Toward Consolidation*, Baltimore/London.
Diamond, Larry (2002), 'Thinking About Hybrid Regimes', in *Journal of Democracy*, 13, 2: 21-35.
Diamond, Larry (2008), 'The Democratic Rollback. The Resurgence of the Predatory State', *Foreign Affairs*, 87, 2: 36-48.
Diamond, Larry/Morlino, Leonardo (eds.) (2005), *Assessing the Quality of Democracy*, Baltimore.
Fish, M. Steven (2001), 'The Dynamics of Democratic Erosion' in Anderson, Richard/Fish, M. Steven/Hanson, Stephen E./Roeder, Philip G. (eds.), *Postcommunism and the Theory of Democracy*, Princeton: 54-95.
Gandhi, J./Przeworski, A. (2007), 'Authoritarian Institutions and the Survival of Autocrats', in *Comparative Political Studies*, 40, 11: 1279-1301.
Hadenius, Axel/Teorell, Jan (2007), 'Pathways from Authoritarianism' in *Journal of Democracy*, 18, 1: 143-156.
Huntington, Samuel (1992), The Third Wave: Democratization in the Late Twentieth Century, Norman, Oklahoma.
Karl, Terry L. (1995), 'The Hybrid Regimes of Central America' in *Journal of Democracy*, 6, 3: 72-86.
Köllner, Patrick (2008), 'Autoritäre Regime – Ein Überblick über die jüngere Literatur' in *Zeitschrift für Vergleichende Politikwissenschaft*, 2: 351-368.
Lauth, Hans-Joachim (2004), Demokratie und Demokratiemessung: Eine konzeptionelle Grundlegung für den interkulturellen Vergleich, Wiesbaden.
Levitsky, S./Way, L. A. (2007), Competitive Authoritarianism: International Linkage, Organizational Power, and the Fate of Hybrid Regimes, Ms.

Lipset Seymour Martin (2000), 'The Indispensability of Political Parties' in *Journal of Democracy*, 11, 1: 48-55.

Merkel, Wolfgang (2004), 'Embedded and Defective Democracies' in Aurel Croissant/Wolfgang Merkel (eds.), Special Issue of *Democratization*: Consolidated or Defective Democracy? Problems of Regime Change, 11, 5: 33-58.

Merkel, Wolfgang (2010), 'Are Dictatorships Returning? Revisiting the 'Democratic Rollback' Hypothesis' in *Contemporary Politics*, 16, 1: 17-31.

Müller, Thomas/Pickel, Susanne (2007), 'Wie lässt sich Demokratie am besten messen? Zur Konzeptqualität von Demokratie-Indizes' in *Politische Vierteljahresschrift*, 3: 511-539.

Munck, Gerardo L. (2009), Measuring Democracy. A Bridge between Scholarship and Politics, Baltimore.

O'Donnell, Guillermo (1988), 'Challenges to Democratization in Brazil' in *World Policy Journal*, 5, 2: 281-300.

O'Donnell, Guillermo (1995), 'Do Economists Know Best?' in *Journal of Democracy*, 6, 1: 23-28.

O'Donnell, Guillermo/Schmitter, Philippe (1986), *Transitions from Authoritarian Rule*, vol.4: Tentative Conclusions about Uncertain Democracies, Baltimore/London.

O'Donnell, Guillermo/Cullel, Jorge Vargas/Iazzetta Osvaldo M. (eds.) (2004), *The Quality of Democracy. Theory and Applications,* Notre Dame: 9-93.

Puddington, Arch (2008), Findings of Freedom in the World 2008 – Freedom in Retreat: Is the Tide Turning?, Freedom House 2008.

Puddington, Arch (2010), 'The Erosion Accelerates, The Freedom House Survey for 2009' in *Journal of Democracy*, 21, 2: 136-150.

Schedler, Andreas (1998), 'What is Democratic Consolidation?' in *Journal of Democracy*, 9, 2: 91-107.

Schedler, Andreas (ed.) (2006), Electoral Authoritarianism: The Dynamics of Unfree Competition, Boulder.

Zakaria, Fareed (1997), 'The Rise of Illiberal Democracy' in *Foreign Affairs*, 76, 6: 22-43.

ARTICLE

Decline of Democracy: Loss of Quality, Hybridisation and Breakdown of Democracy

Gero Erdmann

Abstract The contribution points out that there is hardly any research for the reverse transition, the transition from democracy to non-democratic regimes for more than 30 years. For heuristical purposes, it provides basic data of the decline of democracy, which refers to loss of democratic quality, changes from liberal democracy to hybrid and to authoritarian regimes, during the third wave of democratisation (1974-2008). The stocktaking shows that most of the cases of decline refer to the change in and from young democracies established during the third wave, especially after 1989. Loss of democratic quality and hybridization are the most frequent cases of decline, while the breakdown of democracy has been very rare. Young democracies and poorer countries are more prone to decline than the older and richer cases – aside from a few remarkable exceptions. Finally, the overview argues that the research on the decline of democracy can benefit from the richness of the approaches of transitology, but should also avoid its methodological traps and failures, concluding with a number of suggestions for the future research agenda.

1. Introduction[1]

For more than two decades, transitions from authoritarian regimes to liberal democracies preoccupied politics as well as political science research. The ebb of the third wave of democratisation, the persistence of hybrid and authoritarian regimes and even the resurgence of the latter have not only posed a new political challenge, but have also provided a new research agenda. The 'End of Transition Paradigm' (Carothers 2002) and the 'Backlash against Democracy Promotion' (Carothers 2006) indicate not only a turn for international democracy promoters, but apparently also a significant factual trend in regime development signalled by titles such as 'The Democratic Rollback' (Diamond 2008) and 'Freedom in Retreat' (Puddington 2008) or 'the Erosion Acceler-

---

[1] I would like to thank Jan Sändig, University of Potsdam and former intern at the GIGA Institute of African Affairs for the compilation of the data that were the basis for this article, and three reviewers for their very helpful comments.

ates' (Puddington 2010). This poses the question of whether we are already experiencing a 'reverse wave' (and to what degree), as we experienced after the first and second waves of democratisation (Huntington 1993: 290). Despite the pessimistic tone of the titles quoted above, the evidence is not quite as clear as is claimed. Other authors believe the 'third wave of democratisation' expired in the late 1990s, hence the 'stagnation' in the spread of democracy, but no stagnation in a reverse wave or a resurgence of dictatorships (Merkel 2010). In fact, the number of democracies remained stable while some 'partly free' regimes became 'not free' (Freedom House 2010).[2]

This vague 'trend' notwithstanding, political scientists re-discovered the phenomenon of authoritarian rule some years earlier.[3] Hybrid regimes have attracted the attention of political scientists in a similar way.[4] While the research on non-democratic regimes mainly deals with the status and the self-reinforcing mechanisms of these regimes and why they last, researchers have neglected the way they came into being. For more than twenty years, the research agenda on regime change was shaped by a specific perspective that dealt with the transition from authoritarian rule with its particular set of research questions and issues. However, the converse process – the transition from democracy – was hardly addressed, and this perspective might raise its own issues and specific questions. While the former research question was 'Why have some countries had democratic transitions while others have not?' (Munck 2004: 69), the new question will be 'Why have some democracies experienced declines while others have not?'

Given the scarcity of research on this question, the aim of this article is twofold: First, it will address the question of whether this is a research topic worthy of study at all by taking stock of the various cases of decline of democracy and their regional and socio-economic contexts. Second, it will provide an overview of the current state of research, the various research issues involved, and the various approaches, and sketch out the possible routes of future research. Hence, the overall purpose is to find out whether the conditions for and the processes leading to the emergence of democracy are different from the conditions and processes that cause the decline of democracy, and to detail these conditions appropriately.

Before taking stock of the cases, I shall give a short overview of the literature that relates indirectly and directly to the transition from democracy.

---

2 The conclusion on the 'retreat of freedom' is largely based on developments (decline) in non-democratic regimes ('partly free' and 'not free' in terms of Freedom House). Overall, the number of countries classified as 'not free' (2009 = 47) is still lower than in 1993 (= 55), although it increased from 2008 (= 42); five 'partly free' countries subsequently put into the 'not free' category. The 89 'free' countries of 2009 continued to be the second-highest number ever recorded, topped only by 90 'free' countries in 2006.
3 For an overview, see Köllner 2008. He makes reference to Brownlee 2007; Brooker 2000; Hadenius/Teorell 2007; Schedler 2006; Levitsky/Way 2002; 2007; Gandhi/Przeworski 2007; Snyder 2006; Diamond 2008; Magaloni 2008; 2007; Wintrobe 2007; Lewis 2006; Bogaards 2009.
4 Karl 1995; Bendel/Croissant/Rüb 2002; Diamond 2002; *Journal of Democracy*, 4, 2002.

2. The research problem and the literature

There is a vast amount of literature which deals indirectly with this issue – namely, the research that enquires about the conditions or prerequisites for democractic as well as non-democratic regimes. Most of these studies have a developmental perspective, which might be misleading: They try to find out favourable and unfavourable conditions for the *emergence* of democracy. This scholarship, a large amount of which is based on macro-quantitative research, (which in turn is based on rational choice models), provides substantial – albeit sometimes methodologically questionable – results as to what is more favourable and less favourable for democracy.[5] From this we can learn about the conditions or circumstances under which a democracy is more likely to survive and perhaps even become consolidated – or those under which a democracy may remain instable and be prone to declining into a non-democratic regime again.

At the same time, there are also a number of sociological and political-institution studies in the tradition of the 'Barrington Moore Research Programme' that search for systematic historical explanations based on qualitative comparisons (Mahoney 2003). More recently, new approaches, such as the qualitative comparative analysis (QCA) based on Boolean algebra, have contributed an additional methodological dimension to this field (see Ragin 1987 and 2000; Schneider/Wagemann 2007; Rihoux/Ragin 2009). While the number of configurational factors has been enlarged in these studies, going beyond socio-economic factors, such as the Berg-Schlosser/Mitchell project (Berg-Schlosser/Mitchell 2000; 2002), these approaches remain in the structuralist camp (see Skaaning in this issue as well).

While the research has been vastly enriched on favourable and less favourable conditions of democracy and what makes a democracy endure, we still know very little about the specific constellations of actors and actual process that make a democracy reverse.[6] As suggested above, during the third wave of democratisation, a number of young democracies declined into hybrid and authoritarian regimes. We do not know exactly how many of the young democracies were affected, though, or whether they merely declined into a hybrid state or continued to reverse into an authoritarian regime, nor do we know how often democracies have collapsed and directly turned into autocracies.

So far, research on the decline of democracy whose focus is the *process* of decline has hardly moved beyond Linz's seminal study on the breakdown of democracy (Linz

---

5 For a short overview up to 1992, see Diamond (1992), which covers the following studies: Lipset 1963; Cutright 1963; Olsen 1968; Cutright/Wiley 1969; Jackman 1973; Bollen 1979; 1983; Bollen/Jackman 1985; Thomas/Ramirez/Meyer/Gobalet 1979; Hanon/Carroll 1981; Diamond et al. 1987. See also Lipset/Seong/Torres 1993 and the standard work by Przeworski et al. (1996; 1997; 2000); also Epstein et al. (2006). One fundamental problem particularly with the earlier works is that correlations at a point in time are translated into a development path without any explanation.

6 One of the few experts who have explicitly addressed the issue of democratic decline is M. Steven Fish (2001), who deals with democratic erosion in post-communist countries. Based on simple bivariate regressions, he concludes that 'the normal causes or the usual suspects' do not help to explain the democratic reversal.

1978). Because of the focus on the process, there is an actor or agent orientation. His attempt to systematically describe and conceptually capture the breakdown process addressed cases from the inter-war period in 20th-century Western Europe and in Latin America after World War II. Africa, Asia, the Middle East and Eastern Europe were not included (although Linz did make occasional references to the latter in his overview). Building upon an older research tradition on military coups and military regimes (Feiner 1988; Nordlinger 1977), Paul Brooker (2000: 59ff) suggested an analytical framework for the establishment of military regimes and one-party regimes only, with a focus on motives and opportunity structures of authoritarian-minded actors.

A more recent study takes up – as a rare case – our issue of the 'authoritarian reversal' (Svolik 2007), but relates it to the question of democratic consolidation. The same perspective, which factors might 'help insure new democracies against backsliding', is applied by Epstein et al. (2006: 557) and addressed in Przeworski et al. (2000), which, like the two previous studies, is a macro-quantitative analysis. They all give some valuable hints about possible prerequisites for the decline of democracy, but do not really help us understand the process of decline.

Hypothetically, the reverse process might start with a loss of democratic quality,[7] which is not confined to young democracies, but may affect old ones, too. Loss of quality describes a deterioration of quality in one of the two central dimensions of democracy – freedom and equality – and in an additional one, i.e. the (horizontal) control of power; it describes a negative variation within the democratic regime type. Democracies can decline in quality and change into one of three different regime types: hybrid regimes, authoritarian regimes and totalitarian regimes.[8] The process can be slow and gradual, moving from quality-loss to a hybrid regime, which I call 'hybridisation', and then possibly evolving into other non-democratic regimes. A hybrid regime is understood to be a regime type of its own located between democracy and autocracy and not a diminished subtype of one of the other regimes (Morlino 2009: 276).[9] The decline process can also be fast and short, accelerated through the various phases ending in an authoritarian or totalitarian regime without passing through a hybrid stage at all. I call this process a 'breakdown of democracy'. The overall process starting with quality-loss is termed 'decline of democracy'. The process of decline does not necessarily follow the

---

[7] The quality of democracy is a controversial concept; usually it refers to the fact that democracies differ from each other and that they have different qualities or degrees of democracy ('high'- and 'low'-quality democracies). The move from low to high quality signifies a 'deepening' of democracy. For example, an electoral democracy is of lower quality than a liberal democracy. For a discussion of the problem and a detailed conceptualisation of the quality of democracy see Munck/Verkuilen 2002; Coppedge 2002; Bühlmann/Merkel/Wessels 2008.

[8] Another possible variant of a decline of democracy would be the reversal from a failed transition from an authoritarian regime; this, however, might be viewed as a regime-type change within the authoritarian camp, a possible change between authoritarian subcategories.

[9] Unlike Morlino's definition, a hybrid regime cannot only arise from an authoritarian regime (ibid.: 281), but from a democracy as well. This point rests on the simple observation that democracies can also transition into other types of regimes, not just authoritarian ones.

sequence of steps described. In fact, the decline can stop at any point and remain there, perhaps at a lower level of democratic quality, as a defective or electoral democracy or as a hybrid regime of one of the 'competitive authoritarianism' types. One sequence of the process can be skipped, of course: The decline of quality can be finalised by a coup d'état that establishes an autocratic regime. In this context, one fundamental question is whether a consolidated democracy can possibly experience a decline at all that goes beyond a quality decline towards a hybrid or authoritarian regime. Some concepts of democratic consolidation exclude this possibility by definition (Schedler 1998: 91, 103; Svolik 2008).

3. Taking stock of the situation

Since there is little knowledge about the statistics of democratic decline, I shall make a first attempt at taking stock of the various cases of democratic decline that have occurred during the third wave of democratisation (since 1974), and especially those since the fall of the Iron Curtain in 1989, which gave the third wave an additional push. Apart from taking stock of the number of cases and the types of decline (loss of democratic quality, hybridisation or breakdown of democracy), two other questions will also be addressed: First, an institutional question: What kind of democracies have experienced the decline, young ones or old ones? Second, the classic structuralist question: What kind of countries are affected by a decline in democracy in terms of their socio-economic development?

Such a survey requires well-defined concepts and delineations between the various types and subtypes of regimes, which are not sufficiently provided by previous research (Bogaards 2009).[10] However, for the purpose of this heuristic survey, no detailed discussion of the difficult delineations and thresholds between regime types is required at this stage. Instead, a simple analytical instrument based on the threefold typology of democratic, hybrid and authoritarian regimes linked to data from the Freedom House Index (FHI) will be applied. The FHI category 'free' (with a value of 1.0 to 2.5) can be translated into a liberal democracy, 'partly free' (3.0 to 5.0) into a hybrid regime, and 'not free' (5.5 to 7.0) into an authoritarian regime or dictatorship.[11] The index not only allows a distinction to be made between different types of regimes, but since the categories are scaled, the variation in value can be taken to indicate partial variations in the quality of each regime type. In the quality of democracy, for example, 1.0 indicates a 'higher' quality of democracy than 1.5 or 2.5 – more freedom, in other words.[12] Since

---

10 The problem mainly relates to the creation of subtypes and how they are delineated from other root concepts of either democracy or autocracy. See the discussion about defective democracy and hybrid regimes, for example (Krennerich 2002; Rüb 2002).
11 Until 2003 countries with a value of 3.0 to 5.5 were categorised as 'partly free', while those lying between 5.5 and 7.0 were deemed 'not free'.
12 A note is required here regarding the relationship between the Freedom House Index and the various regime types, especially the concept of democracy. The FHI research questions related to political rights and

the index only has two values with which to capture differences in the quality of democracy, the changes in the FHI data are only a very crude indicator of quality changes.[13]

3.1 Frequency of decline

In order to establish the number of declines in the quality of democracy based on the Freedom House data, I considered the value changes from 1 to 2 and from 2 to 3 in both dimensions, i.e. political rights and civil liberties. Countries with a value of 2 in one and 3 in the other category (which adds up to an average value of 2.5) were still classified as 'free' or democratic. For the third wave, from 1974 to 2008, the data provide 88 cases of negative changes in the quality of democracy in 53 countries worldwide. The number was clearly higher from 1989 to 2008 (58 cases in 43 countries) than for the period before that (see Table 1); some of these countries experienced quality changes several times (see Appendix 1).

As regards the total number of losses in democratic quality in the different regions, Africa was less affected than Europe, followed by Asia and Latin America. The reason why the number is smaller for Africa than for Europe, for example, is very simply due to the small number of democracies in Africa (see Table 1).

The data provide 52 cases of regime change for the third wave, either from democracy to a hybrid form (hybridisation) or to an authoritarian regime (breakdown). The count only includes cases that were classified as 'free' or democratic for at least two years before the hybridisation or breakdown occurred. This requirement should exclude cases with very short spells of democracy after a democratic transition that is viewed as an extended transition conflict (not as an established type of democratic regime).

Significantly, among these 52 cases there were only five cases of a clear breakdown of democracy or a direct transition from democracy to an authoritarian regime, and interestingly, four of those breakdowns happened before 1989. All the other cases were hybridisations, i.e. changes from democracy to hybrid regimes (see Appendix 2).

The 52 regime changes from democracy to non-democratic regimes took place in 40 countries, nine of which were affected by hybridisation twice and one of which under-

---

civil liberties comprise essential elements which are part of all liberal concepts of democracy. The basic questions of the index are very similar to other measurements of democracy; they cover the three dimensions of democracy mentioned above: a) electoral process (three questions), b) political pluralism and participation (four questions), and c) functioning of government (three questions), d) freedom of expression and belief (four questions), e) associational and organisational rights (three questions), f) rule of law (four questions), and g) personal autonomy and individual fights (four questions). The question in sections a to c cover political rights, although the function of government is not 'right', while the other four are related to civil liberties. See http://freedomhouse.org/template.cfm?page=351&anapage= 342&year= 2008; see also Lauth's critical view in Lauth 2004: 269ff.

13 For a much more refined measurement of qualities of democracy, see the democracy barometer project (Bühlmann/Merkel/Wessels 2008), for example.

went hybridisation and then a breakdown more than a decade later. This means these ten countries were re-democratised in between.

Table 1: Frequencies of decline of democracy, 1974–2008

	1974–1988	1989–2008	Total
	Cases / countries	Cases / countries	Cases / countries
A. Decline of quality			
Africa	2 / 2	10 / 7	12 / 7
Asia	4 / 4	14 / 10	18 / 12
Latin America	15 / 12	22 / 16	37 / 21
Europe	9 / 6	12 / 10	21 / 13
B. Change to hybrid regime			
Africa	4 / 4	4 / 4	8 / 8
Asia	9 / 8	10 / 7	19 / 12
Latin America	4 / 4	14 / 10	18 / 14
Europe	1 / 1	1 / 1	2 / 2
C. Change to dictatorship			
Africa	2 / 2	1 / 1	3 / 3
Asia	2 / 2	- / -	2 / 2
Latin America	- / -	- / -	- / -
Europe	- / -	- / -	- / -
D. All regime changes (B & C)			
Africa	6 / 6	5 / 5	11 / 10
Asia	11 / 9	10 / 7	21 / 14
Latin America	4 / 4	14 / 10	18 / 14
Europe	1 / 1	1 / 1	2 / 2

Source: Appendix 1, 2

A few observations should be noted at this point. The first one is the high number of declines of democracies, i.e. the transformation from democratic to non-democratic regimes. The second interesting point is the high degree of regime instability in Latin America indicated by the high number of changes in the quality of democracy combined with the high number of regime changes from democratic to hybrid regimes. This also implies renewed improvements in the quality of democracy and re-democratisation after a hybrid period, however. Despite the fact that Latin American countries were among the first and most successful during the third wave of democratisation up to the point that there was hardly any authoritarian regime left in the region, this still suggests a lastingly high degree of institutional instability, which might provide the basis for future authoritarian reversals. Finally, compared with Latin America, Europe, Asia and Africa stand for regime stability, although for opposite types of regimes: Europe stands for stable democracies, while Africa and Asia stand for the stability of non-democratic regimes. Surprisingly, however, there have only been a few declines in democracy in Africa since the 'wind from the East [shook] the coconut trees' (Omar Bongo, *West Africa*, 9 April 1990) in 1989.

3.2 The institutional or age dimension

Besides asking about the actual number of declines that have taken place, the other crucial questions are: What type of democracies decline? Is the number of losses of democratic quality and/or the hybridisation higher among young democracies than among older ones because they lack institutionalisation or consolidation – as is suggested in the democratic transition literature?[14] For the purpose of this heuristic overview, no elaborated concept of institutionalisation or consolidation is required – apart from the fact that both concepts are controversial and difficult to operationalise. In the definitions of both concepts, time explicitly or implicitly plays a crucial role (e.g. Linz/ Stepan 1996; Merkel 1996; Huntington 1993; Schedler 1998; Schneider/Schmitter 2004).[15] The durability of democracy is used here as a proxy for 'institutionalisation' or 'consolidation' as in macro-statistical studies, although it is quite clear that age is an insufficient indicator of either institutionalisation or consolidation of democracy.

From this institutional perspective, the survey reveals that most of the changes to hybrid regimes took place in young democracies that were established during the third wave of democratisation and especially after 1989. Interestingly, there were only very few cases of hybridisation and breakdown before 1989, a circumstance which can partly be attributed to the smaller number of democracies. During this period, more than two-thirds of the democracies were not affected by a regime change. With the increasing number of democracies after 1989, the democratic stability slightly declined to 63 per cent (see Table 2). However, some older democracies that were established long before 1989 and even before the beginning of the third wave were affected as well. The overall observation for the time under consideration is that the longer a democratic regime endures, the less likely it is to decline into a hybrid regime.

A direct transition (breakdown) from a democracy to an authoritarian regime is even less likely; it has occurred in only five cases (see Appendix 2) and if we include 'extended' declines to authoritarian regimes through a 'hybrid-regime stage' of more than one year, the number of cases increases to nine. Interestingly, in two cases a reversal took place after more than 20 years of democratic rule. These latter cases can hardly be regarded as young democracies.

---

14 For different conceptualisations see Merkel 1996; Huntington 1993: 266f; Schneider/Schmitter 2004: 62.

15 See also the debate in the *Journal of Democracy*, 1996, 7, 2 and 4.

Table 2: Frequencies of regime changes, 1974–2008

Democratic years	Transition from democratic to hybrid / authoritarian regimes, no. of cases*				
	1974–1988		1989–2008		1974–2008
	Cases of decline	Average no of democracies	Cases of decline	Average no of democracies	Total cases of decline
2–5	5		13		18
6–10	4		7		11
11–15	-		4		4
16–20	[4]		3		[7]
More than 20	[3]		3		[6]
Total	16	50	30	69	46

* In a number of cases, the democratic period extended before Freedom House started up in 1972. This is indicated by square brackets. Additional information such as Polity IV Project is used for the assessment. The 16-to-20-year-old democracies were in Columbia, the Fiji Islands, Gambia and Malta.

Source: Appendix 2

The balance corroborates the assumption about a close correlation between the durability and the consolidation or institutionalisation of democratic regimes. It also suggests the operation of a self-reinforcing mechanism that, in the end, contributes to the consolidation of democracy. At the same time, the balance supports the view that most of these democratic regimes were not consolidated because young democracies and countries with a history of varied regime types were mostly affected by hybridisation or the breakdown of democracy.

Since there are a number of democracies that were forced into becoming non-democratic regimes, even after more than 20 years of democratic rule, this raises the issue of consolidation of democracy.[16] Moreover, there were a number of other democracies that collapsed before the start of the third wave after more than 20 years, such as

---

16 These were India, Lebanon, Sri Lanka before the start of the Freedom House assessment for 1972, and later Venezuela, the Solomon Islands and Trinidad and Tobago.

Chile, Uruguay and the Philippines (Huntington 1993: 271). As noted above, age is not a sufficient way of explaining consolidation.[17]

Some of the cases mentioned above are of major interest with respect to the question of whether an authoritarian regression from a consolidated democracy is possible or not. One crucial observation related to this issue is that most of the transitions from democracy occurred outside Europe, viz. in Asia and Latin America. This means that no high-income countries were affected and it brings structural factors into the analysis, which will be briefly considered in the next chapter.

At the same time, it is obvious that since the end of the Cold War, older, established democracies in industrialised countries experienced declines in the quality of democracy, but no hybridisation or breakdown. The crucial observation for the period, however, is that direct regressions to authoritarian regimes are rare, and they only took place in countries with a short experience of democracy (see above and Appendix 2).

Macro-quantitative studies come up with conflicting results on the relationship between the volatility and age of democracies. Przeworski et al. (1996; 1997; 2000), whose work is regarded as a standard in this kind of analysis, found out that new democracies break down more frequently, but if controlled for economic factors, the difference with respect to old democracies disappears. These results are basically confirmed by Epstein et al. (2006), who used a different variable and data set.[18] A different analysis by Svolik based on a new research strategy contradicts the previous surveys and is more in line with the observations above that a democracy's age is associated with greater chances of survival and that young democracies are more volatile than older ones (Svolik 2007).

It is difficult to explain the differences in the research results. Apart from the different research strategies, the studies are all based on different time sets. Przeworski et al. (1996; 1997; 2000) covered the period from 1950 to 1990, Epstein et al. (2006), the period from 1960 to 2000, while Svolik extended the coverage from 1789 to 2001. My observations are confined to the third wave (1974–2008), the latter period of which has been missed out in all other recent studies. In addition, Przeworski et al. applied a dichotomous regime typology, while I used a trichotomous typology that can easily turn out different results, as illustrated by Epstein et al., although not for the question that concerns us here, where they are in line with Przeworski et al., except as regards the relevance of economic factors. Since all these analyses provide information about the correlation between various factors in terms of likelihoods, we can conclude that the age

---

17 The answer to the problem could possibly depend on the definition of consolidation. In some definitions, a regression to a non-democratic regime is excluded; consolidated democracies are regarded as 'immune' to an authoritarian menace by 'securing achieved levels of democratic rule against authoritarian regression' (Schedler 1998: 91, 103; Svolik 2007). Others do not foreclose a possible breakdown or a tendency for deconsolidation (Linz/Stepan 1996: 6; Merkel 1999: 146), which makes their concept somewhat ambiguous.

18 Przeworski et al. (1996; 2000) cover the period from 1950 to 1990, Epstein et al. (2006), the period from 1960 to 2000. Epstein et al. use a trichotomous regime variable (democracy, partial democracy, autocracy), whereas Przeworski et al. use the classical dichotomy of democracy and autocracy.

of a democracy and its economic well-being are crucial to an understanding of their proneness to decline.

Some relevant information related to the time factor and whether democracies are more volatile during different stages of their development is provided by the study conducted by Bernhard et al. (2003). Their study suggests that after a short honeymoon period of about two years, during which young democracies survive economic crisis, they become more vulnerable to poor economic performance before their third parliamentary elections.

3.3 The economic conditions

For a preliminary survey about the socio-economic conditions under which the various declines of democracy occurred, I used the country group data from the World Bank's *World Development Reports* (WDRs) and UNDP's *Human Development Report* (HDR). The WDR groups the world's countries into four categories: low-income countries (LIC), lower-middle-income countries (LMC), upper-middle-income countries (UMC) and high-income countries (HIC),[19] while the HDR only uses three groups: low human development (LHD), medium human development (MHD) and high human development (HHD). The reason that the data from the HDR are included here is because the HDR considers not only an economic factor (per capita income), but also a number of other social factors (such as social equality/inequality, degree of education, etc.) which are assumed to contribute positively to the development and stability of democracies.

Based on these data, democratic quality losses between 1989 and 2008 occurred in 87 per cent of all cases under conditions of high and medium human development or high and medium income (see Table 3).[20] This result is not very surprising since most democracies can be found in these two country groups. Neither the WDR nor the HDR classification show any significant differences; only the more differentiated WDR classification allows the observation that democracies with lower medium incomes are more frequently affected by quality losses than countries in higher income groups. Losses of democratic quality occurred slightly more frequently in middle-income countries than in high-income countries, the latter being the income group with the highest numbers of democracies anyway. However, if the number of cases is related to the number of countries in each income group, countries with high human development were more often

---

19 Classification based on 2005 according to the following figures: low income, $905 or less; middle-income, $906 to $11,115; and high income, $11,116 and above. A further division at GNI per capita $3,595 is made between lower-middle-income and upper-middle-income economies. The benchmarks were lower for previous periods, for example for 2001: low income, $745 or less; middle income, $746 to $9,205; and high income, $9,206 and above. A further division at GNI per capita $2,975 is made between lower-middle-income and upper-middle-income economies (World Bank 2009; 2003).

20 I have confined this part of the analysis to the period after 1989 because the available data for the countries for the period from 1974 to 1989 are sketchy; the categories of country-income groups were not available for the whole period or they were different.

affected than countries with medium human development. The least frequently affected democracies were those of industrialised countries in Western Europe and Asia (see Appendix 3 and 4).

Table 3: Frequency of loss of democratic quality according to country groups, 1989–2008

	Cases	Countries	Average no. of countries in each group*
Low-income country (LIC)	7	5	52
Lower-middle-income country (LMC)	22	19	55
Upper-middle-income country (UMC)	14	11	36
High-income country (HIC)	11	7	39
Total number	54	42	182
Low human development (LHD)	7	5	41
Medium human development (MHD)	23	20	71
High human development (HHD)	25	19	64
Total number	55	44	176

* Based on classification in 1992, 2000/1, 2010; independent countries only.

Source: Appendix 3, 4; World Bank 1992; 2001; 2010; UNDP 1993; 2002; 2010

As regards the hybridisation of democracies, about 80 per cent of the regime changes took place in countries with a medium or low level of human development and also in low and lower-middle-income countries, and none in a high-income country (see Table 4). The single case of a breakdown of democracy occurred in a very poor country (LIC/LHD).

The classification schemes used in the WDR and HDR provide similar results for this analysis. The difference can clearly be attributed to the finer classification of the WDR. The cases of the middle- and low-income groups of the WDR correspond to the low and medium human development level of the HDR. And an examination of cases in relation to the country groups confirms that hybridisation and breakdown of democracy is predominantly a problem for low- and middle-income countries or countries with low to medium human development (see Table 4).[21]

Table 4: Frequency of hybridisation and breakdown of democracies according to country groupings, 1989–2008

Country groups	Frequency of hybridisation, no. of cases, in () no. of countries		
	Hybridisation F – PF	Breakdown F – NF	Average no of countries in each group
Low-income country (LIC)	8	1	52
Lower-middle-income country (LMC)	17 (11)	-	55
Upper-middle-income country (UMC)	7	-	36
High-income country (HIC)	-	-	39
Total	32	1	182
Low human development (LHD)	7	1	41
Medium human development (MHD)	19 (13)	-	71
High human development (HHD)	6	-	64
Total	32	1	176

* Based on classification in 1992, 2000/1, 2010; independent countries only.
Source: Appendix 5, 6; World Bank 1992; 2001; 2010; UNDP 1993; 2002; 2010

The short overview of the decline of democracies corroborates more general findings in macro-quantitative analyses concerning the relationship between democracy and economic development. According to these studies, democracies can emerge under different economic conditions or at different levels of development, and, once installed, these democracies have a better chance of survival in wealthier societies than in poor ones, and are almost certain to survive beyond a certain level of per capita income (Przeworski et al. 2000: 137, 269f, 273). In even stronger terms, the 'probability of a democratic breakdown declines steeply with income' (Boix/Stokes 2003: 525). Strictly speaking, though, these findings provide no explanation about the decline of democracies, but are merely observations of correlations. Nevertheless, the frequency of the quality of the same results strongly suggests a causal relationship as well, and these are 'only' average probabilities.

---

[21] There were only three cases that showed a consecutive loss of quality and a transition to a non-democratic regime within a short period of two to three years: two regressed to a hybrid state and one to an authoritarian regime that might be viewed as one process. Two of the countries belong to the group of middle-income or medium human development countries and one of them to the low-income group (see Appendix 1, 2).

One issue not yet examined here is the relationship between economic performance and the decline of democracy. The world economic crisis of the late 1920s was a major reason for the breakdown of democracies in Europe (see Linz 1978, for example). For developing countries this view was basically repeated by Linz and Diamond (1989), who identified economic crisis as one of the 'most common threats to democracy'. Macro-quantitative analyses confirmed this general wisdom (Przeworski et al. 1996: 42; Epstein et al. 2006: 564f). The evidence is refined by Bernhard et al. (2003), who found that although young democracies can survive economic crisis for a short period immediately after transition, they become more vulnerable to poor economic performance after this 'honeymoon'. All these findings suggest that younger democracies with poor economic growth or economic decline tend to be more prone to regression than democracies with higher rates of economic growth.

All in all, a number of observations are worth recording for the period of the third wave of democratisation, some of which may not seem very surprising:

1. A decline of democracy – as a loss of quality and hybridisation – can occur under all sorts of different economic conditions or levels of development. However, a complete breakdown of democracy becomes less likely the wealthier a country is – in fact, no breakdown has happened in a high-income democracy before.
2. A loss of democratic quality can affect young and old democracies as well as poor and rich ones.
3. The loss of democratic quality does not inevitably lead to a breakdown of democracy ending in a hybrid or authoritarian regime.
4. The decline of democracy to a hybrid regime is one possibility that not only affects young democracies, but older democracies as well, as in the case of India and Venezuela.
5. In addition, no hybridisation or breakdown of democracy has occurred in a high-income country – the decline of democracy in such countries is confined to the loss of democratic quality.
6. The latter two observations re-open the conceptual issue of a consolidated democracy, i.e. whether it can be reversed and not only lose democratic quality, but also deteriorate into a hybrid or authoritarian regime. The empirical evidence for the third wave is very clear: No high-income democracy was affected by hybridisation or breakdown.

An initial conclusion that can be derived from this overview is that the major challenge for the research on the decline of democracy – at least in quantitative terms – is the analysis of the loss in quality of democracy and the transition from democracies into hybrid regimes. The decline of democracy is often a gradual one without a coup d'état or any other significant event such as the cancellation of elections, the prohibition of political parties, the declaration of a state of emergency, the suspension of fundamental political rights, the changing of the constitution, or a major revolt. The absence of such dramatic events makes it difficult to capture and analyse the process of decline and the resulting regime. In fact, after applying a trichotomous regime classification in their macro-quantitative analysis, Epstein et al. (2006: 564f) came to the conclusion that the determinants of transitions to 'partial democracies' (hybrid regimes) 'elude' their understanding. Generally, it should be noted that apart from the latter study, the quantitative analyses are usually based on a dichotomous regime classification and therefore fail to capture a) changes in the quality of democracy and b) regime changes that turn them into hybrid regimes. The only phenomenon captured is the breakdown of democracies into dictatorships.

4. Case-oriented approaches

Przeworski and Limongi have argued that democracies can come into being in many different ways and for many different reasons (1997: 158). The argument can also be reversed: Democracies can decline, lose democratic quality, become hybrid regimes or break down in many different ways and for many different reasons. It is a common view among social scientists that no single variable or factor can entirely explain the transition to or the development of democracy in a country and that democratisation is the result of a combination of causes. The same is true for the decline of democratic quality, the transition from a democracy to a hybrid regime, or the breakdown of a democracy and its transformation into an autocracy. Moreover, the factors that may be responsible for the reverse wave of democratisation may be different from those responsible for a previous wave. Democratic decline in the inter-war period is likely to be different from that during the Cold War and is also different from the cases that have occurred since the fall of the Iron Curtain. Not only has the international environment changed (the international environment being less conducive to democracy during the interwar period than the period following the fall of the Iron Curtain, for example), but the internal factors, the constellation of social forces and the articulation of political ideas and ideologies have changed as well. In the 21st century the societal groups in favour of democracy will be different from those of the early 19th century or early 20th when 'post-feudal' groups still played a crucial political role.

4.1 Structurally biased approaches

Various qualitative, case-oriented studies have tried to address some of the issues just mentioned. Largely different from macro-quantitative, variable-oriented approaches, institutionalist and/or structuralist comparative historical studies – many of which are in the Barrington Moore research tradition – are characterised far more by diversity, but they also pose different problems. The historical periods, the cases, the number of cases, the regions and the various political, social and economic factors selected vary considerably. They often cover Western Europe from the 19th to the 20th century, while others cover Western Europe and some non-European cases (US, Japan and China) or examine Latin American cases from the early and late 20th century. Some analyse several distinct historical periods, e.g. first-wave and third-wave democracies as well as different regions in one study. Some focus their explanation on a specific period and region (e.g. inter-war Europe) while others try to make a general argument. These studies also differ in their focus, some of them concentrating on 'classes' and 'class alliances', others on political parties and government elites as representatives of 'classes' and on various factions among these elites. They disagree about the role of the bourgeoisie and the labour movement – for example, about which class alliance was important and about the autonomy of the state vis-à-vis the dominant classes, and see the relationship between state and civil society in different ways as well (Moore 1966; Collier/Collier 1991; Luebbert 1991; Rueschemeyer et al. 1992; Ertmann 1998; Collier 1999; Mahoney 2001). At the same time, there are a number of critical methodological issues involved that range from case selection and the stringency of the comparative method employed to the historical plausibility of some of the arguments. It should be noted that these studies are confined to Western Europe and Latin America, omitting Eastern Europe, Africa and Asia (apart from Moore). Apart from Collier (1999), they do not deal with the possible decline of third-wave democracies. Hence, they all end up with different results for their particular cases and comparisons, so no generalisation seems to be possible. Although they have improved the analyses by combining quantitative with qualitative methods, by enlarging the scope of factors involved, even including some agency-related elements, they finished by making repeated calls for further refined analyses with more 'variables' to be considered (e.g. Rueschemeyer et al. 1992: 281ff; Collier 1999: 197).

Although a number of studies include the role of actors in certain 'critical' circumstances, and in particular when some try to explain the exceptionality of deviant cases, they leave the structural argument and bring back in the crucial role of actors, strategic choice and contingency, but remain in and maintain the domain of structural arguments. It is only Mahoney (2001; 2003) who – without solving the problem – emphasises the importance of critical junctures and hence of focusing systematically on the process and the choices of actors at particular points in time, i.e. critical junctures, within the framework of a path-dependent analysis.[22]

A Boolean analysis of nine well-known, major theories or hypotheses about the conditions of breakdown or survival of democracies, including a number of those mentioned above, revealed some of the fundamental deficiencies (Berg-Schlosser/De Meure 1994: 276, 274). One familiar conclusion was, again, the call 'to go beyond the analysis of simple and very few factors' by incorporating a 'broader range of elements'. An answer to this challenge is provided by the Berg-Schlosser/Mitchell project (Berg-Schlosser/Mitchell 2000; 2002), which investigated the conditions of breakdown and survival of democracy during the inter-war period in 20th-century Western Europe.

---

22 Interestingly, O'Donnell (1973) in his early case study of the emergence of the bureaucratic-authoritarian state, which is explained structurally by 'politico-economic relationships' (O'Donnell 1978: 6), was using historical institutional arguments linking path-dependent institutional developments with rational choice game theory (critical junctures) to explain the decline of the Argentine democracy between 1955 and 1966 (1973: 115-199) – however without using the concepts of or putting his approach in the historical-institutionalist tradition. He also used some of Linz's (1978) process-oriented concepts (see below).

However, the 'multi-methodological' coverage of eighteen country cases and 63 variables of different structural, institutional and actor-related dimensions, which were ultimately reduced to eight 'supervariables', highlights the magnitude of the endeavour (Berg-Schlosser/De Meur 2002; Berg-Schlosser 2002: 315).[23] Although the research programme was confined to a particular region and to first-wave democracies, a few conclusions are to be mentioned here which could guide our further research:

The first one is that 'none of the single factor approaches [...] accounted for a great deal of variance' (ibid.: 319); the second is, 'socio-economic development and "modernization" alone explain relatively little. The "standard model" [...] of the conditions favouring democracy thus has to include basic elements of a secular and democratic political culture, an effective civil control of the military, and the absence of feudal structures' (ibid.: 322). The third one is, against 'this "structural" background the more specific political processes and actors and their dynamic interactions over time come into play' (ibid.). Although the Berg-Schlosser/Mitchell project went beyond the analysis of 'classical' structural and institutional variables by taking dynamic factors into account, it still has a 'structural bias' in that it investigates the 'conditions' for breakdown or survival. Remarkably, the dynamic elements stem from one of the few process-oriented approaches to the breakdown of democracy, namely the seminal work of Juan J. Linz on the breakdown of democracy (1978).

4.2 Process-oriented approaches

I know of only two research approaches that deal explicitly with the process of democratic decline and that might provide a framework for the analysis of the decline of democracy (Linz 1978; Brooker 2000). Paul Brooker (2000) confines his approach to the emergence of military regimes and one-party dictatorships, which he views as the most important types of modern authoritarian regimes. Considering the number of military and one-party regimes that exist, this seems to be a questionable assumption, however. Brooker picks up the older scholarship on the role of the armed forces and their intervention in politics (Feiner 1988; Nordlinger 1977; Janowitz 1964) and focuses it on a model which is then applied to the emergence of one-party dictatorships. There are several shortcomings of this approach: One is the one-sided focus on autocratic actors and the removal of the civilian sphere and its actors. The second is the failure to explain what type of regime – a democracy, a hybrid regime or a (civilian) authoritarian regime – the armed forces are coming up against, and that the model is confined to transitions into two specific authoritarian regime types that have become rare.

Linz amplified the research agenda established at the time, which focused on either non-democratic actors and movements or on structural causes of democratic breakdowns by including the role of pro-democratic forces. He claimed that historical-

---

23 The 'supervariables' are pre-war democracy, feudalism, economic development, social heterogeneity, democratic political culture, political unrest, the political role of the armed forces, and observance of civil and political rights.

institutional or socio-structural variables as used by approaches in the tradition of Barrington Moore (1974) hardly have any explanatory power with regard to the process of the breakdown of democracy. Hence, Linz' research programme had an explicit focus on agency. Unlike his later *Transition from Democracy* project (Linz and Stepan 1996), he negated the conceptual relevance of institutional and social-structure factors almost completely (Linz 1978: 24ff). Using a number of case studies, his aim was to inductively construct a 'descriptive model' that would capture any recurrent patterns, sequences and crises involved in the process of a breakdown. Linz identified three core 'elements' and five consecutive phases of the breakdown process.

The three core elements were the 'legitimacy', 'efficacy' (output) and 'efficiency' (outcome) of democratic governments, the latter two having an impact on the first. The delegitimation of the democratic government is at the heart of the issue. Aside from analysing the democratic government, the model distinguishes between three groups of actors: the loyal ones, the semi-loyal ones and the disloyal opposition. Most crucial is not the behaviour of the disloyal opposition, but rather that of the semi-loyal, which, is, however, difficult to determine and assess because its questionable 'loyalty' only becomes obvious during the crisis. The role of the semi-loyal opposition becomes crucial because the disloyal opposition is not usually in a position to command the support of the majority and topple a democratic government on its own. Finally, the model identifies five consecutive phases of breakdown: (1) crisis, (2) loss of power, (3) breakdown, (4) takeover, and (5) the 're-equilibration' or reconstitution of the democratic regime shortly before or after the breakdown (Linz 1978: 38ff, 87ff). So far, Linz seems to provide a useful framework for a process-oriented analysis of the decline of democracy. However, a number of problematic issues need to be addressed.[24]

Linz's breakdown model of democracy has hardly been applied to a single case or a comparative study.[25] One reason for this might be that the model is too complex or too abstract to apply in empirical research. However, given the fate of O'Donnell and Schmitter's (1986) phasing scheme regarding the transition from democracy, it is surprising that even Linz's phases of breakdown have not gained wider prominence. In fact, his central concepts of 'legitimacy', 'efficacy' and 'efficiency' are difficult to operationalise, and it is hard to apply them for empirical research in a comparative research design spanning several cases. This problem applies to other important concepts in his framework as well (Schmitter 1980: 850).

In light of more recent studies, which point out that economic recession is an important factor (Svolik 2007: 166; Bernhard et al. 2003; Przeworski et al. 1996: 42), it is

---

[24] Linz claimed that his model can be used for analysing the breakdown of 'consolidated' democracies, and that the model for young democracies would be different (Linz 1978: 8f). Since Linz regarded the short-lived democracies of the inter-war period in Germany, Spain and Portugal as consolidated, it is obvious that his concept then was different from today's concept of consolidation (e.g. Linz/Stepan 1996; Merkel 1996; Huntington 1993; Schedler 1998). According to the latter, all cases considered by Linz would be categorised as unconsolidated democracies.

[25] To my knowledge, only Giovanni Capoccia (2007) has adopted Linz's actor-oriented approach in his study on inter-war Europe without actually using his framework.

obvious that Linz did not sufficiently recognise the relevance of a country's economic performance for the legitimacy of its democratic government, although he complained that this issue had not been conceptually addressed in the literature that was then available.

Acknowledging that a process-oriented approach is required for analysing declines of democracy, Linz's conceptualisation appears to be too complex to be really useful for comparative research.[26] However, at least his sequencing scheme of a breakdown could be a helpful guide for exploring such processes and, perhaps, a starting point to develop it further – just like the one suggested for the transition from authoritarian rule which paved the way for fruitful research.

5. The conceptual issue: Quality and more

Up to this point, the different approaches discussed have addressed the decline of democracy as a regime change, but not as a decline in the quality of democracy. The decline of quality poses a challenge of its own and raises a conceptual issue at the same time. In the case of quality changes, we are dealing with finer nuances or degrees of change than in the case of regime changes. Therefore, an analysis of changes in the quality of democracy not only requires that fine-tuned 'measures' or instruments be used, but also entails a refined conceptualisation of democracy in the first place. Minimal concepts of democracy such as Schumpeter's or Dahl's (Schumpeter 1950; Dahl 1971; Huntington 1993; Przeworski 1999; Munck 2009), which are conveniently used to analyse regime changes, help to distinguish between autocracy and (electoral) democracy, yet they are not very helpful in investigating different degrees of democratic quality.

More complex democracy concepts are required that allow different qualities of democracy to be captured (Coppedge 2002).[27] Solutions for this challenge are provided by Merkel's 'embedded democracy' (Merkel 2004; Merkel et al. 2003) and – viewed at a critical distance – Lauth's 'democracy matrix' (2004: 327ff). Both use a three-dimensional concept of democracy, which comprises freedom, equality and control (checks and balances). Merkel's concept of 'embedded democracy' differentiates these dimensions systematically into five 'partial regimes' of democracy (see also Schmitter 1997: 243): (a) an electoral regime as the core regime, (b) political rights, (c) civil rights, (d)

---

26 Berg-Schlosser/De Meure (1994: 270) provide a different interpretation of Linz's work that is less critical. However, they concede that what they have extracted from his work 'may not reflect exactly what he had in mind in all cases'. They very successfully use Linz's work as a resource for identifying relevant variables concerning the breakdown of democracy.

27 To overcome the conceptual limitations of a minimalist concept of democracy see O'Donnell 2004; Schmitter 2004; Beetham 2004; Rueschemeyer 2004; Powell 2004; Plattner 2004; and Diamond/Morlino 2005.

horizontal accountability and (e) effective power of government.[28] This 'root concept' also provides the analytical framework for the 'Democracy Barometer' of the Swiss 'NCCR Democracy 21' project (Bühlmann et al. 2008), which is confined to 'established democracies of the OECD world'. The Barometer provides a highly differentiated set of components, which have to fulfil nine democratic functions (subcomponents) and a number of variables and indicators for measuring democracy (ibid.: 49ff). However, the Barometer still needs to prove its empirical usefulness, although its root concept is already regularly used for the Status Index of the Bertelsmann Transformation Index (BTI).[29]

The 'embedded democracy' concept has been used for the analysis of the status as well as for the transition process to democracy (Merkel et al. 2006), but not for the transition *from* democracy. However, the concept is not only useful for capturing the status and changes in the quality of democracy at different points in time, but can provide a framework for identifying and analysing the decline of democracies into hybrid and authoritarian regimes (and not only defective democracies). As applied in Merkel et al. (2006), the concept has been combined with a causal analysis, although the latter is mainly concerned with socio-economic factors, institutional structures and 'structural contexts and conditions'. What is still missing is the application of the embedded democracy concept to the decline of democracy in conjunction with a process- and actor-oriented analytical framework.

6. The international dimension

The international dimension of the breakdown of democracy has been largely absent in the discussion up to this point. It was not accounted for in either Linz's or Brooker's model, nor did it play a major role in any of the structural-oriented approaches. The research agenda for the *Transitions from Authoritarian Rule p*roject started in a similar way, but had to be changed later (O'Donnell/Schmitter 1986; Whitehead 1986; 1996a; Pridham 1991; Kneuer 2009). It is possible that external factors might not have been of much relevance during the 1920s and 1930s. However, since the third wave of democratisation and especially since the fall of the Berlin Wall, the international dimension of regime changes could not be neglected any more (see Kneuer 2009 for an overview).

The result of the third-wave stocktaking of decline cases might be significant: While there were five cases of a complete breakdown of democracy for the third wave, there has only been one since 1989 when the Cold War ended (or possibly two extended cases).[30] Although the frequency of hybridisation did not decline, but actually increased

---

28 Lauth's concept has not been applied yet, while Merkel and his collaborators (2006) have used the concept in empirical analysis; see also Bühlmann et al. 2008. For a discussion of the two concepts, see Bogaards 2009.
29 http://www.bertelsmann-transformation-index.de/en/bti/
30 Namely, in Gambia. Two other cases, Nepal and Thailand, could be considered here as well since they passed through a hybrid stage. It should be noted that all other transitions to authoritarian regimes were forced upon hybrid regimes, and coups d'état occurred not only in hybrid, but also in authoritarian regimes – rarely

slightly, both observations suggest that the international environment might have changed and, indeed, might have become more resistant to the decline of democracy. The change in the international environment after 1989 and its assumed impact on democratic decline is highlighted if we compare the third wave with previous waves of democratisation and reversals. Huntington (1993: 290) claimed that far more breakdowns occurred during the first wave and the second 'reverse wave'. For an example from the first reverse wave, only four of the 17 countries that democratised between 1910 and 1931 maintained democratic institutions throughout the 1920s and 1930s (ibid.: 17; Boix/Stokes 2003: 530). As for the second reverse wave, a third of the 32 democracies in 1958 had turned authoritarian by the mid-1970s (ibid.: 21; also Boix/Stokes 2003: 529). This short overview clearly suggests that the international dimension mattered increasingly in a reverse way – *disfavouring* the decline of democracy.

I do not mean to claim that external factors are the cause of regime changes (or that they hinder decline). But if the process of change is the research topic, the analysis has to consider the role of external actors, which might have been the factors that tipped the scales at one point during the struggle between autocratic and democratic camps. Although the challenge of analysing the complexity of the impact of external factors has been acknowledged, it cannot be a reason for ignoring this dimension (Kneuer 2009; Erdmann/Kneuer 2009; Burnell in this volume). The 'return' of authoritarian superpowers such as China and Russia to world politics (Gat 2007) along with the economic expansion of the PRC might become the paragon for other countries – not so much in Europe, but in Africa, Asia and possibly even in Latin America – and hence might have a 'tipping' impact on democratic regimes that struggle for survival in a similar way on democratisation processes.

The problem is how the international dimension can be conceptualised for the analysis of the decline of democracy. It can be considered in two ways, as a structural factor or as a process factor. The international dimension as a structural factor would be what Whitehead (1996b) has termed 'contagion' or 'diffusion' of democracy (Schmitter 1996: 37) or Huntington's (1993: 31–34) 'snowballing' effect. These concepts basically refer to the worldwide formal and informal spread and acceptance of democratic values and attitudes by various means (Rogers 2003; Lauth/Pickel 2009). On the other hand, democracy promotion or assistance can be both,[31] a structural factor or an agency if the external actor intervenes directly, for example with political and economic sanctions or through particular positive measures in support of internal actors.

---

in democracies. However, one caveat needs to be reiterated here: The hybrid category used in the Freedom House Index ('partly free') encompasses a wide spectrum of different regimes, among them 'electoral democracies' and regimes up to the value of 5.5 which is the benchmark to authoritarianism. However, none of the regimes considered here to by hybrid is close to that benchmark.

31 For a discussion of the different terms see Burnell 2000. He distinguishes between democracy promotion in a wider sense that includes all manners of development (even economic and social) assistance, which is viewed as beneficial for the conditions of democracy, and democracy assistance in a narrow understanding that directly impacts 'democracy's political variables' (p. 12).

Unlike many democracies, which often actively promote democratic developments abroad, in the post-Cold War era authoritarian regimes usually do not have an explicit dictatorship export strategy – apart from the previously communist big powers. However, in the case of democratisation conflict in neighbouring countries, they might intervene by supporting non-democratic actors in various ways, as Russia did, in the name of stability (e.g. Bader et al. 2010). The 'contagion' of the Chinese authoritarian success story might be supported directly and even protected by the alternative economic and financial bids and influence provided by China as an alternative to the democracy conditionality of Western donors. Yet, as Peter Burnell points out in this volume, we do not know how we can analyse it or how effectively the international dimension works.

7. Conclusion and desiderata

Systematic and comparative research on the decline of democracy is just beginning. Hence there is not yet a ready-made model or framework available for analysing the various forms of the decline of democracy. The traditional question of whether a structure- or an actor-theory approach is more applicable is hardly an issue anymore. The richness of the transitology research agenda of the last 25 years provides evidence of a rather 'eclectic' theoretical approach that brings 'structure' and 'contingency' together. The multiplicity and refined combination of structuralist, functionalist, institutionalist, historical-institutionalist and actor-oriented approaches have provided fruitful results, as highlighted by Gerardo Munck (2004). Some of the research findings about the prerequisites of democracy and on the transition from authoritarian rule will be indirectly helpful.

A first attempt at taking stock of the decline of democracy, (covering loss of quality, hybridisation and breakdown of democracy since the beginning of the third wave in 1974), reveals a substantial number of empirical cases that deserve scholarly attention. Based on the relatively crude measure of the Freedom House Index, the heuristic survey nevertheless provides some highly interesting results:

1. This topic appears to be particularly rewarding simply because of the frequency of the loss of democratic quality. It not only matters for younger democracies of the third wave, but also for old and established democracies in industrialised countries.
2. A decline of democracy into hybrid regimes occurred less frequently than a decline in quality, but it still occurred in a substantial number of cases. The hybridisation of democratic regimes took place most frequently in young democracies with a medium level of income. Established (or consolidated) democracies in industrialised countries in Europe were spared by hybridisation during the period of the third wave. However, a few democracies outside Europe that endured for more than 20 years, some of which were counted among the established democracies, experienced a democratic decline, regressing to hybrid regimes. This observation raises the topic of the concept of democratic consolidation once again.

3. Surprisingly – especially for transition and democracy sceptics – direct breakdowns of democracy as we know them from the past are rather exceptional cases even outside Europe and there are only a few more cases of breakdowns that made a 'detour' via a hybrid regime.
4. The socio-economic conditions that favour successful democratisation seem to be clearly the same that work against a hybridisation and particularly against a breakdown of democracy: In very general terms, the higher the national income level, the less likely an authoritarian reversal. A similar observation can be made for the impact of the international environment. The more 'democratic' conditions of the post-1989 era have not only favoured democratisation, but also seem to mitigate a reverse wave (although this judgement might be too early): Higher numbers of democracies make authoritarian reversals more difficult.

In regard to any future research on democracy decline, I have a number of suggestions. First, research should avoid the selection bias of the democratic-transition research that mainly focused on positive or successful cases (Munck 2004: 79) – apart from a few exceptions (e.g. Bratton/Walle 1997; Berg-Schlosser/Mitchell 2002; Berg-Schlosser 2008) – right from the beginning. Second, as already pointed out above, the international dimension, which has been ignored in transitology for so long, needs to be included from the outset. Although it is methodologically difficult to provide causal evidence for the effects of a more or less benign international environment for particular regime types, it is highly plausible that the inter-war period in Europe or the Cold War period in general were more benign to autocracies than the period after the fall of the Iron Curtain.

Third, the research on the relationship between social inequality and the broader social heterogeneity (which addresses cultural, ethnic, religious differences, *inter alia*) on the one side and democracy on the other is inconclusive or even contradictory (Acemoglu/Robinson 2006: 61–62; Horowitz 1993; Fish/Brooks 2004; Anderson/Paskeviciute 2006). Some studies cannot find a relationship between the two (e.g. Przeworski et al. 2000; Bollen/Jackman 1985), and others claim inequality makes dictatorships more stable (Muller 1985; 1995) or that democracy is not compatible with high inequality (Dahl 1971; Huntington 1991). Apart from the numerous methodological problems involved in these studies, the fragility of democracies in Africa, Asia and particularly in Latin America, which included cases of hybridisation even after very long periods of democratic rule, suggests that it might be worthwhile to have a closer look at social inequality and heterogeneity. Many of these studies cover only particular periods and are therefore biased toward democracies of industrialised countries which, for example, exclude the fragile inter-war period in Europe (e.g. Przeworski et al. 2000). It can be assumed that in a different specific historical context and at a 'medium' level of development, social inequality and societal heterogeneity might matter much more than at a higher income level.

Fourth, also related to the history problem is another 'explanatory variable', namely the different historical sequencing of competition and participation as Robert H. Dix (1994) pointed out. Perhaps, all those countries that did not follow the 'preferred trajectory' to democracy, in which competition preceded participation during the first wave, might be more prone to democracy decline (hybridisation or loss of quality) than others. At the same time, the question about historical sequences can be extended to other institutional arrangements: for example, the control dimension (the efficacy of the rule of law) in relation to competition and participation, or, more generally, the historical sequencing of the effective institutionalisation of the five partial regimes of democracy. A deeper comparative-historical survey could identify 'critical junctures' and perhaps path-dependent developments that might help to explain the fragility of democratic regimes (Cappoccia/Kelemen 2007; Pierson 2004; Mahoney 2003: 137).

Fifth, the economic crisis needs to be considered more thoroughly, and scholars should focus on how and under which conditions an economic crisis can be turned into a political crisis that will ultimately endanger a democratic regime (because it is not the case that every economic crisis automatically turns into a political crisis for the regime in question).

Finally, it is evident that none of these 'factors' or 'variables' – this is by no means an exhaustive list – is sufficient to explain declines of democracy; the status of the various factors and variables may be that of an intervening variable, or, more generally, they might matter in different ways under different structural and historical conditions. In the end, they provide the lining for the actor analysis in the decline process.

On the conceptual level, the research agenda can hardly rely on a dichotomous regime classification of democracy and dictatorship. Instead, it can make use of the concept differentiation of diminished subtypes developed in the context of research on democratic transition. This also requires that the boundaries between the subtypes of democracy and autocracy based on different 'root concepts' be determined, and that different degrees of quality regarding democracy be established. Moreover, the analysis of different qualities of democracy may require a concept of democracy that extends beyond competition and participation but includes the control dimension.

As the research on democratic transition started with small-n comparisons generating new concepts and new ideas for causal assessments based on process-tracing (Munck 2004: 77f), a similar research strategy ought to be fertile for crafting hypotheses on the decline of democracy. To overcome the challenge of combining quantitative and qualitative methods as indicated for democratic-transition research, a complex methodological mixture based on a QCA application might prove most useful here as exemplified by the Berg-Schlosser/Mitchell project for inter-war Europe. The result suggests similar intra-regional comparisons for other regions such as Africa, Asia, Latin America and Eastern Europe with their own configuration of conditions and of time-specific contexts.

Bibliography

Acemoglu, Daron/Robinson, James A. (2006) *Economic Origins of Dictatorship and Democracy*, Cambridge.
Anderson, Christopher J./Paskeviciute, Aida (2006) 'How Ethnic and Linguistic Heterogeneity Influence the Prospects of Civil Society: A Comparative Study of Citizenship Behavior', *Journal of Politics*, 68, 4: 783-802.

Bader, Julia/Grävingholt, Jörn/Kästner, Antje (2010) 'Would autocracies promote autocracy? A political economy perspective on regime-type export in regional neighbourhoods' Contemporary Politics, 16, 1, 81-100.
Beetham, David (2004) 'Freedom as the Foundation', *Journal of Democracy*, 15, 4: 61-75.
Bendel, Petra/Croissant, Aurel/Rüb, Friedbert W. (eds) (2002) *Hybride Regime. Zur Konzeption und Empirie demokratischer Grauzonen*, Opladen.
Berg-Schlosser, Dirk (2002) 'Cross-Sectional and Longitudinal Analysis' in Berg-Schlosser, Dirk/Mitchell, Jeremy (eds.) *Authoritarianism and Democracy in Europe, 1919-39*, Hampshire: 285-315.
Berg-Schlosser, Dirk (2008) 'Determinants of Democratic Successes and Failures in Africa', *European Journal of Political Research*, 47, 3: 269-306
Berg-Schlosser, Dirk/De Meur, Gisèle (1994) 'Conditions of Democracy in inter-war Europe: a Boolean test of major hypotheses', *Comparative Politics*, 26: 252-279.
Berg-Schlosser, Dirk/De Meur, Gisèle (2002) 'Reduction of Complexity' in Berg-Schlosser, Dirk/Mitchell, Jeremy (eds.), *Authoritarianism and Democracy in Europe, 1919-39*, Hampshire:: 270-284.
Berg-Schlosser, Dirk/Mitchell, Jeremy (eds.) (2000) *Conditions of Democracy in Europe, 1919-39, Systematic Case Studies*, Hampshire.
Berg-Schlosser, Dirk/Mitchell, Jeremy (eds.) (2002) *Authoritarianism and Democracy in Europe, 1919-39*, Hampshire.
Bernhard, Michael/Reenock, Christopher/Nordstrom, Timothy (2003) 'Economic Performance and Survival in New Democracies. Is there a Honeymoon Effect?', *Comparative Political Studies*, 36, 4: 404-431.
Bogaards, Matthijs (2009) 'How to Classify Hybrid Regimes? Defective Democracy and Electoral Authoritarianism', *Democratization*, 16, 2: 399-423.
Boix, Charles/Stokes, Susan C. (2003) 'Endogenous Democratization', *World Politics*, 55, July, 2003: 517-549.
Bollen, Kenneth A./Jackman, Richard W. (1985) 'Political Democracy and the Size Distribution of Income', *American Sociological Review*, 50: 438-457.
Bollen, Kenneth A. (1983) 'Temporal Variations in Mortality: A Comparison of U. S. Suicides and Motor Vehicle Fatalities, 1972-1976', *Demography*, 20: 45-59.
Bollen, Kenneth A. (1979) 'Political Democracy and the Timing of Development', *American Sociological Review*, 44: 572-87.
Bratton, Michael/van de Walle, Nicolas (1997) Democratic Experiments in Africa: Regime Transition in Comparative Perspective, Cambridge.
Brooker, Paul (2000) *Non-Democratic Regimes*, New York.
Brownlee, Jason (2007) Authoritarianism in Age of Democratization, Cambridge.
Bühlmann, Marc/Merkel, Wolfgang/Wessels, Bernhard (2008) 'The Quality of Democracy. Democracy Barometer for Established Democracies', nccr democracy 21, Working Paper No. 10a. National Center of Competence in Research: Challenges to Democracy in the 21st Century.
Burnell, Peter (2000) 'Democracy Assistance: The State of the Discourse' in Burnell, Peter (ed.) *Democracy Assistance. International Co-operation for Democratization*, London: 3-33.
Burnell, Peter (2008)'Is the international environment becoming less benign for democratisation?', Paper prepared to the Annual Workshop of the standing group "Demokratieforschung" (democracy research) of the German Political Science Association, Hamburg 16 October (in this volume).

Capoccia, Giovanni (2005) Defending Democracy. Reactions to Extremism in Interwar Europe, Baltimore.
Capoccia, Giovanni/Kelemen, R. Daniel (2007) 'The Study of Critical Junctures: Theory, Narrative, and Counterfactuals in Historical Institutionalism', *World Politics*, 59, 3: 341-369
Carothers, Thomas (2002) 'The End of the Transition Paradigm', *Journal of Democracy*, 13, 1: 5-21.
Carothers, Thomas (2006) 'The Backlash Against Democracy Promotion', *Foreign Affairs*, 85, 2: 55-68.
Collier, Ruth Berins (1999) Paths towards Democracy. The Working Class and Elites in Western Europe and South America, Cambridge.
Collier, Ruth Berins/Collier, David (1991) Shaping the Political Arena: Critical Junctures, the Labor Movement, and Regime Dynamics in Latin America, Princeton.
Coppedge, Michael (2002) 'Democracy and Dimensions. Comments on Munck and Verkuilen', *Comparative Political Studies*, 35, 1: 35-39.
Cutright, Philips (1962) 'National Political Development: Measurement and analysis', *American Sociological Review*, 28: 253-264
Cutright, Philips/ Wiley, James (1969) 'Modernization and Political Representation: 1927-1966', *Studies in Comparative International Development*, 5: 23-44
Dahl, Robert (1971) Polyarchy: Participation and Opposition, New Haven.
Diamond, Larry et al. (1987) 'Democracy in Developing Countries: Faciliating and obstructing factors' in Gastil, Raymond (ed.) *Freedom in the World: Political and civil liberties, 1987-1989*, New York.
Diamond, Larry (1992) 'Economic Development and Democracy Reconsidered' in Marks, Gary/Diamond, Larry (eds.) *Reexamining Democracy*, Newburry Park: Sage Publication: 93-139.
Diamond, Larry (2002) 'Thinking About Hybrid Regimes', *Journal of Democracy*, 13, 2: 21-35.
Diamond, Larry (2008) 'The Democratic Rollback. The Resurgence of the Predatory State', *Foreign Affairs*, 87, 2: 36-48.
Diamond, Larry/Linz, Juan J. (1989) 'Introduction: Politics, Democracy, and Society in Latin America' in Diamond, Larry/Linz, Juan J./Lipset, Seymour M. (eds.) *Democracy and Development in Developing Countries: Latin America*, Boulder: 1-35
Diamond, Larry/Morlino, Leonardo (eds.) (2005) *Assessing the Quality of Democracy*, Baltimore.
Dix, Robert H. (1994) 'History and Democracy Revisted. Research Note', *Comparative Politics*, 27, 1: 91-105.
Epstein, David L./Bates, Robert/Goldstone, Jack/Kristensen, Ida/O'Halloran, Sharyn (2006) 'Democratic Transitions', *American Journal of Political Science*, 50 (July): 551-569.
Erdmann, Gero/Kneuer, Marianne (2009) 'Externe Faktoren der Demokratisierung: Forschungsperspektiven und Entwicklungspotential' in Erdmann, Gero/Kneuer, Marianne (eds.) *Externe Faktoren der Demokratisierung*, Baden-Baden: 319-338.
Ertmann, Thomas (1998) 'Democracy and dictatorship in interwar Western Europe', *World Politics*, 50, 3: 475-505.
Feiner, Samuel E. (1988) *The Man on Horseback. The Role of the Military in Politics*, London (revised edition 1976, original 1962).
Fish, Steven M. (2001) 'The Dynamics of Democratic Erosion' in Anderson, Richard D./ Fish, Steven M./ Hanson. Stephen E./Roeder, Philip G. *Postcommunism and the Theory of Democracy*, Princeton: 54-95.
Fish, Steven M./Brooks, Robin S. (2004) 'Does Diversity Hurt Democracy?', *Journal of Democracy*, 15, 1: 154-168.

Freedom House (2009) *Freedom in the World. Country Ratings 1972-2009*, http://www.freedom house.org.
Gandhi, Jennifer/Przeworski, Adam (2007) 'Authoritarian Institutions and the Survival of Autocrats', *Comparative Political Studies* 40, 11: 1279-1301.
Gat, Azar (2007) 'The Return of Authoritarian Great Powers', *Foreign Affairs*, July/August: 59-69.
Hadenius, Axel/Teorell, Jan (2007) 'Pathways from Authoritarianism', *Journal of Democracy* 18, 1: 143-156.
Horowitz, Donald L. (1993) 'Democracy in Divided Societies', *Journal of Democracy*, 4, 4: 269-308
Huntington, Samuel P. (1993) The Third Wave. Democratization in the late twentieth century, Norman.
Jackman, Richard (1973) 'On the relation of Economic Development to Democratic Performance', *American Journal of Political Science*, 17: 611-621
Janowitz, Morris (1964) The Military in the Political Development of New Nations: An Essay in Comparative Analysis, Chicago.
Karl, Terry L. (1995) 'The Hybrid Regimes of Central America', *Journal of Democracy* 6, 3: 72-87.
Kneuer, Marianne (2009) 'Externe Faktoren der Demokratisierung – zum Stand der Forschung' in Erdmann, Gero/Kneuer, Marianne (eds.) *Externe Faktoren der Demokratisierung*, Baden-Baden: 9-36.
Köllner, Patrick (2008) 'Autoritäre Regime – Ein Überblick über die jüngere Literatur', *Zeitschrift für vergleichende Politikwissenschaft*, 2, 2: 351-366. ,
Krennerich, Michael (2002) 'Weder Fisch noch Fleisch? Klassifikationsprobleme zwischen Demokratie und Diktatur' in Bendel, Petra/Croissant, Aurel/Rüb, Friedbert W. (eds.) *Zwischen Demokratie und Diktatur,* Opladen: 55-70.
Lauth, Hans-Joachim (2004) Demokratie und Demokratiemessung: Eine konzeptionelle Grundlegung für den interkulturellen Vergleich, Wiesbaden.
Lauth, Hans-Joachim/Pickel, Gert (2009) 'Diffusion der Demokratie – Transfer eines erfolgreichen Modells?' in: Erdmann, Gero/Kneuer, Marianne (eds.) *Externe Faktoren der Demokratisierung*, Baden-Baden: 37-74
Levitsky, Steven/Way Lucian A. (2002) 'The Rise of Competitive Authoritarianism', *Journal of Democracy*, 13, 2: 51-65.
Levitsky, Steven/Way, Lucien, W. (2007) Competitive Authoritarianism: International Linkage, Organizational Power, and the Fate of Hybrid Regimes, Manuscript.
Lewis, Paul H. (2006) Authoritarian Regimes in Latin America: Dictators, Despots, and Tyrants, Lanham, MA.
Linz, Juan J. (1978) 'Crisis, Breakdown, and Reequilibration' in Linz, Juan J./Stepan, Alfred (eds.) *The Breakdown of Democratic Regimes*, London 1978: 3-124.
Linz, Juan J./Stepan, Alfred (1996) Problems of Democratic Transition and Consolidation: Southern Europe, South America and Post-Communist Europe, Baltimore.
Lipset, Seymour Martin (1963) *Political Man. The social basis of politics*, Garden City, New York.
Lipset, Seymour Martin/Seong, Kyoung-Ryung/Torres, John Charles (1993) 'A comparative analysis of the social requisites of democracy', *International Social Science Journal*, 45: 155-175.
Luebbert, Gregory (1991) Liberalism, Fascism or Social Democracy, New York.

Magaloni, Beatriz (2008) 'Credible Power-Sharing and the Longevity of Authoritarian Rule', *Comparative Political Studies* 41, 4/5: 715-741.
Mahoney, James (2001) 'Path-Dependent Explanations of Regime Change: Central America in Comparative Perspective', *Studies in Comparative International Development*, 36, 1: 111-141.
Mahoney, James (2003) 'Knowledge Accumulation in Comparative Historical Research: The Case of Democracy and Authoritarianism' in Mahoney, James/ Rueschemeyer, Dietrich (eds.) *Comparative Historical Analysis in the Social Sciences*, Cambridge: 131-174.
Merkel, Wolfgang (1996) 'Institutionalisierung und Konsolidierung der Demokratien in Ostmitteleuropa ' in Merkel, Wolfgang et al. (eds.) *Systemwechsel 2. Die Institutionalisierung der Demokratie*, Opladen: 9-36.
Merkel, Wolfgang (1999) *Systemtransformation*, Opladen.
Merkel, Wolfgang (2004) 'Embedded and Defective Democracies' in Aurel Croissant/Wolfgang Merkel (eds.) *Special Issue of Democratization: Consolidated or Defective Democracy? Problems of Regime Change*, 11, 5: 33-58.
Merkel, Wolfgang (2010) 'Das Ende der Euphorie. Der Systemwettlauf zwischen Demokratie und Diktatur ist eingefroren' in *Internationale Politik* (Mai / Juni): 18-23.
Merkel, Wolfgang/Puhle, Hans-Jürgen/Croissant, Aurel/Eicher, Claudia/Thiery, Peter (2003) *Defekte Demokratien, vol. 1: Theorien und Probleme*, Opladen.
Merkel, Wolfgang/Puhle, Hans-Jürgen/Croissant, Aurel/ Thiery, Peter (2006) *Defekte Demokratien, vol. 2: Regionalanalysen*, Opladen.
Moore, Barrington (1966) The Social Origins of Dictatorship and Democracy: Lord and Peasant in the Making of the Modern World, Boston.
Morlino, Leonardo (2009) 'Are there hybrid regimes? Or are they just an optical illusion?', *European Political Science Review*, 1, 2: 273-296.
Munck, Gerardo L. (2004) 'Democracy Studies: Agendas, Findings, Challenges' in Berg-Schlosser, Dirk (ed.) *Democratization. The State of the Art*, Wiesbaden: 65-97
Munck, Gerardo L. (2009) Measuring Democracy. A Bridge between Scholarship and Politics, Baltimore.
Munck, Gerardo L./Verkuilen, Jay (2002) 'Conceptualizing and Measuring Democracy. Evaluating Alternative Indices', *Comparative Political Studies*, 35, 1: 5-34.
Nordlinger, Eric A. (1977) *Soldiers in Politics. Military Coups and Governments*, Englewood Cliffs, New Jersey.
O'Donnell, Guillermo (1973) Modernization and Bureaucratic Authoritarianism. Studies in South American Politics, Berkeley.
O'Donnell, Guillermo (1978) 'Reflections on the Parterns of Change in the Bureaucratic-Authoritarian State', *Latin American Research Review*, 13, 1: 3-38.
O'Donnell, Guillermo (2004) 'Why the Rule of Law Matters', *Journal of Democracy*, 15, 4: 20-31.
O'Donnell, Guillermo/Schmitter, Philippe C. (1986) Transitions from Authoritarian Rule: Tentative Conclusions About Uncertain Democracies, Baltimore.
Olson, Mancur (1968) 'Multivariate Analysis of National Political Development', *American Sociological Review*, 35: 699-712
Plattner, Marc F. (2004) 'A Skeptical Afterword', *Journal of Democracy*, 15, 4: 106-110
Powell, G. Bingham (2004) 'The Chain of Responsiveness', *Journal of Democracy*, 15, 4: 91-105
Pierson, Paul (2004) Politics in Time. History, Institutions and Social Analysis, Princeton.
Polity IV Project, Political Regime Characteristics and Transitions, 1800-2009, http://www.systemicpeace.org/polity/polity4.htm

Pridham, Geoffrey (1991) 'International Influences and Democratic Transition: Problems of Theory and Practice in Linkage Politics' in Pridham, Geoffrey, (ed.) *Encouraging Democracy: The International Context of Regime Transition in Southern Europe*, London: 1-29.

Przeworski, Adam (1999) 'Minimalist Conception of Democracy: A Defense' in Shapiro, Ian/Hacker-Cordón, Caiano (eds.) *Democracy's Value*, New York: 23-55.

Przeworski, Adam/Alvarez, Michael E./Cheibub, José Antonio/Limongi, Fernando (1996) 'What makes democracies endure?', *Journal of Democracy*, 7, 1: 39-55.

Przeworski, Adam/Limongi, Fernando (1997) 'Modernization: Theories and Facts', *World Politics*, 49, 2: 155-183.

Przeworski, Adam/Alvarez, Michael E./Cheibub, José Antonio/Limongi, Fernando (2000) *Democracy and Development: Political Institutions and Well-Being in the World, 1950-1990*, Cambridge.

Puddington, Arch (2008) Findings of Freedom in the World 2008 – Freedom in Retreat: Is the Tide Turning?, Freedom House 2008.

Puddington, Arch (2010) 'The Erosion Accelerates, The Freedom House Survey for 2009', *Journal of Democracy*, 21, 2, 136-150.

Ragin, Charles C. (1987) Comparative Method: Moving Beyond Qualitative and Quantitative Strategies, Berkeley.

Ragin, Charles C. (2000) *Fuzzy-Set Social Science*, Chicago.

Rihoux, Benoît/Ragin, Charles C. (2009) Configurational Comparative Methods. Qualitative Comparative Analysis (QCA) and Related Techniques, London.

Rogers, Everett M. (2003) *Diffusion of innovations* (5th ed.). New York.

Rüb, Friedbert (2002) 'Hybride Regime: Politikwissenschaftliches Chamäleon oder neuer Regimetypus? Begriffliche und konzeptionelle Überlegungen zum neuen Pessimismus in der Transitologie' in Bendel, Petra/Croissant, Aurel/Rüb, Friedbert W. (eds.) *Zwischen Demokratie und Diktatur*, Opladen: 99-118.

Rueschemeyer, Dietrich (2004) 'Addressing Inequality', *Journal of Democracy*, 15, 4: 76-90.

Rueschemeyer, Dietrich/Huber Stephens, Evelyne/Huber, John D. (1992) *Capitalist Development and Democracy*, Cambridge.

Schedler, Andreas (1998) 'What is Democratic Consolidation', *Journal of Democracy*, 9: 91-107.

Schedler, Andreas (ed.) (2006) *Electoral Authoritarianism*, Boulder.

Schmitter, Philippe C. (1980) 'Reviewed work: The Breakdown of Democratic Regimes by Juan J. Linz; Alfred Stepan', *American Political Science Review*, 74, 3: 849-852

Schmitter, Philippe C. (1996) 'The International Context, Political Conditionality, and the Consolidation of Neo-Democracies' in Whitehead, Laurence (ed.) *The International Dimensions of Democratization: Europe and the Americas*, Oxford: 27-57.

Schmitter, Philippe C. (2004) 'The Ambiguous Virtues of Accountability', *Journal of Democracy*, 15, 4: 47-60.

Schneider, Carsten Q./Schmitter, Philippe C. (2004) 'Liberalization, Transition and Consolidation: Measuring the Components of Democratization', *Democratization*, 11, 5: 59-90.

Schneider, Carsten Q./Wagemann, Claudius (2007) *Qualitative Comparative Analysis (QCA) und Fuzzy Sets*, Opladen.

Schumpeter, Joseph A. (1950) *Capitalism, Socialism, and Democracy*, New York.

Snyder, Richard (2006) 'Beyond Electoral Authoritarianism: The Spectrum of Non-Democratic Regimes' in Schedler, Andreas (ed.) *Electoral Authoritarianism: The Dynamics of Unfree Competition*, Boulder: 219-231.

Svolik, Milan (2007) 'Authoritarian Reversals and Democratic Consolidation', *American Political Science Review* 102, 2: 153-168.

Thomas, George/Ramirez, Francisco/Meyer, John/Gobalet, Jeanne (1979) 'Maintaining National Boundaries in the World System: The Rise of Centralist Regimes' in Meyer, John/ Hannan, Michael (ed.) *National Development and the World System*, Chicago: 187-209

UNDP (various years), *Human Development Report*.

Whitehead, Laurence (1986) 'International Aspects of Democratization' in O'Donnell, Guillermo/Schmitter, Philippe C./Whitehead, Laurence (eds..) *Transitions from Authoritarian Rule*, Bd. 4: Comparative Aspects, Baltimore/London: 3-47.

Whitehead, Laurence (ed.) (1996a) The International Dimensions of Democratization: Europe and the Americas, Oxford.

Whitehead, Laurence (1996b) 'Three International Dimensions of Democratization' in Whitehead, Laurence (ed.) *The International Dimensions of Democratization: Europe and the Americas*, Oxford: 3-26.

Whitehead, Laurence (2009) 'Democratization and social inequalities', Development & Transition, 12: 5-8.

Wintrobe, Ronald (2007) 'Dictatorship: Analytic Approaches' in Boix, Charles/Stokes, Susan (eds.) *The Oxford Handbook of Comparative Politics*, Oxford: 363-394.

World Bank (various years), *World Development Report*.

Appendix 1: Loss of democratic quality* by region, 1974–2008

	Africa	Asia	Latin America	Europe
1974–1988				
PR 1-2			Bahamas 1980–81 Belize 1983–84	Greece 1984–85 Italy 1975–76 Malta 1976–77 Sweden 1974–75
PR 2-3			Bahamas 1986–87	
CL 1-2			Argentina 1988–89 Barbados 1983–84 Belize 1987–88 Dominican Rep. 1978–79 Dominican Rep. 1983–84 Grenada 1988–89 St. Kitts & Nevis 1986–87	West Germany 1976–77 Italy 1976–77 Malta 1975–76
CL 2-3	Botswana 1979–80 Gambia 1979–8	India 1979–80 Papua New Guinea 1987–88 Solomon Islands 1983–84 Sri Lanka 1977–78	Brazil 1987–88 Colombia 1974–75 Ecuador 1984–85 Jamaica 1975–76 Venezuela 1988–89	Malta 1978–79 Spain 1979–80
PR & CL 1-2	–	–	–	–
PR & CL 2-3				
No. of cases /countries 1974-1989	2 / 2	4 / 4	15 / 12	9 / 6
1989–2007				
PR 1–2	Botswana 1992–93 Gambia 1992–93 Mauritius 1991–92 São Tomé & Príncipe 2002–03	Japan 1992–93 Taiwan 2001–02 Vanuatu 2002–03 Taiwan 2005–06	Argentina 1991–92 Bolivia 2001–02 Peru 2001–02 St. Vincent & Grenadines 1993–94 Suriname 2004–05 Trinidad & Tobago 1999–00 Uruguay 1992–93	Belgium 1995–96 Lithuania 2003–04 Latvia 2006–07
PR 2–3	Benin 2000–01	Mongolia 1991–92	Argentina 1997–98 Chile 1997–98 Dominican Rep. 2002–03	Romania 2003–04
CL 1–2	Mauritius 2005–06	Japan 1990–91 Micronesia 1996–97 Solomon Islands 1992–93	Argentina 1989–90 Belize 2000–01 Costa Rica 1992–93 Dominican Rep. 1989–90 Trinidad & Tobago 1993–94	Ireland 1992–93 Italy 1991–92 Spain 1992–93 United Kingdom 1989–90

	Africa	Asia	Latin America	Europe
CL 2–3	Benin 1998–99 Mali 2005–06 Namibia 1992–93	Israel 1992–93 Israel 1999–00 Nauru 1992–93 Papua New Guinea 1989–90 Samoa 1997–98 Vanuatu 1993–94	Brazil 1989–90 Ecuador 1990–91 Jamaica 1992–93 Jamaica 2000–01 Mexico 2005–06	Bulgaria 1995–96 Greece 1992–93 Italy 1992–93 Italy 2007–08
PR & CL 1–2			Dominican Rep. 2003–04 St. Kitts & Nevis 1993–94	
PR & CL 2–3	Mali 1996–97			
No. of cases / countries 1989–2008	10 / 7	14 / 10	22 / 16	12 / 10
Totals: cases / countries	**12 / 7**	**18 / 12**	**37 / 21**	**21 / 13**

* Change of quality 1–2, 2–3 (1–3 none), PR = political rights; CL = civil liberties.
** Years indicate the change of evaluation in Freedom House.

Appendix 2: Regime changes from democracy to hybrid and authoritarian regimes, 1974–2008*

	Africa	Asia	Latin America	Europe
1974–1988				
F–PF = hybrid	Burkina Faso 1979–80 Gambia 1980–81 Mauritius 1977–78 Seychelles 1976–77	Fiji 1986–87 India 1974–75 Lebanon 1974–75 Maldives 1974–75 Sri Lanka 1974–75, 1980–81 Suriname 1988–89 Turkey 1979–80 Vanuatu 1981–82	Colombia 1988–89 El Salvador 1975–76 Grenada 1978–79 Peru 1988–89	Malta 1980–1981/82
F–NF = authoritarian	Ghana 1980–1981 Nigeria 1982–83	Suriname 1979–80 Thailand 1975–76		
(F)–PF–NF	*Burkina F. 1980–81*		*Grenada 1980–81*	
No. of cases / countries	6 / 6	11 / 9	4 / 4	1 / 1
1989–2008				
F–PF = hybrid	Malawi 1998–99 Mali 1993–94 Zambia 1992–93 Senegal 2007–08	Bangladesh 1992–93 India 1990–91 Nepal 1992–93 Papua New Guinea 1992–93, 2002–03 Philippines 1989–90, 2004–05 Solomon Islands 1999–2000 Thailand 1990–91, 2004–05	Antigua & Barbuda 1990–91 Argentina 2000–01 Bolivia 1994–95, 2002–03 Brazil 1992–93 Dominican Rep. 1992–93 Ecuador 1995–96, 1999–00 Guyana 2004–05 Honduras 1992–93, 1998–99 Trinidad & Tobago 2000–01 Venezuela 1992–93, 1998–99	*Estonia 1991–92*** *Latvia 1991–92*** Slovakia 1995–96
F–NF = authoritarian	Gambia 1993–94			
(F)–PF–NF		*Nepal 2004–05* *Thailand 2005–06*		
No. of cases / countries	5 / 5	10 / 7	14 / 10	1 / 1
Total	11 / 10	21 / 14	18 / 14	2 / 2

* Years indicate the change of evaluation in Freedom House.
** After independence 1 year F, then a) 1 year or 2 years PF, afterwards F (hence not considered for Table 1).

F = free (liberal democracy); PF = partly free (hybrid regime); NF = not free (authoritarian regime).

Source: Freedom House 2009

Appendix 3: Loss of democratic quality by country income groups, 1989–2008

	Low–income, LIC	Lower–middle–income, LMC	Upper–middle–income, UMC	High income, HIC
1.	Benin 1998–99 CL: 2 to CL: 3 Benin 2000–01 PR: 2 to PR: 3	Belize 2000–01 CL: 1 to CL: 2	Argentina 1989–90 CL: 1 to CL: 2 Argentina 1991–92 PR: 1 to PR: 2 Argentina 1997–98 PR: 2 to PR: 3	Belgium 1995–96 PR: 1 to PR: 2
2.	Gambia 1992–93 PR: 1 to PR: 2	Bolivia 2001–02 PR: 1 to PR: 2	Chile 1997–98 PR: 2 to PR: 3	Israel 1992–93 CL: 2 to CL: 3 Israel 1999–00 CL: 2 to CL: 3
3.	Mali 1996–97 PR + CL: 2 to 3 Mali 2005–06 CL: 2 to CL: 3	Botswana 1992–93 PR: 1 to PR: 2	Greece 1992–93 CL: 2 to CL: 3	Ireland 1992–93 CL: 1 to CL: 2
4.	Papua New Guinea 1989–90 C: 2 to CL: 3	Brazil 1989–90 CL: 2 to CL: 3	Latvia 2006–07 PR: 1 to PR: 2	Italy 1991–92 CL: 1 to CL: 2 Italy 1992–93 CL: 2 to CL: 3 Italy 2007–08 CL: 1 to CL: 2
5.	São Tomé & Príncipe 2002–03 PR: 1 to PR: 2	Bulgaria 1995–96 CL: 2 to CL: 3	Lithuania 2003–04 PR: 1 to PR: 2	Japan 1990–91 CL: 1 to CL: 2, Japan 1992–93 PR: 1 to PR: 2
6.		Costa Rica 1992–93 CL: 1 to CL: 2	Mauritius 2005–06 CL: 1 to CL: 2	Spain 1992–93 CL: 1 to CL: 2
7.		Dominican Rep. 1989–90 CL: 1 to CL: 2, Dominican Rep. 2003–04 CL + PR: 1 to 2	Mexico 2005–06 CL: 2 to CL: 3	United Kingdom 1989–90 CL: 1 to CL: 2
8.		Ecuador 1990–91 CL: 2 to CL: 3	St. Kitts & Nevis 1993–94 CL + PR: 1 to 2	
9.		Jamaica 1992–93 CL: 2 to CL: 3 Jamaica 2000–01 CL: 2 to CL: 3	Trinidad & Tobago 1993–94 CL: 1 to CL: 2 Trinidad & Tobago 1999–00 PR: 1 to PR: 2	
10.		Mauritius 1991–92 PR: 1 to PR: 2	Uruguay 1992–93 PR: 1 to PR: 2	
11.		Mongolia 1991–92 PR: 2 to PR: 3	Venezuela 1991–92 PR: 1 to PR: 3	

	Low–income, LIC	Lower–middle–income, LMC	Upper–middle–income, UMC	High income, HIC
12.		Namibia 1992–93 CL: 2 to CL: 3		
13.		Peru 2001–02 PR: 1 to PR: 2		
14.		Romania 2003–04 PR: 2 to PR: 3		
15.		Samoa 1997–98 CL:2 to CL: 3		
16.		Solomon Islands 1992–93 CL: 1 to CL: 2		
17.		St. Vincent & Grenadines 1993–94 PR: 1 to PR: 2		
18.		Suriname 2004–05 PR: 1 to PR: 2		
19.		Vanuatu 1993–94 CL: 2 to CL: 3, Vanuatu 2002–03 PR: 1 to PR: 2		

Source: Freedom House 2009; World Bank, World Development Report (various years)
* no data available for 2 (World Bank) and 3 countries (UNDP).

Appendix 4: Loss of democratic quality by level of human development, 1989–2008

	Low	Medium	High
1.	Benin 1998–99 CL: 2 to CL: 3 Benin 2000–01 PR: 2 to PR: 3	Belize 2000–01 CL: 1 to CL: 2	Argentina 1989–90 CL: 1 to CL: 2 Argentina 1991–92 PR: 1 to PR: 2 Argentina 1997–98 PR: 2 to PR: 3
2.	Gambia 1992–93 PR: 1 to PR: 2	Bolivia 2001–02 PR: 1 to PR: 2	Belgium 1995–96 PR: 1 to PR: 2
3.	Mali 1996–97 PR + CL: 2 to 3 Mali 2005–06 CL: 2 to CL: 3	Botswana 1992–93 PR: 1 to PR: 2	Chile 1997–98 PR: 2 to PR: 3
4.	Mongolia 1991–92 PR: 2 to PR: 3	Brazil 1989–90 CL: 2 to CL: 3	Costa Rica 1992–93 CL: 1 to CL: 2
5.	São Tomé & Príncipe 2002–03 PR: 1 to PR: 2	Bulgaria 1995–96 CL: 2 to CL: 3	Greece 1992–93 CL: 2 to CL: 3
6.		Dominican Rep. 1989–90 CL: 1 to CL: 2, Dominican Rep. 2003–04 CL + PR: 1 to 2	Israel 1992–93 CL: 2 to CL: 3 Israel 1999–00 CL: 2 to CL: 3
7.		Ecuador 1990–91 CL: 2 to CL: 3	Ireland 1992–93 CL: 1 to CL: 2
8.		Jamaica 1992–93 CL: 2 to CL: 3 Jamaica 2000–01 CL: 2 to CL: 3	Italy 1991–92 CL: 1 to CL: 2 Italy 1992–93 CL: 2 to CL: 3 Italy 2007–08 CL: 1 to CL: 2
9.		Mauritius 1991–92 PR: 1 to PR: 2,	Latvia 2006–07 PR: 1 to PR: 2
10.		Micronesia 1996–97 CL: 1 to CL: 2	Lithuania 2003–04 PR: 1 to PR: 2
11.		Namibia 1992–93 CL: 2 to CL: 3	Mauritius 2005–06 CL: 1 to CL: 2
12.		Papua New Guinea 1989–90 C: 2 to CL: 3	Mexico 2005–06 CL: 2 to CL: 3
13.		Peru 2001–02 PR: 1 to PR: 2	Japan 1990–91 CL: 1 to CL: 2, Japan 1992–93 PR: 1 to PR: 2
14.		Romania 2003–04 PR: 2 to PR: 3	Spain 1992–93 CL: 1 to CL: 2
15.		Samoa 1997–98 CL:2 to CL: 3	St. Kitts & Nevis 1993–94 CL + PR:: 1 to 2
16.		Solomon Islands 1992–93 CL: 1 to CL: 2	Trinidad & Tobago 1993–94 CL: 1 to CL: 2
17.		St. Vincent & Grenadines 1993–94 PR: 1 to PR: 2	United Kingdom 1989–90 CL: 1 to CL: 2
18.		Suriname 2004–05 PR: 1 to PR: 2	Uruguay 1992–93 PR: 1 to PR: 2
19.		Trinidad & Tobago 1999–00 PR: 1 to PR: 2	Venezuela 1991–92 PR: 1 to PR: 3
20.		Vanuatu 1993–94 CL: 2 to CL: 3, Vanuatu 2002–03 PR: 1 to PR: 2	

Source: Freedom House 2009; UN, Human Development Report (various years)

Appendix 5: Change from democratic to hybrid regime by country income groups, 1989–2008

	Low-income, LIC	Lower-middle-income, LMC	Upper-middle-income, UMC	High-income, HIC
F – PF:				
1.	Bangladesh 1992–93	Bolivia 1994–95, Bolivia 2002–03	Antigua & Barbuda 1990–91	
2.	India 1990–91	Dominican Rep. 1992–93	Argentina 2000–01	
3.	Malawi 1998–99	Ecuador 1995–96, Ecuador 1999–00	Brazil 1992–93	
4.	Mali 1993–94	Fiji 1999–2000	Estonia 1991–1992	
5.	Nepal 1992–93	Guyana 2004–05	Trinidad & Tobago 2000–01	
6.	Senegal 2007–08	Honduras 1992–93, Honduras 1998–99	Venezuela 1992–93, Venezuela 1998–99	
7.	Solomon Islands 1999–2000	Latvia 1991–92		
8.	Zambia 1992–93	Papua New Guinea 1992–93, Papua New Guinea 2002–03		
9.		Philippines 1989–90, Philippines 2004–05		
10.		Slovakia 1995–96		
11.		Thailand 1990–91, Thailand 2004–05		
F–NF:				
1.	Gambia 1993–94			

Source: Freedom House 2009; World Bank, World Development Report (various years)

Appendix 6: Change from democratic to hybrid regime by level of human development, 1989–2008

Low	Medium	High
F – PF:		
1. Bangladesh 1992–93	Bolivia 1994–95, Bolivia 2002–03	Antigua & Barbuda 1990–91
2. India 1990–91	Dominican Rep. 1992–93	Argentina 2000–01
3. Malawi 1998–99	Ecuador 1995–96, Ecuador 1999–00	Brazil 1992–93
4. Mali 1993–94	Fiji 1999–2000	Estonia 1991–1992
5. Nepal 1992–93	Guyana 2004–05	Slovakia 1995–96
6. Senegal 2007–08	Honduras 1992–93, Honduras 1998–99	Venezuela 1992–93
7. Zambia 1992–93	Latvia 1991–92	
8.	Papua New Guinea 1992–93, Papua New Guinea 2002–03	
9.	Philippines 1989–90, Philippines 2004–05	
10.	Solomon Islands 1999–2000	
11.	Thailand 1990–91, Thailand 2004–05	
12.	Trinidad & Tobago 2000–01	
13.	Venezuela 1998–99	
F–NF:		
1. Gambia 1993–94		

Source: Freedom House 2009; UN, Human Development Report (various years)

ARTICLE

Quality Criteria for Democracy. Why Responsiveness is not the Key

Hans-Joachim Lauth

Abstract Responsiveness, a basic principle of democracy, its relevance as well as our understanding of it are examined and widely discussed. There are two reasons for this choice. Firstly, the quality of democracy and with it the regression of democracy are often linked to responsiveness in public debates. Secondly, by such examination, we are considering crucial definitions of democracy, which have given direction to research into Comparative Democracy (Dahl, Lijphart). In both discussions, it is often ignored that the quality of democracy also reveals itself via the criterion for responsibility. This can come into conflict with the responsiveness criterion. Which then are the criteria necessary to solve the conflict in terms of democratic quality? Moreover, it should be discussed in how far the responsiveness criterion – despite its undisputed relevance – is of limited suitability in making democratic quality accessible. Put another way, under what circumstances can responsiveness (or its related procedures) be a suitable criterion for determining the quality of a democracy? Does a lower degree of responsiveness always indicate a loss of democratic quality? To structure this discussion the article reflects fundamental issues of conceptualizing democracy at the beginning.

1. On the relevance of quality criteria

If we consider the current debate on democratic developments, we see that after years of euphoria, things have clearly come back down to Earth. This scepticism has less to do with the fact that for some time, the number of democracies has no longer increased; and more with dissatisfaction with existing democracy becoming evident. This can be observed at various levels. At an empirical level, dissatisfaction manifests itself when we draw upon survey values of dissatisfaction with the functioning of democracy's existing institutions. In new democracies as well as in established ones, the lack of trust is obvious. This dissatisfaction, or rather this sceptical evaluation, can likewise be seen in academic studies. Thus many new democracies are judged to be either deficient or defect, as they often and recognizably show insufficiencies in their democratic working. However, established democracies have also become the subject of criticism, as the Post-democracy debate has shown most pointedly (Crouch 2008). In all the cases mentioned here, the quality of democracy is the focus of interest. It has thus risen to become a central *topos* of current Democracy research.

This central importance of this term is not surprising, because determining the quality of democracy means nothing more than clarifying how democracy is to be measured. Judgements concerning the state of democracy stand and fall on this. Whatever measurement is chosen, be it a slender or demanding definition – decides upon the number of democracies as well as it does upon the purported quality. The closer the empirical findings lie to this benchmark, the higher the democratic quality will be judged. If the threshold is to be lowered, then it becomes incapable of differentiating between the individual quality of those democracies who have stepped above the threshold. Accordingly, the findings cluster together, as they do for example with *polity* findings in the area of established democracies. If the bar is set too high, it is possible that the empirical cases hardly reach it. Because of its relevance, it is obvious that the benchmark itself must be the subject of careful deliberation. Surprisingly however, in the area of empirical Democracy research, this does not happen very often. Rather, ad hoc definitions of democracy are frequently employed, which prejudice the subsequent assessment in advance. This is true even for the area of democracy measurement, which should be sensitive to this question. Despite this, there is an increasing body of study which deals more carefully with this basic question; in so doing, it brings the debate more firmly into the realm of Political Philosophy.

As examples, two volumes of selected works are of special mention, namely *The Quality of Democracy* (2004), edited by Guillermo O'Donnell, Jorge Vargas Cullell and Osvaldo M. Iazzetta, and *Assessing the Quality of Democracy* (2005), edited by Larry Diamond and Leonardo Morlino. This latter work takes up the discussion of the former. In the introduction, Diamond and Morlino attempt to compile a synthesis of different views on democracy. They identify eight dimensions, namely *rule of law, vertical and horizontal accountability, participation, competition, responsiveness, freedom and equality*. This clearly goes further than Robert Dahl's pioneering suggestion of 1971 (Polyarchy), who, with competition and participation, brought two dimensions into the debate, although the proposal of Diamond/Morlino is limited, when one takes into account suggestions concerning social democracy. If we investigate Diamond/Morlino's suggestion more closely, it rapidly becomes evident that the term 'dimension' itself remains unclear. Thus the individual dimensions vary in terms of their degree of abstraction (and with it their range). For example, 'freedom' could also be understood as a heading for 'competition' and 'vertical accountability'. At the same time, not all dimensions are conceived separate of each other, and thus overlap. Finally, they are either substantiated to varying degrees, or remain vague. Although this proposal enriches the discussion, there remains a lot to clarify. This task is necessary not only to measure the quality of democracy, but also to identify possible regressions of its quality.

2. The Quality of Democracy – Methodical Solution Strategy and Findings

In order to accurately define a synthesis of the democracy debate, it is essential to systematically reconstruct the democracy term using clear rules (cf. Lauth 2004: 24-28). In this, the following basic assumption is taken: democracy is a societal construct. Central ideas are introduced and aggregated by public debate and defined more accurately in academic debate. The latter, for its part, orientates at the same time towards lines of historical development in reference to Political Philosophy on the one hand and real-historical processes on the other. Despite large differences in their concrete design, a normative core underlies all these considerations; this core refers to the idea of the sovereignty of the people. The more precise the ideas on democracy become, the more strongly the normative core is interpreted and supplemented, thus suggestions vary accordingly.

For a systematic view of the discussion surrounding Democracy Theory, the following pragmatic rules of analysis are suggested to determine the quality of democracy:

(1) Abstraction. Here, the normative bases are reconstructed as far as possible in their basic abstract forms from current assumptions on democracy.

(2) Modularization. At this second level, central components or modules of democracy are identified at a lower level of abstraction, situated at the level of institutional design. In this way, institutions relevant to democracy are cited as examples.

(3) Construction. Abstraction and modularization are combined. In so doing, the following rules should be observed:
   a) Coherence (or validity of content). The institutional components must correspond to the normative bases of the abstract level.
   b) Parsimony. In order to limit the variance at the construction level and to make possible the linking for as many variants of democracy as possible, only necessary components must be considered.
   c) Functional equivalents should be identified and integrated within a single component.

   Put in simple terms, we must clarify which institutional forms are relevant in realising the normative bases by avoiding an institutional bias.

(4) We must further differentiate between elements inherent to democracy and those which constitute necessary and promotional factors.
   a) necessary factors (Brennan 2003): these are factors which, without being a democratic characteristic specifically, represent a necessary condition for democratic quality (the state, for example). Here, in principle, the strict causal link is relevant – if the necessary condition is lacking, the quality of democracy cannot exist. As in empirical Social Sciences, we are confronted rather with gradual findings; an analogous causal relationship should be that

the weaker the necessary condition, the lower the democratic quality. Keeping this relationship in mind does not mean that the reverse interrelation must exist. The existence of a necessary factor (such as state) does not imply that a democracy is also present.

b) promotional and obstructive factors. Here, it is hypothetically assumed that the existence of promotional or obstructive factors (for example the degree of socio-economic development) improves or worsens democratic quality. There exists no compellingly logical correlation: democratic quality can only be partially determined by the extent of promotional factors. Thus a democracy with high quality is possible even with a medium degree of socio-economic development (Costa Rica and Uruguay being examples), even though this is rather the exception, or at a high level of socio-economic development, the quality of democracy can be low (cf. the Weimar Republic). For this reason, the investigation of promotional and obstructive factors tends to prove hypotheses concerning the stability and dynamism of the quality of democracy.

c) sufficiently obstructive factors. Here, it is hypothetically assumed that the existence of obstructive factors worsens democratic quality. Here initially, the relationships are similar to those in 4b. However in the case of a strong presence of obstructive factors (for example when corruption becomes an informal institution), these can constitute a sufficient pre-condition for the weakening of democratic quality. At this point, we should reiterate the socio-economic preconditions necessary for democracy, which since Lipset's time (1959) have been subject to hefty debate (Muno 2001). Even surely, when it is exaggerated to set a comprehensive welfare state as a prerequisite for high democratic quality, the lack of minimum social standards (education, income, employment) means limitations on participation in the political process.[1] In this sense, low levels of social development must constitute sufficiently obstructive factors, or formulated another way, minimum social standards are necessary conditions for the extent of democratic quality.

The clear analytical separations should not belie the fact that the empirical relationships are at times more complex. Thus a high degree of socio-economic development initially constitutes a promotional factor. However, from a certain low level of development, this can also be interpreted as an obstructive factor. Finally, it can even be perceived as a necessary condition, if at a very low level of development, bare survival is not ensured. This variable, the degree of socio-economic development transforms itself, according to the degree of its realization reached, into a necessary, obstructive, or promotional condition.

---

1 No general norms can be ascribed to minimum social standards, as these can vary context-specifically and in terms of their composition. However the extent of general education does provide a useful approximation.

(5) Avoidance of *conceptual stretching* (Sartori 1970). Up to now, our considerations as presented here show, that to determine the democratic quality, not only must the democracy definition be included (as in 1-3 above), but also all factors (as in 4) have to be taken into account, which effect the working of democracy. In this way, both necessary and sufficient factors have to be included in the analysis. Due to the increase in complexity that this implies, it is important to reflect thoroughly upon all of these relationships, so as to avoid a conceptual stretching, in which conditioning factors also become included within the democracy concept.

As far as determining democratic quality is concerned, at what results do we arrive when we critically evaluate current empirical Democracy research (cf. O'Donnell/ Vargas Cullell/Iazzetta 2004, Diamond/Morlino 2005, Merkel et al. 2003, Lauth 2004, Schmidt 2006, Bühlmann et al. 2006) by means of the rules as discussed above?[2]

Two terms are situated prominently at the level of abstract dimensions – those of freedom and equality; to be more precise, individual political freedom and individual political equality. No relevant conception of democracy is sufficient without reference to both of these dimensions. When both of these basic principles are taken seriously, it is logical to consider the idea of political and legal control. Consequently, the notion of democracy is understood as a limited form of rule. Democracy finds its limits in the guarantees of individual freedom and equality. The majority is not allowed to dispose freely of the basic rights of the minority. The understanding of freedom halts the freedom of the individual at its limits that is to say as soon as it violates the freedom of others. Defining what control at this level should be is essential, as in turn, it serves to orientate how basic institutional principles are determined. Here, control operates at a political and at a legal level. At the legal level, the basic principles of the rule of law are already established at this level of abstraction; they are subsequently defined fully at institutional level. So that an adequate employment of legal control may be possible, possibilities of political control are themselves essential; some authors even view these as having priority (Schmitter 2005). We should bear in mind however that political control finds not only its limits, but also its most potent weapon, within the framework of the rule of law. This short reflection underlines three dimensions of democracy: political liberty, political equality and political and judicial control.

At this abstract level, two further basic principles can be discerned below these dimensions:

(1) If democracy is based upon the sovereignty of the people, in the sense of a collective form of individual self-government, then government action intrinsically bears reference to the preferences of the participants; this reference finds its expression in the notion of responsiveness. According to this, democratic decisions should take full account of the preferences of all citizens.

---

2 This cannot be attempted fully within the framework of this essay. For a more comprehensive discussion, cf. Lauth, 2004, Ch.1.

(2) If democracy is a limited form of rule, which finds its justification in upholding its own basic principles and central characteristics, then governing is aligned towards the principle of responsibility. For this reason, democratic decisions must reflect long-term perspectives and protect their own basic principle (that of civil rights and freedoms). Responsiveness and responsibility are two basic principles which should be guaranteed through the institutional character of democracy.

With the institutional forms, the dimensions and principles of democracy find their full expression. Here, the institutional minimum orientates itself towards the institutional guarantees (see Dahl 1971), which include electoral law as well as freedom of organization and of communication. This list is extended through the characteristic of 'an effective government'. For the democratic process does not arrive at its completion with the formulation of decisions, but rather with their implementation. The responsiveness towards the preferences of the *demos* must also be expressed in the performance of the political system (cf. Scharpf 1970; Benz 2003). By implementing political decisions, however, we must give appropriate consideration to the scope for political action.[3] The smaller this becomes, the stronger a democracy's ability to shape and define, and with it, its quality is compromised. With it, the means of argument is also created through which globalization and debt can be understood as a weakening of democratic quality. However not only the input as well as the output components, but also the dimension of control demands institutional safeguards which it finds under the rule of law and within the politically biased mechanisms of *accountability*. This division follows the systematic separation between legal and political control (Lauth 2004: 86). According to these considerations, the following six institutions can be named, each representing a complex institutional patchwork.

- Active and passive electoral law (universal, free, equal and secret)
- Freedom of organization
- Freedom of communication
- Effective Government
- Rule of law
- (Political) mechanisms of accountability.

At this stage, a more precise understanding of the designated institutions could be discussed, in which discrepancies between various approaches would certainly become more evident. However, the rules as discussed above should at least lead to a narrowing down of the bandwidth of possible results. In the discussion of necessary institutions, reference to functional equivalents could serve as a guide. The central question is which

---

3 It should be pointed out that predetermining the content of output so as to determine democratic quality – the better the socio-economic data, the higher democratic quality – is not feasible. The point of reference is citizens' preferences. Only one exception is worthy of note, however. All those decisions which negatively affect the functioning of democracy itself, as well as their implementation, are to be included in determining democratic quality in a negative manner.

institutions can make possible the realization of central dimensions and principles. These remain constant, whilst the character of the institutions indeed vary, and can also include informal institutions. Thus electoral law is not a reference to representation, but also includes procedures of direct democracy. Which relationship mix shows itself as the most productive for preference transfer, is to be decided in concrete cases. The same can be said of electoral law, located in the spectrum between proportional and majority voting.

Reconsidering the rules of analysis leads us to the fourth and fifth points of the verification criteria, which refer to promotional, obstructive, sufficient and necessary conditions. As the clarification of the meaning of promotional and obstructive factors requires empirical investigation, the necessary conditions should be named at this point. To these belongs the rule of law, as mentioned, and without which all democratic regimes show a weakening in their quality. However transparency must also be mentioned, without which a democratic political process cannot function. This begins when forming preferences, covers the law of organization and communication and includes control. Inversely, the undermining of democratic processes through a high degree of corruption and similar informal practices is a condition sufficient to reduce democratic quality.

Do good governing and good political results belong to this quality? This question is not easy to answer. Firstly, it can be seen that many characteristics of a high quality democracy correspond to the criteria of *Good Governance* (independently of the World Bank/OECD/EU/BMZ version), thereby showing a close relationship between both (Conzelmann 2003). This must not necessarily mean however that good political results are always to be expected, as in this process, we must reckon with further intervening factors (such as extent of resources, the international economy, etc.). Furthermore, it would have to be clarified what is to be understood at all by good political results. In this regard, we have so far discussed the two leads of responsiveness and responsibility. However these must not necessarily be consistent with each other. This will be made clear in the next chapter.

With regard to Diamond/Morlino, it still remains to be clarified where exactly participation is to be situated. Other types of political regime also know forms of participation. Thus on its own, participation in general is not a characteristic of democracy, but rather the specific modus of democratic participation. This is shown in the realization of the dimensions and principles through the specific set of democratic institutions which for their part, are all directed at participation. For this reason, participation can be understood as the essential form which makes democratic characteristics possible, integrating all of these. At the end of our reflections the suggested, pragmatic rules of analysis demonstrate their capacity to systematize Diamond and Morlino's concept (2005).

Considering all proposals about dimensions, democracy is best understood as basing on the three dimensions of political liberty, political equality and political and judicial control. To list all relevant characteristics of a democracy does not mean that the highest level of democratic quality is achieved when all are comprehensively developed. Rather, possible trade-offs must be considered at all levels. These are motivated significantly through the tense relationship between dimensions situated at the highest level of abstraction.

The best known area of conflict concerns the tension between freedom and equality, which has given rise to serious ideological and philosophical debate (cf. Held 1987: 86ff; Reisinger 1997: 40pp). The loss of balance of both dimensions in democracy in favour of equality is seen by Tocqueville as a central threat to freedom. Freedom and equality come all the more heavily into conflict with each other, the stronger substantial demands are linked to the notion of equality. The criticism of social, participative and feminist Democracy Theory of its liberal variant delivers a multi-faceted view. According to these, the realization of participation options (as an expression of freedom rights) firstly requires the creation of equal opportunities through material transfer or quota rulings. In the view of classical liberalism however, it is precisely such mechanisms which curtail the unlimited implementation of liberal human rights.[4] However, even to forego a material linking of formal freedom rights for the purpose of allowing the dominance of liberal values fails to relieve the tension, as Zippelius (1991: 325) stresses: "On the other hand, a certain measure of equality also in real development opportunities, is indispensable, in order to maintain freedom as universal freedom over time." In the debate surrounding both directions, it is hardly this basic understanding which is controversial, rather the defining of the 'certain degree'. Some orientation criteria have already been touched upon in the discussion concerning the necessary social preconditions for democracy.

Tension also exists between the dimensions of freedom and of control. The spread of control mechanisms narrows down the individual and / or collective freedom domains for the purpose of bureaucratic juridification, which reglements and restrains the room for political organization and action. In turn, any extension of the freedom dimension occurs at the expense of possibilities of control; this is demonstrated in the decreasing possibility of horizontal *accountability*. The tension is echoed in the diverging imperatives of responsiveness and *responsibility*. At the abstract level, this tension is expressed in the limitation of political majority rule through the rule of law and constitutional law.

At the same time, with its complex procedural rules, democratic rule offers a solution to the conflict between freedom and limitation of power. This conflict however always remains latent and manifests itself more strongly when the balance between both poles shifts. Even when control in the democracy operates indispensably according to principles of the rule of law, the formulation in constitutional law of related rights still has sufficient scope for action to leave for political decisions, should free self-determination still be possible. For its part, unlimited freedom tends towards the tyranny of the majority (or of the rulers), when it fails to observe the limitations set by the rule of law. In this way, democracy is expressed within both dimensions; however this becomes distorted when either begins to dominate. Even when democracy is appropriately expressed

---

4 Correspondingly, Habermas (1996 : 304) states : "the 'wrong' classifications (*to reduce gender discrimination – the author*) lead namely to normalising readjustments to one's life, turning the intended compensation into renewed discrimination, turning bailment of freedom into loss of freedom."

within the balance between freedom and control, it remains to be defined what its correct degree is within the specificity of each dimension.[5]

What potential for tension can be said to exist between equality and control? Even the strict implementation of the equality principle can reduce the effectiveness of the control dimension, if in so doing, a permanent and general participation by the *demos* were to be combined with it, without delegation to specific bodies. An efficient organization of control mechanisms, which in particular demands the inclusion of functionally specialized institutions, reduces the equality of participation in issues concerning control. The functional differentiation tends towards the concentration of control in the hands of highly qualified elites. Accordingly, Alexy (1998: 244) states: 'That only constitutional court jurisdiction represents real control, does not mean that the solution to the issue of control has been found. The disadvantages of constitutional court jurisdiction could be greater than the advantages in terms of the control of the democratic process that it brings. The disadvantages lie within the dangers of a constitutional court paternalism (*Habermas*), which could entail the transition from a parliamentary legislative state to one based on the jurisdiction of the constitutional court (*Böckenförde*).' In order to avoid an elite form of democracy in this dimension, a high degree of transparency of the political process and cooperation on the part of the citizen through information is required.

The effect of a dominant control dimension upon equality then becomes obvious if a constitutional court assuming such a degree of authority develops towards the ideal of the ruler of philosophers, as Plato understood it (Höffe 1999: 184).[6] With the elite conception of rule that this entails, the equality of political participation inherent within democracy is effectively undermined. Control - especially when it draws upon the authority to exercise authority – requires a strong measure of moderation, limiting the activity of the constitutional court to aspects of constitutional *law*, thus leaving open issues of constitutional *policy*, as advocated by Höffe (1999). The difficulty involved in identifying and respecting this limit in individual cases points to a further limitation debate inherent to democracy.

These considerations on the potential for tension between the three dimensions can be summarized thus: in principle, an 'optimal' or 'perfect' democracy cannot be based upon the comprehensive realization of all three dimensions; rather, it is expressed by an appropriate, gradual implementation, maintaining a balance between them. Falling short of their limits as well as exceeding them are both problematic.

Finally, defining what this balance should be is the expression of a continuing debate within society and must remain contingent to historical situations. In its quest for the balance between the three dimensions, democracy, or rather its citizens (seen as players), fall into the sheer paradoxical situation of having to continually agree upon the

---

[5] Across the historical development of democracy, a growth in the relevance of the control dimension can be observed, which indeed curtailed freedom domains and was expressed most clearly in the commitment of the sovereign to constitutional law.

[6] According to Alexy (1998: 244) this danger can only be banished through a 'successful embedding of constitutional court jurisdiction within the democratic process.'

rules of the game, without abandoning the game in the process. The only way out of this is for the solutions seen hitherto at the game's basic rule level to no longer be generally available. All three dimensions would then constitute a categorical orientation, which could no longer be cheated, of which the shape and balance would continually be redrawn anew. The openness sought through this approach does not mark a weakness in democracy, but rather outlines its inherent potential for development and problem-solving, and portrays the character of democracy as a *boundary* concept. Within it, the limits of the three dimensions (and with these the extent of those norms which are given up and which are upheld), are to be continually redefined, without forfeiting their identity.

A possible optimization of the relationship between the three dimensions of democracy points to the extension and further development of the deliberative character of democratic procedures. These represent the sole possibility of an appropriate and differentiated mediation between these competing, and simultaneously complementary, dimensions. Whilst not being able to expand upon this discussion here, we should note that the upper domain of the profile of the three dimensions cannot be interpreted linearly according to the motto 'the more, the more democratic'. At the same time, this profile should not fall below a lower threshold. For their classification within a well working democracy, it is unimportant to what extent the individual dimensions are developed, as long as all three dimensions display their core characteristics at a satisfactory level. If the single dimensions are not existent to a satisfactory but sufficient degree, we speak of a deficient democracy. If the characteristics of the single democratic components lie below this threshold, we cannot speak of a democracy. Following these remarks, it is possible to research a possible decline in democratic quality.

The character of the three dimensions in the upper spectrum however serves to establish profiles of empirical findings within the domain of working democracy, whereby the targeted indicators in the upper 'threshold range' should show themselves to be necessarily sensitive to the potential target conflicts (cf. Lauth 2004, ch. 3.3.2). For the basic determining of a (working) democracy, this idea should find consensus, as opposed to competing ideals which as a rule favour specific extents and weightings of the dimensions (be these towards liberal, social or jurisdictional democracy). At the same time, these observations give an indication as to the scope for interpreting the basic dimensions. Although linked with differing profiles, they maintain a basic consensus.

3. Responsiveness – a core basis for democracy?

In the following, we will examine and discuss more closely a basic principle, namely responsiveness, its relevance as well as our understanding of it. There are two reasons for this choice. First, in general public debate, the quality of democracy and with it the regression of democracy is often linked to this, as common complaints concerning politicians demonstrate: 'They do what they want' and 'They should listen to the people more'. Secondly, by such examination, we are considering a crucial definition of democracy, which has given direction to research into Comparative Democracy. The definition referred to here is that of Robert Dahl, which he puts forward in his work on Polyarchy. Dahl (1971: 2) defines democracy using the central characteristic of responsiveness: „I should like to reserve the term ‚democracy' for a political system, one of the characteristics of which is the quality of being completely or almost completely responsive to all its citizens." The stronger it is in evidence – the stronger citizens' preferences are observed – the more we can speak of a democracy. This view is reflected within many conceptions of democracy and forms a fundamental argument in the defence of direct democracy (Saward). As Lijphart (1984: 1pp.) stresses, "complete responsiveness" is the ideal "to which democratic regimes should aspire". In the same way, Saward (1994: 14) makes the term the focus of his understanding of democracy thus: "A political system is democratic to the extent that, and only to the extent that, it involves realization of responsive rule". As previously mentioned, Diamond and Morlino (2004: 30) see responsiveness as one of "eight different dimensions of democratic quality".

In both discussions, it is often ignored that the quality of democracy also reveals itself via the criterion of responsibility. This can come into conflict with the responsiveness criterion. Which then are the criteria necessary to solve the conflict in terms of democratic quality? Moreover, it should be discussed in how far the responsiveness criterion - despite its undisputed relevance – is of limited suitability in making democratic quality accessible. Put another way, under what circumstances can responsiveness (or its related procedures) be a suitable criterion for determining the quality of a democracy, and when not? Does a lower degree of responsiveness always indicate a loss of democratic quality?

Let us look more closely at Dahl's deliberations (1971: 2), in which he understands democracy as a political system "completely or almost completely responsive to all its citizens". Responsiveness is the key term with which Dahl links governmental action to the preservation of the preferences of all citizens, whereby in his conception of Polyarchy, he sees the receptiveness of elected representatives for exactly these preferences as being guaranteed by eight functional conditions.[7]

The criteria include the political system's *input* as well as *output* functions, whereby both are interconnected in terms of their content.[8] Government's activities are linked to citizens' preferences, whereby here not only voting citizens or the majority of citizens, but all citizens are meant. However no certain definition of content is linked to responsiveness; rather, the expectation is expressed of congruence in the content of citizens'

---

[7] These eight criteria (Dahl 1971: 3) are: "1. Freedom to form and join organizations, 2. Freedom of expression, 3. Right to vote, 4. Eligibility for public office, 5. Right of political leaders to compete for support and for votes, 6. Alternative sources of information, 7. Free and fair elections, 8. Institutions for making government policies depend on votes and other expressions of preference".

[8] In determining the eight functional conditions, the input side does outweigh, however output activities are included within the eighth criterion, that of "policies". It should be pointed out however, that Dahl 1989 (221pp. and 233) no longer gives this criterion, taking only input aspects into account. This does not mean however, that the "responsiveness" idea has been dropped. It is incorporated via the quality of the democratic process alone (Dahl 1989: 108-118).

preferences and of government action. Even when with this, no explicit reference to a conception of social equality is established, the *responsiveness* as made possible through procedure implies the striving for, and the possible realization of a *common good* (cf. Dahl 1989: 299-308). Here, the equality dimension with equal consideration of all interests is stressed: "I assume further that in order for a government to continue over a period of time to be responsive to the preferences of its citizens, considered as political equals, all full citizens must have unimpaired opportunities:

1. To formulate their preferences,
2. To signify their preferences to their fellow citizens and the government by individual and collective action,
3. To have their preferences weighted equally in the conduct of the government that is weighted with no discrimination because of the content or source of the preference" (Dahl 1971: 2).

With equal consideration of all interests, Dahl does not link any egalitarian development to the detriment of freedom, as was feared by Tocqueville.[9] Finally, it is the institutional guarantees as mentioned, and the procedures of the democratic process resulting from these, which likewise defend freedom or, to be more precise, with those of citizens themselves defend their freedom.

Saward (1994: 13pp.) takes up the same category, which in reference to May he calls "responsive rule", observing it together with a substantially understood political equality, as being the second core dimension of democracy. He calls for the observance of "responsive rule" (output) in legal decisions and administrative action. Saward sees this as being guaranteed through the procedure of direct democracy. In order to achieve responsiveness, preferences should be recognized via democratic procedures and as far as possible – as demanded by Dahl – taken account of in the same way. Even when Saward names procedures different to those as given by Dahl, in the conceptions of both, these constitute the only convincing way of systematically 'creating' a more comprehensive degree of responsiveness.

However, in how far can or should procedures guarantee responsiveness to its full extent? The following reservations can be mentioned, whereby the procedures of indirect democracy are more strongly affected as those of the direct type:

(1) the construction and the application of the procedures (and their societal bases);
(2) the qualifications and motivations of those holding office and of the intermediary organizations (parties) which underline an empirical argument;
(3) losses due to friction during implementation or capacity problems;

---

9 It is however obvious that the equal consideration of all preferences does not exclude the establishment of rules designed to create social justice (to express it cautiously). As an essential basis of democratic decision of the individual in terms of preference communication, Dahl understands that individual having the possibility of being able to obtain comprehensive information about the object of the decision and about possible alternatives. Logically, the prerequisite for this is a comprehensive and egalitarian communicative infrastructure.

(4) moreover, one must examine "responsiveness" with regards to its principle – can it really describe the core idea of democracy, as Dahl (1971: 2) claims ? It needs to be debated whether responsiveness can be observed at all as being a desirable aim of democratic rule. However before discussing this question, let us examine the three restrictions more closely. The normative limits of responsiveness are to be treated.

(1) The first restriction deals with problems of collective choice and lies at the limits of the procedures themselves, which yield different results according to the method of preference communication in use, thus indicating the manipulability of the majorities, as Manfred Schmidt (1995a: 181 – 194) describes in detail. For example Riker (1980) stresses in his criticism of majority rule, that even slight manipulation of decision-making procedures can have lasting influence upon the result.[10] Classic examples of the technical construction of results are the Ostrogorski Paradox and the Condorcet Paradox.[11] With a view to these arguments, Hadenius (1992: 19) deduces that "(...) no complete, reliable reflection of individual preferences is possible. 'The instrument' to measure the opinion (...) always dictates the result to some extent."

Procedures can also encounter limitations, because citizens' preferences are so disparate in modern societies that they cannot be aggregated free of contradiction and thus can never all be satisfied (see Arrow's Impossibility Theorem (1951)).The impossibility in satisfying all interests lies not only in the conflictual structure of claims, but also in their instability. When looking at responsiveness, it should therefore be considered that not all interests are exogenously determined and relatively stable, but that they are also changed, formed, even created through the political process itself. Moreover the argument concerning insufficient representativeness of interests on the political agenda could be cited; from a critique of pluralism, this was brought into the debate for good reasons, and was reinforced by the arguments of Mancur Olson in his deliberations about the logic of collective action. According to this, not all interests have an equal chance of being articulated and aggregated.

Furthermore, a loss of responsiveness is inherent to the representation principle (as also Saward rightly stresses). Block offers of preferences continually stand for election in the form of candidates or parties (cf. Scharpf 1970: 79). It is rather the hypothetical exception for a voter's complete bundle of preferences to precisely match the analogous offer. As a rule, the party or candidate receives those votes which by comparison to the others show the greatest match with its own preferences. The loss in this transfer of

---

10 In this way, according to critics, reasonable policy would not only have to consider the interests of voting citizens, but would also have to include all persons affected by a decision. This would include – as the problem of environmental protection shows – future generations in the deliberations (cf. Guggenberger / Offe 1984). An overview of the central arguments against democracy by the majority can be found in Schmidt (1995a: 198-201).

11 According to the Ostrogorski Paradox, only the applied decision-making rule and type of vote concerning alternatives can decisively affect the decision. Thus majorities are created artificially. Even with the Condorcet Paradox, only the voting procedure decides the result in cases of cyclical or unstable majorities. Examples are given in Schmidt (1995a: 181-186); cf. also Scharpf (2000: 259-269).

preferences is all the greater, the more individualistically a society is structured.[12] For with individualization, even value clusters which form collective identity lose significance; previously, within classes and milieus structured by societal *cleavages*, such clusters made possible a clearer transfer of preferences to those parties organized along these lines of conflict (cf. Lipset / Rokkan 1967). These binding value clusters, which were common to voters and candidates alike during the phases of mass parties, were accompanied by relatively firm connections to target preferences within specific *policy fields*. The breakup of such strongly homogenous preference structures, also not without their relevance for direct democracy procedures, underlines the necessity to complement traditional representative procedures by means of other forms of participation in the further development of democracy. These are to be found on the agendas of discussions concerning plebiscitary procedures, deliberative models and Civil Society. The quality of such complements can be seen in how far they are capable of harnessing through argument the heterogeneity of individual preferences with the societal processes of debates that such complements induce, and to translate these into consistent programmes. Elections alone have only limited capacity to inform us of the electorate's true preferences (Powell 2005: 64).

(2) With procedures constrained by limitations, we must include a further aspect which concerns the qualifications and motivations of those holding office. Democratic election cannot guarantee the consideration of applicants who are capable, be it cognitively or also willingly, to carry out the duties of their office in a responsive way. The problem of principle linked with this (of incompetent and of self-interested holders of office) is reduced by the periodical character of elections in thus far, as these provide the possibility of revising obvious mistakes in appointments and to achieve greater responsiveness. If this opportunity is available, the problem is reduced. This idea also follows the Economic Theory of Democracy (Downs 1968) in its *response* approach through *input* and *output*. According to this, elected carriers of mandates and parties attempt to make good their election promises, through which they are elected, in order to secure re-election. For this reason, through the performance of government, preferences (of 'victorious' citizens) are largely taken into account and thus the responsiveness of the political system assured. In this way, the *response* approach informs us about the relative satisfaction of voters; however, it says nothing about the focus of preferences in terms of their content, and little about democratic quality. For example, political market structures can be distorted by oligopolistic structures. A guarantee on offer to all existing preferences does not exist. The victorious party can only represent that offer which is the least 'bad'. Most problematic are those cases in which responsiveness is systematically undermined by cartels of elites or in which the chances of change are limited.[13]

---

[12] It is thus unsurprising when Economic Decision Theory points out that "the less chances, stable majorities and objectively consistent programmes are to be found, the larger the societal differentiation and the more heterogeneous the electorate" (Schmidt 1995a: 182).

[13] A problem can arise when there is a general lack of suitable candidates. It is exactly this which Maihold (1996: 67) diagnoses for many Latin American democracies: "The format of actors is not covered by the

The quality of procedures in the sense of a functioning democracy surely remains unachieved when political decisions – as Offe (1996: 146) formulates in following the deliberations of Bobbio and Zolo – present themselves merely as "an *artefact* of cartels of elites and of media strategies" and when the citizen is understood as being merely a surface onto which manipulative strategies of elites are projected.

Responsiveness cannot only continue to refer uniquely to target preferences, but also to strategies, of which the pursuance will serve the realization of the said preferences. In this, target and strategy preferences must not necessarily correspond to each other. In which case however is responsiveness more firmly assured – when preferred strategies are applied, but are unsuccessful, or when by means of undesired strategies preferred aims are achieved? These strongly diverging possibilities in the interpretation of the same phenomenon underline the problem of linking responsiveness directly to the performance of a democracy. When a loss in responsiveness is to the detriment of democracy, then criticism should directed at insufficiencies in democratic procedures, and not at the form of the output.

(3) In the debate concerning the first reservation, numerous procedure-specific difficulties in preference aggregation were pointed out. However, even when an appropriately unifying or successful compromise of all interests concerned can be found, it cannot be guaranteed that the intended aims will be achieved. Not only has Policy Research pointed at numerous restrictions in implementation (Héritier 1993; Schmidt 1997; Mayntz 1997). In the same way, the debate concerning the steering capacities of political systems has indicated problems in political planning. Without wishing to spread general scepticism, steering deficits cannot be overlooked (Luhmann 1984; Wilke 1992). Such difficulties can lie in the authority, way of working and organization of bureaucracy, in the disruptive intervention by concerned actors, or in uncalculated or intended secondary effects. Many points touch upon the theme of effective government, whereby one aspect has a direct link with preferences.

By this, it is implied that citizens' preferences are appropriately acknowledged by political decision makers, and that the latter have the will to implement the decision taken. How should a failure of implementation be interpretated, itself due to an unrealistic setting of preferences? Could the fact that utopian aims are being pursued then be an expression of insufficient democratic quality? In one sense, this would be true, as it could be suspected that the discrepancy represents the result of insufficient deliberation within the political process. One would have to judge otherwise if a utopian aim were consciously being pursued in order to set a corresponding symbol, which in the long run would contribute to the realization of that aim.

---

institutional arrangements of democratic society, to the extent that not only can noticeable performance deficits be seen within political parties and party systems, but also a very limited fulfilling of the intermediary tasks of associations and interest groups". Maihold (1996 : 66) underlines that he does not see the deficits as lying within the institutional design, but "rather are attributable to the lack of development of actor-specific qualities in Latin American societies, which do not necessarily correspond to the institutionally prescribed format".

Further, the discharging of responsiveness alone does not avouch the rationality of decisions. Greven (1993: 411) rightly underlines the fact that a democracy cannot guarantee any reasonable solutions, even when – as Holmes (1995: 303) and Beetham (1996: 33) stress – the embedding of decisions within democratic procedures and public debate can serve to increase their effectiveness and rationality. Through a qualitative improvement in procedures, rationality of decisions can be achieved, as is the subject of discussion within the context of deliberative democracy models.

If indeed democracies are capable of producing unreasonable solutions, the judgement of (socio-economic) performance is not suitable as a criterion with which to classify regimes. Even in authoritarian regimes, it is wholly possible for results to be produced which can prove to be useful for the development of the country and for these to be supported by the majority of the population. In certain instances, authoritarian regimes even aim to achieve this, as next to the ideological foundation of the regime, the generation of output provides the only way of enhancing its legitimacy (in the sense of a specific legitimation). However their way to systematically knowing the preferences of the population (and with these, essential aspects of a potential common good) is barred. The blindness towards the wishes of the citizen, itself attributable to the logic of the functioning of many regime systems in Socialist states, illustrates this inability (cf. Offe 1994: 90 pp.). As the population for its part has limited possibilities of articulating its needs due to authoritarian limitation of participation, no adequate input can take place. Another obstacle to the fulfilment of preferences of the majority is that every autocratic government endeavours to satisfy individual needs which are not in the interests of the majority (Faust 2007).

(4) After showing limits of preference communication and realization, the question remains to be discussed whether at all responsiveness is always desirable and in how far this represents in reality a core characteristic of democracy. Two problems of principle arise, concerning on the one hand the normative form of preferences themselves and how far they correspond to each other as well as the time of policy-making on the other.

(4a) The first reservation arises from the question of whether the government should show itself as being responsive towards all preferences without regard to which interests are expressed. Can responsiveness be wished for when with regard to certain values, it is accompanied by negative policy effects (outcomes), when the rights of minorities are restricted or when the democratic system or the rule of law are called into question ? How can or should one react, when fundamentalist majorities who go against democracy become apparent within society ? In such a dilemma situation, there is obviously no satisfactory solution. Responsiveness towards preferences situated outside the basic democratic consensus, as well as their negation means a temporary suspension of democratic procedures at the least. The question (or the dilemma) illustrates that preferences must be judged using inherent limits within the framework of democracy, and that responsiveness cannot be extended to all preferences.

The problem of preferences which impair democracy is included by Dahl (1989: 307; cf. Ch. 8, 13) in as far as he links the formulation of preferences to cognitive standards, which are largely supposed to exclude such dispositions. For an appropriate expression of individual preferences, he believes that "each citizen ought to have adequate and equal opportunities for discovering and validating (within the time permitted by the need for a decision) the choice on the matter to be decided that would best serve the citizen's interests. (...) A person's good or interest is whatever that person would choose with the fullest attainable understanding of the experience resulting from that choice and its most relevant alternatives". These demands, set by this criterion of "enlightened understanding" are however so high that empirically, they can hardly be effective, for as a rule, it is not possible to act upon such assumptions, which demand a high capacity of abstraction. If it can be shown that responsiveness can only be secured by employing high (unrealistic) standards upon democracy-impairing preferences, another solution would have to be sought. Amongst 'realistic' conditions, the selection of 'problematic' conditions is not assured, the more so as numerous possibilities of (populist) manipulation exist. The discharging of responsiveness does not then guarantee per se a result compatible with democracy. Responsiveness as a purely formal principle is not sufficient to characterize a democracy; in addition, the normative qualification of preferences from a Democracy Theory perspective is essential.

One principle limitation of responsiveness is marked by the concept of responsibility, which considers the responsibility of those in government and orientates towards the stability of democracy. Przeworski's (1988: 61 pp.) definition of democracy can illustrate this. According to his definition, democracy is an 'organised uncertainty' within fixed basic assumptions. For Przeworski et al. (1996: 50 pp.) democratic is "a regime in which governmental offices are filled as a consequence of contested elections. Only if the opposition is allowed to compete, win, and assume office is a regime democratic". Accordingly, three characteristics distinguish a democratic regime, namely "ex ante uncertainty ... ex post irreversibility ..., and repeatability". The latter characteristic, that of repeatability, logically excludes the removal of democratic procedures. In a democracy, no material content can be defined *a priori*; this is due to the uncertainty inherent within the democratic decision-making process, as it is precisely such content which can only be confirmed *a posteriori*, as a result of the procedure. However, if the characteristic of repeatability, as considered by Przeworski et al., is taken seriously, certain results can be excluded. One would have to exclude those decisions which in turn undermine the bases of chosen procedures. In this way, the target horizon of democratic action which works according to the responsibility principle, does not remain completely undefined.

(4b) Finally, it should be pointed out that the strategy of fulfilling as many preferences as possible, that is to say of taking account of the interests of the majority at the time of the election decision, can be counterproductive for this group if the decision-making context has significantly changed. Should 'surveys' therefore take place continually, and should these refer to aims or means ? Barring the factual difficulties which concern not only continuous surveys, but also the mediation of a sufficient decision-making basis, one is in so doing embarking upon the path to a direct democracy. If this is understood as being a solution path (as Saward does), then it must be shown that direct procedures are more suitable in reducing the problem of adequate preference determination than are representative ones. Whether however such demonstration of supremacy could be successful, is rather doubtful. At the very least, deliberative forms of direct democracy would have to be introduced; these are clearly different from common survey techniques.

Besides this, the problem of continual preference determination also arises when the decision-making context remains stable, but the preferences change. As generally, one must assume changes of the attitudinal as well as of the contextual type, the problem of finding a continual and responsive adaptation increases. Apart from the fact that such a participation project would exhaust all the time capacities of the participants, the ability to plan political decisions would no longer exist.[14]

4. Conclusion

As a result of these considerations, we can conclude that despite its undoubtedly democratic core, the responsiveness of a government is suitable only in a limited way as an expression of democratic quality. This path, without inclusion of the responsibility principle, shows itself consistently to be a dead-end. Or to express it another way, to define democracy solely through responsiveness is as much a dead-end as it would be to ignore it. Complete responsiveness can neither be guaranteed, nor from a Democracy Theory perspective would it always be useful. The unconsidered connection back to the wish of the voter cannot be the decisive criterion for defining democracy. Responsiveness refers to two of democracy's core components, the *input* and *output* sides; both must be included in defining democracy. As the present deliberations have illustrated however, the latter of these can only be considered in its negative limitation. The qualification of policy results is based upon the democratic quality of the decision-making process, upon the 'normative compatibility' of the decision with democratic values as well as upon the ability to implement that decision administratively. The consideration of performance also points limits to democracy. This does not yet guarantee per se development which is socially just, economically prosperous as well as ecologically sound.[15] However, by means of its procedures, it does offer better possibilities than do authoritarian regimes, of making, in a considered way, the preferences of the citizen the basis of policy. Whether social justice becomes reality is no expression of democratic quality, as it is based more upon the expressed preferences of the electorate, and upon the transformation of these preferences into binding political decisions.

---

14 In the process of continual decision-making which accompanies this, the "enlightened understanding", as Dahl calls for, could not be realized, as preferences and political results would be incalculable.

15 When during fundamental system change and transformation processes, the wishes of the population are founded upon these *issues*, disappointment is guaranteed. To reduce such disappointment, democracies must be able to show themselves capable of at least striving for these goals. Otherwise, it could happen that shifts in preferences take root amongst the population at the political level and that even authoritarian developments are then welcomed, should they perceive these as being more effective in achieving their objectives.

In this exceedingly pointed emphasis upon responsiveness, Dahl's definition of democracy (1971) shows itself indeed to be problematic, as this term is neither empirically viable, nor (in the sense of *complete responsiveness*) does it outline an objective which is theoretically possible or indeed desirable. Consequently, it fails to figure even once in the index in Dahl's later reflections upon democracy (1989). Despite this, the basic idea does not disappear, which is linked to the procedural understanding of 'responsiveness', as has been outlined. On the contrary, in his examination of the meaning of quality for the democratic process, Dahl (1989: 307) stresses this sole, plausible interpretation for the situative determination of the *common good*. It is not a matter of eliminating this term from Democracy Theory, but simply of explicating its problem and limits or preconditions. It is also worth including the basic idea that government action is coupled with the wishes and needs of the population within the analysis of democratic Government, and within the reflective interpretation perspective as offered here. Responsiveness can be portrayed as being compatible with democracy in as far as democratic procedures can be consolidated through deliberation, and at the same time, the added security of the rule of law is available.

At this point, no explication of deliberative procedures can be offered which addresses all of the differing facets (Habermas 1992, Dryzek 2002, Bohman/Rehg 1997). However, an indication needs to be given, which makes the implications for the intermediary domain clearer, and refers to the institutions dealing with freedom of organization and of communication. In classifying its core characteristics and tasks to the dimensions of political freedom, political equality and judicial control, this domain is already essentially outlined. However with regard to possible deliberative characteristics, the element of stability must also be mentioned. This concerns in particular intermediary organizations – parties and Civil Society, which primarily take on the tasks of the articulation as well as the aggregation of interests. In order to take on these functions appropriately, firm organizational structures are essential, capable of guiding structured communication processes. If parties are incapable of this, due to their own fragility and lack of organizational stability, then no contribution to the deliberative consideration of the political process can be expected. Such incapability is illustrated by populist parties, uninterested in any form of exchange through argument, but far more in manipulating public opinion by addressing and pushing certain themes. In the same way, clientelist parties are hardly capable of this task, as their internal communication process is steered by personal loyalties. Apart from the tendency to instability of person-oriented patterns of organization, in such contexts a debate based upon a programme is paid lip-service. In many fledgling democracies of central Eastern Europe, this phenomenon is well illustrated by person-oriented parties (cf. Lauth 2008; Kneuer in this issue).

Thus considering democratic quality in fledgling democracies involves the careful documentation and analysis of the democratic process. The study of the necessary institutions forms an essential basis of this task. However at the same time, we must also examine the actors who bring these institutions to life. At the individual level, this concerns their attitudes and cognitive expertise; at the meso level, we must consider the organisational and communication structures of intermediary organizations (Powell 2005: 63). Employing current typologies of parties and of Civil Society is not always useful, as these hardly cover informal structures systemically. Such structures can significantly hamper the functioning of such collective actors (for positive approaches, see Betz/Erdmann/Köllner 2004). These latter considerations demonstrate that the definition of the measurement of democratic quality is a work in progress, and must remain so. Even when agreement can be reached at abstract levels, shape and form of the institutional domain must be defined. This concerns the exact functioning as much as it does the indicators and methods of measurement employed for the purpose.

Therefore making assumptions about regressions of democracy is no easy task. In this article, we have stressed central criteria which should be considered when measuring democracy. The main point of discussion has focussed on the relevance of responsiveness. It could be demonstrated that measuring the quality of democracy should not rely only on these criteria. Full responsiveness cannot exist, neither for empirical and methodological reasons, nor for normative criteria. If responsiveness is measured for example by the indicator "satisfaction with the performance of the democratic government" one should reflect upon the result very carefully. A low degree of such a satisfaction does not indicate automatically a regression of democratic quality. The analysis of such processes should always include several indicators of the main dimensions, always bearing in mind that democracy is a boundary concept sensitive to potential target conflicts.

Bibliography

Alexy, Robert (1998) 'Die Institutionalisierung der Menschenrechte im demokratischen Verfassungsstaat' in Gosepath, Stefan/Lohmann, Georg (eds.) *Philosophie der Menschenrechte*, Frankfurt/ Main: 244-264.

Arrow, Kenneth (1951): *Social Choice and Individual Values*, New Haven.

Beetham, David (1994) 'Key Principles and Indices for a Democratic Audit' in Beetham, David (ed.) *Defining and Measuring Democracy*, London: 25-43.

Beetham, David (1996) ‚The Democratic Audit: Grundprinzipien und Schlüsselindikatoren politischer Demokratie' in Campbell, David F.J./Liebhart, Karin/Martinsen, Renate/Schaller, Christian/Schedler, Andreas (eds.) *Die Qualität der österreichischen Demokratie. Versuche einer Annäherung*, Wien: 19-44.

Benz, Arthur (2003) 'Föderalismus und Demokratie. Eine Untersuchung zum Zusammenwirken zweier Verfassungsprinzipien'; *polis* 57 FernUniversität Hagen.

Betz, Joachim/Erdmann, Gero/Köllner, Patrick (2004) *Die gesellschaftliche Verankerung politischer*

Parteien. Formale und informelle Dimensionen im internationalen Vergleich, Wiesbaden.

Bohman, James/Rehg, William (Hrsg.) (1997) *Deliberative Democracy. Essays on Reason and Politics*, Cambridge/Mass./London.

Brennan, Andrew (2003) 'Necessary and Sufficient Conditions', *Stanford Encyclopedia of Philosophy*, in http://plato.stanford.edu/entries/necessary-sufficient/.

Bühlmann, Marc/Merkel, Wolfgang/Müller, Lisa/Wessels, Bernhard (2008) 'Quality of Democracy. Democracy Barometer for Established Democracies. Working Paper No. 10a:', National Center for Competence in Reaserach - Democracy, Universität Zürich und WZB. Quality Criteria for Democracy. Why Responsiveness is not the Key 79

Conzelmann, Thomas (2003) 'Auf der Suche nach einem Phänomen: Was bedeutet Good Governance in der europäischen Entwicklungspolitik?', *Nord - Süd aktuell* 3: 468-477.
Croissant, Aurel/Thiery, Peter (2000) 'Defekte Demokratie. Konzept, Operationalisierung und Messung' in Lauth, Hans-Joachim/Pickel, Gert/Welzel, Christian (eds.) *Demokratiemessung,* Opladen: 89-111.
Crouch, Colin (2008) *Postdemokratie,* Frankfurt/Main.
Dahl, Robert A. (1971) *Polyarchy. Participation and Opposition,* New Haven/London.
Dahl, Robert A. (1989) *Democracy and its Critics,* New Haven/London.
Diamond, Larry/Morlino, Leonardo (2004) 'The Quality of Democracy. An Overview', *Journal of Democracy* 4: 14-25.
Diamond, Larry/Morlino, Leonardo (eds.) (2005) *Assessing the Quality of Democracy,* Baltimore.
Downs, Anthony (1968) *Ökonomische Theory der Demokratie,* Tübingen.
Dryzek, John S. (2002) Deliberative Democracy and Beyond, Oxford.
Faust, Jörg (2007) 'Democracy's Dividend: Political Order and Economic Productivity', *World Political Science Review* 2: Article 2. DOI: 10.2202/1935-6226.1019.
Greven, Michael (1993) 'Ist die Demokratie modern? Zur Rationalitätskrise der politischen Gesellschaft', *Politische Vierteljahresschrift* 3: 399-413.
Guggenberger, Bernd/Offe, Claus (eds.) (1984) *An den Grenzen der Mehrheitsdemokratie,* Opladen.
Habermas, Jürgen (1992) 'Drei normative Modelle der Demokratie: Zum Begriff deliberativer Politik' in Münkler, Herfried (ed.) *Die Chancen der Freiheit,* München/Zürich: 11-24.
Habermas, Jürgen (1996) 'Über den internen Zusammenhang von Rechtsstaat und Demokratie' in Habermas, Jürgen (ed.) *Die Einbeziehung des Anderen. Studien zur politischen Theorie,* Frankfurt/Main: 293-305.
Hadenius, Axel (1992) *Democracy and Development,* Cambridge.
Held, David (ed.) (1987) *Models of Democracy,* Cambridge.
Héretier, Adrienne (ed.) (1993): *Policy-Analyse. Kritik und Neuorientierung* (PVS-Sonderband 24), Opladen.
Höffe, Otfried (1999) 'Wieviel Politik ist dem Verfassungsgericht erlaubt?' in *Der Staat 2*: 171-193.
Holmes, Stephen (1995) 'Constitutionalism' in Lipset, Seymour M. (ed.) *The Encyclopedia of Democracy,* London: 299-305.
Lauth, Hans-Joachim (2004) *Demokratie und Demokratiemessung. Eine konzeptionelle Grundlegung für den interkulturellen Vergleich,* Wiesbaden.
Lauth, Hans-Joachim (2008) 'Qualität und Konsolidierung der Demokratie im Osten Europas' in *Zeitschrift für Staats- und Europawissenschaften* 1: 101-122.
Lauth, Hans-Joachim/Pickel, Gert/Welzel, Christian (eds.) (2000) *Demokratiemessung. Konzepte und Befunde im internationalen Vergleich,* Wiesbaden.
Lijphart, Arend (1984) *Democracies: Patterns of Majoritarian and Consensus Government in Twenty-one Countries,* New Haven.
Lipset, Seymour M./Rokkan, Stein (eds.) (1967): *Party Systems and Voter Alignments,* New York.
Lipset, Seymour M. (1959) 'Some Social Requisites of Democracy: Economic Development and Political Legitimacy' in *American Political Science Review* 1: 69-105.
Luhmann, Niklas (1984) *Soziale Systeme. Grundriß einer allgemeinen Theorie,* Frankfurt/Main.
Maihold, Günter (1996) '"Erblinden" die Institutionen und versagen die Akteure? Regierbarkeit und Zukunftsfähigkeit der Demokratie in Lateinamerika' in Bodemer, Klaus/Krumwiede,

Heinrich-W./Nolte, Detlef/Sangmeister, Hartmut (eds.) *Lateinamerika Jahrbuch 1996*, Frankfurt/Main: 62-91.

Mayntz, Renate (1997) 'Politische Steuerung und gesellschaftliche Steuerungsprobleme' in Mayntz, Renate (ed.) *Soziale Dynamik und politische Steuerung*, Frankfurt/Main: 186-208.

Merkel, Wolfgang/Puhle, Hans-Jürgen/Croissant, Aurel/Eicher, Claudia/Thiery, Peter (2003) *Defekte Demokratien, Bd. 1: Theorie*, Opladen.

Muno, Wolfgang (2001) 'Demokratie und Entwicklung', Institut für Politikwissenschaft, Abt. politische Auslandsstudien und Entwicklungspolitik, Dokumente und Materialien 29, Mainz.

O'Donnell, Guillermo/Cullell, Jorge V./Iazzetta, Osvaldo M. (eds.) (2004): *The Quality of Democracy*, Notre Dame.

Offe, Claus (1994) *Der Tunnel am Ende des Lichts: Erkundungen der politischen Transformation im Neuen Osten*, Frankfurt/Main/New York.

Offe, Claus (1996) 'Bewährungsproben – Über einige Beweislasten bei der Verteidigung der liberalen Demokratie' in Weidenfeld, Werner (ed.) *Demokratie am Wendepunkt*, Berlin: 141-157.

Powell, G. Bingham (2005) 'The Chain of Responsiveness' in Diamond, Larry/Morlino, Leonardo (eds.) *Assessing the Quality of Democracy*, Baltimore: 62-76.

Przeworski, Adam (1988) 'Democracy as a Contingent Outcome of Conflicts' in Elster, Jon/Slagstad, Rume (eds.) *Constitutionalism and Democracy*, Cambridge: 59-80.

Przeworski, Adam/Alvarez, Michael M./Cheibub, Jose Antonio/Limongi Neto, Fernando Papaterra (1996) 'What makes Democracies Endure' in *Journal of Democracy* 1: 39-56.

Reisinger, William M. (1997) 'Choices Facing the Builders of a Liberal Democracy' in Grey, Robert D. (ed.) *Democratic Theory and Post-Communist Change*, Englewood Cliffs/NJ: 24-51.

Riker, William H. (1980) 'A Reply to Ordeshook and Rae' in *American Political Science Review* 2: 456-458.

Sartori, Giovanni (1970) 'Concept Misformation in Comparative Politics' in *American Political Science Review* 4: 1033-1053.

Saward, Michael 1994 'Democratic Theory and Indices of Democratization' in Beetham, David (ed.) *Defining and Measuring Democracy*, London: 6-24.

Scharpf, Fritz W. (1970) *Demokratietheorie zwischen Utopie und Anpassung*, Konstanz.

Scharpf, Fritz W. (2000) *Interaktionsformen. Akteurzentrierter Institutionalismus in der Politikforschung*, Opladen.

Schmidt, Manfred G. (2006) *Demokratietheorien. Eine Einführung*, Wiesbaden.

Schmidt, Manfred G. (1995) *Demokratietheorien. Eine Einführung*, Opladen.

Schmidt, Manfred G. (1997): 'Komplexität und Demokratie. Ergebnisse älterer und neuere Debatten' in Klein, Ansgar/Schmalz-Bruns, Rainer (eds.) *Politische Beteiligung und Bürgerengagement*, Bonn: 41-58.

Schmitter, Philippe C. (2004) 'The Ambiguous Virtues of Accountability' in Diamond, Larry/Morlino, Leonardo (eds.) *Assessing the Quality of democracy*, Baltimore: 18-31.

Wilke, Helmut (1992) *Ironie des Staates. Grundlinien einer Staatstheorie polyzentrischer Gesellschaft*, Frankfurt/Main.

Zippelius, Reinhold (1991) *Allgemeine Staatslehre*, München.

ARTICLE

Is the international environment becoming less benign for democratisation?[1]

Peter Burnell

Abstract In order to know whether the international environment is becoming less benign for democratisation this article argues that we must first establish how we would know if such a trend is happening or not, before going on to what it means and the implications for democratisation. Although the answer to the headline question is probably a qualified yes, more analytical and much empirical research is needed to compare the international context for democratisation on the one side and authoritarian resilience or resurgence on the other.

In 2003 Philippe Schmitter (2003: 28) said the causal impact of the international context 'is often indirect, working in mysterious and unintended ways through ostensibly national agents'. Today, there is no reason to believe that much has changed. The international environment is large and multifaceted: There is far more to it than international democracy promotion and democracy assistance more narrowly defined. And the international environment's relationship with actors, institutions and conditions inside countries is interwoven in such complex ways that the good sense of even just posing the question 'is the international environment becoming less benign for democratisation?' might itself be questioned, let alone the wisdom of any proposed answer.

Rather than a simple yes or no, then, this article offers some reflections on how to go about trying to find out whether the international environment is changing in ways that matter and the direction of that change, uncovering what is involved in trying to address the issue. After a framing introduction (Section 1), the article consists of four main parts: Section 2 shares some definitions and fundamental assumptions; Section 3 suggests how to modernise the analytical framework for examining the influence of the international environment; Section 4 compares international aspects of authoritarian renewal with those of democracy's advance; Section 5 argues that the existence of weak and insignificant states may be no less important than the international spread of authoritarian rule. A conclusion (Section 6) offers final remarks.

---

[1] Final version of article submitted March 2010.

1. Introduction: Why now?

Posing the question 'is the international environment becoming less benign for democratisation?' clearly assumes that the international environment matters. And, probably more than that, that the environment matters more now than formerly or than scholars used to think. This could be because of the progress that democracy has made over the last two decades, which leads countries to become more open to external influence. However none of this means that the international environment is now more benign.

Indeed, whereas in the mid-1990s a growing awareness of the potential significance of the international dimensions of democratisation started as a reaction against what previously looked like an almost exclusive focus on democratisation's *domestic* causes and conditions, so interest now is fuelled by an awareness that the environment has changed. The most relevant changes date from the outset of the 1990s and the prospect of a benign new world order. In late 2001 this expectation moved sharply to a sense of disorder, fuelled by 9/11 and other acts of international terrorism. The 'security first' response by leading states in the West adversely affected both the internal commitment to individual liberties inside countries, including theUnited States, and their international politics, notably the securitisation of foreign policy in general and likewise the securitisation of their approach to democracy-promotion specifically. President Obama's foreign policy initiatives so far have yet to convince anyone that a broadly neo-realist approach will not now predominate. Some writers have even mused about the chances of a new cold war –in which a more assertive and illiberal regime in Russia, China's growing international presence, and a supporting cast of smaller illiberal regimes like Iran cloud not just the prospects of democratisation but possibly the outlook for international peace too.

A parallel and related shift in consciousness is leaning away from what some writers in the 1990s recognised as the making of new international norms. These norms comprised a right of all societies to democratic rule irrespective of their rulers' position and, moreover an emerging right *and* even duty of the 'international community' to protect, defend and restore democracy as well as to support the establishment of new democracies (Halperin and Galic 2007). These expectations of a new normative international regime are now complicated by renewed emphasis on state-based notions of national sovereignty. These notions closely peg the legal entitlement of international coercive intervention in domestic affairs to the restrictive clauses enshrined in the United Nations Charter (Chapter 1, Article 2; Chapter 7, Articles 39–42), with modest extra leeway in situations of alleged war crimes, genocide, ethnic cleansing and other human rights abuse. It has become harder to mobilise broad-based international consensus even over softer approaches to international intervention in the name of democratisation (Whitehead 2009).

The foregoing might look bad enough for democratisation; yet further developments make the situation appear even worse. These include the growing obsolescence of the *unique* influence that European Union (EU) enlargement has exerted on political regimes to its east through the political conditionalities enshrined in the Copenhagen Agreement (1993), because further expansion will be very limited. Another factor is the substantial drop in morale in the international democracy-promotion industry, which owes only in part to the tarnishing of its image by a somewhat tenuous association with President Bush's rhetorical justification for forced regime change in Afghanistan and Iraq and the subsequent diminution of US credibility (Burnell 2008b). By the time President Obama can put some distance between himself and the legacy of his predecessor and signal a strong positive new strategy, the West could find other more pressing issues crowding the foreign relations agenda – Iran's attainment of nuclear weapons capability for example.

The global economic retrenchment in 2008–09 and, perhaps more significant in the longer term, the emergence of unsustainable public debt in the US and elsewhere are other developments whose negative implications for spreading democracy have attracted comment.[2] But we should not forget the boom in the commodities trade that benefited several authoritarian and semi-authoritarian rentier regimes, in the Persian Gulf for instance. Vulnerabilities to democratically conditioned international financial assistance and trade were reduced. A corollary of these developments is tougher economic conditions for some of the poorest fragile democracies, especially the oil importers. Whether these prove more problematic in the long run than the major structural economic (not just financial) problems now facing the US and some other advanced, post-industrial democracies is a moot point. But from the viewpoint of several African and Middle Eastern countries, the United States' scramble to secure diversified sources of oil has already undercut a consistent approach to promoting democracy in those nations.

Only ten years ago democracy was declared to be a universal value (Sen 1999); only five years ago international democracy-promotion was said to be a world value (McFaul 2004). On both counts we cannot be so sure now; the number of doubters is increasing. Indeed, the chances that a *vicious* circle spiralling downwards might be replacing a *virtuous* circle cannot be lightly dismissed: As the international environment becomes less benign, so the democratic momentum inside countries weakens in consequence; and when the democracies weaken, so their chances of exerting a favourable influence on democratisation elsewhere suffer too.

2. Assumptions

A number of assumptions made in the article warrant clarification.

First, although democracy continues to be a contested concept, scholarly consensus views democratisation as progress towards liberal democracy understood as something more than just free and fair elections: It includes recognition of essential civil liberties and respect for the rule of law, as well. Just like 'defective democracies', authoritarian/semi-authoritarian regimes fall short in varying degrees: De facto political power is

---

2 .Svolik's (2008) statistical survey identifies economic recession as the primary factor associated with reversals of democracy to authoritarian rule.

usually concentrated in the hands of a select few who do not have to account properly for how they use power and to what ends.

Second, the international environment may have become less (or conversely more) benign not just for democratisation but more generally, including for political stability, governmental effectiveness and national security. Not only democracies but many kinds of government and regime are challenged by such developments as the worldwide economic slowdown, potential proliferation of weapons of mass destruction and growing climate instability. The current millennium has seen increasing tension among large states (including within the transatlantic alliance), and a transformation is under way from the relative order of a unipolar world briefly present in the 1990s to the greater uncertainties of whatever is taking its place, whether multipolarity or more profound fragmentation. Claims like 'analysts now routinely refer to American hegemony' (Clark 2005: 733) now seem outdated.

Third, the choice of baseline for considering trends in the influence of the international environment will affect the results. The same point applies to how far into the future we want to speculate on the prospects. The first half of the 1990s was perhaps a golden age for democratisation. Comparing 2010 with periods either more than 21 years ago or less than 10 years ago probably makes the present look more favourable (or less unfavourable) to the spread of democracy than comparisons with the mid-1990s. Comparing a verdict on today with what we now know about the early 1990s could prove less unfavourable than comparing the verdict with beliefs widely held at that time, but which now seem misguided. A particularly salient baseline is 2001: The terrorist events of '9/11' had profound consequences both for international relations and the way world politics is understood, as well as for international democracy-promotion specifically.

Empirical judgements about the international environment in any given period are influenced by comparisons with other periods, and may fluctuate over time, but no less pertinent is that conceptions of the environment – the way analysts construct the most relevant parameters – evolves too. In part, this evolution stems from a learning effect: a calculated response to discovering that former frameworks and old lenses are too limiting or have been previously misapplied. In addition the evolution in our conceptions has happened because the world really has changed, and comprehension of that change requires new ways of thinking. To illustrate, prior to social science's discovery of globalisation, the international environment was constructed in largely state-centric terms, the dominant feature being relations between national states. When theorising about international politics, many scholars found that a (neo-)realist perspective offered a very good fit, especially during the height of the cold war period. Since the end of the cold war the world order has begun to look much less simple: The role of multilateral, transnational and supra-territorial forces, the place of multilevel actors and arrangements for polycentric governance have attracted increasing attention in recent years. This meant that not just states and inter-governmental bodies but international, non-governmental institutions came to be recognised as significant parts of the mix. Finally, the way the international environment is conceived may change because of shifts in whose view demands attention: Is it (still) the view from the West or is there more acceptance now of views from elsewhere? Certainly the views from Moscow and Beijing and the global

South in general are probably better known now than a decade or so ago, as they tend to be articulated more forcefully these days. So, assessments of the international environment cannot be divorced entirely from the question of 'whose (interpretation of the) international environment are we considering?': Where you sit matters.

Fourth, obviously the international environment is no monolith. When modelling the external influences on politics in states, the regional and even sub-regional contexts should be distinguished, alongside ideas about a global space, universal trends and such actors as the United Nations. Both an exposure to influence and the direction of that influence are variable, depending on place, time and circumstance.[3] For example, new states in the Balkans en route to becoming full members of the EU are more susceptible to influence and more likely to be influenced in a pro-democratic direction than is North Korea. Of course what constitutes a region and its borders is itself dependent on the context. Georgians themselves might look westwards, and the West views Georgia as an emerging (albeit increasingly troubled) democracy. But objective reality also says that Russia is a powerful neighbour, and Russian Prime Minister Medvedev eyes Georgia as part of a region where Russia has 'privileged interests'.

A consolidating view in the democratisation literature is that, generally speaking, the regional context has become more important, compared to the binational and global contexts (for example Schmitter 2001: 40), and that institutions like the Organization of American States (OAS), African Union (AU) and Organisation for Security and Co-operation in Europe (OSCE) could well be democratisation's first line of support and defence in the future (Diamond 2008: 332).[4] Differences between locations in terms of whether the international environment increasingly matters and whether it has become more favourable are inevitable. Clearly, for countries that have recently joined (or still have realistic hopes of joining) the EU, the immediate regional political environment probably seems more favourable now than it did 20 years ago, but for states in the Caucasus and Central Asia it looks less benign than 15 years ago. In the Middle East, the outlook for democracy seems not to have changed much at all, the debacle in Iraq notwithstanding, if only because a major roadblock – settlement of the Israel-Palestine dispute – still awaits resolution. Africa's unimpressive efforts to prevent Zimbabwe's slide into crisis lowered expectations that South Africa could be a regional engine of political and not just economic progress. And in the Bush administration's preoccupation with Islamist-linked terrorism and the Middle East, US attention was distracted from the return of politically destabilising and potentially illiberal tendencies in parts of the Americas, most notably among Andean countries, although the democratic consolidation experienced in countries like Chile and Brazil must be considered a success story for the region too.

---

3. 'Looking for universal global influences that affect all countries alike is probably as ill-conceived as assuming identical and independent processes within each country' (Gleditsch and Ward 2006: 916).

4. Pevehouse (2002) showed that regional organisations whose members share strong democratic credentials provide a 'commitment device' that guards against democratic backsliding. However, the 'neighbourhood effect' that Brinks and Coppedge (2006) discuss may be either supportive or corrosive, according to the politics of the neighbours (see Bader, Grävingholt and Kästner 2010 forthcoming).

Fifth in the list of main assumptions that underpin this article, there is no presumption here that the nature of the international environment is decisive for democratisation; no assessment by itself can tell us all we need to know about what moves the dependent variable. A consensus that bridges leading academic writers on democratisation like Diamond (2008: Chapter 5) and think-tank experts on democracy promotion like Thomas Carothers maintains that domestic processes matter most for explaining democracy (and anti-democratic outcomes). These processes include political factors such as governance and those related to socio-economic condition. A nuanced formulation says it is 'external–internal interactions, rather than external factors per se, which are more accurately said to shape domestic outcomes' (Morlino and Magen 2009: 29), but there is little agreement on whether this is equally true for the short run (democratic opening and transition, or their opposites) and the long run (whether democratic consolidation or deconsolidation). For example, Schmitter's (2001: 40) claim that 'external intervention will have a greater and more lasting effect on the consolidation of democracy than upon the transition to it' could be difficult to reconcile with the more familiar proposition that external actors have the greatest leverage at key turning points in a country's political transformation. And yet Schmitter's assessment does not deny that in the long run domestic influences, such as popular and elite consensus on democratic values, will outweigh other influences, foreign ones included.

However, even if Whitehead (2004: 155) was correct to doubt (even before the present historical juncture) that international initiative can actually create a democratic regime notwithstanding the presence of favourable local conditions, strong international consensus and ample practical support, the converse – that international circumstances can inhibit a democratic breakthrough or make democratic consolidation difficult – may yet hold true. Perfect symmetry in the way international influences exert an effect is improbable. The potential to be a positive influence for democratic progress and the potential to be a negative influence may vary not only across locations but also with respect to the pace and direction of political change – towards or away from democracy – either stronger on the positive side than on the negative side, or vice versa.[5] A timely, if ambitious, exercise would turn existing reflections on the comparative influence of democratisation's domestic and international dimensions towards comparing domestic and international influences separately on democratic regression or decay, transitions to and consolidation of authoritarian and semi-authoritarian rule.

Finally, these days any inquiry into politics that goes beyond the micro-level must must be aware that the boundaries between the domestic and the foreign, the internal and the external, the endogenous and the exogenous are thought to be more fuzzy than half a century ago. And just as the international system itself is not a purely objective given but rather is constructed, at least to some extent, by actions and views formed at different levels, so the manner in which the levels and their degree of separation are understood are also under permanent review. The increasing penetration of national and sub-national spaces by extra-national and transnational forces, ideas and institutions,

---

5.Burnell (1998: 22-25) signalled that symmetry may be absent but critical analysis has been slow to turn from pro-democratisation to anti-democratisation influences.

makes this possible. The foreign policies of states still impact on the international scene, but the states themselves change as a result of engagement with the outside world. Even so, it is still worth it to hang on to the idea of dependent and independent variables in world politics, and to look for relations between the two, even as the different components increasingly come to reflect varying measures of constitutive interdependence.

3. Modernising the analytical framework

Interest in establishing whether a changing international environment harms democratisation raises the question 'how would we know?'

One approach would be to try to establish first the international requisites (prerequisites, even) of democratisation, much in the same way as Lipset (1959) wrote about democracy's social requisites half a century ago. There have been few, if any, substantial attempts to do this. Dahl (1998:145–88), for instance, in his survey of 'conditions favorable and unfavorable' to democracy concentrated on the absence of hostile foreign intervention – surely more a prerequisite than a requisite. Anyway, the narrow focus of such an approach is not adopted here.

Another temptation would be to look first at trends in the number of examples of the different types of political regime and proceed on the assumption that the more democracies there are in the world, (however uneven their 'democraticness' and the fact that some are still democratising), the more favourable the international environment, if only because of the neighbourhood effect (see Brinks and Coppedge 2006; Gleditsch and Ward 2006).[6] Starr and Lindborg (2003: 516) went so far as to claim that the greater the number of democracies, the larger the feedback loop that strengthens the diffusion of consolidated democracy. A combination of enhanced capacity for collective self-defence by the larger number of democracies and positive transnational spill-over effects from democratisation suggest that the international environment both comes to matter more at the same time as it becomes increasingly benign. Nevertheless, the apparent stalling of democratisation worldwide in recent years – or even worse, what is now being called a 'freedom recession' – that is discussed elsewhere in this journal issue also indicate that the positive dynamic contained in ideas of feedback is not inevitable. More emphatic reversals of history's first two 'waves' of democratisation bear this out.

Another tempting strategy for addressing the question of 'how would we know?' would be to note the number of intergovernmental as well as national and sub-national organisations that now formally include democratic development as part of their mission statement or official goal. The number of autonomous and semi-autonomous (publicly funded) 'democracy institutes' and 'democracy foundations' has never been higher, and looks to increase.

---

6. The theory associated with Mansfield and Snyder (2005) that democratisation of a country is a hazardous process threatening to international peace looks perverse in its implications if peace is considered helpful to democratisation. However the theory is controversial.

However, the international environment and its capacity to exert influence are more than just distinctive patterns of organisational innovation and the presence of parallel trends across broad swathes of states, although these are important. The international context for democratisation consists of a larger and more complex mosaic of different kinds of actors, events, trends, conditions, prevailing sentiments or beliefs and informal as well as formal institutions. Theorists of international relations vigorously contend the relative significance of these categories, according to whether they subscribe to a (neo-)realist, liberal, neo-Marxist, social constructivist, feminist or other paradigm. For some theorists, states still make the greatest impact; for others it is now the activities of non-state actors (transnational networks of non-governmental actors, or civil society, as well as inter-governmental instruments) that cry out for attention; and yet others believe more attention should be paid to the way norms and valuea are sometimes diffused spontaneously. Alternatively they subscribe to the view that not just ideas in general but identities in particular both shape and are shaped by what happens, and must be understood contextually. In practice, however, the challenge of assessing the international environment of democratisation has not been a major focus of attention of any of these, with the partial exception of studies of the European Union's influence on prospective new member states. Instead, the wider international environment's influence on democratisation has been addressed most directly in a smaller – almost niche – literature that exists outside the grand swirl of abstract international relations theory debate. First, Huntington (1991) devoted 20 pages to the new policies of external actors and demonstration effects, or 'snowballing', in explaining democratisation's 'third wave'. But the two foremost, Laurence Whitehead (1996; 2001; 2004) and Philippe Schmitter (2001) came later. They set the pace in offering more detailed analytical frameworks that shed light on how the international environment (independent variable) might matter for democratisation (dependent variable), which in turn reveals something more about why the international environment matters and whether it actually does have an effect.

Briefly, Whitehead's pioneering framework (1996) had three main components: contagion, control and conditionality, to which he later (2001) added consent; consent was further subdivided into four distinct themes. Schmitter's (2001) more elaborate framework distinguishes trends, events and waves. It goes on to list an inventory of 'propositions-cum-hypotheses' – no less than 15 headings and 18 sub-headings, which is said to be not all-inclusive. Neither framework offers a key for comparing the relative weight of the different dimensions and propositions and of the information that their application might reveal. We have few guidelines for arriving at overall judgments about whether, how far or fast the sum total of international dimensions of democratisation on balance is becoming more or less favourable. But there are some clues as to particular international mechanisms or combinations deemed insufficient to produce sustainable democratic transition, even in favourable domestic circumstances (examples include Schmitter (2001) specifically on contagion and consent). Most recently, however, the challenge of assessing international influence has taken on a whole new dimension.

(i) The international dimensions of multi-directional regime change

In reality, regime change viewed analytically as the dependent variable now turns out to be not one but several distinct phenomena. Commentators on international politics have begun to notice both that the 'democratic project' may be in trouble and that international factors could be partly responsible (examples are Yom and Al-Momani 2008; Ambrosio 2008; and a special issue of *Contemporary Politics*, 16: 1, 2010) . These international factors demand both theoretical and empirical investigation.

We can turn on its head the approach that starts with the international environment and investigates its (pro-democratic) effects. In other words we can set out instead from the 'dependent' variable – states, political regimes and regime changes in their full variety – and ask how if at all these are affected by international developments. This substitution leads a more variegated landscape to come into view. The dependent variable now is multifarious: democratic transition, democratic consolidation, and democracy's qualitative improvement together with the reverse of all of these plus authoritarian and semi-authoritarian resilience and revival. There could be international influence on all of these; moreover, potentially, the most relevant aspects of the international environment could differ for each case, just as an identical international variable could affect fundamentally different regimes in different ways. In this plural multi-directional universe of cases the choice of *dependent* variable requiring explanation might be expected to influence the way the *independent* variable (the international environment) is actually framed. So the way ideas about the international environment and its effects are conceived and then executed may both vary over time and be non-uniform across the full spectrum of regime change movements towards and away from democracy and political stasis.

In principle the familiar proposition that says the influence of the international environment has become more important as a consequence of democratisation begins to look less tenable, if democratic backsliding really is happening now. In practice the reality may be less straightforward. To illustrate, Russia moved back in an authoritarian direction as it became both more globally integrated and more assertive on the regional and world stage. China now scores higher on the standard indices for economic and political globalisation than many small democracies combined. But China is not about to succumb to international norms of liberal democracy. In a similar vein Chile is globally much less-integrated but no-one seriously suggests that its democracy is unstable and likely to weaken. In fact, it is China's potential to exert an anti-democratic influence in places like Myanmar and its trading partners in Africa that has recently drawn concern in the West.

So, the way the international influences are studied will change too. In respect of formulating strategies for promoting democracy, Carothers (1997) has long argued that to be successful they must be grounded in a credible theory of democratisation, i.e. one that explains how democracies come about. The reach of Carothers' insight can be extended: reflection not just on the effects of democracy–promotion on democratisation but on the influence of the international environment in general on democratisation would benefit from making stronger connections with appropriate theories of democratisation. Furthermore, irrespective of whether a credible theory (or theories) of democratisation already exist, if the international dimensions of regime changes towards authoritarian rule are to be fully understood, then a plausible theory of de-democratisation – of the reasons why authoritarian and semi-authoritarian regimes can be revived or persist – is also required. This task remains a work in progress.Pioneering work on the breakdown of democratic regimes by Linz and Stepan (1978) did not consider international aspects; more recent analysis by Gandhi and Przeworski (2007) examined domestic political causes only; and while Diskin, Diskin and Hazen (2005) found a robust correlation between democratic collapse and 'foreign involvement in domestic politics', the study's value is limited because the study does not fully elucidate the foreign variable or explain how it was operationalised

(ii) Influences: active and passive, direct and indirect

A complementary and parsimonious addition to existing frameworks for analysing democratisation's international influences, and going beyond any one type of regime or direction of regime change, would distinguish between direct and indirect influence and between active and passive influence. Direct influence on regimes has immediate political effect; in contrast, indirect influence on regimes works through intervening variables, for instance the state of the economy. Active influences are those that are intended to influence the type of regime and/or direction of regime change. Examples include deliberately taking sides in a domestic political struggle, trying to remould the dominant values or helping to reshape political structures and institutions. In all cases the actual effects may not necessarily correspond with the intentions and may even be counter-productive or . Influence that is passive does not have origins in any specific policy to influence politics (although external actors may still welcome the effects); hence passive influence shares some affinities both with Levitsky and Way's (2005) notion of linkage (ties to the West) and Nye's (2001) original formulation of 'soft power' (the ability of a country's culture, ideals and policies to influence others by attraction and without deliberate resort to bribery or coercion), but is not synonymous with either idea. Levitsky and Way (2005) shared with Nye a bias towards explaining democracy's spread. And although Nye's (2001) original formulation of 'soft power' allowed for unintended effects, a great deal of the considerable debate it has spawned focuses on how government policy (mainly US policy but increasingly that of China as well) might secure, manipulate and enhance soft power to achieve intended effects, such as through public diplomacy, foreign aid. The avoidance of using hard power unnecessarily or in a clumsy way making has also became a common recommendation, .with particular reference to military interventions of the kind witnessed in Iraq.

Proposed initially for the purpose of critiquing international democracy-promotion (Burnell 2006), the fourfold typology of active, passive, direct and indirect influences can be applied to studying the influence abroad not only of established democracies but of all other regimes too. Moreover this typology encompasses the many different kinds of external influences, both favourable and unfavourable, that cannot be attributed to any conscious design. The typology can be applied in a non-ideological way: It is detached from normative commitments to democracy and from the orientation towards offering policy advice on how to advance democracy – something that has been so prevalent throughout the democratisation literature including the international dimensions. Of course intentionality can only be attributed to conscious state or non-state actors. This is hardly a shortcoming; on the contrary, the active versus passive distinction draws attention to where a regime – irrespective of type or trajectory – may be influenced by such factors as learning or examples from abroad. The regimes may react negatively, or alternatively seek to emulate or to modify and adapt – to use Acharya's (2004) term, 'localise' – foreign norms, values and practices to become more congruent with the established situation inside the country. The forces that propel domestic political change can be structural conditions, or events and trends in the international sphere as much as the policies, decisions or models offered by external actors and international institutions.

All four permutations – direct and active; direct and passive, indirect and active; indirect and passive - are feasible. In each case the effect might be favourable (or becoming less unfavourable) or conversely unfavourable (or becoming more favourable) to democracy and democratisation and to their alternatives, or to maintaining the status quo. Examples of some of the cominations are: applying overt and covert political strategies of aggression aimed at bringing about 'regime change' (active, that is to say intentional, and direct); attempting to subvert a regime by applying economic sanctions or more constructively contributing to internal conflict-resolution (active and indirect); the effects of undirected social learning and international demonstration effects (passive and direct); and of market-based transactions in trade and international finance, whose impact on modernisation and development have consequences for the regime (passive and indirect).

In sum, a modernised analytical framework must be able to capture structural as well as policy-based sources of influence, both controlled events and random happenings in the international environment, and do this without confinement to any particular region, set of countries or regimes as the source of influence (namely, the West) or any particular direction in terms of regime change (e.g. democratisation). It must capture the relationships whereby democracies sometimes encourage authoritarian tendencies in other countries (at times knowingly and quite deliberately) and other relationships whereby the actions of an autocracy help to advance democracy elsewhere (including by highlighting autocracy's vices). That said, there is currently a surge of interest in what has come to be called backlash or pushback against democracy and against the international promotion of democracy

4. Comparing international strategies for securing democracy's advance and maintaining or renewing authoritarian rule

Comparing the impact that the democracies and democratisation have on the prospects for democracy elsewhere with the impact that authoritarian/semi-authoritarian regimes have on the prospects for authoritarianism/semi-authoritarianism elsewhere offers an exciting intellectual prospect. Could one be a mirror image of the other? Just as the deliberate promotion of democracy abroad is only one of many ways in which the international environment may affect democracy's progress around the world, so defensive measures of resistance at home are not the only way that non-democratic regimes actively try to protect themselves against external democratising influences, in general, and international democracy-promotion, specifically. The international effects – intended and unintended – may be far reaching. Do authoritarian and semi-authoritarian regimes seek to promote look-alike regimes abroad, in the same way that Western democracies appear keen to encourage the spread of Western-style liberal democracy? (Bader, Grävingholt and Kästner 2010 offers one of the very first theoretical attempts to address this question; Burnell 2010a offers a different analytical approach). If the answer is yes, are the reasons and motivations behind the parallels and the practical modus operandi also broadly comparable? One possible contrast is that whereas democracies seek to influence a change of regime towards democracy and yet will accept continuity of the same politicians and many of same policies in government (where the rulers learn to play the new democratic game successfully), autocracies might be more interested in ensuring that the rulers of a neighbouring state are friendly, if necessary by conniving to bring about a change of rulers. They are less concerned with influencing the type of political regime another state employs. Yet even where a government is externally influenced in this way and without any impact on the type of regime it might still be argued that the possibility of enjoying full democratic self-rule has still been compromised, so making the contrast seem less compelling.

A related argument says that democracies promote democracy abroad out of a sincere attachment to its universal value whereas the rulers of non-democracies are preoccupied more narrowly with personal ambitions of holding on to power at home, and will subordinate foreign policy to that end. However, even this contrast may be overdrawn, for at least two reasons, which I detail below.

First, on the one side there is Kagan's (2008) argument that authoritarian rulers might have a genuine belief in the merits of strong authoritarian rule – if not merely for their own sake then for the political stability and security that it can bring to a country (almost any country) so benefitting its economic prospects as well. For Kagan (2008) Russia's and China's leaders 'are not simply autocrats. They believe in autocracy....Today the autocrats pursue foreign policies aimed at making the world safe, if not for all autocracies, then at least for their own' (Kagan 2008). Preserving a sense of national identity and independence (important in the case of China), or protecting traditional culture and cherished religious beliefs (as in some Islamic countries), or even advancing social justice (Cuba and perhaps Venezuela) may be examples of the earnest intentions of autocratic regimes, which fear both the cultural standardisation that globalisation represents as well as the social inequalities that could come from increased integration into the world capitalist system. In any case the vigorous defence by authoritarian and semi-authoritarian regimes of traditional absolutist ideas of national sovereignty and non-interference in domestic politics (see Whitehead 2009) itself comes pretty close to a universalising claim, albeit at times resting on pragmatic foundations, such as in the case of Russia which seeks to influence politics of Georgia. (On China's nuanced attitude towards interference in other countries' politics see Kleine-Ahlbrandt and Small 2008.)

A second reason for questioning the crude contrast between the altruism of democracies' approach to foreign affairs and the personal selfishness of autocrats is that democracies clearly are motivated in their enthusiasm to see democracy spread by a variety of instrumental reasons meant to aid their own interests. Furthermore they are much less enthusiastic (unhelpful, even) where they believe their own interests might be threatened. (Their cold war diplomacy provides ample testimony to that.) Their democracy-promotion since the late 1980s has been explained in terms of security reasons (the democratic peace thesis; cutting the roots of international terrorism), economic reasons (pursuing the synergy that political liberalisation is said to have with economic liberalisation and the opening of markets and investment opportunities to international capital), and an unvarnished drive for hegemony imperialism. And where their core foreign policy objectives come into conflict with their attempts to democratise another regime, the support for democratic reform is sacrificed as a matter of course – that much is agreed to by American observers of the US like Thomas Carothers, and by Europeans writing about Europe (for example Jünemann and Knodt 2007). Direct and indirect means, active engagements as well as unintended effects have helped prop up some non-democracies, just as the non-democracies continue to do business with the West in ways that are mutually advantageous.

If in regard to conducting relations with regimes abroad the differences in terms of what both democracies and non-democracies do, and what their policy motives are, are not entirely clear-cut, then something similar can be said about the 'how', i.e. the policy modalities. A simple contrast between, on the one side, democracies willing to be assertive in exporting democracy (whether by coercion, conditionality or democracy assistance), that is to, say an outward-leaning orientation, and, on the other side, authoritarian or semi-authoritarian rulers digging in defensively at home, that is to say an inwards-leaning orientation, does not conform to the facts either. There are democracies whose commitment to exporting democracy is generally lukewarm or barely visible at the best of times; in contrast, as Ambrosio (2008) showed in respect of Putin's Russia, the route to authoritarian renewal at home can stretch beyond domestic strategies like 'regime insulation', to bolstering authoritarian regimes outside (Belarus, for example), subverting democracy abroad (as in Ukraine); and coordinating international action with like-minded regimes (as in the Commonwealth of Independent States, and Russia together with China and former Soviet republics in Central Asia forming the Shanghai Cooperation Organisation). Detailed comparison of the foreign policy behaviour of non-democracies with the foreign policy of Western democracies assessed as approaches to domestic regime maintenance, and the comparative evaluation of their effectiveness, is perhaps well overdue. This can be said notwithstanding all the methodological and other difficulties that have beset even just the evaluation of democracy assistance (see Burnell 2008a), let alone other ways of intervening and interventions directed at anti-democratic ends (on the comparative evaluation of democracy promotion and autocrayc promotion see Burnell 2010b).

(i) Is socialisation any different?

There is perhaps one area – possibly crucial in the long run – where an important difference between democratic and anti-democratic diffusion still remains. The spread of liberal democratic values does not need to be actively promoted by governments or, even by non-governmental organisations from outside. Spontaneous diffusion, or something akin to market forces, can spread ideals of liberal democracy at the base societal level, even if the permeability of national borders is a necessary (but not sufficient) condition. Social learning or acculturation can take place automatically. But in contrast to certain fundamentalist religious beliefs, racism, and xenophobia, it is difficult to see how the political values of authoritarian rule are so easily carried across borders at the popular level, through socialisation.

Certainly, authoritarian regimes (Syria, for example) make use of examples of foreign political instability and social chaos (e.g. in post-Hussein Iraq) as a way of persuading their own citizens to acquiesce in firm rule. And some autocracies are happy to promote beliefs resembling their own: Saudi government funding of *madrasas* in Pakistan for example. But authoritarian and semi-authoritarian regimes are just as likely to try to heavily regulate – if not actually prevent – inward flows of authoritarian-leaning values, especially any they judge threatening. Both Chinese and Russian government sensitivity to imported Islamic fundamentalism, and former Pakistani President Musharraf's unsuccessful attempts to control the *madrasas* bear this out. And notwithstanding improved relations between China and Russia in recent years the cultural dissimilarities between the two are strong, and mutual suspicions go back a long way.

So the relevant question is, can there be a form of authoritarian socialisation capable of operating across borders in any way comparable to the socialisation of more liberal democratic values? Arguably, at least some of the values, beliefs and attitudes that might fit authoritarian socialisation do not so much reject liberal democracy head on as they pursue different focuses, such as where a particular religious credo, commitment to national unity or some other social value supplies the defining concern. The implications for type of rule or political regime, while of course important, are contingent (and variable): where a certain kind of regime does fit the norms it is embraced not for itself but in consequence of values and beliefs pertaining to other areas of human existence. This scenario looks different from the structure of democratic socialisation at least in its guise of normative political suasion.

Even so, the opinion that in the 1990s in the competition between political ideologies, freedom and democracy have now irrevocably triumphed does look more dubious now, even when backed by arguments that even autocrats now resort to (spurious) claims of either being democrats or aiming for democracy, and stage-manage (neither free nor fair) elections. This doubtful kind of evidence is certainly not tantamount to accepting that only liberal democracy bestows political legitimacy. And even though authoritarian socialisation is underdeveloped as a theoretical concept, illustrative vehicles like Russian (language) media's presence in Central Asia are not hard to find.

But perhaps even more portentous than discordant views over whether liberal democracy has finally won the battle of ideas is the re-emergence of profound disagreements about what fluctuations in the ideational struggles really signify. The point here is a reference to the claim that what moves international politics is not ideological contestation at all but rather a competition for power between national states, with which particular ideological leanings happen to be associated. Just as the 1990s were favourable to the spread of democracy chiefly because 'freedom-loving' nations in North America and Western Europe were on top, (in terms of military capability, international political influence and economic power), so now the movement towards a more multipolar world must produce consequences for the relative status of different value systems, given that emerging poles do not endorse the West's enthusiasm for democracy (Kagan 2008) or for democracy promotion. (India for example is comparatively reticent.) It is worth noting that in addition to claiming that international politics is moving back towards a scenario resembling much of the former centuries (i.e. competition for power between states), so this deployment of a (neo-)realist perspective on international politics itself constitutes a return to the past, reminiscent of Huntington's remark (1984: 2006): 'In large measure, the rise and decline of democracy on a global scale is a function of the rise and decline of the most powerful democratic states'. Clearly the constructivist turn in the analysis of international politics, which made such inroads in European scholarship in recent years, has not captured every international relations theorist, any more than has liberal democracy become universally adopted as an ideology. A further implication is that the influence of multilateral and transnational governmental and non-governmental organisations – including many that were caught up in the most recent wave of democratisation and have actively supported the spread or defence of democracy – do not now count for as much as globalisation theories have been prone to emphasise. And their ability to help democracy spread may count for even less.

The validity or invalidity of Kagan's remarks notwithstanding, all analysts must now take far more account of the interplay of moves and counter-moves between pro-democratisation impulses and anti-democratisation impulses on the international stage. This refers not just to conflicts between the calculated actions of democracies and the predominantly democracy-favouring intergovernmental and non-governmental actors on the one side, and the deliberate actions of authoritarian and semi-authoritarian counterparts on the other. It also means investigating the passive or unintended effects, including how the domestic politics and inward-oriented policies of regimes of contrasting types constitute also the external environment for other states, where influences can flow across borders even in the absence of a foreign policy to direct them. A leading example is the economic success that has come to be associated with China, just as Western affluence has served as a passive influence for liberal democracy before the financial chaos and economic recessions of 2008–09 dented the image. The point is worth making even though the actual causal link connecting political regime type to economic development performance occasions much disagreement among social scientists, not just in regard to autocratic rule but in regard to democracy as well.

Against this background, then, Schmitter (2001: 46) looks very prescient to conclude that 'if there is one overriding lesson to be gleaned from the contemporary international context for democratisation, it is that this context is subject to rapid change in both the magnitude and direction of its impact'. Added to which the lens through which this context is studied seems no less likely to change back and forth. Furthermore, drawing attention to the uncertainty of the future prompts speculation that an observed increase in external influence by a few prominent regimes that are not liberal demiocracies, like China and Russia might look worrying for democracy, but this is not the only threat. For far more numerous are states whose own domestic political situations are far less certain, and where political weakness, not strength, merits closet attention.

5. Weak and insignificant states are part of the international (dis)order too

Their size and other advantages, including some shared economic and security interests with the West, not only help China and Russia resist Western attempts to spread liberal democracy but also give them a strong international presence. However China and Russia are exceptions, and concerns that they are responsible for transmitting – deliberately or otherwise – anti-democratic impulses to other countries should be kept in perspective, for reasons illustrated below.

One reason is that the great majority of all states that Freedom House calls either not free or only partly free countries, or their nearest equivalents in the Bertelsmann Transformation Index (autocracies and defective democracies), are actually too small or too insignificant in geopolitical terms to spread alternatives to democracy in any sustained way. A number of them are too unstable to have the capability let alone the inclination. The Bertelsmann Foundation (2008) for instance identified 27 fragile states (defined as places where the state's monopoly of the use of force is not guaranteed and its administrative structures are barely operable), of which ten are autocracies and seven failed states. Indeed issues of state capacity and government effectiveness rather than regime type may provide a much more insightful lens through which to examine not simply a state's internal politics but its external effects as well. The earlier mistake that viewed all countries as candidates for democratisation and thereby viable 'targets' for international democracy-promotion should not be repeated now by pumping up the profile of the engines of authoritarian contagion. A balanced survey would recognise the problems both weakness and strength pose for democracy. This includes societies where relative indifference from outside states to issues like chronic food insecurity, environmental calamities or economic debility make political instability there that much more likely. The danger that such states will be unable to hold on to their own newly democratised institutions or, worse, unwittingly export instability and their domestic conflict to neighbouring countries, (and in doing so threatening other fragile new democracies), should not be ignored.

Very few of the world's autocracies and defective democracies, or 'not free' states and 'partly free' states, are serious candidates for exporting non-democratic models. For most of them, including the likes of Cuba, Venezuela, Iran, Saudi Arabia and, perhaps, even Russia their likely intentions and their actual reach are regional or sub-regional, not global. By comparison the great majority of non-democracies have to rely more on whatever advantages can be derived from weakness (Schelling 1980) – weakness of the state, or of the regime, or of the government, and maybe of all three. But therein also lies the possibility that interference by foreign powers – whether nearby authoritarian rulers seeing an opportunity to influence political convergence towards their own type of regime, or Western intervention that seeks to fend off political regime changes that might threaten their own core foreign policy interests – will constitute an international obstacle to democratisation. This last scenario has ample precedents including the West's extensive and ongoing financial, economic, political and military support of the regimes in Egypt and Jordan, whose rulers can manipulate Western anxieties that free and fair elections might bring radical Islamists to power (see Yom and Al-Momani 2008). Multinational cooperation that enlists China and major democracies in trying to prevent North Korea from economic and political collapse provides a different but no less telling example.

In sum, the realities of state failure and largely ineffective or just weak regimes and those that can profit by appearing to have these defects, and the external consequences, should occupy attention in studies of the changing international environment for democratisation, alongside the growing attention only now being given to the influence of non-democracies on the spread of authoritarian rule and deliberate attempts to export autocracy specifically. The respective weight that should be attached to these two sources of threat to democratisation is up for debate. But in any case the two are not mutually exclusive in the case of a country like Afghanistan, where the Taliban's return to power could renew that country's status as an exporter of terrorism, with the maintenance of Pakistan's fragile democracy very much in the firing line.

6. Concluding remarks

The approach this article has taken, while ranging widely, has not resorted to falling back on one or other of the grand causal theories whose reductionism warrants a much more straightforward conclusion than offered here.

For instance there are the theories that say that as long as capitalism remains globally hegemonic the world either is safe for democracy or, conversely, cannot produce any true model of democracy other than very low-intensity or elitist versions unworthy of being called democracies. Questions about the impact of the international environment then become ancillary to questions about the survival of international capitalism.

Then there is the view that says globalisation is an unstoppable train, undermining national sovereignty and usurping power over the livelihoods and lives of ordinary people. And that even where globalisation is not transferring power to non-elected and unaccountable institutions of global and regional governance, it may be used as a pretext – by political leaders of all kinds – to wrestle greater autonomy for the state from society. All of which means that democracy, which was devised for states when national sovereignty had much substance, may no longer be viable at least in its present institutional form, and that the time has come to think more imaginatively about how to infuse democratic values, principles, and practices into the transnational and supra-territorial structures of power – social and economic as well as political. (Scholte 2008 is an example of a constructive response.) Some will argue that the relevance of these factors can only grow as the most salient challenges facing humankind become increasingly trans-territorial and supra-national – global climate change, for instance. A passing observation here is that although democracy was devised for and, perhaps, may not now be able to transcend state and sub-state levels of political organisation, defending national sovereignty and non-intervention features strongly in the pronouncements of the leading illiberal (semi-)/authoritarian regimes.

Rather than setting out from foundations rooted either in theories of globalisation or competing literatures in international relations theory, this article has had the more modest goal of seeking to up-date the more purpose-built frameworks for identifying ways in which national politics may be influenced by the international context, (away from as well as towards democracy), drawing special attention to unintended effects. It has not shown how to compare the significance of the different influences or calculate an overall *net* effect – exercises that pose daunting challenges and which demand further study. A conclusion that said something like 'the international environment is now twice as benign as it was twenty years ago', or '10% less favourable than it was in 1999', or '5% more (or less) favourable than we imagined it would be when predictions were being made about 2010 several years ago', would be very satisfying from a social science point of view. But the toolkits to reach such findings and make them compelling do not exist. And as with Hegel's celebrated owl of Minerva, conclusive answers to inquiries about today's – or even yesterday's – international environment for democratisation may become available only later, if ever.

Although the main theoretical and methodological shortcomings to knowledge are unlikely to be resolved any time soon, research can be expected to move in the direction of explaining not simply authoritarian persistence or increase but the contribution made by the international influences, even though systematic comparative evaluation of international strategies for domestic political regime maintenance or expansion by authoritarian and democratic regimes is likely to take much longer.

There should also be more interest in turning the question around: not 'has the international environment become less benign for democratisation?', but instead 'have democratisation and the increase in democracies been as benign for the international system as was expected?' Is the end of the most recent wave(s) of democratisation such a bad thing after all? What are the consequences for international peace, for globalisation, and for the political capacity to address the mitigation of global warming? Even as the perceived threat of international terrorism begins to recede, so the challenge of slowing global warming and adapting to all its potentially harmful consequences (political consequences included) begins to take on massive importance. The United Nations summit on climate change in December 2009, judged a failure by many critics, adds weight, even if it did not prove to be what some called the 'last best chance' to devise a solution. By comparison, the state of democratisation around the world could soon be relegated closer to the margins of the international agenda, and international attempts to promote democracy might follow suit.

However, if the international environment has become less favourable and could deteriorate even further, the outcome need not prove fatal to democracy or democratisation so long as the international influences remain secondary to domestic ones. Dahl

(1998: 148) said of the late twentieth century: 'Never in human history had international forces – political, economic, and cultural – been so supportive of democratic ideas and institutions'. Hindsight confirms that for the decade following the fall of the Berlin Wall the international context was indeed exceptionally favourable, perhaps uniquely so, for democracy's advance. And dating from the moment when decisions were taken to force regime change in Afghanistan and Iraq the international situation began to change dramatically. However, whereas on the one side Dahl did not claim the positive international changes he observed were sufficient causes, on the other side the impact of more recent and much less benign changes should be assessed with due regard to regional and other contextual variations. The environment may now be markedly less helpful to democratic opening and transition in general but only very modestly less favourable to the further democratic development of the newly consolidated liberal democracies, compared to just a few years ago. The old argument that struggle is vital if a society is to attain freedoms and go on to defend them tenaciously (Mill 1867) adds a yet further twist: Even what looks like bad news may turn out to be a cause for celebration, if the response is right.

Certainly the contemporary view of the world as seen from Moscow and Beijing might be thought to underwrite renewed interest in taking a neo-realist perspective on international politics – one that emphasises national interest defined in terms of power, and where democratic socialisation and the analyses founded on constructivist views more generally have less purchase than before. Some readings of President Obama's approach to foreign policy also point in this direction. But even if the doctrine of non-interference in domestic politics does now impede democracy's spread more than would have been predicted a few years ago, that may not be enough to secure a country that is not a liberal democracy, like Iran, from internal implosion of the regime or a successful revolution carried about by forces in the society at large. Indeed, for some countries like Yemen, for example, an increase in political instability may now seem more likely than movement towards stable autocracy, constituting a threat as much as an opportunity for democratisation, at home and abroad. Nevertheless, the experience of failing to anticipate momentous, world-shaping events like those in 1989 and in 2001, along with the voicing of short-sighted hubris about democracy's future in the early 1990s, stand as a caution against forecasting the future too confidently. If events matter, then it is also true that actors and actions matter. Governments and the orientation of political leadership can change abruptly, sometimes taking everyone by surprise.

So although on balance the reasoning in this article tends towards a somewhat less benign assessment of the international environment now and for the near future when compared to a decade ago, further ahead the picture might look completely different.

References

Acharya, Amitav (2004) 'How Ideas Spread. Whose Norms Matter? Norm Localization and Institutional Change in Asian Regionalism', *International Organization* 2: 239-275.
Ambrosio, Thomas (2008) Authoritarian Backlash. Russian Resistance to Democratization in the Former Soviet Union, Aldershot.

Bader, Julia/Grävingholt, Jörn/Kästner, Antje (2010) 'Would Autocracies Promote Autocracy? A Political Economy Perspective on Regime Type Export in Regional Neighbourhoods', *Contemporary Politics 1:* 812-100.
Bertelsmann Foundation (2008) 'Bertelsmann Transformation Index 2008', in http://www-bertelsmann-transformation-index.de [accessed on December 12, 2008].
Brinks, Daniel/Coppedge, Michael (2006) 'Diffusion is No Illusion. Neighbour Emulation in the Third Wave of Democracy', *Comparative Political Studies* 4: 463-89.
Burnell, Peter (1998) 'Arrivals and Departures: a Preliminary Classification of Democratic Failures and their Explanation', *Commonwealth and Comparative Politics* 3: 1-29.
Burnell, Peter (2006) 'Promoting Democracy Backwards', Madrid: Fundación Para Las Relaciones Internacionales Y El Diálogo Exterior Working Paper 28.
Burnell, Peter (2008a) 'From Evaluating Democracy Assistance to Appraising Democracy Promotion', *Political Studies* 2: 414-34.
Burnell, Peter (2008b) 'International Democracy Promotion: a Role for Public Goods theory?', *Contemporary Politics* 1: 37-52.
Burnell, Peter (2010a) 'A New Autocracy Promotion?', Madrid: Fundación Para Las Relaciones Internacionales Y El Diálogo Exterior Working Paper 98.
Burnell, Peter (2010b) 'Promoting Democracy and Promoting Autocracy: Towards Comparative Evaluation', *Journal of Politics and Law* 2: 3-14.
Carothers, Thomas (1997) 'Democracy Assistance: the Question of Strategy', *Democratization* 3: 109-32.
Clark, Ian (2005) 'Globalization and the Post-cold War Order' in Baylis, John/Smith, Steve (eds.) *The Globalization of World Politics,* Oxford: 727-742.
Dahl, Robert (1998) *On Democracy,* New Haven.
Diamond, Larry (2008) *The Spirit of Democracy,* New York.
Diskin, Abraham/Diskin, Hanna/Hazan, Reuven (2005) 'Why Democracies Collapse: the Reasons for Democratic Failure and Success', *International Political Science Review* 3: 291-309.
Gandhi, Jennifer/Przeworski, Adam (2007) 'Authoritarian Institutions and the Survival of Autocrats', *Comparative Political Studies* 11: 1279-1301.
Gleditsch, Kristian/Ward, Michael (2006) 'Diffusion and the International Context of Democratization', *International Organization* 4: 911-33.
Halperin, Morton/Galic, Mirna (eds.) (2007) *Protecting Democracy. International Responses,* Lanham.
Huntington, Samuel P. (1984) 'Will More Countries Become Democratic?', *Political Science Quarterly* 2: 193-218.
Huntington, Samuel P. (1991) The Third Wave: Democratization in the Late Twentieth Century, Norman OK/London.
Jünemann, Annette/ Knodt, Michéle (eds.) (2007) *European External Democracy Promotion,* Baden-Baden.
Kagan, Robert (2008) The Return of History and the End of Dreams, New York.
Kleine-Ahlbrandt, Stephanie/Small, Andrew (2008) 'China's New Dictatorship Diplomacy: is Beijing Parting with Pariahs?', *Foreign Affairs* 1: 38-56
Levitsky, Steven/Way, Lucan (2005) 'International Linkage and Democratization', *Journal of Democracy* 3: 20-34.
Linz, Juan/Stepan, Alfred (eds.) (1987) *The Breakdown of Democratic Regimes,* Baltimore.
Lipset, Seymour (1959) 'Some Social Requisites of Democracy', *American Political Science Review* 1: 69-105.

Mansfield, Edward/Snyder, Jack (2005) Electing to Fight. Why Emerging Democracies Go to War, Cambridge.
McFaul, Michael (2004) 'Democracy Promotion as a World Value', *The Washington Quarterly* 1: 147-63.
Mill, John. Stuart (1867) 'A Few Words on Non-intervention' in Mill, John Stuart *Dissertations and Discussions, Volume 3,* London: 153-78.
Morlino, Leonardo/Magen, Amichai (2009) 'Methods of Influence, Layers of Impact, Cycles of Change' in Magen, Amichai/Morlino, Leonardo (eds.) *International Actors, Democratization and the Rule of Law,* Abingdon: 27-51.
Nye, Joseph (2005) Born to Lead: the Changing Nature of American Power, New York.
Pevehouse, Jon (2002) 'With a Little Help from My Friends: Regional Organizations and Democratization', *American Journal of Political Science* 3: 611-26.
Schelling, Thomas (1980) *The Strategy of Conflict,* Cambridge.
Schlumberger, Oliver (2008) *'International Factors in the Resilience of Authoritarianism'*, Presentation to panel on 'Promoting autocracy?, World International Studies Conference, July 25, 2008, University of Ljubljana.
Schmitter, Philippe (2001) 'The Influence of the International Context upon the Choice of National Institutions and Policies in Neo-democracies' in Whitehead, Laurence (ed.) *The International Dimensions of Democratization,* Oxford: 26-50.
Scholte, Jan A. (2008) 'Reconstructing Contemporary Democracy', *Indiana Journal of Global Legal Studies* 1: 305-50.
Sen, Amartya (1999) 'Democracy as a Universal Value', *Journal of Democracy* 3: 3-17.
Starr, Harvey/Lindborg, Christina (2003) 'Democratic Dominoes Revisited: the Hazards of Governmental Transitions, 1976-96', *Journal of Conflict Resolution* 4: 490-519.
Svolik, Milan (2008) 'Authoritarian Reversals and Democratic Consolidation', *American Political Science Review* 2: 153-68.
Whitehead, Laurence (1996) 'Concerning International Support for Democracy in the South' in Luckham, Robin/White, Gordon (eds.) *Democratization in the South. The jagged wave,* Manchester/New York: 243-73.
Whitehead, Laurence (2001) 'Three International Dimensions of Democratization' in Whitehead, Laurence (ed.) *The International Dimensions of Democratization.* Oxford: 3-25.
Whitehead, Laurence (2004) 'Democratization with the Benefit of Hindsight: the Changing International Components' in Newman, Edward/Rich, Roland (eds.) *The UN Role in Promoting Democracy. Between Ideals and Reality,* Tokyo/New York: 135-165.
Whitehead, Laurence (2009) 'Democracy and Sovereignty: an Awkward Coupling' in Burnell, Peter/Youngs, Richard (eds.) *New Challenges to Democratization,* London/New York: 23-41
Yom, Sean/Al-Momani, Mohammad (2008) 'The International Dimensions of Authoritarian Regime Stability: Jordan in the Post-cold War Era', *Arab Studies Quarterly* 1: 39-60.

ARTICLE

The United States of America – a Deficient Democracy

Josef Braml and Hans-Joachim Lauth

Summary The United States of America are an example that also established democracies show deficiencies in the quality of democracy. This is illustrated in this article in a "democracy matrix" which marks the significant problems. The efforts of U.S. President George W. Bush to democratize the world through military means have led to a marked decline in the quality of American democracy. It remains to be seen whether Bush's successor, Barack Obama, will be able to repair the collateral damage of the Global War on Terror and reverse the deterioration of the former model democracy's image. President Obama has promised that his administration will restore the glory of the charter written by America's founding fathers and guarantee the rule of law and human rights. So far, President Obama's attempts to put his solemn words into action have not yet materialized. The outcome of these ongoing efforts will be very important, because repairing some defects could demonstrate that the American government has different choices – even in times of war.

1. Introduction: Terminology and Research Question

The quality of established democracies has been the subject of academic research for only a few years. More recently, the research has focused on the decline of the American democracy and the debate has centered on whether the signs of a deficient democracy are already present in the United States.[1] The term "deficient (or defective) democracy" refers explicitly to the quality of a democracy.[2] Using terms such as "deficient" or "defective" democracy implies that the typically accepted standards of democracy are only partially present.[3] Such a classification is distinguishable from other common ty-

---

1 Chalmers Johnson (2004) went so far as to claim that the American democracy had committed "suicide."
2 The terms "defective" and "deficient" are used here as synonyms. Although the term "defective" is rather inappropriate, because it is associated with an inability to function (Lauth 2004), we use the term because its use has already been established in scientific literature.
3 Deficient subtypes of democracies are "diminished subtypes" (Collier/Levitsky 1997), which are oriented around the criterion of the qualitative "functioning." This modifies the basic concept to the extent that its components are only insufficiently present, but not completely missing (the number of criteria studied is the same). If the basic concept includes free and fair elections, the modified subtype has only limited free and fair

pologies of democracies that refer to ideal types such as parliamentary and presidential democracies or consensus and majoritarian democracies.

Beginning in the late 1980s, with the research of so-called democracies of the "third wave" (Huntington 1991), democracies were typologized according to quality criteria. Research conducted on different regions showed that new democracies differed from established ones in how they functioned, even when they had a similar institutional structure. This divergence from the ideal type of democracy was described by a variety of terms: "delegative democracy" (O'Donnell 1994), "illiberal democracy" (Zakaria 1997) and "enclave democracy" (Merkel 1999).

The study of new democracies led in turn to a more precise analysis of established democracies. Consequently, research interest in the field shifted to questions concerning the factors that cause democracies to regress and the means for optimizing established democracies. Researchers shifted their attention to the *measurement of democracy*, i.e. the defining of a standard and its operationalization. The measurement of democracy had two goals: one was the classification of a *regime*, i.e. whether a particular regime was a democracy or autocracy. The second goal was to assess the quality of a democracy on a scale which compared empirical characteristics to an agreed upon standard. The choice of standards determines the results of the analysis. Because of the critical role played by the standards, they require not only a precise explanation, but also a (normative) justification.

This article will use social science tools in order to more closely examine the applicability of the current democracy models. (Lauth 2004: 227-237; Munck/Verkuilen 2002). Whether a democracy model is convincing is judged according to the criteria of the internal coherence and plausibility as well as its correspondence to the central arguments of the democratic theory debates in the field of political philosophy.[4]

In following pages, the main approaches to measuring democracy are presented and discussed (Chapter 2). Then, the political system of the United States will be analyzed using a measurement scheme that meets the above-mentioned criteria (Chapter 3), and anticipated developments will be discussed (Chapter 4), highlighting problematic aspects of American democracy as it exists today.

2. Freedom, Equality and Control: Development and Standards for the Measurement of Democracy

2.1 Fundamental Concepts

The measurement of democracy, still a relatively new discipline, was founded in the 1960s. Qualitative and quantitative measuring systems must be distinguished from each other. The most prominent example of the quantitative variant, espoused by the Finnish

---

elections, such as through limitations on the right to vote (as was the case in Switzerland until the introduction of the right to vote for women in 1971).

4 The methodological quality of the measuring of democracy is only outlined here. For a more complete discussion, refer to Schmidt 2008; Lauth 2004; Müller/Pickel 2007.

researcher Tatu Vanhanen, conceptualizes democracy in the sense of the two-dimensional polyarchy model of Robert Dahl (1971). This method has its own global dataset (Vanhanen 2003, 1990, 1984). However, this methodology – as the author himself highlights (Vanhanen 1990: 30) – permits one to reach only very general conclusions about the quality of a democracy. Researchers who prefer to use qualitative measurement methods evaluate the regime features that they consider relevant, which in turn are quantified. There are two data sets of this type, which are widely used to support these qualitative measurements: *Polity* and *Freedom House*.[5]

The *Polity* project, which has been updated into multiple versions, is widely used because of both its global perspective and the fact that its dataset goes back the furthest in time (Jaggers/Gurr 1995; Gurr et al. 1990). However, this methodology also has its problems. The individual indicators cannot be clearly distinguished from each other, and the distances between the individual categories (on the measurement scale) are not always the same. This diminishes the reliability and validity of the results. In addition, this method does not take into account some important aspects of democracy, such as civil liberties and rights. Moreover, this method does not effectively differentiate between the qualities of established democracies. Therefore, almost all of the established democracies are lumped together in one category.

The *Freedom House* "Freedom of the World" project is not designed to measure democracy. Nevertheless, it is often used for this purpose, because it relies on data that can also be used to analyze the quality of democracy and reflects a global perspective (Gastil 1991). *Freedom House* does not explicitly measure the quality of a democracy but rather the degree of political rights and civil liberties on the basis of criteria, which have been slightly modified over the course of the years.[6] Freedom House analysts evaluate countries, assigning scores for each of the criteria on a scale from 0 to 4. The total points received determines whether a country is rated as *"free,"* *"partly free"* or *"not free."* A principal problem of the Freedom House rating system is the lack of transparency of the ratings. This problem is made worse, because the respective concepts which underlie the ratings are insufficiently precise. Therefore, the ratings can only be verified in a very limited manner, even though, meanwhile more details beyond the aggregate results are made available for review.

In German speaking countries, in addition to the concept of the "democracy matrix" (Lauth 2004), which is explained in detail below, the concept of the "embedded democracy" (Merkel et al. 2003) has also been developed.[7] As with the *Polity* and *Freedom*

---

5 The *Democratic Audit* should also be mentioned. Using this method, individual case studies are carried out – the most extensive was done on Great Britain (see Beetham/Weir 2000, 1999). Because of the methodology – the rejection of any quantification (also of the results) and a somewhat relativistic opening of the standards – it is however less useful for comparative research.

6 The current list is available at: http://www.freedomhouse.org/.

7 The *Bertelsmann Transformation Index (BTI)* (Bertelsmann Stiftung 2004) should be included. Its measurement components – as with the concept of *Embedded Democracy* – also assess the quality of democracy. Two other concepts, the *NCCR* and the *BTI Reform Index* (Bühlmann et al. 2008; Brusis 2008, have not yet been fully developed.

House, the *Embedded Democracy* method also has a fundamental problem: the lack of reflection on threshold values (see Lauth 2002), which allow for quantitative results to be typologically organized. Rationales are provided for certain thresholds only in very limited cases, even though the thresholds are decisive for the classification. Furthermore, the concept is intended to measure deficient democracies and borderline authoritarian regimes, making it less suitable for analyzing established democracies.

Further research is necessary to refine the different types of democracy. A key starting point for this research is the identification of the institutional sources of defects, found in formal and informal institutions. This is supplemented by providing the exact description of a model, in other words a situation, in which the institutions to be studied function optimally.

2.2 Varying Concepts of Democracy: Participation, Competition and/or Control

The measurement of democracy is based on two different understandings or *concepts of democracy*. The first set of authors follows more or less explicitly the Dahlian concept of polyarchy. While some extend the concept into another dimension to include the *separation of powers* or *civil liberties and rights* (see Gasiorowski 1996; Arat 1991), others either consciously or implicitly reduce it to one dimension (Elklit 1994; Coppedge/Reinicke 1991). Others retain both dimensions – *participation* and *competition* – from Dahl (Vanhanen 2003, 1990, 1984).[8]

The second set of authors (Beetham et al. 2002; Saward 1994; Hadenius 1992) has developed its own democracy models or draws on other considerations (Gurr et al. 1990; Bollen 1980). These authors highlight, above all, aspects of *equality* and – somewhat less frequently – *control*, which are hardly mentioned by Dahl.

In spite of the differing points of view, it is still possible to identify commonalities. Most concepts have a *multidimensional* model of democracy. Viewed from a broader perspective, *political freedom* and *political equality* stand out as the two central dimensions, although with varying emphasis, namely a stronger focus on the freedom dimension. *Control*, in the sense of *horizontal accountability* regarding the rule of law, is used by very few authors, although it is present in all complex models.[9]

---

8 At times, the inclusion of the rule of law in the concept of democracy is explained merely functionally. But the systemic connection between rule of law and democracy is hardly called into question in the more recent analysis of democracy. Yet, not all analysts agree – especially those who continue to take close guidance from the two dimensions by Dahl. (Coppedge/Reinicke 1991; Vanhanen 1984). However, these authors overlook the fact that the legal and constitutional guarantee of human rights is inseparably connected to the core of democracy. Even a democratic majority cannot abolish these fundamental rights. (Schmitter/Karl 1991: 81). Democracy does not mean the unrestricted rule of the majority, but is limited by the inalienable rights of the individual.

9 Additional dimensions used in some other models can generally be subsumed in these trias without difficulty, as long as they remain within the realm of procedural democracy. See the discussion by Diamond/Morlino 2005.

Although different interpretations concerning the weight given to the dimensions exist, the current relevant measures of democracy contain the above-mentioned three dimensions.[10] The *three-dimensional concept of democracy*, which refers to *political freedom*, *political equality*, and *political and legal control*, corresponds to the (normative) democratic fundamentals.

2.3 The "Democracy Matrix" as a Basis for Determining the Quality of a Democracy

For most methods, the measurement of the level of intermediation by political institutions remains imprecise (Beetham 1994; Hadenius 1992). Taking a step further and broadening the polyarchy concept, which Dahl had focused on the two major dimensions of democracy (competition and participation),[11] five key institutions[12] can be identified, which are essential to the functional elaboration of the concept of democracy (see Lauth 2004: 183-185):

(1) Decision-making processes (elections),
(2) Institutional intermediation,
(3) Public communication,
(4) Effective rule of law,
(5) Setting and implementation of laws.

A combination of the five institutional variables and the three dimensions of democracy discussed above in Chapter 2.1 (freedom, equality, and control) yields a matrix of 15 fields, which systematically includes all of the elements of a democracy (see diagram 1). This matrix is based on the following definition of democracy: "Democracy is a form of government based on the rule of law, which allows for the self-rule of all citizens in accordance with the sovereignty of the people, by guaranteeing meaningful participation of those citizens in the appointment of positions of political decision-making (and/or the decisions themselves) in free, competitive and fair means (for ex-

---

10 On the other hand, little attention is given to the tension that exists between the three dimensions. (See Lauth 2004: 96-101).
11 The eight criteria of Dahl are (1971: 3): "1. Freedom to form and join organizations, 2. Freedom of expression, 3. Right to vote, 4. Eligibility for public office, 5. Right of political leaders to compete for support and for votes, 6. Alternative sources of information, 7. Free and fair elections, 8. Institutions for making government policies depend on votes and other expressions of preference." For Dahl, polyarchy is a synonym for real existing democracies; he reserves the term democracy for an (utopian) ideal type of democracy.
12 Rüb (1994: 116) offered the following definition: "Political institutions *in the narrow sense* are the constitution, which determines the fundamental features of the political system, and the regime itself (president, parliament, ministries, administration/bureaucracy, federal structure etc.), but also basic political and democratic rights, electoral regimes, and constitutional jurisdiction. Political institutions *in the broader sense* (...) are laws for political parties and associations, the structure of the mass media, and the political communication, general laws etc."

ample elections), and ensuring opportunities of continuing influence in the political process and checks on political power. Democratic participation in the political rule thus manifests itself along the dimensions of political freedom, political equality, and political and legal control." (Lauth 2004: 100).

Diagram 1: The 15 Field Matrix of Democracy

Dimensions / Institutions	Freedom	Equality	Control
Decision-making Processes	Free Elections and Referenda 01 1/1	Equal Opportunity to Participate and Parity of Votes 06 1/2	Control by an Election Commission 11 1/3
Institutional Intermediation	Freedom of Association 02 2/1	Equal Rights to Organize and Take Political Action 07 2/2	Control by means of Associations, Interest Groups, Parties, and Civil Society/Grassroots Organizations 12 2/3
Public Communication/Public Opinion	Freedom of Speech/Expression 03 3/1	Equal Opportunity to Participate 08 3/2	Control by means of an Independent Media 13 3/3
Effective Rule of Law	Open Access to the Legal System 04 4/1	Equal Rights and Treatment in the Legal System 09 4/2	Effective Administration of Justice and Constitutional Jurisdiction/Litigation 14 4/3
Setting and Implementation of Laws	Effective Government (Parliament, Rational Bureaucracy) 05 5/1	Equal Treatment by the Parliament and Administration/Bureaucracy 10 5/2	Separation of Powers /Checks and Balances (Parliamentary Opposition, a Second Chamber, Auditor, Budget Controls etc.) 15 5/3

Source: Lauth (2004: 186).

The United States of America – a Deficient Democracy

The individual matrix fields will be specified with predominantly qualitative values, and, to a lesser extent, quantitative values. According to the underlying understanding of institutions, both the formal, legal form and the shape they take in practice need to be examined. In the study of rights and rules, there are thus three levels to consider: (1) the *existence of laws* (codification), (2) the opportunity to *put the laws into practice* in the sense of administrative and institutional capacity (necessary conditions) and (3) *suppression of laws* through formal or informal intervention (the extent of violation of law). However, the extent to which citizens do exercise their rights is not examined, because this approach – as voter turnout reveals – conceals a variety of problems. The same can be said of evaluating the effectiveness of rules, if they are of a permissive character. However, if rules are mandatory, the violation of laws is treated as an indicator that needs to be taken into account.

One measures control in a slightly different manner as compared to the freedom and equality dimensions. Here one also must ask if these take place in practice, because the mere lack of evidence of the violation of control rules does not necessarily prove the existence of functioning, active mechanisms of control. Therefore, there is also a fourth level to examine: (4) to what extent *control rights are used*. With regard to institutional supervisory authorities, this level examines the drafting of regular reports or similar proof of the corresponding activities. Does the parliament use its various control mechanisms, are journalists actively and independently investigating stories, do members of the civil society take advantage of the opportunity to engage in public criticism or take legal action?

Different types of actors require different standards to evaluate their level of control. In official institutions the supervision duties fall into the category of binding rules, and a failure to perform these duties is considered to be a rule violation. This standard does not apply to civil society actors, because they are not obligated to exercise control. In the latter case, what matters to the value placed on the quality of control is not the number of individuals exercising control, but rather the observed effectiveness of the entire control apparatus.

The quantification is based on a scale from 1 to 5, where 1 (*very good*) corresponds to a fully developed feature of democracy and 5 corresponds to the *incomplete/unsatisfactory* development of that feature. Each value is separated by equal intervals. The values are roughly analogous to grades (in the German school system) as follows: 1 = *very good*, 2 = *good*, 3 = *satisfactory*, 4 = *sufficient*, 5 = *incomplete/ unsatisfactory*. Scores from 1 to 4 are indicators of a democratic regime, 5 indicates autocratic/authoritarian tendencies (see Lauth 2004, Chapter 3.3). It is important to note that a failure to reach a *threshold value* (with respect to one field) cannot be offset, i.e. made up for, by stronger "performances" in other categories. So all fields are weighed equally. There are three main rules for using the democracy matrix to classify regimes (assuming that there are values for all 15 fields):

Rule 1: If any matrix value is scored *incomplete/unsatisfactory,* a country cannot be classified as a democracy in the overall assessment. Conversely, a country will be classified as a democracy, only if all of the measured values are at least *sufficient.*

Rule 2: If any matrix value is scored *sufficient*, the regime will be labeled as a deficient democracy (provided that none of the other matrix values is *unsatisfactory*).

Rule 3: If no matrix value is lower than *satisfactory*, the country will be classified as having a functioning democracy.

The delineation between categories flows from the substantive quality of the individual characteristics. In the case of a *sufficient* score, which reflects a borderline *deficient democracy*, it is important to highlight the institutional causes of defects. However, deficiencies should not undermine the basic foundations for the functioning of formal institutions, otherwise a democratic regime would not qualify for the necessary standard.

Under this methodology, regimes are classified into three types – authoritarian regimes, functioning democracies, and deficient democracies – which reflect a specific functional logic (see Lauth 2004: Chapter 1.3.2.). The threshold is developed for each indicator, i.e. according to *sub thresholds.* A further consideration, which is necessary to verify or reproduce the measurement, is the point in time and scope of the measurement. The following discussion covers the most noticeable and significant features of the time period during the eight year administration of George W. Bush, after the attacks of September 11, 2001. The assessment takes into consideration not only the changes but also the fundamental characteristics of the political system during that time period. Different observations inside one matrix field are added up and quantified into one value.

3. The Quality of American Democracy: Strengths and Weaknesses

The application of the democracy matrix to the United States after 2001 leads to mixed results (for the following discussion also see the quantitative conclusion of diagram 2). Most of the findings are rated with good or satisfactory, but four ratings reached only sufficient. Applying our rules, the political regime must be classified as a deficient democracy. In the following the individual fields of the matrix are examined, by institution. There are different – institutional, behavioral as well as situational (war on terrorism) – factors explaining the assessment of each matrix value.

The United States of America – a Deficient Democracy

Diagram 2: Strengths and Deficiencies of American Democracy, 2001-2008

Dimensions / Institutions	Freedom	Equality	Control
Decision-making Processes	Free Elections and Referenda good	Equal Opportunity to Participate and Parity of Votes satisfactory	Control by an Election Commission satisfactory
Institutional Intermediation	Freedom of Association very good	Equal rights to Organize and Take Political Action good	Control by means of Associations, Interest Groups, Parties and Civil Society/Grassroots Organizations satisfactory
Public Communication/Public Opinion	Freedom of Speech/Expression good	Equal Opportunity to Participate satisfactory	Control by means of an Independent Media sufficient
Effective Rule of Law	Open Access to the Legal System sufficient	Equal Rights and Treatment in the Legal System sufficient	Effective Administration of Justice and Constitutional Jurisdiction/Litigation satisfactory
Setting and Implementation of Laws	Effective Government (Parliament, Rational Bureaucracy) good	Equal Treatment by the Parliament and Administration/Bureaucracy satisfactory	Separation of Powers /Checks and Balances (Parliamentary Opposition, a Second Chamber, Auditor/Budget Controls, etc.) sufficient

3.1 Decision-making Processes (Elections)

The institutions of decision-making (elections) have worked well with only minor qualifications. For example, some convicted felons have permanently lost the right to vote.[13] With respect to the right to run for office, it is important to note that there are significant financial barriers to mounting a successful campaign, which prevent or deter a significant portion of the population from running for office. Furthermore, the irregularities during the voting and vote counting for the 2000 presidential election, and resulting legal battles that ultimately determined the winner created some lingering doubts about the integrity of the system. To this day, a number of commentators still question the quality of voting systems and deem them to be unsatisfactory. Nevertheless, the Supreme Court decision of December 12, 2000 (*Bush v. Gore*) was almost universally accepted, including by the loser Al Gore, and thus eventually provided George W. Bush with the legitimacy, which the elections had initially denied him. Some electoral reforms improved the transparency of voting and vote counting in the following years.

Bush's re-election in 2004, in which the incumbent received a majority of the popular vote in addition to a majority in the Electoral College, finally removed all doubts: The majority of Americans trusted George W. Bush with a second term in office. In addition, a number of Congressmen and Senators road Bush's coattails into office, leading to strong Republican majorities in both houses of Congress in addition to Republican control of the White House, resulting in the rare constellation of a "united government" (Sundquist 1988: 613-635).

The congressional elections of 2006 demonstrated that the voters could also withdraw this "political capital" – as Bush enthusiastically had described it after his re-election. Even though Bush himself was not up for re-election, the midterms were deemed to be a referendum on his policies and administration. The loss of the congressional majority to the Democrats re-established a "divided government" (Sundquist 1988: 613-635), i.e. the executive and the legislative branches were "controlled" by different parties. This also created the conditions for an effective exercise of the system of "checks and balances" by the competing branches of government.[14] Resuming all findings we can speak of a well working institution with only small deficiencies. The importance of this electoral institution is even greater if we do not look only at the national elections but also at the myriad of elections on state and local levels.

---

13 Approximately 5.3 million Americans, who are convicted felons, have for a limited period of time, or permanently, lost the right to vote. For African-Americans, 13% of the males have lost the right to vote – seven times higher than the national average. See: Felony Disenfranchisement Laws in the U.S.; http://www.sentencingproject.org/Admin%5CDocuments% 5Cpublications%5Cfd_bs_fdlawsinus.pdf (as of 04.06.2009).

14 Richard E. Neustadt (1990: 29) accurately describes the American political system as "government of separated institutions sharing powers." Charles O. Jones (2005: 24) further specifies Neustadt's expression as "separated institutions sharing and competing for powers."

3.2 Institutional Intermediation

In the system of "checks and balances," political parties – with the exception of their role in elections – are of secondary importance (Weaver/Rockman 1993: 1-41). They have gained, however, more influence in the recent years due to ideological cleavages. The numerous, well-financed interest groups and civil society organizations (Berry 1999), which represent political preferences within the decision-making process, are, nevertheless, more important. Intermediary institutions are also an expression of fundamental civil rights and liberties, such as free speech and freedom of association, and make control by civil society possible. Although well financed pressure groups have better access to the political decision process, poor or marginal groups can also influence the political agenda. It is more difficult for them, however, to effectuate a comprehensive control.

The expertise and opinions of a number of public intellectuals in universities, think tanks and grassroots organizations have a significant influence on the debate and decision-making process.[15] These intellectuals cooperate with the media to set the political agenda, and influence perceptions among decision-makers and the population, by identifying threats and analyzing or making claims about the "nature" of these threats. The power of these "threat interpreters" and "knowledge producers" can be constrained by a diverse supply of competing interpretations. Consequently, in the so-called marketplace of ideas, competition and pluralism constitute an important component for liberal democracies.

During the general public insecurity that followed in the aftermath of the attacks of 9/11/2001, the importance of the guidance provided by experts increased. According to Winand Gellner (1995: 12), the collective desire to reduce real or imagined dangers leads people to assign credibility to experts and depend on their opinions for seemingly reliable solutions.[16] Regarding foreign policy, two different interpretative frameworks compete for primacy: the contextualist and the essentialist. From a *contextualist* perspective, the widespread anti-Americanism and sometimes deep hatred in parts of the Muslim world are interpreted as a reaction to specific foreign policy decisions and actions by the United States. Even Francis Fukuyama, who was regarded as a leading neoconservative intellectual before he distanced himself from the neoconservative movement (Fukuyama 2006a; 2006b), views the "war on terror" as a *classic counterinsurgency war* (Fukuyama 2004). This assessment corresponds to empirical studies, according to which nearly all terrorist attacks in the time period from 1980 to 2003

---

15 Think Tanks play a central role in America's marketplace of ideas, since parties play – with the exception of their function during elections – a secondary role. So-called *advocacy tanks*, think tanks with a particular political agenda (literally: interest oriented think tanks), that often acquire the legal status necessary to lobby the political base (*grassroots lobbying*), strategically cooperate with like-minded politicians, journalists, and business representatives in *issue networks* to put their political goals into practice. See Gellner (1995: 254); Braml (2004a: 50-70).

16 Also see Dahl (1989: 75) and Rothman/Lichter (1987: 383-404). Douglas/Wildavsky (1982) also pointed out that cultural factors influence risk perception.

reflect a strategic goal, namely to force modern nation states to withdraw their militaries form territories that the terrorists regard as their own. While terrorist organizations frequently use religious motives for recruitment, Islamic fundamentalism is not seen as the actual root of all evil. Rather, according to this view, the military operation in Iraq and the American military presence – in other words, the attempts of the Bush administration to confront terrorism abroad with military means – are part of the same problem. These strategies are deemed to be ill-suited to pacify the Middle East or democratize the region (Pape 2005).

Contrary to the contextualists, the *essentialists* perceive a totalitarian threat of an existential nature that must be eliminated by any means necessary. In February 2004, for example, the neoconservative columnist Charles Krauthammer (1991) explained the verification of his thesis from the early 1990s: Thank God that America used the historical window of opportunity created by the "unipolar moment" after the demise of the Soviet Union, to fortify its unipolar position of power and is now prepared. The visionary Krauthammer sees his views confirmed by history, especially since evil has once again shown its ugly face in the form of an existential threat by Arab-Islamist terrorism:

> "On September 11, 2001, we saw the face of Armageddon again, but this time with an enemy that does not draw back. This time the enemy knows no reason. Were that the only difference between now and then, our situation would be hopeless. But there is a second difference between now and then: the uniqueness of our power, unrivaled, not just today but ever." (Krauthammer 2004: 19).

This allusion to an existential and decisive battle was intended to resonate with Evangelical Christians – the core of the Bush administration's electoral base[17] (Braml 2004b; 2005) – and to mobilize them to provide for the security of America worldwide, if necessary with military means.[18]

This controversy reflects a more fundamental change. In today's marketplace of ideas, various conceptions of ideas compete. As far back as the 1980s, the traditional pragmatic approach with its empirical methodology has increasingly given way to ideology and religious convictions (Smith 1989: 186). Beside the partisan factor, religious convictions are important for the government's legitimation. In view of the lack of bipartisan support preceding the Iraq war – 84 percent of partisans of the Presidents party supported the war; among the Democrats only 37 percent of respondents agreed with George W. Bush's course (Newport 2003) – the support of his own party was all the more important. Differentiated analyses further show that besides party affiliation reli-

---

17 In the presidential elections of 2004, white Evangelical Christians once again formed the foundation of George W. Bush's electoral victory, providing over 40 percent of the entire vote for Bush.

18 Republican followers tend to support the use of military means more than Democrats – especially the hard core of Evangelical Christians. Compared to the average population, they rely more on military strength than on diplomacy to achieve peace (Kohut et al. 2000: 130-133). According to a survey, so-called "strength issues" – military strength and toughness in the "War on Terror," against "evil" – play a very important role for white Evangelicals. Ninety-three percent find it "extremely/very important" to keep America's military strong. (Greenberg/Berktold 2004: 18-20, Questionnaire: 6-8).

gious factors were decisive for the support of the President's war strategy: Of Americans who responded to a Gallup poll that they considered religion was "very important," 60 percent supported the war. In contrast, only 49 percent of those that declared that religion was "not very important" to them answered affirmatively (Newport 2003).

3.3 Public Communication

After the 9/11 attacks, patriotic sentiments and religious convictions, amplified by insecurity and fear, also affected the ability of many in the news industry to differentiate and draw rational conclusions. This enabled Bush, as Commander-in-Chief, to legitimize a war – waged in violation of international law and considered to be unnecessary by most security experts (e.g. Haass 2009) – against Saddam Hussein's regime, based on dubious claims (weapons of mass destruction in the hands of Saddam Hussein that could be passed on to terrorists)[19] and religious convictions.[20] This war also contributed to his re-election.[21] All of this occurred without provoking sustained criticism from established media outlets such Fox or CNN. The finding is different with respect to the conduct of several national newspapers in the primarily domestic debate about the restriction of personal freedom for the sake of security. In particular, the *New York Times* and the *Washington Post* have strongly criticized the infringement on personal freedom by the executive, and the failure of Congress.

Even after it became clear that Saddam Hussein did not possess weapons of mass destruction, white Evangelical Protestants – the electoral base of the Republicans – insisted that the Iraq war was "justified;" seven out of ten Evangelicals (72 percent) supported the concept of preventative war. (Green 2004: 34). Misperceptions – e.g. that Saddam Hussein was responsible for the 9/11 attacks; that there was proof of coopera-

---

19 To prepare the nation for war, President Bush, in his State-of-the-Union address on January 29, 2003, linked the situation in Iraq once again with the existential threat that weapons of mass destruction in the hands of terrorists posed to the United States: "Imagine those 19 hijackers with other weapons and other plans – this time armed by Saddam Hussein. It would take one vial, one canister, one crate slipped into this country to bring a day of horror like none we have ever known." (White House 2003).

20 "And we go forward with confidence, because this call of history has come to the right country (...) Americans are a free people, who know that freedom is the right of every person and the future of every nation. The liberty we prize is not America's gift to the world, it is God's gift to humanity. We Americans have faith in ourselves, but not in ourselves alone. We do not know – we do not claim to know all the ways of Providence, yet we can trust in them, placing our confidence in the loving God behind all of life, and all of history. May He guide us now. And may God continue to bless the United States of America" – these were the concluding remarks of the American President's State-of-the-Union address in preparation for the war. (White House 2003).

21 Leading up to George W. Bush's re-election – which initially appeared to many observers as uncertain because of the Iraq war – it became clear that, even after the invasion, people frequently attending church were more likely to support the war than less religious Americans. (National Annenberg Election Survey 2004: 2, 5, 7).

tion between Iraq and Al-Qaeda; that weapons of mass destruction were found after the invasion and even used against U.S. troops by Saddam Hussein's regime – are significantly more common among regular viewers of the "news" of the Fox News Network than among listeners of quality media, such as National Public Radio (Program on International Policy Attitudes 2003).

By scarcely criticizing the Iraq War and only partially fulfilling their function of control, the media – especially in the most effective medium, TV – contributed to the isolation of critical voices from intellectual, in particular academic, circles, and missed the opportunity to influence the public agenda (see Massing 2004 in connection with newspapers). These observations are mainly responsible for the week rating in this matrix field.

The lack of control facilitates the absence of transparency and tendencies among top governmental officials to manipulate information (see Wilzewski 2006). As an initial matter, the opportunities to participate in the public discourse are not equal. This gives the President the opportunity to dominate public discourse, especially in times of crisis. In his role as Commander-in-Chief of the armed forces, the President wields even more influence as the "interpreter-in-chief" (Stuckey 1991), because he can and is expected to frame the public perception of events.[22] The President can take advantage of his *bully pulpit*,[23] i.e. his ability to direct public opinion from the White House, to mobilize the public in support of his political agenda, not least to counter his institutional opponent, Congress.

President Bush interpreted the 9/11 attacks as a declaration of war and responded with the "Global War on Terror." The attacks on New York and Washington were not perceived as terrorist acts, but acts of war. (Europe, in contrast, did not interpret the attacks as a declaration of war.) Bush also interpreted the military operation against Iraq as a further battle in the long-term and world-wide "War on Terror." In this context, the fundamental constitutional principles of individual freedom were re-interpreted in light of domestic security concerns within the legal framework of a war.

3.4 Effective Rule of Law

A liberal democracy based on the *rule of law* ties government's powers to existing law – subject to *judicial review*, thereby guaranteeing the *individual liberties* of its citizens as well as non-citizens. Personal freedoms are also a basic condition for a "responsive democracy" and constitute an inviolable area, removed from majority rule and a potential "tyranny of the majority." The fear of the founding fathers, *the federalists*, of a *tyranny of the majority* (the negative example was revolutionary France) is apart from

---

22 Ernst-Otto Czempiel (1996: 91) notes that for understandable reasons, "American society listens in particular to its President, when attempting to assess situations of conflict in foreign policy."

23 President Theodore Roosevelt (1901-1909) coined this phrase, to illustrate the president's institutional advantage and resources to influence public opinion.

federalism the central cause for the early emergence of judicial review, which itself is not explicitly laid out in the constitution (Pasquino 1998: 44).[24]

However, from the point of view of the Bush administration, the terrorist attacks of 9/11 justified the transformation of civil law, with its traditional emphasis on individual freedoms, into wartime law, with collective security taking precedence over everything else. Thus there is a common theme for the various problem areas: Less emphasis was placed on the criminal responsibility of individual perpetrators and their prosecution for their crimes, in favor of focusing on the prevention of future attacks. According to Attorney General Ashcroft the "culture of inhibition" before September 11, 2001, "was a culture that so sharply focused on investigations of past crimes that it limited the prevention of future terrorism."[25]

The "Ashcroft doctrine of prevention" (see Gorman 2002b) manifested itself in a policy that targeted certain groups of potentially dangerous people and systematically denied them admission to the United States, deported them, or "removed them from the street" to place them in "preventive detention." Potential informants were detained as *material witnesses*. The military tribunals – which the President had created by executive order without the consent of Congress – were also considered to be weapons in the "War on Terror." As Pierre-Richard Prosper, Ambassador-at-Large for War Crimes Issues, explained to the Senate on behalf of the State Department: "The Military Order adds additional arrows to the President's quiver." (Prosper 2001). Even abuse and torture were accepted by the Bush administration as appropriate preventative measures and used by security agencies in some cases to supposedly prevent further attacks. The line between civilian criminal prosecution and prevention on one hand, and military operations and self-made law of war on the other, became increasingly blurred. This is the reason why the emerging change of paradigm in the interpretation of the protective role of the state not only affected the understanding of democratic rule of law, but also the functioning of the political system of checks and balances, which is supposed to guarantee individual civil liberties.

As demonstrated by the Bush government's handling of individual rights, which drew international attention (see Braml 2003a for more details) – the status of captured members of the Taliban and Al-Qaeda, the establishment of military tribunals, the capturing and "preventive detention" of suspicious foreigners – show that those in charge distinguished between two classes of people with different rights: American citizens and "non-Americans."[26] Although the constitutional provisions of *due process* and *equal*

---

24 See Hudson (2004: 69-77) for a short historical overview of the evolution of judicial control of executive and legislative acts in the United States.

25 As Attorney General Ashcroft put it on October 1, 2002, in an address to the U.S. Attorneys Conference in New York (see Gorman 2002a for excerpts).

26 In addition, flaws have existed for some time concerning the treatment of different social groups. Access to the legal system is more difficult for socially marginalized groups, and they are treated differently by the Judiciary. For example, wealthy parties to trials have much better prospects to succeed in court than members of marginalized groups, as is proven by statistics and trial reports (Coker 2003; Cole 1999).

protection protect the individual liberty of "any person,"[27] the Bush administration – contrary to the prevailing legal opinion and previous judicial interpretations – believed that foreigners present in the United States were not entitled to the same legal protection as citizens of the United States. If foreigners were classified as terrorist suspects, they even forfeited this "lower standard." They were treated as outlaws if they were not fortunate enough to be present in the sovereign territory of the United States – as was the case with the captured Taliban and Al-Qaeda militants kept at the U.S. Marine Base at Guantanamo Bay (Cuba).

In the course of the "Global War on Terror," the Bush administration – partly with the support of Congress, as evidenced by the *Military Commissions Act of 2006* – de facto stripped terrorist suspects of the right to have their detention reviewed by a competent court. By suspending the writ of habeas corpus, it not only suspended a fundamental right of liberal democracies, but also ignored the balance of power in the political system of checks and balances. The decision about who is entitled to which rights was made *a priori* by the executive. The Bush administration also attempted to avoid the control of judicial and legislative branches of government. A number of observers feared that this dangerous practice would lead down the path to the dismantling of the system of checks and balances.

Consequently, in its ruling of June 12, 2008 the Supreme Court held that key provisions of the *Military Commissions Act of 2006* were unconstitutional and that the process established by the executive and Congress a year earlier in the *Detainee Treatment Act of 2005* was legally insufficient. By the slimmest majority (5 to 4 votes), the Supreme Court ruled in the case of Lakhdar Boumediene (*Boumediene et al v. Bush et al*), who was imprisoned at Guantanamo Bay, that Article 7 of the law signed by the President in October 2006 did not comply with the constitutionally guaranteed "privilege" of habeas corpus, since the provisions enacted by Congress and the President, denied so-called "enemy combatants" the right to have their detentions reviewed by a federal court. According to the Supreme Court, the "*Writ of Habeas Corpus*" is essential to the protection of individual liberty and an indispensible mechanism to monitor the separation of powers. With its ruling, the Supreme Court defended its own power of control in the system of checks and balances.

As in earlier rulings, the justices only addressed the issue of basic responsibilities,[28] but they refrained from instructing the executive branch and Congress how to apply

---

27 The most important *civil liberties* are guaranteed in the first ten amendments to the constitution. These principles, which are also subsumed under the name *Bill of Rights*, were incorporated as a whole into the constitution on 12/15/1791. After the civil war, additional amendments were added, the 14th amendment being particularly significant for the protections of the individual liberties of "any person" – regardless of citizenship.

28 Even before, the Supreme Court had spoken forcefully with regard to the legal status of an American citizen detained in Afghanistan, Yaser Esam Hamdi (*Hamdi et al. vs. Rumsfeld*), and with regard to the legal claims of non-Americans at the U.S. Naval Base at Guantánamo Bay, Cuba (*Rasul et al. vs. Bush*). In these rulings of June 28, 2004, the Supreme Court rejected the practice of the executive to deny judicial review and to decide unilaterally who was entitled to which rights. The Supreme Court made clear that judicial review of

these rule of law principles to other cases. It remains up to Congress to carry out its function of control, which has been confirmed in several Supreme Court rulings. However, the Democratic chairman of the Senate Judiciary Committee, Patrick J. Leahy, (quoted in Congressional Quarterly (CQ) Today Midday Update, 7/21/2008), reacted to requests for legislative directives from Attorney General Michael Mukasey – who called on Congress to establish new guidelines for the legal process applying to Guantanamo detainees – by stating that the issue would be taken up more in detail and more responsibly following the end of Bush's term in office (after the congressional and presidential elections).

The evaluation of the effective rule of law demonstrates the worst result of all institutions. The executive under President George W. Bush reinterpreted both the rule of law and the system of checks and balances to maximize the powers of the presidency. As in the past, both the Supreme Court and the Congress did not effectively check the imperial tendencies of a wartime president. Especially the legislative branch has again not lived up to its constitutional duty.

3.5 Setting and Implementation of Laws

Unlike the legislative branch in parliamentary systems, Congress has generally a strong institutional position vis-à-vis the executive in the political system of the United States; although it exercises its powers cautiously in times of a national threat, because every Congressman and Senator is expected to decide in favor of national security. While members of Congress are not party soldiers, but independent political entrepreneurs, when it comes to granting the Commander-in-Chief "patriotic powers" so that he can provide for the "defense of the homeland" in times of war, they stand by his side. The conservative Republican Bob Barr, a former member of the House Judiciary Committee and one of the most prominent defenders of civil liberties, explained that pressure from the electorate severely limited Congress' room for maneuver:

> "It's very difficult to get members of Congress to do anything that might appear to the untrained eye (...) not to be going after the terrorists (...) A lot of the members think the folks back home will feel we're not tough enough." (Bob Barr quoted in Dlouhy/Palmer 2001: 2784).

---

executive decisions was an essential element of the American system of checks and balances. In its decision *Hamdan vs. Rumsfeld* the court once more rejected the president's claims. In the decision of June 29, 2006 the majority repeatedly defended its own responsibility and declared the military tribunals illegal because they violated international law, namely the Geneva Conventions, and they were not explicitly authorized by Congress. The court rejected the unilateral approach of the President, but not the legality military tribunals. (The question whether the detention of the plaintiff at the prison camp was lawful, was not examined, either.) Instead, the Supreme Court demanded that the executive cooperate with Congress to find a feasible way of handling military tribunals.

The concern for the protection of individual liberties and the institutional balance of power remains secondary when compared to the fears articulated by the public – as long as there is or appears to be danger. In October 2001, 85 percent of Americans expected further attacks in the United States in the following weeks (see figure 1). This indicated a latent danger that a "tyranny of the majority" was willing to sacrifice constitutional rights, human rights, individual liberties and civil rights (especially of minorities) on the altar of national security. There are not many Congressmen or Senators willing to fight for the personal liberties of non-Americans let alone terrorist suspects.

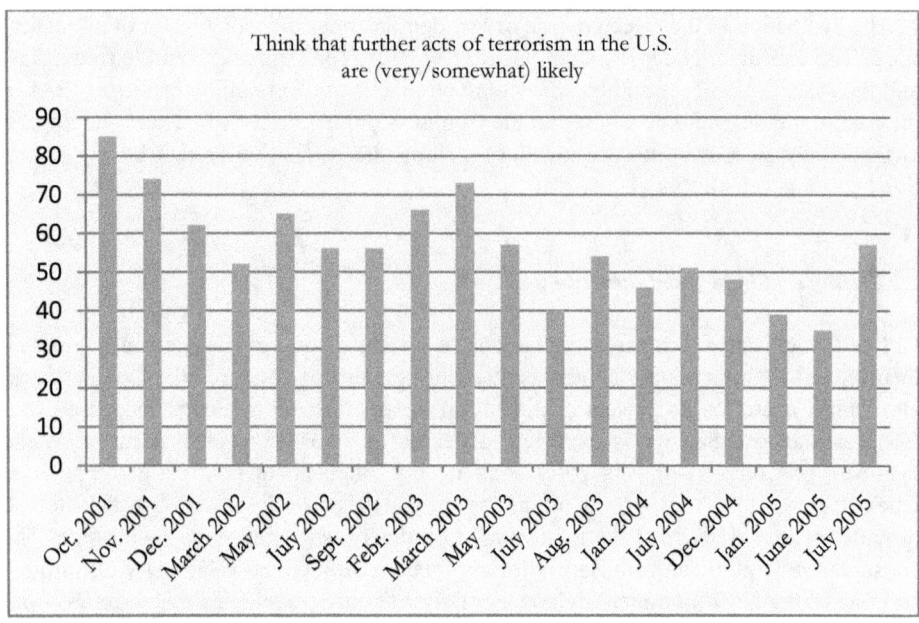

Source: Gallup surveys (Saad 2005).

Figure 1: Expectation of Further Attacks in the United States (In Percent), October 2001 - July 2005

It is therefore not surprising that the *Patriot Act*, which created a series of significant restrictions of civil liberties, faced little resistance when it was pushed through the legislative process on Capitol Hill. The public pressure to act increased even more when, on October 11, 2001, the FBI (Federal Bureau of Investigation) warned that further terrorist attacks were imminent. In the light of this "clear and present danger,"[29] Congress refrained from making significant changes to the Patriot Act.[30] The debate in Congress

---

29 According to F. James Sensenbrenner Jr. (R-Wisconsin), the chairman of the House Judiciary Committee (Palmer 2001b: 2399).

30 At least some of the steps initially considered by the administration were softened. For example, in the version introduced by the executive, it would have sufficed, if the attorney general "ha[d] reason to believe,"

was kept to a minimum; many members of Congress approved the package without even knowing its contents.[31] The *Patriot Act* provided the Commander-in-Chief with legislative cover for his subsequent actions in the "War on Terror." In his remarks before Congress, Attorney General Ashcroft even went as far as linking criticism of the restrictions on civil liberties to treason (Ashcroft 2001: 309-317).

In the meantime, the developments provoked public criticism from a group that calls itself "Patriots to Restore Checks and Balances." (See Lichtblau 2005). Former Republican Congressman and spokesperson for the group Bob Barr built a bi-partisan coalition for the protection of civil liberties. The group encompassed the *American Civil Liberties Union* on the left and conservative leaders of economic libertarianism around Grover Norquist, president of *Americans for Tax Reform*, and "the late" Paul Weyrich, chairman of the *Free Congress Foundation*. Bob Barr hoped that it would be easier for Representatives and Senators to adopt the goals of the coalition, because the members of Congress would receive more effective political cover than if only the *American Civil Liberties Union* or the far right supported the goals (Eggen 2005: A21). The group hoped that by presenting a different political viewpoint that competed with the institutional opinion leadership of the White House, the electoral base would exert counter-pressure on individual Representatives and Senators to get Congress to ignore the Bush administration's (lead by the new attorney general Alberto Gonzales and Director of the FBI Robert Mueller III) push to extend the provisions of the *Patriot Act* that were due to expire at the end of 2005.[32]

The attacks on the London transit system of July 7, 2005 changed the playing field, because they provoked a renewed fear of further attacks in the United States, which had been reduced since 9/11 – even after a notable rise of insecurity during the Iraq war – to relatively low levels (see figure 1). President Bush used the London attacks to his advantage, reminding his fellow citizens of the terrorist danger and pressuring the members of Congress to extend the expiring provisions of the *Patriot Act* (White House 2005a). Before the month of July was over, both houses of Congress passed their versions of the *Patriot Act* extensions. In both versions, 14 of a total of 16 expiring provisions were supposed to become permanent. Even two of the most controversial provi-

---

that the suspect was a terrorist to detain him or her for an indeterminate time period. In the version adopted by Congress, the Attorney General now needs "reasonable grounds." But even this requirement ultimately depends on his discretion; and it would be difficult to provide sufficient evidence to challenge his opinion and the security measures enacted as a consequence. See "Sec. 412. Mandatory Detention of Suspected Terrorists; Habeas Corpus; Judicial Review" of the *USA Patriot Act*. (http://www.cdt.org/security/ usapatriot/011026usa-patriot.pdf (download on 5/20/2009).

31 The Senate passed its bill after only three hours of debate on the floor, without having referred it to the relevant committees. In the House, Republican Speaker J. Dennis Hastert (Illinois) under strong pressure from the White House simply replaced the version reported out of the committees with a new version, which was pushed through the full House of Representatives on the same day (Palmer 2001a: 2533; 2001b: 2399).

32 The opposition called in particular for the prohibition of secret investigations of private homes and companies (so-called *sneak and peek searches*) and the surveillance of libraries. Another goal of this ad-hoc coalition of opposition was to return to a more narrow definition of terrorism.

sions – the wire-tapping of private persons and the secret review of the files of business persons and private organizations – were due to be extended: in the House version by ten years and in the Senate version by four years. The Senate version also included stricter controls on the authorization of secret inspections (Perine/Stern 2005: 2126). But efforts by Democratic Representatives to limit the extension of all expiring provisions to four years failed (Sandler/Perine 2005: 2044).

In mid-December 2005, the *New York Times* (Risen/Lichtblau 2005: A1) disclosed that the President and the executive branch acting under his orders (in particular the National Security Agency, NSA) had secretly wire-tapped telephone conversations and international communications of U.S. citizens without judicial authorization. This disclosure raised expectations that during the negotiation of the two bills in the conference committee some of the more extreme restrictions on personal freedom would ultimately be left out of the final version of the bill. Hopes were further raised because four Republican Senators agreed with the Democratic criticism in the Senate, making a filibuster to delay the vote possible. For his part, President Bush also proceeded more cautiously. The President managed to slow down the process, and obtained two short-term extensions of the present law and maintained its position in the ongoing negotiations about the reauthorization of the Patriot Act and in the controversy about the "Terrorist Surveillance Program," as the President called it.[33] In the process Bush repeatedly stressed the danger facing the United States: "America remains at risk (...) [w]e cannot let the fact that America hasn't been attacked in four and a half years since September 11, 2001, lull us into the illusion that the threats to our nation have disappeared. They have not", alluding to an allegedly disrupted terrorist plot to destroy the *Library Tower* in Los Angeles (the highest building on the American West Coast) with a freight plane (quoted in Baker/Eggen 2006: A04).

According to surveys by *Associated Press-Ipsos* (quoted in Shrader 2006), President Bush succeeded in the course of his struggles with Congress to secure the support of his base, especially white Evangelicals, for his relentless position in the "War on Terror." Karl Rove, election strategist and "architect" of recent Republican electoral victories, also participated in the debate, declaring that the issue of national security would once again be placed in the center of political attention in the run-up to the mid-term elections in November 2006 (VandeHei 2006: A07). The Democratic electoral strategist under President Clinton, Dick Morris (2006) also pointed out to his colleagues that swing voters based their electoral decisions on security issues, stating "I believe the Democrats drove voters back to his [President Bush's] camp with their attacks on the Patriot Act and the administration's wiretapping policies." Both sides of the political spectrum thus employed the scare tactic of upcoming elections and showed that the

---

33 It became clear rather quickly that the executive would not go quietly: "My personal opinion is it was a shameful act for someone to disclose this very important program in a time of war. The fact that we're discussing this program is helping the enemy," declared President Bush who went on the political offensive by implying that someone had committed treason. The Department of Justice opened a criminal investigation to find out who had leaked the existence of secret wire tapping program to the media. (See Shane 2005: A1).

majority of Americans was still not as concerned about personal liberties, but rather influenced by their demand for security.

By mid-February 2006 both houses of Congress were able to agree on a compromise that had the support of the White House. On March 9, 2006, President Bush signed into law the renewed authorization of the *Patriot Act*, the so-called *USA PATRIOT Improvement and Reauthorization Act of 2005 (H.R. 199)*, which permanently extended all of the original provisions except for two.[34] With few changes,[35] the Bush administration was able to accomplish all of its goals. Furthermore, in signing the bill into law, the President claimed the authority to interpret it. In a *signing statement*, Bush specified that he would not comply with the law's requirements to report to Congress[36] if the information would affect the foreign relations, national security, and the flow of information within the executive branch or the executive branch's ability to carry out its constitutional duty to protect the country (White House 2006). The *New York Times* (2/11/2006) concluded that Congress had resisted, but in the end succumbed to pressure from the White House.

There were also efforts in Congress to outlaw the "cruel, inhuman, and degrading" treatment of so-called "enemy combatants." In particular the Republican Senator John McCain (Arizona), who had been tortured during his time as a prisoner of war in Vietnam, ensured that the "prohibition of torture" was included in the bill of *Department of Defense Appropriations Act* in December 2005. After prolonged resistance by the White House, President Bush signed the *Detainee Treatment Act of 2005* as part of the *Department of Defense Appropriations Act of 2006* (Title X, H.R. 2863).[37] However, he expressed his interpretation of the so-called McCain amendment:

"The executive branch shall construe Title X in Division A of the Act, relating to detainees, in a manner consistent with the constitutional authority of the President to supervise the unitary executive branch and as Commander in Chief and consistent with the constitutional limitations on the judicial power, which will assist in achieving the shared objective of the Congress and the President, evidenced in Title X, of protecting the American people from further terrorist attacks." (White House 2005b).

---

34 Allowing the FBI to deploy so-called *roving wiretaps* (wide-ranging and unspecified wiretaps on telephone and emails) and the examination of business documents were only extended for four years.

35 Henceforth, the confiscation of business documents (a so called *gag order*) can be challenged; however, the concerned parties must wait for at least one year and prove that the government acted in "bad faith." Moreover, recipients of so called *National Security Letters* – the security services' orders (issued without court order) to make available (electronic) documents – do not have to disclose their attorney's name to the *FBI*. Libraries, which do not have access to the internet, are exempted from secret service investigations by means of *National Security Letters* (see Sandler 2006: 703).

36 Lawmakers originally intended that the President regularly reports to Congress about the FBI's use of comprehensive competences, in order to prevent the abuse of power.

37 See http://jurist.law.pitt.edu/gazette/2005/12/detainee-treatment-act-of-2005-white.php (download on 5/24/2009).

According to this statement, the power of the President as Commander-in-Chief requires a subordinated and subservient role of Congress and the courts as far as the protection of the Unites States is concerned. The *New York Times* (1/15/2006) helped to decipher the core message of George W. Bush's signing statement: "Whatever Congress intended the law to say, he intended to ignore it on the pretext the commander in chief is above the law. [...] Mr. Bush (...) seems to see no limit to his imperial presidency." Along the same lines, the *Washington Post* (1/11/2006) criticized the "unchecked abuse" and warned: "Without aggressive monitoring – and possibly further action – by Congress, illegal abuse of foreign prisoners in the custody of the United States is likely to continue."

Apart from the so called "prohibition of torture," the *Detainee Treatment Act* contains a bipartisan amendment by Senators Lindsey Graham (R-South Carolina) and Carl Levin (D-Michigan). The amendment limits the opportunities of Guantánamo inmates to make judicial claims in American courts. Moreover, the Bush administration interpreted the law as an ex-post legitimization of the use of military tribunals, which the President had already authorized by executive order in November 2001 (Richey 2006). The executive branch also claimed that it could authorize military tribunals, even without the support of Congress. Paul Clement, Solicitor General, explained the position of the Bush administration during his oral argument before the Supreme Court in the case of the Guantánamo prisoner Salim Ahmed Hamdan (quoted in Lane 2006: A01): "Even if Congress's support for the President's Military Order were not so clear, the President has the inherent authority to convene military commissions to try and punish captured enemy combatants in wartime – even in the absence of any statutory authorization." This once again demonstrated the view of the White House, which Press Secretary Ari Fleischer explained at the very beginning of Bush's term: "The way our nation is set up and the way the Constitution is written, war time powers rest fundamentally in the hands of the executive branch." (Fleischer quoted in Milbank 2001). To avoid any misunderstanding, Attorney General John Ashcroft (2001) was even clearer when he explained to Congress: "I trust, as well, that Congress will respect this President's authority to wage war on terrorism and defend our nation and its citizens with all the power vested in him by the Constitution and entrusted to him by the American people."

In times of extreme danger, the President assumes the role of a "protective patron", and as Commander-in-Chief he is the center of attention. The patriotic *rally around the flag* effect results in an enormous increase in power and trust in the President and the executive branch. The office of the President symbolizes national unity, and the White House is viewed as place people can turn to for support and certainty in times of crisis. With the attacks of 9/11, the already existing will of the executive branch to limit the powers of Congress, which had steadily increased over previous three decades (see Wilzewski 1999 for more on the "triumph of the legislature"), was catalyzed and legitimated. Immediately after assuming office, President Bush and his followers left no doubt that they intended to strengthen the position of the executive branch at the cost of the legislative branch's powers. This White House offensive was designed to push Congress – which had gained strength during the tenure of Bush's predecessor Bill Clinton – back into an inferior role. After the attacks on New York and Washington, Americans generally believed that this "power grab" was justified, even necessary in the light of the real threat to domestic security. In this long-term "Global War on Terror", the President established himself as a permanent Commander-in-Chief. George W. Bush was also successful in projecting himself into the national discourse as a "protective patron" who saved the traumatized nation from further attacks (for a more comprehensive treatment, see Braml 2003b: 35-39).

4. Conclusion and Prospects for American Democracy

Besides its strengths, the frame of reference of the "democracy matrix" also shows the *specific* and probably *temporary* deficits of American democracy, which risked losing its liberal character in the aftermath of the terrorist attacks of 9/11 and in the course of the Global War on Terror. Therefore, the Americans attempts to make the world safe for democracy with military means had unintended consequences for its own democracy – namely domestic insecurity and the serious infringement of civil liberties. The analysis of the changed domestic conditions indicated that the United States understood and interpreted domestic and international law in a way that is problematic for the standing and reputation of a presumably "liberal" democracy.

Under the pretext of a national threat, political power, especially that of the President, was significantly expanded. As long as Congress remains on the defensive, the horizontal checks and balances cannot function properly. The behavior of the Democratic majority, elected in 2006, has contradicted the assumption that the dominance of the President was due merely to a "culture of submission" among the Republican majority in Congress.[38] In contrast, it seems plausible to assume that in times of threats to national security the general weaknesses of the American political system become apparent, in particular in the form of massive infringements on civil liberties. As long as an imminent danger exists or is perceived, the American people are apparently ready to sacrifice personal freedom (especially that of non-Americans) in exchange for security. The founding fathers' concern about the "tyranny of the majority" is all the more relevant in the current context, because in the modern American media democracy (see Hils 2004: 13-21) the opinion of the majority can both be misunderstood and manipulated.

This places the actors and institutions that can influence the political and public perception of threats squarely in the middle of the debate. While public criticism was only rarely prohibited or directly inhibited by the state, the "patriotic" reporting, especially of TV networks, made critical commentators appear as unpatriotic outcasts. The media outlets who came closest to exercising the control function were the national print media. The critical question is, whether public pressure – not least motivated by a somewhat more critical news media (as in the context of the torture allegations and abuse at the military prison at Abu Ghraib), balanced expert analysis and staying true to prin-

---

38 Hils/Wilzewski (2006: III) argued "that a separate, extraordinarily strong sub-culture of submission exists among Republicans, which ceteris paribus has the effect that a legislative controlled by the Grand Old Party cannot maintain its institutional position in questions of war and peace to the same degree as a Congress dominated by Democrats."

ciples (not least by the members of Congress) – triggers a counter-impulse, which reinstates the balance of power between the political branches and swings the pendulum back in the direction of more civil liberties, as has often occurred in American history.

Throughout American history there were phases of external threats, which caused the balance of power to shift in favor of the executive branch. In a thorough analysis of this phenomenon in "All the Laws but One: Civil Liberties in Wartime" William Rehnquist, Chief Justice of the U.S. Supreme Court until his death in early September 2005, warned of the danger that in times of war the Commander-in-Chief is tempted, to expand the interpretations of the Constitution beyond what was intended by the Founding Fathers (Rehnquist 1998: 224). From his historical experience, however, the Chief Justice had little confidence that his colleagues would show the executive branch the limits which had to be maintained: "If the decision is made after the hostilities have ceased, it is more likely to favor civil liberty than if made while hostilities continue." As long as the Global War on Terror continues, the Roman maxim *inter arma silent leges* will also remain valid in the political system of the United States.[39] Even if the law has not been completely silent, its expression so far remains weak. The Supreme Court as a (in its own understanding) non-political institution shows restraint in times of crisis and war – it does not want to undermine the Commander-in-Chief.

So far the Supreme Court has not forcefully interfered with the Commander-in-Chief, but has limited its role to defend its own *raison d'être*, once again in its last ruling of July 2008 (*Boumediene et al v. Bush et al*), with a slim majority of five votes to four. The two judges appointed by President Bush, Samuel A. Alito and Chief Justice John G. Roberts, Jr., have approved the assumption of powers and the President's strategy in the "Global War on Terror." Future appointments to the Supreme Court not only have consequences for the composition of future majorities, but also for decisions which will affect fundamental rights, which can be decisive for the quality of American democracy.

Summing up, the variation of the quality of democracy is mainly dept to the war on terrorism. Only in the matrix field of decision making process (electoral system) we can observe a small improvement which is not connected with the war. Effective rule of law and the control of the executive by the legislative and judiciary powers, however, have deteriorated significantly. Congress' and the Supreme Court's control potentials were diminished by the two institutions' reluctance to exercise their powers. This behavior was, in turn, strongly influenced by public opinion, which was dominated by the presidential public discourse. It is the behavior of the Bush-Administration, disrespecting the rule of law and aiming to increase presidential powers at the expense of the other branches, which give reasons for both concern and hope. In times of war, the president has an opportunity and an incentive to increase the power of the White House. Yet it is also possible that a president with a different mindset and interpretation of its role can choose differently – especially if the perceived threat to national security abates. History has shown that the pendulum swings back. The current decrease of the quality of the American democracy may again prove temporary.

---

39 "When the weapons speak, the laws are silent." Or: "In war, the law is weak." (Cicero, Speech for Milo).

Consequently, the presidential election of 2008 was crucial in two respects: In his interaction with Congress, Bush's successor will have four or, in case of his re-election, possibly eight years to initiate a new phase in the implementation of the living constitution, but also the opportunity to influence the interpretation of the constitution well beyond his time in office through the appointment of judges for life terms. The election of Barack Obama as the 44th President of the United States is cause for optimism, especially because in his inauguration speech the constitutional lawyer came to a devastating conclusion about his predecessor's security policy: "We reject as false the choice between our safety and our ideals." Under President Obama's leadership America is supposed to be restored to its former glory of the charter written by its founding fathers and guaranteeing the rule of law and human rights. Obama criticized the policies of his predecessor George W. Bush stating that "[t]hose ideals still light the world, and we will not give them up for expedience's sake." (Obama 2009). President Obama has promised that his administration will restore the glory of the charter written by America's founding fathers and guarantee the rule of law and human rights. This promise is made more important because American society, acting as a role model through its political freedoms and openness, influences the worldwide perception of what a democracy should be and the understanding of international law and international order (see Braml 2003c: 115-140; Lauth 2006: 77-108).

President Obama's succeeding in keeping his promise to lead America back to the virtuous path of the rule of law will depend on the perception of threats within the United States, because collective security concerns continue to guarantee that national security will be a priority. Almost three-fourths of Americans (71 percent) still condone the torture of terrorist suspects (Pew Research Center 2009).[40] Whether the desire for protection and the general consciousness of war will be fed by the construction of essentialist world views, continued warnings, attack or wars, remains to be seen.

Literature

Arat, Zehra F. (1991) Democracy and Human Rights in Developing Countries, Boulder/CO.
Ashcroft, John (2001) 'Statement of Hon. John Ashcroft, Attorney General of the United States' in U.S. Congress, 107/1, Senate, Committee on the Judiciary, Department of Justice Oversight (ed.) *Pre-Serving Our Freedom While Defending Against Terrorism (Hearing, 6. December),* Washington D.C.: 309-317.
Beetham, David (ed.) (1994) *Defining and Measuring Democracy,* London (et al.).
Beetham, David/Weir, Stuart (1999) *Political Power and Democratic Control in Britain,* London.
Beetham, David/Weir, Stuart (2000) 'Democratic Audit in Comparative Perspective' in Lauth, Hans-Joachim/Pickel, Gert/Welzel, Christian (eds.) *Demokratiemessung: Konzepte und Befunde im internationalen Vergleich,* Opladen: 73-88.
Beetham, David/Bracking, Sarah/Kearton, Iain/Weir, Stuart (eds.) (2002) *International IDEA Handbook on Democracy Assessment,* The Hague et al.

---

[40] Religious attitudes are again significant: Church attendance correlates with the willingness to tolerate torture. (See Pew Research Center 2009).

Berry, Jeffrey M. (1999) *The New Liberalism. The Rising Power of Citizen Groups*, Washington, D.C.
Bertelsmann Stiftung (ed.) (2004) *Codebuch: Bertelsmann Transformation Index 2003: Auf dem Weg zur marktwirtschaftlichen Demokratie*, Gütersloh.
Bollen, Kenneth A. (1980) 'Issues in the Comparative Measurement of Political Democracy', *American Sociological Review* 3: 370-390.
Braml, Josef (2003a) 'USA: Zwischen Rechtsschutz und Staatsschutz. Einschränkung persönlicher Freiheitsrechte', *Stiftung Wissenschaft und Politik* Research Paper S 05, Berlin.
Braml, Josef (2003b) 'Machtpolitische Stellung des Präsidenten als Schutzpatron in Zeiten nationaler Unsicherheit' in Adomeit, Hannes/Alexandrova, Olga/Asseburg, Muriel/Braml, Josef/Möller, Kay/Müller, Friedemann/Rudolf, Peter/van Scherpenberg, Jan/Schmidt, Peter/Schneckener, Ulrich/Schwarz, Klaus-Dieter/Thränert, Oliver/Gudrun Wacker (eds.) *Zwei Jahre Präsident Bush: Beiträge zum Kolloquium der Stiftung Wissenschaft und Politik in Berlin am 13. Februar 2003 (SWP Research Paper S 9)*, Berlin: 35-39.
Braml, Josef (2003c) 'Rule of Law or Dictates by Fear. A German Perspective on American Civil Liberties in the War against Terrorism', *Fletcher Forum of World Affairs* 2: 115-140.
Braml, Josef (2004a) *Think Tanks versus "Denkfabriken"? U.S. and German Policy Research Institutes' Coping with and Influencing Their Environments*, Baden-Baden.
Braml, Josef (2004b) 'Die religiöse Rechte in den USA: Basis der Bush-Administration?', *Stiftung Wissenschaft und Politik* Research Paper S 35, Berlin.
Braml, Josef (2005) *Amerika, Gott und die Welt. George W. Bushs Außenpolitik auf christlich-rechter Basis*, Berlin.
Brusis, Martin (2008) 'Reformfähigkeit messen? Konzeptionelle Überlegungen zu einem Reformfähigkeitsindex für OECD-Staaten', *Politische Vierteljahresschrift* 1: 92-113.
Bühlmann, Marc/Merkel, Wolfgang/Weßels, Bernhard (2008) 'The Quality of Democracy. Democracy Barometer for Established Democracies', *National Centre of Competence in Research* Working Paper 10a, Zürich.
Bush, George W. (2003) State of the Union Speech, The White House January 28, 2003.
Bush, George W. (2005a) Remarks by the President on the Patriot Act, The White House July 20, 2005.
Bush, George W. (2005b) President's Statement on Signing of H.R. 2863, the Department of Defense, Emergency Supplemental Appropriations to Address Hurricanes in the Gulf of Mexico, and Pandemic Influenza Act, The White House December 30, 2005.
Bush, George W. (2006) The President's Statement on H.R. 199, USA PATRIOT Improvement and Reauthorization Act of 2005, The White House March 9, 2006.
Coker, Donna (2003) 'Foreword: Addressing the Real World of Racial Injustice in the Criminal Justice System', *Journal of Criminal Law and Criminology* 93: 827-879.
Cole, David (1999) *No Equal Justice. Race and Class in American Criminal Justice System*, New York.
Today Midday Update (2008) 'Mukasey Asks Congress to Clarify Detainee Rights', *Congressional Quarterly* July 21, 2008.
Collier, David/Levitsky, Steven (1997) 'Democracy with Adjectives: Conceptual Innovation in Comparative Research', *World Politics* 3: 430-451.
Coppedge, Michael/Reinicke, Wolfgang H. (1991) 'Measuring Polyarchy' in Inkeles, Alex (ed.) *On Measuring Democracy: Its Consequences and Concomitants*, New Brunswick NJ: 48-68.
Czempiel, Ernst-Otto (1996) 'Kants Theorem. Oder: Warum sind die Demokratien (noch immer) nicht friedlich?', *Zeitschrift für Internationale Beziehungen*, 1: 79-101.

Dahl, Robert (1971) *Polyarchy: Participation and Opposition,* New Haven CT/London.
Dahl, Robert (1989) *Democracy and Its Critics,* New Haven CT/London.
Diamond, Larry/Morlino, Leonardo (eds.) (2005) *Assessing the Quality of Democracy,* Baltimore.
Dlouhy, Jennifer/Palmer, Elizabeth (2001) 'New Assertions of Executive Power Anger, Frustrate Some on Hill', *Congressional Quarterly Weekly* 59:45: 2784.
Douglas, Mary/Wildavsky, Aaron (1982) *Risk and Culture,* Berkeley CA et al.
Eggen, Dan (2005) 'Patriot Act Changes to Be Proposed: Gonzales Will Seek to Respond to Critics, Get Law Renewed', *Washington Post* April 5, 2005: A21.
Elklit, Jørgen (1994) 'Is the Degree of Electoral Democracy Measureable? Experiences from Bulgaria, Kenya, Latvia, Mongolia and Nepal' in Beetham, David (ed.) *Defining and Measuring Democracy,* London et al.: 89-112.
Fukuyama, Francis (2004) 'The Neoconservative Moment', *The National Interest* June 1, 2004.
Fukuyama, Francis (2006a) 'After Neoconservatism', *New York Times* February 19, 2006.
Fukuyama, Francis (2006b) 'The Paradox of International Action', *The American Interest* 3: 7-18.
Gasiorowski, Mark J. (1996) 'An Overview of the Political Regime Change Dataset', *Comparative Political Studies* 4: 469-483.
Gastil, Raymond Duncan (1991) 'The Comparative Survey of Freedom: Experiences and Suggestions' in Inkeles, Alex (ed.) *On Measuring Democracy: Its Consequences and Concomitants,* New Brunswick NJ: 21-36.
Gellner, Winand (1995) *Ideenagenturen für Politik und Öffentlichkeit: Think Tanks in den USA und in Deutschland,* Opladen.
Gorman, Siobhan (2002a) 'There Are No Second Chances', *National Journal* December 21, 2002.
Gorman, Siobhan (2002b) 'The Ashcroft Doctrine', *National Journal* December 21, 2002.
Green, John (2004) *The American Religious Landscape and Political Attitudes: A Baseline for 2004 (September),* in http://pewforum.org/publications/surveys/green-full.pdf [accessed on 5/20/2009].
Greenberg, Anna/Berktold, Jennifer (2004) 'Evangelicals in America', *Religion and Ethics News Weekly* April 5, 2004.
Gurr, Ted Robert/Jaggers, Keith/Moore, Will H. (1990) 'The Transformation of the Western State: The Growth of Democracy, Autocracy, and State Power since 1800', *Studies on Comparative International Development* 1: 73-108.
Haass, Richard N. (2009) *War of Necessity, War of Choice. A Memoir of Two Iraq Wars,* New York.
Hadenius, Axel (1992) *Democracy and Development,* Cambridge.
Hils, Jochen (2004) 'Zwischen Hyperdemokratie und "Minderheitstyrannei": Die USA zu Beginn des 21. Jahrhunderts', *Center for North American Studies* Arbeits- und Forschungsbericht 1, Frankfurt/Main.
Hils, Jochen (2006) 'Missionary Foreign Policy? Demokratie und gewaltsamer Demokratieexport der USA aus der Sicht der liberalen Theorie der Internationalen Beziehungen' in Hils, Jochen /Wilzewski, Jürgen (2006) (eds.) *Defekte Demokratie – Crusader State? Die Weltpolitik der USA in der Ära Bush,* Trier: 21-75.
Hils, Jochen/Wilzewski, Jürgen (2006) 'Second Image Reconsidered: Die parlamentarische Kontrolle von Militärinterventionen der USA in den 1990er Jahren', *Kaiserslautern Occasional Working Paper in Political Science* 1, Kaiserslautern.
Hils, Jochen /Wilzewski, Jürgen (2006) (eds.) *Defekte Demokratie – Crusader State? Die Weltpolitik der USA in der Ära Bush,* Trier.

Hudson, William E. (2004) *American Democracy in Peril: Eight Challenges to America's Future*, Washington D.C.
Huntington, Samuel P. (1991) *The Third Wave: Democratization in the Late Twentieth Century*, Norman/OK.
Jaggers, Keith/Gurr, Ted R. (1995) 'Transitions to Democracy: Tracking the Third Wave with Polity III Indicators of Democracy and Autocracy', *Journal of Peace Research* 4: 469-482.
Johnson, Chalmers (2004) *Der Selbstmord der amerikanischen Demokratie*, München.
Jones, Charles O. (2005) *The Presidency in a Separated System*, Washington D.C.
Kohut, Andrew/Green, John/Keeter, Scott/Toth, Robert (2000) *The Diminishing Divide: Religion's Changing Role in American Politics*, Washington D.C.
Krauthammer, Charles (2004) *Democratic Realism: An American Foreign Policy for a Unipolar World*, Washington D.C.
Krauthammer, Charles (1991) 'The Unipolar Moment', *Foreign Affairs (America and the World Edition)* 1: 23-33.
Lane, Charles (2006) 'Court Case Challenges Power of President. Military Tribunals', *Legitimacy at Issue* March 26, 2006: A01.
Lauth, Hans-Joachim (2002) 'Die empirische Messung demokratischer Grauzonen: Das Problem der Schwellenbestimmung' in Bendel, Petra/Croissant, Aurel/Rüb, Friedbert (eds.) *Zwischen Diktatur und Demokratie: Zur Konzeption und Empirie demokratischer Grauzonen*, Opladen: 119-138.
Lauth, Hans-Joachim (2004) *Demokratie und Demokratiemessung: Eine konzeptionelle Grundlegung für den interkulturellen Vergleich*, Wiesbaden.
Lauth, Hans-Joachim (2006) 'Deficient Democracies: Qualität und außenpolitische Relevanz der Demokratie aus der Sicht der empirischen Demokratietheorie' in Hils, Jochen/Wilzewski, Jürgen (eds.) *Defekte Demokratie – Crusader State? Die Weltpolitik der USA in der Ära Bush*, Trier: 77-108.
Lauth, Hans-Joachim/Pickel, Gert/Welzel, Christian (2000) 'Grundfragen, Probleme und Perspektiven der Demokratiemessung' in Lauth/Pickel/Welzel (eds.) *Demokratiemessung: Konzepte und Befunde im internationalen Vergleich*, Opladen: 7-26.
Lichtblau, Eric (2005) 'Coalition Forms to Oppose Parts of Antiterrorism Law', *New York Times* March 23, 2005.
Massing, Michael (2004) 'Now They Tell Us', *New York Review of Books* February 26: 43-49.
Merkel, Wolfgang (1999) 'Defekte Demokratien' in Merkel, Wolfgang/Busch, Andreas (eds.) *Demokratie in Ost und West*, Frankfurt/Main: 361-381.
Merkel, Wolfgang/Puhle, Hans-Jürgen/Croissant, Aurel/Eicher, Claudia/Thiery, Peter (2003): *Defekte Demokratie. Vol. 1: Theorie*, Wiesbaden.
Milbank, Dana (2001) 'In War, It's Power to the President', *Washington Post* November 20 2001: A1.
Morris, Dick (2006) 'How the Left Saved Bush', *FrontPageMagazine.com* January 4, 2006, in http://www.frontpagemag.com/Articles/ReadArticle.asp?ID=20769 [accessed on 5/24/2009].
Müller, Thomas/Pickel, Susanne 2007 'Wie lässt sich Demokratie am besten messen? Zur Konzeptqualität von Demokratieindizes', *Politische Vierteljahresschrift* 3: 511-539.
Munck, Gerardo L./Verkuilen, Jay (2002) 'Conceptualizing and Measuring Democracy: Evaluating Alternative Indices', *Comparative Political Studies* 1: 5-34.
National Annenberg Election Survey (2004) 'Blacks, Hispanics Resist Republican Appeals But Conservative White Christians Are Stronger Supporters than in 2000', *Annenberg Public Policy Center of the University of Pennsylvania* July 25, 2004.

Neustadt, Richard E. (1990) *Presidential Power and the Modern Presidents. The Politics of Leadership from Roosevelt to Reagan*, New York/Toronto.
Newport, Frank (2003) 'Support for War Modestly Higher among More Religious Americans: Those Who Identify with the Religious Right Most Likely to Favor Military Action', *Gallup Poll Analyses* February 27, 2003, Washington D.C.
N.N (2006) 'The Imperial Presidency at Work', *New York Times* January 15, 2006.
N.N. (2006) 'Another Cave-In on the Patriot Act', *New York Times* February 11, 2006.
Obama, Barack H. (2009) Inaugural Address, January 20, 2009, in http://www.whitehouse.gov/blog/inaugural-address/ [accessed on 5/20/2009].
O'Donnell, Guillermo (1994) 'Delegative Democracy', *Journal of Democracy* 1: 55-69.
Palmer, Elizabeth (2001a) 'Terrorism Bill's Sparse Paper Trail May Cause Legal Vulnerabilities', *Congressional Quarterly Weekly* 59:41: 2533.
Palmer, Elizabeth (2001b) 'House Passes Anti-Terrorism Bill That Tracks White House's Wishes', *Congressional Quarterly Weekly* 59:39: 2399.
Pape, Robert (2005) Dying to Win: The Strategic Logic of Suicide Terrorism, New York.
Pasquino, Pasquale (1998) 'Constitutional Adjunction and Democracy. Comparative Perspectives: USA, France, Italy', *Ratio Juris* 1: 38-50.
Perine, Keith/Stern, Seth (2005) 'Senate Passes Patriot Act Renewal', *Congressional Quarterly Weekly* 63:31: 2126.
Pew Research Center (2009) The Religious Dimensions of the Torture Debate, Washington, D.C.
Program on International Policy Attitudes (2003): *Misperceptions, The Media and the Iraq War*, October 2, 2003, University of Maryland.
Prosper, Pierre-Richard (2001) 'Statement of Hon. Pierre-Richard Prosper, Ambassador-At-Large for War Crimes Issues, Department of State, Washington, D.C.' in U.S. Congress, 107/1, Senate, Committee on the Judiciary, Department of Justice Oversight (eds.) *Pre-Serving Our Freedom While Defending Against Terrorism (Hearing, December 4)*, Washington D.C.: 135-141.
Puhle, Hans-Jürgen (2005) 'Democratic Consolidation and "Defective Democracies"', Paper for a Conference on "Defekte Demokratie – Crusader State? Die Weltpolitik der USA in der Ära Bush," April 28-30 , 2005, Lambrecht/Pfalz.
Rehnquist, William H. (1998) *All the Laws but One: Civil Liberties in Wartime*, New York/Toronto.
Richey, Warren (2006) 'At Court, a Terror Case Rife with Tough Issues', *Christian Science Monitor* March 27, 2006.
Risen, James/Lichtblau, Eric (2005) 'Bush Lets U.S. Spy on Callers Without Courts', *New York Times* December 16, 2005: A1.
Rothman, Stanley/Lichter, Robert (1987) 'Elite Ideology and Risk Perception in Nuclear Energy Policy', *American Political Science Review* 2: 383-404.
Rüb, Friedbert (1994) 'Die Herausbildung politischer Institutionen in Demokratisierungsprozessen' in Merkel, Wolfgang (ed.) *Systemwechsel 1: Theorien, Ansätze und Konzeptionen*, Opladen: 111-137.
Saad, Lydia (2005) 'Americans Reject Extreme Anti-Privacy Security Measures', *Gallup Poll Analyses* August 8, 2005, Washington D.C.
Sandler, Michael/Perine, Keith (2005) 'Chambers Tweak Patriot Act Provisions', *Congressional Quarterly Weekly* 63:30: 2044.
Saward, Michael (1994) 'Democratic Theory and Indices of Democratization' in Beetham, David (ed.) *Defining and Measuring Democracy*, London et al.: 6-24.

Shane, Scott (2005) 'Criminal Inquiry Opens Into Leak in Eavesdropping', *New York Times* December 31, 2005: A1.
Shrader, Katherine (2006) 'Poll: Surveillance Wins Some More Backers', *Associated Press* February 9, 2006.
Schmidt, Manfred G. (2000) *Demokratietheorien: Eine Einführung*, Opladen.
Schmitter, Philippe C./Karl, Terry Lynn (1991) 'What Democracy Is... and Is Not?', *Journal of Democracy* 3: 75-88.
Smith, James Allen (1989) 'Think Tanks and the Politics of Ideas' in Colander, David C./Coats, Alfred W. (eds.) *The Spread of Economic Ideas*, Cambridge: 175-194.
Stuckey, Mary (1991) *The President As Interpreter-In-Chief*, Chatham/NJ.
Sundquist, James L. (1988) 'Needed: A Political Theory for the New Era of Coalition Government in the United States', *Political Science Quarterly* 4: 613-635.
VandeHei, Jim (2006) 'Cheney Says NSA Spying Should Be an Election Issue', *Washington Post* February 10, 2006: A07.
Vanhanen, Tatu (1984) The Emergence of Democracy: A Comparative Study of 119 States, 1850-1979, Helsinki.
Vanhanen, Tatu (1990) *The Process of Democratization: A Comparative Study of 147 States, 1980-1988*, New York et al.
Vanhanen, Tatu (2003) *Democratization: A Comparative Analysis of 170 Countries*, London/New York.
N.N (2006) 'Unchecked Abuse', *Washington Post* January 11, 2006: A20.
Weaver, R. Kent/Rockman, Bert A. (1993) 'Assessing the Effects of Institutions' in Weaver, R. Kent/Rockman, Bert A. (eds.) *Do Institutions Matter? Government Capabilities in the United States and Abroad*, Washington, D.C.: 1-41.
Wilzewski, Jürgen (2006) 'A Preset Crusade: Die Bush-Administration und der Präventivkrieg gegen den Irak' in Hils, Jochen/Wilzewski, Jürgen (2006) (eds.) *Defekte Demokratie – Crusader State? Die Weltpolitik der USA in der Ära Bush*, Trier: 425-460.
Wilzewski, Jürgen (1999) *Triumph der Legislative: Zum Wandel der amerikanischen Sicherheitspolitik 1981-1991*, Frankfurt/Main/New York.
Zakaria, Fareed (1997) 'The Rise of Illiberal Democracy', *Foreign Affairs* 6: 22-43.
Zakaria, Fareed (2003) *The Future of Freedom: Illiberal Democracy at Home and Abroad*, New York.

ARTICLE

Deficits in Democratic Quality? The Effects of Party-System Institutionalisation on the Quality of Democracy in Central Eastern Europe[1]

Marianne Kneuer

Abstract This study aims to illustrate the contribution of parties and party systems to the quality of democracy. Does an instable party system make a difference for democratic quality in a country regarded as a consolidated democracy? Does the deficient functioning of parties and party systems influence democratic quality? If so, to what extent? To answer these questions, this article will examine the degree of institutionalisation over the two post-autocratic decades of the eight new, post-socialist democracies in Central Eastern Europe that entered the EU in 2004. I will then discuss whether the performance of the party systems affects the quality of democracy, and which aspects in particular may be affected.

1. Introduction

After the first wave of euphoria and the very optimistic visions of the "victory of democracy" as the only remaining form of political regime, in the course of the 1990s it became evident that the results of these post-communist democratisations were ambivalent. Scholars began to broaden the typology of democracy versus autocracy by identifying different types of "adjective" democracies in the grey zone of hybrid forms in between consolidated democracies and non-democratic regimes, and they began to elaborate different concepts in order to typologise these forms of non-consolidated democracies.

Furthermore, the evidence that democratisation does not imply an automatic and linear development towards consolidation, and that democratization processes can be slowed down, paralysed or even reversed, turned the attention of students increasingly from studying regime transition to evaluating and explaining the character of democratic regimes (Diamond/Morlino 2005: ix, O'Donnell 2004: 9). The scrutiny of democracy quality supposes that beyond the institutionalisation of democratic structures during

---

[1] The author thanks Martin Brusis for the invaluable exchange and three anonymous reviewers for their helpful comments.

transition and the more complex and long-enduring consolidation process, additional aspects contribute to a stable, legitimate, and broadly accepted and supported democratic regime. Although the interest in these qualitative aspects of democracy arises from analysing and evaluating newly democratised countries in order to better grasp their state of consolidation, the question of democratic quality also applies to established democracies.

There is a growing interest in analysing and assessing the quality of democracy, but there is not much research on the topic. Main references are the studies of Altmann and Pérez-Liñan (2001), Beetham (2002, 2004), O'Donnell, Cullel and Iazzetta (2004), and Diamond and Morlino (2005). In terms of democracy definitions, these approaches differ in the parsimony of their concepts: Altmann and Pérez-Liñan mainly follow Dahl's concept of polyarchy and find three dimensions of the quality of democracy: effective civil rights, effective participation, and effective competition, and thus present quite a parsimonious approach (2002: 88), while the other concepts are considerably more complex. Beetham's framework, which is reflected in the Democratic Audit of the International IDEA Handbook on democracy assessment (Beetham/Bracking/Kearton/Weir 2002), comprises fourteen sections summarised under four main points: citizen rights, representative and accountable government, civil society and popular participation, and democracy beyond the state (2004: 7). Diamond and Morlino pursue quite a broad, comprehensive approach that goes beyond the minimalist approach of Altmann and Pérez-Liñan but still does not reach the level of substantial democracy definitions that include social and economic criteria. Diamond and Morlino elaborate eight dimensions, which they attribute to three levels: The procedural level embraces rule of law, participation, competition, and accountability; the content level contains two dimensions: civil and political freedoms as well as political equality; and finally, the result level is responsiveness measuring the extent to which public policies correspond to citizens' demands and preferences (2005m: xii). The concept of "Human Development" by O'Donnell (2004) is the most comprehensive and ambitious.[2]

Juxtaposing these three concepts, it becomes evident that a large number of the different quality criteria are connected to the role of parties and the functioning of the party or party system-related mechanisms. In the table below, the aspects and mechanisms where parties are involved as important actors are in italics:

---

[2] The comprehensiveness of the "human development" concept is less systematic and difficult to grasp in a chart. Therefore it is not included in Table 1.

Table 1: Concepts of Quality of Democracy

Altmann/Pérez-Liñan	Beetham, IDEA Handbook	Diamond/Morlino
Effective civil rights *Effective participation* *Effective competition*	Citizen rights Nationhood and citizenship Rule of law and access to justice Civil and political rights Economic and social rights	Procedural level Rule of law *Participation* *Competition* *Horizontal accountability* *Vertical accountability*
	Representative and accountable government Free and fair elections *Democratic role of political parties* *Government effectiveness and accountability* Civilian control of the military and police Minimising corruption	Content level Civil and political freedoms Political equality
	Civil society and popular participation Media in a democratic society *Political participation* *Government responsiveness* Decentralisation	Result level *Responsiveness*
	Democracy beyond the state The international dimension of democracy	

Own compilation on the basis of Altmann/Pérez-Liñan (2001), Beetham (2004), IDEA Handbook (2002), Diamond/Morlino (2005). The italics indicate the involvement of parties in the specific aspect.

Notwithstanding the difference in the presented approaches (see Table 1), the concepts all agree in some essential aspects: They all emphasise the basic conditions of civil and political rights (freedom, equality) and the central relevance of participation and competition. On the basis of the case studies, Diamond and Morlino conclude that competition and participation emerge as key causal aspects in the performance of other dimensions (Diamond/Morlino 2005: xxxv). Moreover, two approaches (Beetham/IDEA and Diamond/Morlino) also agree on the importance of rule of law, accountability, and responsiveness. Beetham and IDEA additionally include the performance and output dimension in terms of government effectiveness and minimising corruption. Other scholars also consider the regime's performance (Diamond 1999:77, Kitschelt/Mansfeldova/Markowski/Tóka 1999; 383, 403). On the basis of these approaches, and taking into account the aspects most common among them, three dimensions of democratic quality crystallise: 1) the dimension of civic and political rights, which would also cover the rule of law and could be considered the *constitutional and control dimension*.[3] 2) the *procedural dimension*, which targets the democratic process on the input level as well as on the decision-making level; 3) the *output dimension*, which reflects the effectiveness of the regime's performance.

Table 2: Three Dimensions of Quality of Democracy

Freedom and control dimension	Procedural dimension	Output dimension
Effective civil rights Effective political rights Rule of law	Participation Competition Accountability Responsiveness	Government effectiveness

Own compilation on the basis of Table 1 and Kitschelt/Mansfeldova/Markowski/Tóka (1999)

Kitschelt, Mansfeldova, Markowski and Tóka (1999) state:

> "A comparison of the quality of emerging democratic polities therefore is well advised to focus on the relations of representation and executive governance that congeal around electoral competition in general and political parties in particular." (44)

The study of Kitschelt, Mansfeldova, Markowski and Tóka, which discusses party systems and the quality of post-communist democracies, focuses therefore "on one central and indispensable aspect of any democracy, the dynamics of party competition" (383).

Given the parties' relevance to democratic processes and governance, of course, does not say anything about the way parties and party systems are performing. That is the starting point for this study, which aims to illuminate the contribution of parties and party systems to the quality of democracy.[4] The central questions of this study are: Can an instable party system make a difference to democratic quality in a country regarded as a consolidated democracy? And do instable party systems influence democratic quality?

So far there is no elaborated framework for tracing the influence of parties and party systems on democratic quality. This article takes the same starting point as that of Kitschelt, Mansfeldova, Markowski and Tóka, but poses the research question differently: While they address the *causes* of different arrangements and competition structures of party systems (49), I look at the *consequences*. Hence, the party systems are the independent variable.

---

[3] This dimension indicates the quality of how the provisions for the protection of the individual rights and their control (as well as the control of the state power) are implemented.

[4] Parties and party systems have to be distinguished conceptually. Although this analysis focuses on the stabilisation of party *systems*, we cannot avoid mentioning *parties*. Parties are neither regarded here individually, as in their origins, structure and development, nor is their institutionalisation analysed (as by Randall/Svasand 2002). I refer to parties as indispensable actors in the party systems and as interactive elements for a) the party–citizen linkage, b) inter-party competition and c) government-building or opposition.

For the analysis, the new democracies in post-socialist Central Eastern Europe constitute an appropriate sample.[5] The countries that entered the European Union in 2004 can largely be considered consolidated and stable. Regarding the party systems, through the 1990s their development was marked by features like high volatility and fragmentation. The party systems' instability after 1989 was neither surprising nor worrying, yet it was widely supposed that stabilisation would take place in the near future in the course of the overall consolidation of the democracies. On the other hand, some scholars raised doubts about prospects of party system consolidation in Central Eastern Europe. Mair not only highlighted the instability of the party systems of the emerging, post-communist party systems, but he also found that they differed from established democracies in respect to the democratisation process, the character of the electorate, and the patterns of competition (1997: 175ff). Mair thus raised the question of whether these party systems "will [...] settle down over time and whether they will also become consolidated" (Mair 1997: 197). Actually, in the first post-autocratic decade, features like high volatility, weak rootedness of parties in society, low trust in parties, sometimes quite low electoral turnouts, and weak links between parties and interest organisations did not improve as expected. The prime weakness was the level of institutionalisation of the party system, which was (and is) low even in relation to other new democracies (Toka 1997: 115, Mainwaring 1998) and has therefore been classified as partially institutionalised (Lewis 2001b: 201).

To assess the degree of consolidation of the party systems, I refer to the concept of institutionalisation generated by Mainwaring and Scully (1995) and further developed by Mainwaring (1998, 1999) and Mainwaring and Torcal (2006). Stability is considered equally important to consolidation as a high degree of institutionalisation is and instability equally important to consolidation as a low degree of institutionalisation. I assume a continuum from highly to weakly institutionalised party systems. This study will examine the whole post-autocratic period. I first provide a complete overview of the development of Central Eastern European party systems' institutionalisation, and then I introduce the time dimension in order to effectively assess the progress or regression of this institutionalisation.

Chapter 2 dwells on party systems' relevance to the quality of democracy. Chapter 3 presents the empirical analysis of the party systems institutionalisation in the NMS-2004. In Chapter 4, I discuss how the stated traits of the CEE party systems impact the different dimensions of democratic quality. And finally, conclusions are provided about the relevance of party systems in the interplay of democratic consolidation and democratic quality.

---

5 Estonia, Latvia, Lithuania, Poland, Czech Republic, Slovakia, Hungary, Slovenia. Synonymously I use the expression CEE (Central Eastern Europe), CEE countries or NMS-2004 (New Member States entered in 2004).

2. Do parties and party systems matter for democratic quality?

The broad consensus is that parties play an important role in the functioning of democracies. Parties are considered to constitute the vital link between government and governed, and, in contrast to other intermediary institutions like interest groups or civil society, parties fulfill not only *social* functions, such as articulating, integrating society, and aggregating and channelling the citizen's interests and demands, but also *political* functions such as organising competition and channelling participation in elections, as well as *governmental* functions: structuring political agendas, formulating and implementing policy formulation, recruiting key governmental and legislative posts, generating governments. These governmental functions also include the opposition's task of controlling the executive. Concerning the relevance of parties and party systems, seminal studies with theoretical and conceptual approaches and empirical analyses are legion. However, there is less research about the role of parties and party systems in democratising countries. There is "considerable uncertainty about the role of parties in the process of democratization" and therefore the nature of their role remains "something of an open question" (Lewis 2001a: 547, 562). A closer look at democratisation studies shows that they have so far not focused on parties and party systems as intensively as they have on other dimensions, such as, for example, institutional designs. So we find few conceptual approaches about the role of party systems in democratisation, and especially in democratic consolidation.

The premise of this study is that there are different levels of consolidation. Linz and Stepan defined three levels of consolidation: behavioural, attitudinal and constitutional (1996: 6ff). Behavioural consolidation assumes that no significant actor pursues non-democratic alternatives, attitudinal consolidation assumes that a strong majority of the public believes that democratic procedures and institutions are the most appropriate way to govern collective life in a society, and constitutional consolidation assumes that governmental and non-governmental forces subject the resolution of conflict to democratic rules and procedures. Parties are thought of as one element of "political society" alongside elections, electoral rules, political leadership, inter-party alliances, and legislatures. This political society contributes to the habituation to norms, procedures of democratic conflict regulation, and to its institutional routinisation. Moreover, Linz and Stepan believe political society should be responsible for conducting intermediation and structuring compromise. However, parties and intermediary institutions, in general, are not integrated explicitly into the definition of consolidation.

Wolfgang Merkel added a fourth level to Linz and Stepan's now commonly recognised definition – namely, "representative consolidation", which targets the territorial and functional representation of interests (Merkel 1999: 145). Merkel argues that the constellations and activities of the actors (parties, party systems, and interest groups) not only influence the consolidation of norms and structures, but also impact the configuration of constitutional consolidation, as well as attitudinal and behavioural consolidation. Hence, the performance of parties and party systems not only influences the consolidation of the representative level, but also potentially contributes to or impedes the consolidation of the other levels, especially the attitudinal and behavioural ones.

This suggests that consolidation is an interactive process between the four identified levels, whereby parties and party systems have a potential influence – positive or negative – on the other levels. Each level, however, might develop at a different pace; it is even quite likely that the levels of consolidation do not advance simultaneously. Scholars point to the fact that especially the attitudinal patterns that involve a democratic political culture that is system-supportive for the new democracy refer to a long-term process (Pridham 1995: 169). Constitutional consolidation, in contrast, can be reached more easily and quickly. The level of representative consolidation and its interplay with the other levels has not been researched sufficiently so far; likewise, how the different actors on the level of representative consolidation are linked. Among all actors – including interest groups, media, and civil society – parties and party systems play an outstanding role that cannot be compensated for by the others. Only parties can translate interests and preferences into policy proposals and are involved in their implementation, and the party systems reflect how the competition for policies is structured and performed. Party systems indicate the linkage to society and the patterns of conflict regulation among the political elite. On the other hand, the degree of consolidation of the parties and party systems may also influence on other intermediary actors.

The assessment of the role of party systems in consolidation is, however, contentious. One could argue that there is a fundamental relationship between the performance of party systems and those of the new democratic systems (Pridham/Lewis 1996: 5). On the other hand, Schmitter argues that democracies can be well consolidated without a stable party system, or even the other way round, "that party systems can remain unconsolidated for some time – perhaps indefinitely", and this would not necessarily mean that the regime as a whole has failed to consolidate itself (Schmitter 2001: 74). This fits with the finding of many empirical studies (Morlino 1995 for Southern Europe, Toka 1997 for Central Eastern Europe) which have shown that the presence of institutionalised parties and party systems is not a necessary condition for successful consolidation. Apparently, the assumptions in this controversy are too narrowly conceived. Eventually, deconsolidation or being a sufficient condition for consolidation is not a precise yardstick. In fact, no study has thus far observed a deconsolidation in Central Eastern Europe although the party systems were not stable or not as stable as expected. And it would be very difficult to attribute democratic regression in other regions solely and in a monocausal way to the lack of consolidation of party systems.

Mainwaring and Scully, who generated the concept of party-system institutionalisation and tested it for Latin America, come to the conclusion that "institutionalizing a party system matters a great deal" (1995: 34). Later, Mainwaring – comparing Latin America to post-socialist countries – puts it more concretely: "It has become apparent that democracy can survive with weakly institutionalized party systems, but weak institutionalization harms the quality of democracy and the prospects for democratic consolidation" (Mainwaring 1998: 79). Along those lines, Toka states that "the *quality* of democracy is important enough to justify the development of a strong party system, even if the latter does not contribute to the *consolidation* of democracy" (1997: 121; italics in original). Finally, Schmitter, too – after showing the deficient performance of parties in fulfilling their functional duties and guessing that they would reduce their leading roles in electoral structuration, symbolic identification, party governance, and interest aggregation – writes: "What this implies for the quality of these neodemocracies is another issue!" (2001: 86)

Thus the question becomes: What consequences do weak party systems and the party performance in these systems have on the quality of democracies? Hence, the next step is to capture and systematically analyse the functioning of the party systems and their degree of institutionalisation in Central Eastern Europe.

3. The party systems in CEE and their institutionalisation

Aside from the Czech Republic and Hungary, all CEE countries have more than five parties in parliament and therefore must be classified as extreme multi-party systems.[6] The development of the party systems since the first elections shows the dynamics and variation. It is remarkable that in the first two or three terms the patterns were quite stable, as there was a large group of countries with a dominant party (Czech Republic, Estonia, Hungary, Lithuania and Slovakia). In Slovenia the main feature was the high number of parties of support with narrow margins, although in the political reality, the LDS (Liberal Democracy of Slovenia) formed part of every government from 1992 till 2004 and thus was the dominant party. Poland and Lithuania were exceptions, having had many parties, yet very soon a bipolar structure emerged.

However, this apparent stability of competition patterns was challenged after three or four elections that caused changes ranging from soft to cataclysmic. The soft version of reshuffling is the transformation of the party system of a dominant party into a bipolar structure, such as in the Czech Republic and Hungary where a second force (the Czech Social Democrats (ČSSD) and the Hungarian Conservatives (FIDESZ)) gained more political profile and voter support. A much more fundamental change took place in the rest of the countries where either the former bipolarity (Poland, Lithuania) or the former dominance of one party (Slovakia, Slovenia, Estonia) experienced a centrifugal movement and thus produced a tripolar structure. Major players, often formerly government parties, disappeared suddenly and completely (e.g. the Polish post-solidarity party AWS in 2001, the Latvian Way in 2002, and the Slovakian Social Democrats, SDL, also in 2002), or experienced significant declines in their status (e.g. the Lithuanian Homeland

---

6 For party-system classifications, Sartori constitutes the classic reference; refinement, however, was indicated in order to describe adequately the increased diversity of party systems that emerged in the so-called "third wave of democratisation" since 1974, or to capture the nuances within the categories, especially the category of multi-party systems (Wolinetz 2004, 2006). Refinements were suggested by different authors (Ware 1996, Siaroff 2000). Ware uses six categories but does not differentiate between limited (3–5 parties) and extreme pluralism (6–8 parties) as Sartori did. This is problematic in that, especially in new democracies, not every party system is a two or two-and-a-half party system – but almost all are multi-party systems. Siaroff's typology consists of eight categories. His typology has the advantage of capturing the difference between "moderate" and "extreme" multi-party systems and of being more sensitive to change over time, two aspects important for the analysis of developments in new democracies.

Union in 2000, the Estonian Koonderakond in 1999, the Polish Social Democrats, SLD, in 2005), while at the same time new parties rushed into the political arena, aggregating a considerable amount of votes and seats (see also Table 7). Many of these newly entered parties – for instance, the Estonian Res Publica in 2005 and the Latvian New Era in 2002 – directly took over governmental responsibility. In Lithuania and Slovakia in particular this phenomenon occurred in almost every election. In many countries the main losers were the left parties, namely the communist-successor parties, which took over a traditional social-democratic profile. The observation in the Lithuanian case – that the lack of unity between the traditional parties broadened the political opportunities for new challengers – can be applied to almost all the countries (Krupavicius 2007: 1026). These new contenders can be put into one of two groups: Firstly, many of these new parties advocate being center parties. By doing this, the parties try either to benefit from the diminishing importance of the cleavage or to offer an alternative to the communism–anti-communism polarisation. Actually, the new contenders are characterised by a diffuse ideological programme and a more technocratic orientation. The only programmatic aspect is their predominantly economical liberalism (see PO, SDKU, Res Publica, National Revival Party, ANO, SaS). Secondly, parties with a clear nationalist approach entered the arena: in Poland, for instance, the PiS, the League of Polish Parties, and Samoobrona, the latter of which, although not a new party, has suddenly become extremely successful; in Slovakia, the Slovak National Party (SNS) and the orthodox communists (Communist Party of Slovakia (KSS)); in Hungary, the JOBBIK.

Only in the Czech Republic and Hungary has the bipolar competition between two parties settled down, although the recent elections in 2010 changed this picture. In both countries, two new parties entered parliament: In the Czech Republic, TOP99 and VV gained a significant share (one third) of seats, and thus changed the balance of conservatives and social democrats. In Poland, the polarisation between the post-solidarity and the post-communist parties after ten years and three elections seems to have been replaced by the two post-solidarity parties, PiS and PO, which nevertheless do not represent a simple left–right divide. This new bipolarity, though, could give way to a more stable competition pattern in the future. In Slovenia the reshuffling occurred with some delay: In the last election in 2008, the long-dominant party LDS was assigned a marginal role and a new antagonism between the center-right Slovenian Democratic Party (SDS) and the center-left Social Democrats (SD) became apparent. The Baltic states did not develop such a clear bipolar structure; this is especially true for Lithuania and Latvia due to the "odd combination of increasing fragmentation and decreasing polarization" (Ramonaite 2005: 86), making a competitive political space difficult. In Estonia, we have to wait and see if a form of bipolarity will establish itself. The last elections in 2007 could be a first step. In Slovakia, the recent election in 2010 diminished the nationalist pole, which may point to a more centripetal trend; on the other hand, new parties are still entering and hindering the settlement of the competition structure. All in all, the second decade stirred up the power balance in the new party systems in Central Eastern Europe more than it contributed to a stabilisation of the competition patterns.

Table 3: Party-System Types in NMS-2004 (1990–2010)

Type of party system	CZ	EE	HUN	LV	LT	PO	SK	SLO
Two-party system								
Moderate multi-party systems: Two-and-a-half party system								
Moderate multi-party systems with 1 dominant party	1990		**2010**		1992 1996	2001		
Moderate multi-party systems with 2 large parties	1998 2006		2002 2006			1997		
Moderate multi-party systems with a balance of power among the parties	2002 **2010**			**2010**			**2010**	
Extreme multi-party system with 1 dominant party	1992	1992 1995	1990 1994	1993	**2008**		1992 1994 2006	2000
Extreme multi-party system with 2 large parties	1996		1998			1993 2005 2007	1998	2004 **2008**
Extreme multi-party system with a balance of power between the parties		1999 2003 **2007**		1995 1998 2002	2000 2004	1991	1990 2002	1992 1996

Own compilation. Bold years indicate the actual state after 2006 the last election.

Looking at the number of parties, a significant reduction has not taken place either in absolute terms or in terms of effective number of parties (fragmentation). There is no country in which the absolute number of parties reduced in a significant way. In Lithuania, the number of parties even increased. The fragmentation displays a mixed record: Only three countries show a gradual and steady reduction (Estonia, Slovenia and Poland), whereas compared to the first election, fragmentation slightly increased in Latvia and doubled in the Czech Republic and Lithuania. Taking the average since the first elections, all countries display a high fragmentation of electoral parties except Hungary (see Table 3).[7]

Both the classification of the party systems and the analysis of the fragmentation point to the continuing dynamics of the party landscape, but behind these data there is even more fluidity. Thus the Polish party system actually comprises six parties, as it did in 1997, but only two of them have had a permanent parliamentarian representation since then; the rest are new parties or split-offs. The cases of the Czech and Hungarian party systems also show that stability in terms of number of parties does not reveal much about the de facto fluctuation in the decline and disappearance of parties, the emergence of new parties, and the fissions and fusions of parties. Hence, all these phenomena significantly shape the essence of party systems. Scholars often relate "stabili-

---

7 Fragmentation is considered low <3, medium 3–5, and high >5.

Deficits in Democratic Quality? 143

ty" of party systems to a low effective number of parties or to a low electoral volatility. These indicators, however, are not sufficiently meaningful.

Table 4: Absolute and Effective Number of Parties in the NMS-2004 (1990–2010)[8]

		1st	2nd	3rd	4th	5th	6th	7th	Ø
CZ	P	4	8	6	5	5	5	5	5.4
	ENEP	3.5	7.29	5.41	4.63	4.8	3.88	6.94	5.2
EE	P	7	7	7	5	6			6.4
	ENEP	6.6	6.03	6.88	5.43	5.02			6.0
HUN	P	7	6	5	4	5	5		5.3
	ENEP	6.71	5.5	4.64	2.84	2.7	3.13		4.2
LV	P	8	9	6	6	7			7.2
	ENEP	6.26	9.96	7.03	6.8	7.51			7.5
LT	P	5	9	7	7	10			7.6
	ENEP	3.83	7.92	5.58	5.78	8.9			6.4
PO	P	9	6	5	7	6	6		6.5
	ENEP	13.83	9.79	5.0	4.5	5.86	3.32		7.05
SK	P	7	5	7	6	7	6	6	6.28
	ENEP	5.85	6.14	5.9	5.33	8.86	6.11	5.54	6.21
SLO	P	8	7	7	8	7	7		7.60
	ENEP	8.46	6.34	5.15	5.91	4.94			6.16

Own compilation. Numbers from first elections until 1998 from Siaroff (2000), numbers from 1998 on based on own calculation.

In order to assess the form and the performance (interaction) of party systems, we would need more indicators. Mainwaring and Scully (1995) introduced the concept of institutionalisation and thereby a concept for analysing and comparing party systems beyond the classical indicators. Institutionalisation is defined as a process "by which a practice or organization becomes well established and widely known, if not universally accepted" (Mainwaring/Scully 1995: 4). Moreover, institutionalisation is meant to produce stable party systems that can support and enhance the democratic consolidation of the political system on the whole, yet Mainwaring and Scully argue that party-system institutionalisation is important to democratic consolidation (ibidem: 1). Mainwaring and Scully create a dichotomy of institutionalised versus inchoate party systems and establish four criteria for assessing party systems: stability in patterns of inter-party competition; party roots in society; legitimacy of parties and elections; and party organisation. Mainwaring and Torcal suggested applying a continuum model because it is more appropriate to show progress or regression (Mainwaring/Torcal 2006: 237).

In order to get more accurate indicators, Mainwaring and Scully's concept has been modified and refined, especially in terms of operationalisation (Mainwaring/Torcal 2006, Jones 2007, Croissant 2008). With the same intention, I suggest two more criteria be met. Measuring the inter-party competition only by volatility gives a limited view of

---

[8] The absolute number of parties is counted as parties with >3% of vote. The effective number of electoral parties is calculated according the Laakso-Taagepera formula.

the possible fluidity and dynamics such as the emergence, splits, and mergers of parties. The index of volatility, as Sikk argues, is blind to the parties involved contributing to it (Sikk 2005: 39). Therefore, I added more indicators in this category: new contenders entering parliament and split-offs during the term.[9] Second, Mainwaring and Scully dwell on the criterion "party organisation" merely in a descriptive manner. Actually, this criterion is difficult to operationalise. I add two indicators, which reflect party loyalty and party discipline: the factional defection of deputies (party-hopping), and the number of independents – not elected independent candidates but rather the number of parliament members who become independents during a term.

Table 5: Indicators for Measuring Party-System Institutionalisation

Criteria	Indicators
Stability in patterns of inter-party competition	-Volatility -*New contenders entering parliament** -*Split-offs**
Party roots in society	-Party age -Party identification -Party membership
Legitimacy of parties and elections	-Trust in parties
Party organisation	-*Fractional migration of deputies** -*Independent deputies**

Own compilation.
*Indicators in italics are generated by the author and added to the model of Mainwaring/Scully (1995).

3.1 Inter-party competition

Again, a high degree of dynamism in electoral volatility during the transition period is nothing unusual. Voters still have to develop a party loyalty, and parties have to form a party identity. A low party attachment in the first elections, therefore, is not surprising. In the future, this volatility is expected to reduce. The experience of the first (e.g. post-war Germany) and second waves (Southern Europe) of democratisation shows that in the first fifteen years in Western Europe, a standard of approximately 12% to 14% of volatility had been reached. Regarding the NMS-2004, such a settling down did not occur. Although there is a general decreasing trend, the numbers remain high – consi-

---

9 I speak of "contenders" in order to avoid confusing this indicator with "genuinely new parties" (Sikk 2005: 399). In regards to inter-party competition, it is less important if a newly entering party is "genuinely new". If a party was founded in 1992 and has been operating with little success since then, but ten years later suddenly receives approximately 10% of the votes, this is significant for the competition pattern. The same applies to parties entering parliament after a merger or a split (such parties would be mostly excluded according to Sikk's definition). These parties are new contenders anyway and may thus cause changes in the competition structure and in government-building.

derably higher than in the EU-15; the calculations of Jungerstam-Mulders show an average of 30.6% in the new and 12% in the old EU-Members States (2006: 15).[10] Only Hungary, with 8.1%, scores remarkably low on the volatility scale, even lower than many Western European countries.

Volatility is generally interpreted as an indicator of a lack of social anchoring of parties. Mainwaring (1998) points to the correlation of floating voters and weak roots of the parties in society: The attachment to a party and the constant support across different elections over time preclude the shifting of preferences from one election to the other. Such an attachment requires that parties be deeply rooted in society. Though, the proliferation of parties, as well as the changing offers in the form of newly emerging parties, split-offs, or mergers, make it difficult for voters to act consistently and strategically. The elites repeatedly present new alternatives to the electorate – certain politicians several times in different parties or functions – which hinders the forming of a party's programmatic profile and in consequence the voters' abilities to develop a more permanent party identification. Likewise, the rapid rise and fall of parties, as well as their continued regrouping, prevents citizens from developing firmer party attachments, and thus citizens tend to vote based one short-term factors. Moreover, new parties cannot, of course, be judged on the basis of their previous record (Toka 1998: 592). On one side, the low trust in established parties and low party affiliation of the voters may nurture the emergence of new parties and charismatic politicians acting in a populist manner. Political entrepreneurs seek their political fortunes with new parties, desert their existing ones, and experiment with new alliance configurations. The success of such new formations in turn feeds the notion that other parties could also succeed with this strategy (Millard 2004: 127). On the other hand, recent studies prove that volatile electoral behaviour is not the cause but rather the product of the inconsistent behaviour of the political elite:

> "Elites may not bother to build strong party organizations and develop grassroots connections. They also may not present clear choices or stand for identifiable values, and thus frequently merge, split, dissolve, and create parties that lead to continuing party system instability. Voters simply are not given a chance to vote consistently because the choices with which they are presented differ significantly from election to election." (Tavits 2008: 541)

---

10 Numbers for the elections between 1994 and 2003.

Table 6: Volatility in the NMS-2004 (in %)

	2nd/1st election	3rd/2nd election	4th/3rd election	5th/4th election	6th/5th election	7th/6th election	Ø
CZ	20.2	24.2	16.1	19.7	18.3	31.3	21.6
EE	47.7	26.9	31.4	21.8			32
HUN	21.8	31.0	19.2	07.1	22.7		20.4
LV	51.4	32.5	39.4	32.6			39
LT	41.5	59.3	64.6	33.2			49.65
PO	29.4	63.9	55.8	34.0	25.3		41.7
SK	52.8	23.3	20.2	48.7	39.4	23.8	34.7
SLO	25.3	24.4	18.7	22.2			22.7

Own compilation based on Siaroff 2000 (data 1990–1998) and own calculations.

Constant fluidity of the party systems remains characteristic for the countries analysed, again with the exceptions of Hungary and the Czech Republic. There are three main traits that contribute to this fluidity: 1) the success of new parties, 2) the fissions and fusions of parties, and 3) the instability of parliamentary clubs/factions caused by the party-hopping or factional migration of deputies during the term. The aforementioned reshuffling of the party systems and their power balances was a result of the surprising decline of "traditional" parties and the surprising success of new parties. In Poland, Slovakia, Lithuania and Latvia this resulted in an almost 50% exchange of the parliamentary seats (see Table 7). The second aspect, the fission and fusion phenomenon, consists of split-offs (see Table 8) and mergers. The splitting of a party is often due to conflicts in the leadership of a party and can also occur when a popular protagonist believes he/she has a good chance on his/her own. Mergers and rebranding of parties in some countries has reached an unmanageable state because of the constant recomposition of splinters, renamed parties, mixing up of alliances, etc., such as is the case in Lithuania and Latvia. Furthermore, parties contract electoral alliances in which the parties remain organisational independent. Although such alliances are different to mergers, they may be a prestage of a merger, yet sometimes the parties within such alliances may decide to fuse. Finally, party-hopping means that individual deputies switch parties, parliamentary clubs, or factions during the term. They may migrate from one party to another or become independent members of parliament. Moreover, there is not only defection of deputies, but also expulsion from the party – in CEE a more common practice than in Western Europe – causing the diminishing of the faction or club. The phenomena of factional migration and independent deputies are analysed in the context of party organisation (see Tables 9 and 10).

Deficits in Democratic Quality?

Table 7: New Contenders Entering the NMS-2004 (1990–2010)

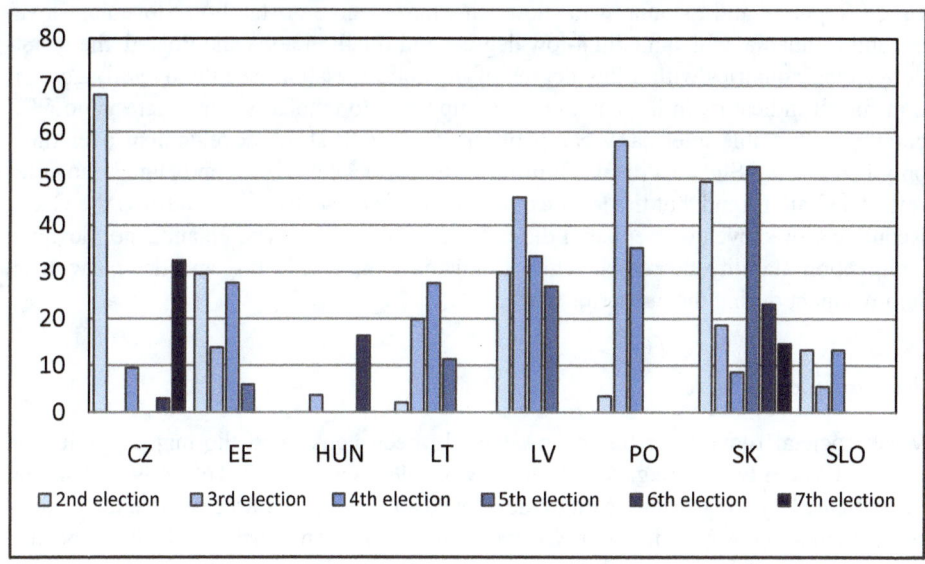

Own compilation and calculation. The columns reflect the seat share (in %) of newly entered contenders (defined as parties that did not have parliamentarian representation in the term before) for all elections (except the first) held in the countries. Electoral alliances are not counted. 0=There has not been any entry of a new contender in this election.

Table 8: Split-offs during a Term in the NMS-2004 (1990–2010)

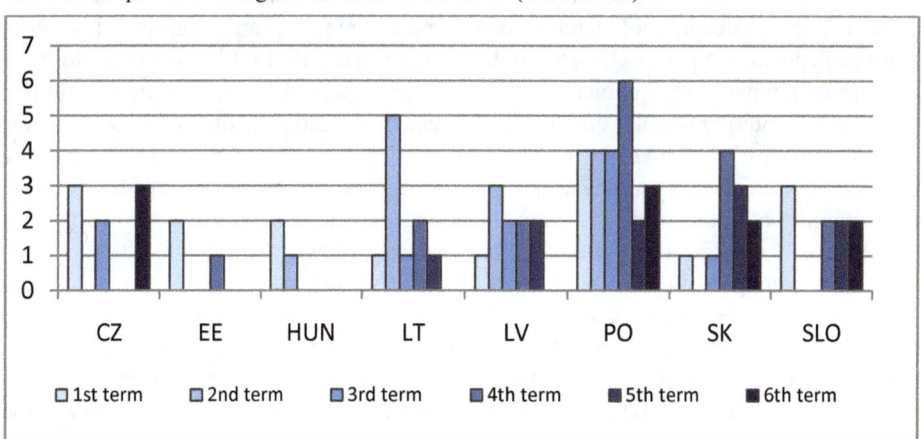

Own compilation and calculation. The columns reflect the number of split-offs of parliamentary factions/clubs/groups during the term. For Slovenia there were no data available for the second and third terms.

The analysis of the inter-party competition crystallises three groups: Hungary, the Czech Republic and Estonia, who show a medium degree of stability; Slovenia, Slovakia and Lithuania, with a medium-low degree; and finally, Latvia and Poland, the worst-performing countries with a low degree of institutionalisation (see the overall aggregation for all indicators in the Annex). It is important to emphasise that there is no CEE country with stable inter-party competition. If we look at the development over time, only Estonia and Slovenia display a linear stabilisation. The Czech and Hungarian cases reflect a similar trend, but the last election in 2010 represents a clear setback: the Czech Republic scored even worse than it did in the first term. In Latvia, Poland, and Slovakia, competition stability decreased while Lithuania experienced ups and downs with an improvement during the last term.

3.2 Party roots in society

Weak societal roots of parties have generally been considered the major problem in Central Eastern Europe (e.g. Agh 1996, Lewis 1996, Segert 1997, Toka 1997). This can be explained by their origin, as they developed in a top-down process as elite projects rather than in the way common in Western democracies. The parties in the post-socialist democracies mainly developed as "parties in the state". The parties have so far failed in their task of reaching out to society. Parties and their founders aspire less to represent their constituents, communicate with voters, and serve public interest. They prefer office-seeking strategies to policy-seeking strategies. Parties thus have been characterised as "uncoupled" (Lawson, 1999) or as "floating" (Rose et al. 2001) above society in the form of volatile electoral platforms lacking distinctive programme definition and structure. Hence, floating voters and a weak rooting of the parties in society are correlated. When parties are deeply rooted, most voters support the same party over time. Likewise, party rootedness and personalism are linked (Mainwaring 1998). If voters begin to identify less with a party, their choices might be based on personalities. Eclectic recruitment practices like putting popular but unaffiliated persons – and sometimes novices – on the party list undermines the voters' and the partisans' programmatic party orientation. The proliferation of lists and candidates and the lack of clear programmatic profiles diminish the capability of voters to develop an attachment to a party and to make strategic choices. The clarity and focus of value-based choices would lower the volatility (Toka 1998b: 607). This is supported by the findings of Mainwaring and Torcal, who demonstrate that ideological links between voters and parties, though important, are not the only means by which voters become attached to parties and by which parties consequently become rooted in society. If there is a weak link between voters' ideological and programmatic positions and their preferred party, voters are more likely to drift from one party to the next (2006: 211f).[11]

---

11 Mainwaring/Torcal's figures do not include Slovakia. Furthermore, they found that this hypothesis does not apply to the Czech Republic, where electoral volatility remains moderate to high despite high ideological structuring (2006: 211).

In fluid party systems, individual personalities dominate at the expense of party organisations; charismatic, often populist, party leaders and short-term mobilisation before elections prevail, while issue-orientation and defined programmatic profiles are lacking. Programmatic party competition is often replaced by clientelistic or personalistic mechanisms of mobilisation; charisma, clientelism, and patronage, however, hinder stable political competition and its institutionalisation (Tiemann 2006: 29, Mainwaring/Torcal 2006: 215ff). Mainwaring and Scully (1995: 9) analyse societal party roots by examining the difference between presidential and legislative voting. This method is, however, only partially applicable to CEE since, first, presidents are not directly elected in every country, and second, presidents of CEE countries do not have the same constitutional position as in Latin America. The second and more applicable indicator used by the authors is party age (1995: 13), although that indicator needs to be modified. Few of the Central Eastern European parties qualify as historic, as is the case in Latin America. Cases where those parties have attracted stronger than average loyalty are difficult to weigh because this effect can be attributed to historical continuity or to the organisational encapsulation of voters (Toka 1997: 104f). For the purposes of the present analysis, I therefore consider the age of parliamentarian parties since their (re-)founding after regime change and the proportion of parties in current parliaments in which the parties are ten years of age or younger (see Table 9). Only Hungary and Slovenia dispose of a high continuity of parties in parliament. In the Czech Republic and Hungary the last election changed the picture significantly; in the 2006 elections, the number of young parties would have been zero. In Poland, the high number can be traced back to the fundamental reshuffling in the Polish party system in 2001, when the important parties of the first post-autocratic decade more or less disappeared, giving way to the main new contenders PO and PiS, who hold about 80% of the seats. Hence, the majority of the countries have a medium share of young parties.

Table 9: Party Age in the NMS-2004

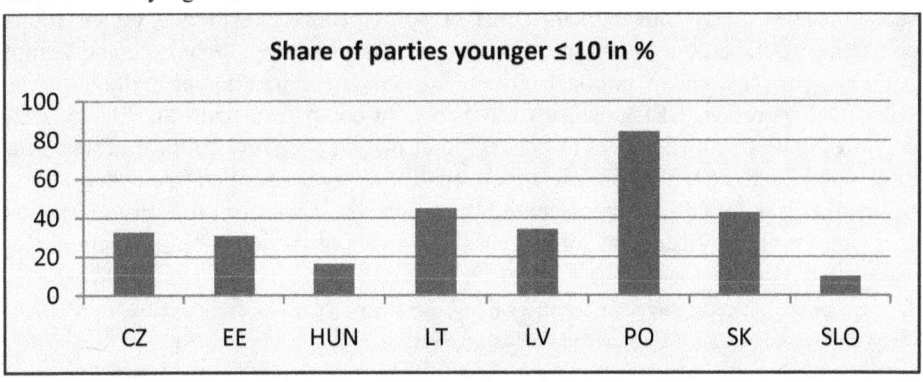

Own compilation and calculation. The party age is calculated as a seat share (in %) of parliamentary parties ten years old or younger in the last election of each country.

According to Mainwaring and Scully, party roots are furthermore measured in terms of partisan identification and party membership. In respect to these two indicators, the main problem is the data situation.[12] Comparing the sources available, I noted an increase in party identification, sometimes only slightly (in Poland and Hungary), sometimes significantly (in the Czech Republic and Slovenia).[13] The level of party identification varies from around 30% (Slovenia) to double that (Czech Republic). All in all, party identification in the NMS-2004 is lower than it is in the rest of the EU (Gabriel 2008: 205), and it is stabilised at low levels (Webb/White 2007b: 351). The data on partisanship are, however, too limited, and more and regular scores are needed to conceive a more convincing account of party attachment (Lewis 2008: 10). The data situation is quite similar regarding party membership: It is difficult to get data and impossible to get continuous numbers. Moreover, the question is if numbers of party membership are meaningful in the first place.

Table 10: Party Membership in the NMS-2004

Party Membership Rate in %	CZ	EE	HUN	LT	LV	PO	SK	SLO
	2.2	3.4	2.0	2.0	1.2	1.5	2.3	n.n.

Own compilation on the basis of Webb/White 2007b.

Party membership is rather low: The average is 2.3%, which is significantly lower than in established democracies (5.5%).[14] This is consistent with the fact that mass parties did not evolve in Central Eastern Europe, as I show below. Kitschelt et al. expected framework or cadre to dominate, rather than mass parties. Moreover, they argue that mass party membership was no longer a critical feature that affected the quality of democracy anyway (1999: 395ff). Indeed, reduced involvement as a party member can be substituted by other, conventional forms of participation, like joining organisations, contacting politicians, or non-conventional forms like protesting, organising and signing petitions, participating in political strikes, etc. Given such different methods of involvement, however, CEE countries score low. In comparison with the EU-15, CEE countries have the lowest level of conventional participation and political protest (Gabriel/Völkl 2008: 282, 285). Political protest is chosen twice as often by Southern Europeans than it is by CEE citizens, three times more by Western Europeans and almost four times more by Scandinavian citizens. The levels of participation illustrate a deep

---

12 There are no continuous data series for all eight countries from 1990 until today. Therefore, party identification is discussed here but not included in the data aggregation.

13 This is based on data from the Comparative Study of Electoral Systems (CSES) of 1996/98 and that of 2001/02 and the European Electoral Studies (EES) of 2004. There were no data for the Baltic states from CSES.

14 It is difficult to obtain reliable numbers on party membership. Therefore, data from different sources can differ quite a bit. The data used here are based on Webb/White 2007: 348f, who calculated 2.3%. Own calculations for the eight here considered countries were slightly lower (2.1%).

cleavage between the EU-15 and the NMS. Only Slovenia is moving toward the EU-15 in this regard. The party roots are still shallow in general.

3.3 Legitimacy of parties

It has been observed that trust in political institutions is generally decreasing in Europe and that parties, in particular, are regarded more skeptically. But, again, the trust of the NMS-2004 is significantly lower – since the EU accession, twice as low – than in the rest of the EU. There are only two countries with a positive trend, namely Estonia and Slovakia. Slovakia's very low score in 2001 (6%) tripled in 2009 and thus represents the highest trust level in CEE; Estonia displays comparable progress. The rest of the countries experienced a decrease in trust levels, which, in Hungary, Latvia, and Poland was rather remarkable as it reduced by half in each of those nations.

This distrust of parties and representative institutions in general does not mean that citizens question the existence of parties and parliament. Apparently they believe that even *bad* elected representatives are better than *no* elected representatives. Thus approximately three-quarters of the EU-NMS reject getting rid of parliament and closing down parties (Rose 2007: 116). But again, more data are needed.

Table 11: Trust in Parties in the NMS-2004 from 2001–2009

	2001	2002	2003	2004	2005	2006	2007	2008	2009	Ø
CZ	12	11	13	10	11	14	11	12	12	12
EE	12	13	18	15	18	16	22	19	17	17
HUN	18	24	20	13	14	14	8	8	9	13
LT	7	8	11	9	5	8	7	10	5	8
LV	7	9	18	9	8	9	7	5	2	8
PO	14	10	6	3	7	7	8	7	7	8
SK	6	11	11	8	7	16	13	16	18	12
SLO	12	16	14	16	14	20	13	17	9	15
Ø NMS-2004	11	13	14	7	10	10	11	12	10	11
Ø EU15	17	18	15	16	19	19	25	29	25	20

Own compilation based on the Candidate Countries Barometer (CEEB) autumn 2001 and 2002, spring 2003 and 2004, and Eurobarometer (EB) 64, 66, 68, 70, 72.

3.4 Party organization

Country experts continuously report on the weak organisational structure of the Central Eastern European parties (Segert/Machos 1995, Segert/Stöss/Niedermayer 1996, Pridham/Lewis 1996, Dawisha/Parrot 1997, Lewis 2000, Jungerstam-Mulders 2006, Webb/White 2007, Bútora/Gyárfášová/Mesežnikov/Skladony 2007, Bos/Segert 2008). Only the Czech Republic seems to be an exception, yet we can recognise an increased organisational capacity there. Moreover, the Czech parties have managed to establish a monopoly of the decision-making process (Kopecky 2006: 125ff). Communist-successor parties principally had an advantage, disposing of a better infrastructure, a broader member base, and more resources. This advantage also applied to the non-reformed communist parties like the KSČM in the Czech Republic, the KSS in Slovakia and the LSP in Latvia. The term "cartel party" often is applied to CEE countries. This party model implies that, first, parties are professional organisations that depend on the state for their survival, e.g. through state funding, and second, that parties slowly retreated from society. Thus, cartel parties reduce their functions to governing and mainly orient themselves towards the maintenance of executive power (Katz/Mair 1995, Krouwel 2006). Due to the fact that most NMS-2004 parties rely on state funding and that they are definitely not deeply rooted in society, I suggest classifying them as cartel parties, though the direction of development is different from the traditional model of cartel parties: The NMS-2004 parties are not moving towards the state and decoupling from society, but were primarily created in parliament as top-down parties, or by individual persons or small elite groups, and thus emphasise the party in office rather than on the ground (Mair 1997: 183f). On the other hand, this elite-based origin of the parties, their weak organisational structure, and a candidate-centred orientation combined with clientelistic networks and particularistic rewards points to them being a modern "elite parties". To adequately illuminate the different party models in CEE, one would need to conduct a much more thorough examination.

It is quite clear and also generally agreed upon that the "mass party" model does not exist in CEE. Electoralist parties prevail, and these can be classified as catch-all, programmatic, or personalistic parties (Gunther/Diamond 2001). Programmatic electoralist parties are mainly those "traditional" parties that predominantly originate from the first post-autocratic decade or as social democratic, conservative, confessional (Christian democratic) forces or as representatives of particular interests, such as agrarian parties. Catch-all electoralist parties, defined by their shallow organisation, a superficial and vague ideology and predominantly vote-maximising orientation, arose in almost all CEE countries as a new phenomenon during the described turmoil after the first three or four elections. These are parties that often demonstrated a certain anti-establishment attitude and declared themselves to be "center" parties. It is difficult to distinguish some of these parties from the personalistic or populist parties that also mushroomed at the beginning of 2000. Common traits of all electoralist parties are: 1) that they utilise modern campaigning techniques (especially television) and prefer to use the media rather than party-member mobilisation, and 2) that a personalistic appeal prevails. The only exception might be the ideological or interest-based parties like Christian democrats, greens, or agrarian parties, which have a relatively loyal and clearly defined group of supporters and therefore need less modern campaigning.

In a highly institutionalised party system, parties should not only be well organised but also have loyal party elites and a solid party discipline in the legislature (Mainwaring/Scully 1995: 16). The fission and fusion phenomenon I discussed earlier gives evidence about the loyalty of party elites. Personal animosities, the popularity of a person with good prospects for the next election, and sometimes having to deal with a party leader with an authoritarian style can all be reasons for leaving a party and founding a new one. While in the Czech Republic (until 2010), Hungary, Slovenia, and Estonia the number of such split-offs is negligable, in the other CEE countries, split-offs continue to be common (see Table 8).

Table 12: Factional Defection during the Term in the NMS-2004 (1998–2009)

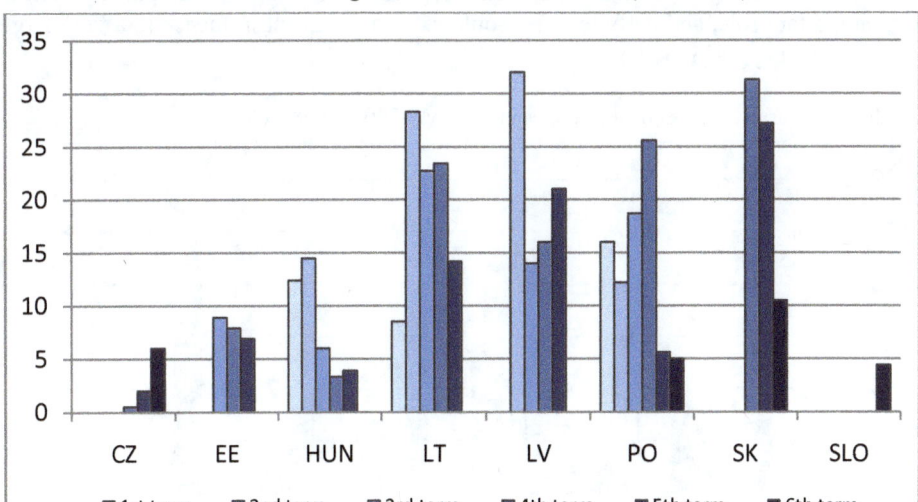

Own compilation. The columns reflect the seat share (in %) of deputies who defected from their parliamentary faction/club/group. The difference between the strength of the parliamentary faction/club/group at the beginning and the end of the term is accounted for. Multiple migration of one deputy is not taken into account. There were no numbers available for the first three terms in the Czech Republic, for the first two terms in Estonia and Latvia, and for all but the last term in Slovenia (2004–2008).

Likewise, the defection of deputies in some countries is a frequent practice, and most remarkable there are cases where deputies even migrate more than once. In Lithuania, 18 deputies – almost 13% of the assembly – changed factions more than three times in the 2004 term (and that number does not take into account the renaming of parties). Sometimes, not only individual deputies but whole groups defect. They either become independents, individually migrate to another party, or found a new party which then would be defined as a split-off. Thus, the number of independents is also interesting to examine. There was a peak of factional migration of around 30% during the reshuffling of the third and fourth elections which then dropped in all countries. Sometimes, an increase in transfer of deputies and thus of independent parliamentarians took place at the end of a given term. These often massive decompositions in the parliament occur because deputies are weighing their best chances for reelection (f.e. in 2009 in the

Czech Republic after announcing early elections[15]). The independents in the NMS-2004 are predominantly deputies who defected during the term and not unaffiliated candidates who ran for election. The average for the last two terms and the current term is remarkably high, between 4.5% (Hungary) and almost 17% (Slovakia). All in all, the hypothesis of the mid-1990s turned out to be right: Parties would continue to develop as formations with loose electoral constituencies, party membership would play a relatively unimportant role, and party leaders would exert a dominant influence to a very large extent (Kopecky 1995: 517f).

Table 13: Share of Independent Deputies in the NMS-2004 (1998–2009)

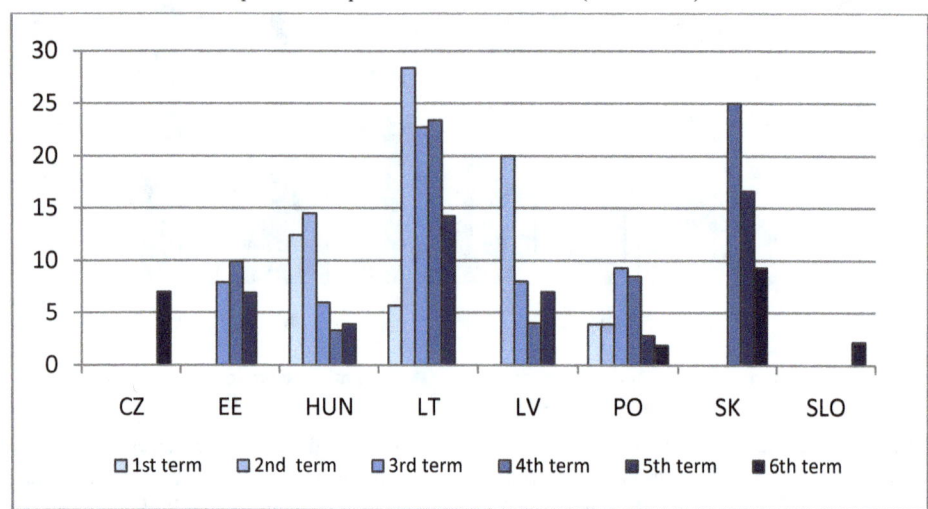

Own compilation. The columns reflect the seat share (in %) of independent deputies at the end of the term. There were no numbers available for the first three terms in the Czech Republic, for the first two terms in Estonia and Latvia, and for all but the last term in Slovenia.

In respect to the criterion party organization – which reflects the organisational level of the parties but also the behaviour of the party elite – three groups crystallise (similar to the criterion "inter-party competition"): a medium-ranking group made up of the Czech Republic and Poland, directly followed by Hungary; the medium-low-ranking Estonia; and the worst-performing, low-scoring group made up of Latvia, Lithuania and Slovakia, who all lack, in addition, any improvement over the course of time. Poland and Hungary present a clear development towards more stability.

Regarding the aggregated results of all four criteria (see Annex) the picture is different, although, again, three groups appear. Again, no country displays a high or even medium-high degree of institutionalisation. Out of all the countries, Hungary is the only one with a medium institutionalised party system, although in the last three terms Hungary's stability has decreased. Latvia and Lithuania have weakly institutionalised party systems,

---

15 The elections initially planned for autumn 2009 were postponed until June 2010.

Deficits in Democratic Quality?

and, in addition, there is no clear trend towards improvement. The remaining five countries display levels of institutionalisation between medium and medium-low. It is evident that even if some traits like fragmentation and volatility improve, the partial institutionalisation of the party systems persists in most CEE countries. Likewise, the countries could neither reach a solid state of party organisation, nor fully stabilise inter-party competition. Moreover, the socio-economic cleavage has not become as dominant as one might have thought (Jungerstam-Mulders 2006: 245). All cases – including the more stable ones – are shaped by a conflictive competition pattern dominated by personalism, often combined with populism and clientelistic structures, and a vote- and office-seeking orientation. In those cases where a clear-cut, highly identifiable governmental alternative emerged, there is a high level of polarisation, which is not pre-determined by the attitudes of the citizens but rather produced by conscious actions of the parties (Enyedi 2006: 198). The main problems in the performance of the party systems turned out to be their persistent fluidity, highly conflictual inter-party competition (which goes along with behavioural polarisation), and the low party–citizen linkage.

Table 14: Party-System Institutionalisation (PSI) of the NMS-2004[16]

1,0 (high)	1,5 (medium-high)	2,0 (medium)	2,5 (medium-low)	3,0 (low)
		HU EE SLO SK PO CZ	LV LT	

4. Instability of party systems and the implications for the quality of democracy

What are the concrete implications for the quality of democracy in these countries? Looking at the three dimensions of democratic quality described in the first chapter, we can trace implications mainly to the procedural and output dimensions.

Regarding the *procedural dimension,* parties have a monopoly on accountable and responsive representation. Jungestam-Mulders states that in CEE, parties have a monopoly on public office positions, but their representative performance is poor. Parties are governing rather than representative agents (Jungerstam-Mulders 2006: 249). This statement is underpinned by the findings of my analysis, which points to several deficits in this respect. Split-offs, defections (including expelling), and party-switching of deputies between elections do not only impede the structuring of alternative choices for voters and hinder a strong and stable citizen–party linkage. The shallow party discipline

---

[16] According to Mainwaring/Scully, institutionalisation is calculated by the scale from high (1.0), medium-high (1.5), medium (2.0), medium-low (2.5) to low (3.0). I follow Mainwaring/Torcal (2006: 207) who suggest applying a continuum model because it is more appropriate to show progress or regression.

and the predominance of office-seeking goals (often combined with a populist or polarizing approach) pose a serious problem for representation, yet, they question the responsibility of the individual legislators, they undermine his/her retrospective accountability and reduce the predictability of the programmatic input. It seems trivial to indicate the idea of representation in this context: Independently of the electoral system, and if the voter decided explicitly for a certain candidate (or a list) and independently of the question if the voter took his decision primarily because of the programme of the party or on the basis of the individual candidate, the elected deputy represents a certain party programme and hence the preferences of the citizens who voted for him. The person elected assumes the responsibility to represent these preferences in the parliament and additionally in government or opposition in order to advocate for a certain policy formulation. Voters would judge this deputy and his party in the next elections based on his record. If individual deputies switch parties, if a group of deputies leave their party and establish a new one, or remain independents, a serious violation of the assumed responsibility can occur, especially if the factional transfer is not based on a decision of "consciousness" as the "last option" but instead due to the intention to improve the chances for the next election. Thus, the excessively vote-seeking orientation of the political elite leading to factional migration and split-offs, combined with diffuse programmatic offers, seriously undermines representativeness (Webb/White 365). While party break-ups and fusions in the run-up to elections are less problematic because voters are potentially able to include these new perspectives into their strategic choices, party-hopping and party-splitting have more severe implications during the term: Voters learn to be more uncertain about the relevance of the act of choosing and voting itself. They may learn that programmatic orientations of individual politicians are fluid. Hence, this will make a party–voter linkage difficult and may even lead to voters learning to regard voting as irrelevant. The degree of split-offs and defections during term cast a damning light on the function of representation in parliament.

This finding is also underscored by the aspect of recruitment of political personnel and office-holders: In programmatic parties like the Czech ČSSD and ODS, the Hungarian SzDSz and FIDESZ parties nominate their candidates according to their electoral appeal and – similar to in Western democracies – a potential candidate's position in the party (support of important factions) also plays a role. In personalistic parties it goes without saying that the charismatic party leader is the dominant figure. The support in the party is achieved by a person-centred, often authoritarian style as well as by a clientelistic reward system. In the young democracies of the NMS-2004, these parties' leaders are sometimes the founders of the parties themselves (see Vladimir Mečiar and HZDS, Lech and Jaroslaw Kaczynski and PiS), and whether they would allow (or survive) an elite exchange or reshuffling of the top posts remains an unanswered question. We can observe a third case of recruitment in the Czech Republic and in Hungary, where expert governments were installed in spring 2009. The Czech Prime Minister Topolanek, who resigned after a vote of no-confidence, was followed by Jan Fischer (who was appointed by the president, Vaclav Klaus); the Hungarian government had been in crisis since Ferenc Gyurscany lost the majority in 2008, and when he resigned, he installed an expert government led by the former minister of economy, Gordon Bajnai. In Hungary independent prime ministers were nominated in the past: Ferenc Gyurscany himself and his predecessor, Peter Medgyessy.

In CEE, political novices and independents entering the political arena is not generally unusual. High-profile personalities, often without political experience or party affiliation, try to benefit from their popularity or recognition by initiating a new party: like the Latvian President of the National Bank Einars Repse (New Era), the Estonian President of the National Bank Siim Kallas (Reform Party), the Slovak media mogul Pavel Ruzko (ANO), the TV-men Arunas Valinskas (Lithuanian National Resurrection Party) and John Radek (VV, Czech Republic). The position of unaffiliated and inexperienced party leaders is weaker in the policy-making process (when the support of the party is needed) and in sustaining the government (in critical situations, the loyalty of the party will be low).

A further phenomenon are businessmen – or "oligarchs" who form parties like the lithuanians Viktor Uspaskich (Lithuanian Labour Party) and Rolandas Paksas (Liberal Democratic Party, now: Order and Justice), the Latvians Ainars Šlesers (New Party) and Andris Škele (People's Party), one of the richest persons in Latvia. These "oligarchs" belong to the economic elite of the country and seem to strive to political power in order to expand their influence. Often they own media (journals or TV stations) so they are able to influence the public opinion. Oligarchs' parties survive more easily yet the financial flow from private sources is guaranteed. Moreover, great expenditures during the electoral campaigning are possible. Likewise, parties commonly enrich their lists with prominent or popular persons. It has become a problem, especially in the Baltic States, that prominent persons on lists for European Parliament or municipal/regional elections do not fill the positions after having been elected. Sometimes, political leaders who rely on their special popularity even are involved in several party foundings (e.g. Paksas in Lithuania was involved in founding or merging three parties, the Latvian politician Ainars Šlesers in two).

Moreover, the instability of elite behaviour damages accountability. The more frequent the changes in the party structure (defection, party-hopping, etc.) and government (coalition break-ups, new prime ministers, etc.), the fewer the possibilities of retrospective accountability and responsiveness. Accountability requires transparency in political procedures; citizens need to comprehend the programmatic rationale and to reconstruct the actions of the representatives. Inconsistent political elites that switch parties (possibly even more than once) or found new parties during the term hinder transparency and loosen the link between the representative and the voter. On the other hand, responsiveness is often artificially constructed in the form of populism or hypermobilisation (see Hungary). Actually, both phenomena – lack of accountability and responsiveness, and populist mobilisation – rupture the "chain of responsiveness" (Powell 2005) rather than enforce it. Populist parties are apparently more well suited only for mobilising citizens or for channelling voters' preferences, assuming that populist approaches reflect "the voice of the people". But there are some risks: Populist and personalistic strategies may attract voters who may at first feel more well represented, but the moment the candidate loses popularity or trust, voter alienation increases (Gunther/Diamond 2001: 29). Eventually, populism can even produce more apathy after the successful mobilisation.

Regarding the patterns of competition, Mair's prognosis – that elites in the post-communist democracies will prove substantially more conflictual and adversarial than is usually the case in established democracies – can also be witnessed in the second post-autocratic decade after 1989 (1997: 193). It can be observed that elites do opt for conflictual rather than coalescent strategies. Interestingly, this applies also, or especially, to the most institutionalised cases. Consequences of this adversarial elite behaviour are a) problems in the governing coalition, b) a government's majoritarian style, or c) the opposition's obstructive style (f.e. excessive use of votes of no confidence or of referendum). Thus in the Czech Republic, the small majority and the difficult governing situation of PM Topolanek was permanently challenged by votes of no confidence (five in two years), which finally succeeded. Thus the Czech opposition produced the collapse of the government during the time the Czech Republic held the all-important EU presidency, thereby consciously damaging the country's image and position in the EU. Repeatedly organising referenda is another method of weakening the government that, for example, the Hungarian opposition employed in 2007. Three referenda were initiated against the reform projects (health care and education) of the government. Moreover, Hungarian FIDESZ opposition attacked a reform that, as a liberal-conservative party, it normally would have endorsed. The success of the polls led to the demission of the responsible minister, the withdrawal of the coalition partner, and thus to a minority government being replaced finally by a caretaker government and an independent, technocrat prime minister. As a result, Hungary, for a period of one year, was "administered" rather than "governed", and the reform projects were put on hold.

A rough conclusion could be drawn that the major problems in competition are the low willingness to accommodate and the persisting adversarial attitudes of the political elite. There is competition, but not about programmes or issues, but rather competition of a highly conflictual and highly personalistic nature. Weakening or even overthrowing the incumbent takes precedence over policy orientation, public interest, and the common good. This type of prioritising affects the public perception of the political elite, which is reflected in the decreasing trust in political parties, parliaments, and governments. Moreover, the elite behaviour is not likely to enhance the already weak linkage between party and electorate. Competition is not sufficiently accompanied by a responsible way of conflict settlement and what Schmitter and Karl call "contingent consent" (1996: 57). Competition must go hand in hand with cooperation, or, actors "must cooperate in order to compete" (53).

This leads us to the aspects of participation. I did not include the indicator of voter turnout in this analysis, yet it is considered as contentious (Parry/Moyser 1994). Regarding the tendency of turnout rates, there has been a clear decrease in voter turnout over the course of the twenty post-autocratic years. Only one country, Hungary, remained at the same level. The already notorious group of Slovakia, Latvia, and Lithuania displays significant drops (from 24% to 40%). Poland, on the other hand, began at a very low level (43.2%), so the highest electoral participation level ever, 53.88%, which occurred in the last election represents an increase. Although electoral participation also is declining in Western Europe, the NMS-2004 lags behind the EU-15 by approximately 10%. Moreover, the level of involvement in alternative political activities, such as protests, is

Deficits in Democratic Quality?

also low in CEE. The decreasing electoral participation along with the low participation in other aspects, including membership in interest organisations, underscores the fact that the deficits of parties regarding their social functions can barely be compensated for by other intermediary organisations.

Parties and party systems channel input from society and transport it into the decision-making process. It is widely acknowledged that the role of parties in terms of in the aggregation of interests, the mobilisation of voters, and the integration of citizens has decreased in general. Parties cannot claim to have a monopoly on those functions, as Schmitter states (2001). Thus, it is plausible to point to the other intermediary systems like interest organisations, which can partially fulfill the parties' social functions, and where established democracies or new democracies in other regions are concerned, this may be the case. In Central Eastern Europe, however, social organisations and civil society barely constitute a functional substitute, as they have their own – often significant – weaknesses. Therefore it is doubtful that they could assume these functions and thus compensate for the deficits of parties and party systems. In Central Eastern Europe interest organisations have an especially weak position, not only as input givers, but also as agencies for output functions such as policy-making. The same applies to civil-society structures that only contribute marginally to the political arena. Indeed, in some countries there is even a tendency of parties to monopolise the control of decision-making, such as in the Czech Republic where parties influence all major areas of the government, or in Slovakia where former Prime Minister Fico openly expressed his negative opinions of NGOs and the media.

If interest groups and civil society do not substitute or compensate for these deficits of parties and party systems, who will do so? To a large extent, functions like agenda-setting, issue-structuring and social integration are fulfilled by electronic media, primarily television. This does not bode well if we look to the prevailing low-quality television in many countries. As electoralist parties dominate in CEE, voter mobilisation likewise takes place via media, again mainly via television. Parties generally attach less importance to enrolling citizens and prefer to draw on loose networks of supporters at election time, whom they mobilise using the mass media as a means of communication. Personalistic and populist parties depend equally on television for their campaigning, which focuses on presenting the candidate or the populist message to the maximum number of citizens possible. Hence, the only intermediary entity that substitutes for parties in most social functions is television; social organisations and civil society do not.

The instability of party systems also has consequences for *government effectiveness.* Most of the time, high levels of fragmentation make it necessary to build coalitions, coalition governments being the predominant type of government in CEE. In order to obtain a majority, most governments need at least three parties, often even more than that. Such broad coalitions imply a high degree of heterogeneity and the intrinsic risk of internal frictions, which can result in the breakaway of one coalition partner or, in the worst case, the end of the coalition. The most common reason for the dissolution of governments is indeed a change in the composition of the coalition.[17] In the case of minority governments, a breakaway of partners is even more likely to finish the government and to produce early elections. Split-offs and deputy-switching can influence the delicate power balance in the government. The Dzurinda II government in Slovakia (2002–2006) is a good example of the melting away of coalition partners – first in 2003, then in 2005 and finally in 2006 – with the consequence of early elections. The same happened in Latvia in 2006 with the exodus of the chairman of the parliament, which caused the founding of the Civic Democracy Party and led to a fragile majority (71:141). The Czech Republic, where since 1998 government-building has been difficult due to small margins or stalemate situations, also illustrates that the defection of even just one member of parliament can change the balance of power. Thus the government from 2002 to 2006 had a one-vote majority;[18] the result of the 2006 elections was a stalemate of 100 to 100, and the extremely difficult task of government-building was only possible with the silent support of two opposition deputies. Analysis of the coalition-building in Central Eastern Europe emphasises that the "traditional" approaches tested for Western Europe cannot fully explain the variation between the countries (Nikolenyi 2004, Grotz 2007). There is a partial correlation between the stability of the cabinet and the fragmentation of the party system, a finding confirmed by the fact that the Polish and Slovak governments are less stable than the Czech and Hungarian governments. What cannot be verified, however, is whether the type of government is the decisive factor, meaning that minimum winning coalitions or minority governments are more stable than surplus coalitions.

Therefore, the precarious forming and sustaining of stable majorities in several cases in CEE countries also impacts executive effectiveness. Splitting also endangers the remaining factions; due to the generally weak cohesion of the parties, deputies may feel motivated to switch to the new club. Defections can even lead to the dissolution of factions. Moreover, new parties entering government responsibility are definitely more challenged in forming and sustaining effective governments (Schmitter 2001: 79). This also applies to the lack of experience of novices. Popular candidates with no experience in politics who decide to stand in elections often promote a sort of "anti-establishment", "fresh", and often "anti-corruption" policy and are able to gain broad electoral support due to their renown and alternative campaigning styles (especially when they are TV personalities). However, these novices, once elected, may fail to fulfill the high expectations they evoked when they were campaigning. Often they do not even enter the next elections, or they turn to populist methods. Moreover, novices may perform weakly in realising their policy programmes and projects, as they have, of course, generally no experience in policy-making processes, in achieving the necessary consensus, and in forming and maintaining coalitions. They are also generally inexperienced in leading a party, and often unprofessional approaches of novices lead to party splits or defection in one's own party or to tensions between coalition partners. In some countries (Poland,

---

17 This and the following calculations are mainly based on the excellent data collection of Müller-Rommel/Schultze/Harfst/Fettelschoß (2008).

18 Later it grew to a two-vote majority due to the desertion of an ODS deputy.

Slovakia, Latvia, Lithuania) broad and heterogeneous coalitions exist that demand a high degree of consensus orientation as well as leadership skills that novices often lack.

The analysis shows that deficits in party-system institutionalisation definitely have implications for the procedural and effective government dimensions of democratic quality. The examination of the impact on the policy output goes beyond this study. A future research programme would have to look thoroughly at the correlation between instable party systems, executive effectiveness, and policy output.

5. Conclusion: Why the stability of party systems matters

The first task of this study was to examine the degree of institutionalisation of the party systems in Central Eastern Europe. The result is that the majority of the party systems still cannot be evaluated as institutionalised. In two cases (Lithuania and Latvia) the question is if there is evidence that they will ever reach a high degree of institutionalisation. Estonia and Slovenia are on a path towards stability. But only Estonia displays steady and consistent progress in party-system institutionalisation while the rest of the countries are taking slow steps or experiencing ups and downs. The Czech Republic and Hungary constitute two remarkable cases, yet while their party systems displayed an advanced institutionalisation in the first decade of post-autocratic rule, since 2004 however we have been observing signs of a decreasing stability. In Poland and Slovakia the evolution of the party systems in the last two decades has not shown a clear trend; especially in Slovakia the development in the near future remains rather open. This picture does not reflect any regional similarities within the group of the Visegrad countries and within the group of the Baltic countries. This also emphasises that early relations with the EU and early association – as was the case with the Visegrad countries – did not have an influence on a homogenous party-system development in the region.

The study's second intention was to trace whether the performance of the party systems affects the quality of democracy and, if so, which aspects are affected. The main finding is that the fluidity of the party system has consequences for the procedural dimension as well as for the dimension of government effectiveness. Lack of both accountability and transparency will be crystallised as a central problem as long as the erratic elite behaviour produces this considerable flux in the competition structure and the parliamentary representation.

This concluding chapter returns to the question of how party systems' stabilisation, democratic consolidation, and democratic quality are linked. Does weak party-system institutionalisation harm the quality of democracy and the prospects for democratic consolidation, as Mainwaring argues (1998: 79)? Are strong party systems important for the quality of democracy even if they do not contribute to the consolidation of democracy? (Toka 1997: 121). Regarding the NMS-2004, relevant democracy indices prove that these countries are consolidated democracies disposing of stable and functioning institutions (see Nations in Transit, Bertelsmann Transformation Index). Our analysis shows that consolidation however is not accomplished on the representative level, especially as regards the parties and party systems. That means we have to regard consolidation as a process in which the four levels evolve non-simultaneously. Even if the constitutional level is advanced in consolidation, the others may not be.

Pridham differentiates between negative consolidation, including the containment or reduction of serious challenges to democratisation on one side, and positive consolidation, which refers to the "deeper levels of the overall process", the attitudinal patterns, and the inculcation of democratic values on the other side (Pridham 1995: 168f). While negative consolidation may be achieved in a shorter time span, positive consolidation refers to a long-term change. This highlights the fact that different levels of consolidation may proceed at different rates and involve different sets of actors. During transition and negative consolidation, the emphasis is on elite settlement and elite management, whereas positive consolidation implies developing linkages between the new political system and society, developing predictable and accountable interplay between the different regimes, and internalising patterns of behaviour and attitudes based on democratic norms. This development of linkages may occur with delay, but it is necessary for positive consolidation. In this respect, the representative level has an eminent relevance; weak institutionalisation of parties and party systems, interest organisations, and civil society will not present a danger for the overall consolidation, but for the *positive* consolidation. As I elaborated in the last chapter, the deficits in the party systems in the CEE countries cannot be compensated for by the other intermediary actors. Thus the prospects for positive consolidation are reduced by this weakness on the representative level.

What does this mean for the quality of democracy? Is there a correlation between the degree of party-system institutionalisation and a specific dimension of democratic quality: the freedom and control dimension, the procedural and the effective government dimension? To test this, I correlated the scores for party-system institutionalisation (PSI) that resulted from this analysis and the three World Bank Governance Indicators (WBGI), which match quite well with the three compiled dimensions: rule of law (freedom and control dimension), voice and accountability (procedural dimension), government effectiveness (effective government dimension). Furthermore, I tested the indicators National Democratic Governance and Judicial Framework indicator by Nations in Transit to target the procedural dimension.[19]

---

19 Correlations have been tested for the years 1996, 2000, 2004 and 2009 referring to the five mentioned indicators. In this paper cannot be provided all the results; Table 15 shows a representative example. The World Bank Governance Indicator "Rule of Law" captures perceptions of the extent to which agents have confidence in and abide by the rules of society, and in particular the quality of contract enforcement, property rights, the police, and the courts, as well as the likelihood of crime and violence. "Voice and accountability" captures perceptions of the extent to which a country's citizens are able to participate in selecting their government, as well as freedom of expression, freedom of association, and a free media. "Government effectiveness" captures perceptions of the quality of public services, the quality of the civil service and the degree of its independence from political pressures, the quality of policy formulation and implementation, and the credibility of the government's commitment to such policies. The National Democratic Governance Indicator by Nations in Transit (Freedom House) captures inter alia the stability of the governmental system; legislative and executive transparency; and, the ability of legislative bodies to fulfill their law-making and investigative responsibilities.

The most interesting finding is that time and the degree of consolidation actually play a central role. While there was only a weak correlation between accountability and party-system institutionalisation in 1996, it grew stronger in the second decade: The direction of the correlation effectively inverted from 1996 to 2000 and the years after. In the 1990s, the party-system stability did not result in better accountability; thus Estonia and Latvia, for example, ranked equal in this aspect although Estonia's party system was far more stable. Since 2000, however, countries with more stable party systems have also scored high in accountability (see Table 15). This is similar as regards to rule of law. The high performers in rule of law have at the same time higher institutionalised party systems. Regarding national democratic governance, the change is even more drastic: While in the first decade, the influence of stable party systems was almost insignificant, in 2009 the countries with the best PSI scores are the best performers in national governance. Hence, instable party systems affected the freedom and control and the procedural dimensions of democratic quality little in the first post-autocratic decade, but very much in the second. In this relatively coherent picture, the last indicator – government effectiveness – breaks away. In the first decade, more effective governments correlated strongly with strong party systems; in the second decade it continues to be manifest but clearly less significant. Poland is a good example with a very weak party system and the weakest national governance performance in 1996. In 2000 and 2004, however, Poland scored significantly better in governance effectiveness but not in party-system stability.

These results indicate that instable party systems influence not only the procedural dimension, but also the freedom and control dimension. Government effectiveness, on the contrary, seems less affected by instable party systems. An explanation is that the fluid and conflictual competition – also in the parliamentary representation – is compensated for by a concentration in the executive. The weak party coherence and discipline and the low relevance of programme orientation attenuates the parties' capacity to steer the policy formulation and policy-making process, which is then taken over by the government, often accompanied by informal and clientelistic structures and procedures at the expense of representativity and transparency.

This leads to the conclusion: The more the consolidation progresses, the more manifest the correlation becomes between the stability of the party system and the quality of democracy. This finding supports the argument of the non-simultaneous consolidation process of the different levels. Deficits of the party systems during transition and the beginning consolidation can be present but – as our analysis shows – the impact is only perceptible and measurable in the medium and long run. Deficits in the institutionalisation of party systems – and intermediary actors in general – do not interfere in the overall consolidation or stability of a young democracy. But regarding consolidation as a process on four levels, our conclusion is that more the overall consolidation proceeds, the more the lack of institutionalisation on one level or more levels critically manifests and affects the deepening of democracy and thereby the quality of democracy. Moreover, the lacking consolidation on the representative level may influence the other levels, like e.g. the behavioural dimension and hinder its consolidation. This interaction between differently advanced levels of consolidation and their consequences for the democratic quality has to be considered in further studies. Hence, there are some more problematic aspects involved: Weak intermediary actors and low citizen participation are correlated to a low degree of input agency and input capacity. This could pose a problem in the sense of a debilitation of the input legitimacy. Future studies must examine the impact on democratic quality if this only partial institutionalisation of the representative level remains long-lasting or permanent. A central question then will be if deficient party system stability in the long run causes legitimacy problems.

Table 15: Correlation between Accountability and Party System Institutionalization (PSI)

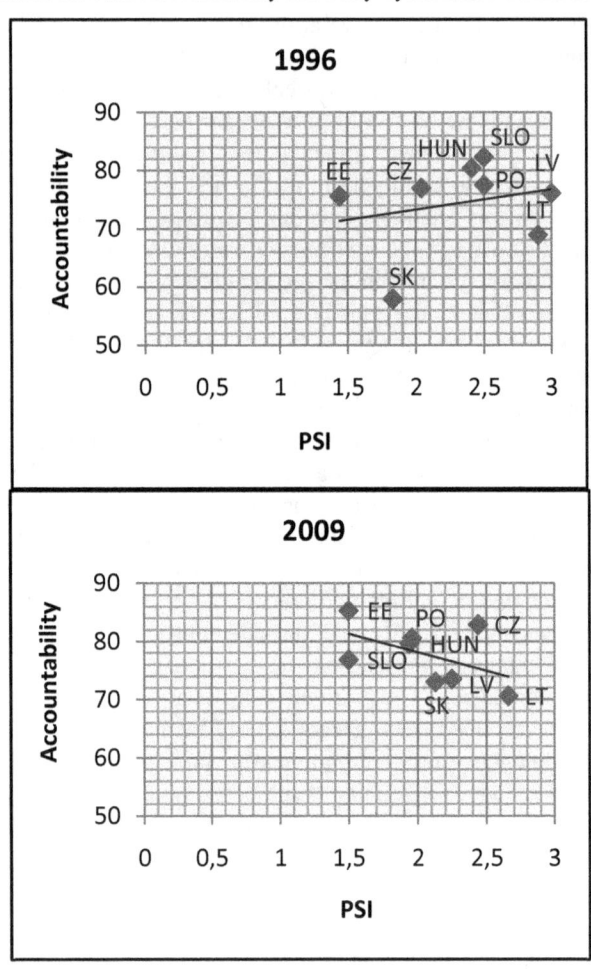

Calculated on the basis of a Spearman Correlation Coefficient.

Annex

Aggregated indicators

Criterion 1 – Stability of inter-party competition:
Volatility: The scale for volatility is low (≤10%), medium-low (>10≤15%), medium (>15≤20%), medium-high (>20≤25%), high (≥25%). Low volatility scores 1.0 and so forth.
New contenders entering: The scale for new contenders entering is low (≤5%), medium-low (>5≤10%), medium (>10≤15%), medium-high (>15≤20%), high (≥20%). Low seat share of new contenders scores with 1.0.
Split-offs: The scale for split-offs is low (0), medium-low (1), medium (2), medium-high (3), high (≥4). Low number of split-offs scores 1.

Criterion 2 – Party roots in society:
Party age: The scale for party age is low (≤12.5%), medium-low (>12≤25%), medium (>25≤37.5%), medium-high (>37.5≤50%), high (>50%). High seat share of "old parties" scores 1.0.
Party membership: The scale for party membership is low (≤1.5%), medium low (>1.5≤2%), medium (>2≤2.5%), medium high (>2.5≤3%), high (≥3%). High percentage of party membership scores 1.0.

Criterion 3 – Legitimacy of parties and elections:
Party trust: The scale for party trust: low (≤10%), medium-low (>10≤20%), medium (>20≤30%), medium-high (>30≤40%), high (≥40%). High percentage of trust scores 1.0.

Criterion 4 – Party organisation:
Factional defection: The scale for factional defection is low (≤3%), medium-low (>3≤6%), medium (>6≤9%), medium-high (>9≤12.5%), high (≥12.5%). Low share of factional defection scores 1.0.
Independents: The scale for independents is low (≤3%), medium-low (>3≤6%), medium (>6≤9%), medium-high (>9≤12.5%), high (≥12.5%). Low seat share of independents scores 1.0.

The values reflect the average of each criterion (AV C1, AV C2, AV C3, AV C4) for each term/election. The columns go from the current term/last elections (top) to the first term/second election (down). AV tot is the overall average of all four criteria in the time period from 1990 to 2010. In the case of Slovenia, there were no data available for Criterion 2 and only few data on Criterion 4. Therefore the value is not as robust as the others.

Party system institutionalisation indicators for the NMS-2004 1990–2010

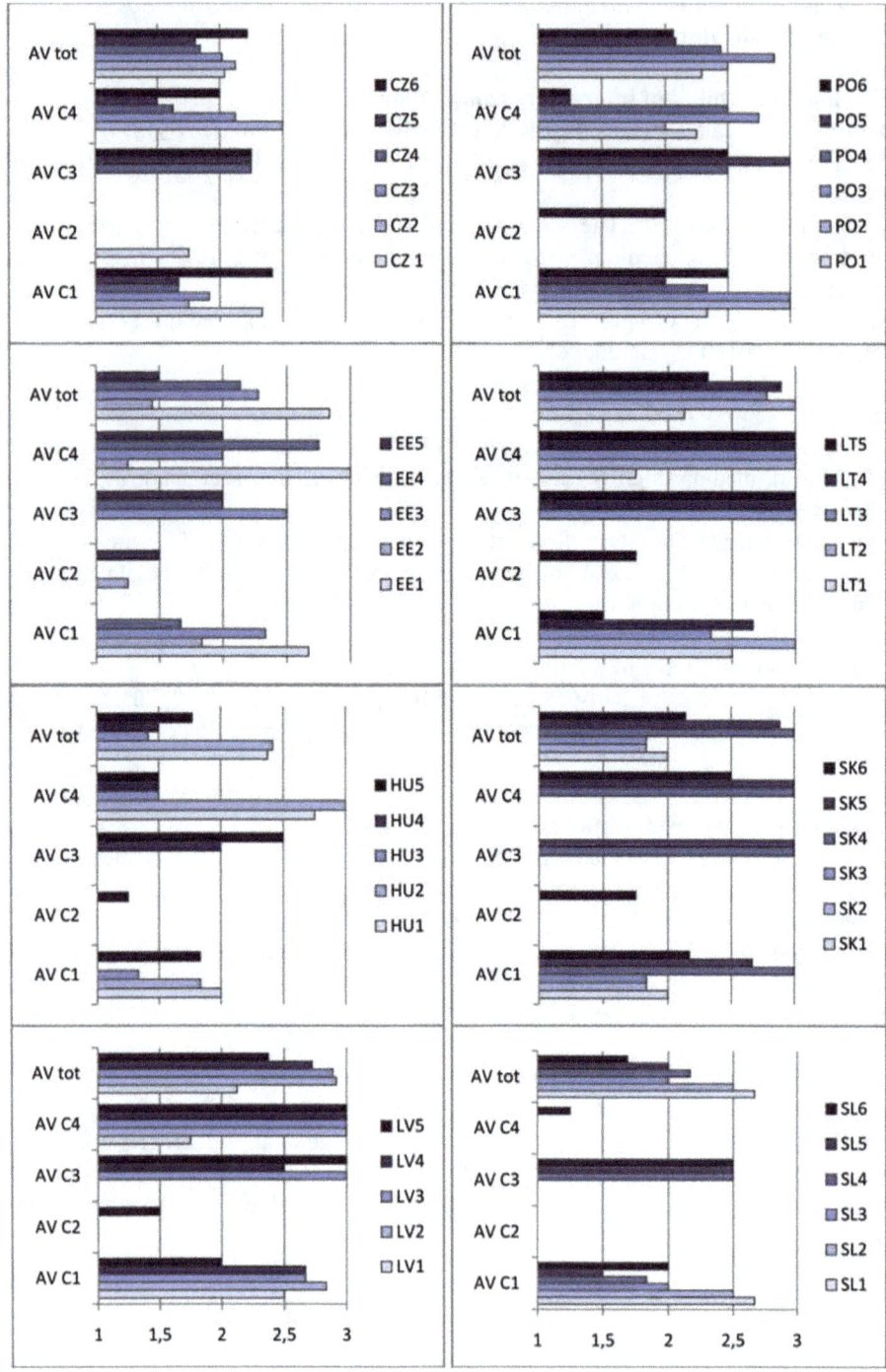

Bibliography

Agh, Attila (1996)'The development of East Central European party systems: From „movement" to cartels' in Szabó, Máté (ed.) *The Challenge of Europeanization in the Region: East Central Europe*, Budapest: 247-64.

Altmann, David/Pérez-Liñan, Aníbal (2001) 'Assessing the Quality of Democracy: Freedom, Competitiveness and Participation in 18 Latin American Countries', Kellogg Institute working paper, Notre Dame.

Armingeon, Klaus/Careja, Romana (2008) 'Institutional change and stability in postcommunist countries 1990-2002', *European Journal of Political Research* 4: 436-466.

Bartolini, Stefano/Mair, Peter (2001) 'Challenges to Contemporary Political Parties' in Diamond, Larry/Gunther, Richard (eds.) *Political Parties and Democracy*, Baltimore/London: 327-343.

Beetham, David (2004) 'Towards a universal framework for democracy assessment', *Democratization* 2: 1-17.

Beetham, David (ed.) (1994) *Defining and Measuring Democracy*, London/Thousand Oaks/New Delhi.

Beetham, David/Bracking, Sarah/Kearton, Iain/Weir, Stuart (2002) *International IDEA Handbook of Democracy Assessment*, The Hague et al.

Biezen, Ingrid van (2003) Political Parties in New Democracies. Party Organization in Southern and East-Central Europe, Basingstoke et al.

Bos, Ellen/Segert, Dieter (eds.) (2008) *Osteuropäische Demokratien als Trendsetter?* Opladen/Farmington Hills.

Bútora, Martin/Gyárfášová, Olga/Mesežnikov, Grigorij/Skladony, Thomas W. (eds.) (2007) *Democracy and Populism in Central Europe. The Visegrad Elections and Their Aftermath*, Bratislava.

Coppedge, Michael (2004) 'Quality of Democracy and Its Measurements' in O'Donnell, Guillermo/Cullel, Jorge Vargas/Iazzetta, Osvaldo M. (eds.) *The Quality of Democracy. Theory and Applications*, Notre Dame: 239-248.

Croissant, Aurel (2008) 'Die Parteiensysteme neuer Demokratien in Ostasien: Merkmale, Typen und Institutionalisierungsgrad', *Zeitschrift für Vergleichende Politikwissenschaft* 1: 95-124.

Dahl, Robert A. (1972) Polyarchy: Participation and Opposition, Yale.

Dawisha, Karen/Parrot, Bruce (eds.) (1997) *The consolidation in East-Central Europe*, Cambridge.

Diamond, Larry/Morlino, Leonardo (eds.) (2005) *Assessing the Quality of Democracy*, Baltimore.

Diamond, Larry/Morlino, Leonardo (2005) 'Introduction' in Diamond, Larry/Morlino, Leonardo (eds.) *Assessing the Quality of Democracy*, Baltimore: ix-xliii.

Diamond, Larry (1999) *Developing Democracy. Toward Consolidation*, Baltimore/London, 1999.

Enyedi, Zsolt (2006) 'The Survival of the Fittest: Party System Concentration in Hungary' in Jungerstam-Mulders, Susanne (ed.) *Post-Communist EU Member States. Parties and Party Systems*, Aldershot: 177-203.

Enyedi, Zsolt/Tóka, Gábor (2007) 'Party Politics in Hungary' in Webb, Paul/White, Stephan (eds.) *Party Politics in New Democracies*, Oxford: 147-179.

Gabriel, Oscar W. (2008) ‚Politische Einstellungen und politische Kultur' in Gabriel, Oscar W./Kropp, Sabine (eds.) *Die EU-Staaten im Vergleich. Strukturen, Prozesse, Politikinhalte*, Wiesbaden: 181-215.

Gabriel, Oscar W./Völkl, Kerstin (2008) ‚Politische und soziale Partizipation' in Gabriel, Oscar W./Kropp, Sabine (eds.) *Die EU-Staaten im Vergleich. Strukturen, Prozesse, Politikinhalte*, Wiesbaden: 268-299.

Grotz, Florian (2007) ‚Stabile Regierungsbündnisse? Determinanten der Koalitionspolitik in Ostmitteleuropa', *Osteuropa* 4: 109-23.

Gunther, Richard/Diamond, Larry (2001) 'Types and Functions of Parties', Diamond, Larry/Gunther, Richard (eds.) *Political Parties and Democracy*, Baltimore/London: 3-40.

Helms, Ludger (1995) 'Parteiensysteme als Parteienstruktur. Zur methodisch-analytischen Konzeption der funktional vergleichenden Parteiensystemanalyse', *Zeitschrift für Parlamentsfragen* 26: 642-657.

Jungerstam-Mulders, Susanne (ed.) (2006) Post-Communist EU Member States. Parties and Party Systems, Aldershot.

Katz, Richard S. (2008) 'Political parties', in Caramani, Daniele (ed.) *Comparative Politics*, Oxford: 293-317.

Katz, Richard S./Mair, Peter (1995) 'Changing models of party organization and party democracy: The emergence of the cartel party', *Party Politics* 1: 5-28.

Kitschelt, Herbert P./Mansfeldova, Zdenka/Markowski, Radoslav/Gabor Toka (1999) *Post-Communist Party Systems, Competition, Representation, and Inter-Party Cooperation*, Cambridge.

Kopecky, Peter (2006) 'The Rise of the Power Monopoly: Political Parties in the Czech Republic' in Jungerstam-Mulders, Susanne (ed.) *Post-Communist EU Member States. Parties and Party Systems*, Aldershot: 125-147.

Kopecky, Petr (1995) 'Developing party organizations in east-central Europe: what type of party is likely to emerge?', *Party Politics* 1: 515-534.

Krouwel, André (2006) 'Party models' in Katz, Richard S./Crotty, William (eds.) *Handbook of Party Politics*, London et al.: 249-270.

Krupavicius, Algis (2007) 'Lithuania', *European Journal of Political Research* 46: 1019-1031.

Lang, Kai-Olaf (2007) 'Populism in 'Old' and 'New' Europe. Trends and Implications' in Bútora, Martin/Gyárfášová, Olga/Mesežnikov, Grigorij/Skladony, Thomas W. (eds.) *Democracy and Populism in Central Europe. The Visegrad Elections and Their Aftermath*, Bratislava: 125-141.

Lawson, Kay (1999) 'Cleavages, Parties, and Voters' in Lawson, Kay/Römmele, Andrea/Karasimeonov, Georgi (eds.) *Cleavages, Parties and Voters. Studies from Bulgaria, the Czech Republic, Hungary, Poland, and Romania*, Westport: 19-34.

Lewis, Paul (ed.) (1996) Party Structure and Organization in East-Central Europe, Cheltenham.

Lewis Paul (2000) Political parties in Post-communist Eastern Europe, London.

Lewis, Paul (2001a) 'The 'Third Wave' of Democracy in Eastern Europe. Comparative Perspectives on Party Roles and Political Development', *Party Politics* 5: 543-565.

Lewis, Paul (ed.) (2001b) *Party development and democratic change in post-communist Europe. The first decade*, London/Portland, OR: 199-212.

Lewis, Paul (2008) 'Party System Institutionalization in East Central Europe: Empirical Dimensions and Tentative Conclusions', Paper prepared for ECPR Joint Session of Workshops, Rennes 2008 (unpublished manuscript).

Linz, Juan J./Stepan, Alfred (1996) *Problems of Democratic Transition and Consolidation*, Baltimore/London.

Mainwaring, Scott (1998) 'Party Systems in the Third Wave', *Journal of Democracy* 3: 67-82.

Mainwaring, Scott/Scully, Timothy R. (1995) 'Introduction. Party System in Latin America' in Scott Mainwaring/Scully, Timothy R. (eds.) *Building Democratic Institutions. Party Systems in Latin America*, Standford: 1-34.

Mainwaring, Scott/Torcal, Mariano (2006) 'Party system institutionalization and party system theory after the third wave of democratization' in Katz, Richard/Crotty, William (eds.) *Handbook of Party Politics*, London et al.: 204-228.

Mair, Peter (1997) Party System Change. Approaches and Interpretations. Oxford.

Mair, Peter (2008) 'The Challenge to Party Government', *West European Politics* 1: 211-234.

Merkel, Wolfgang (1999) *Systemtransformation*, Opladen.

Mesežnikov, Grigorij (2007) 'The Visegrad Group Elections of 2005-2006: Trends in Party Systems and Coalition Behavior' in Bútora, Martin/Gyárfášová, Olga/Mesežnikov, Grigorij/Skladony, Thomas W. (eds.) *Democracy and Populism in Central Europe. The Visegrad Elections and Their Aftermath*, Bratislava: 9-19.

Gunther, Richard/Montero, José Ramón/Linz, Juan J. (eds.) (2002) *Political Parties. Old Concepts and New Challenges*, Oxford.

Morlino, Leonardo (1995) 'Political Parties and Democratic Consolidation in Southern Europe' in Gunther, Richard/Diamandouros, P. Nikiforos/Puhle, Hans-Jürgen (eds.) *The Politics of Democratic Consolidation*, Baltimore /London: 315-389.

Müller-Rommel, Ferdinand/Schultze, Henrike/Harfst, Philipp/Fettelschoß, Katja (2008) 'Parteienregierungen in Mittel- und Osteuropa: Empirische Befunde im Ländervergleich (1990-2008)', *Zeitschrift für Parlamentsfragen* 39: 810-831.

Mungiu-Pippidi, Alina (2007) 'EU Accession Is No "End of History', *Journal of Democracy* 4: 8-17.

Nikolenyi, Csaba (2004) 'Cabinet Stability in Post-Communist Central Europe', Party Politics 2: 123-150.

O'Donnell, Guillermo (2004) 'Human Development, Human Rights, and Democracy' in O'Donnell, Guillermo/Cullel, Jorge Vargas/Iazzetta Osvaldo M. (eds.) *The Quality of Democracy. Theory and Applications,* Notre Dame: 9-93.

Perry Geraint/Moyser, George (1994) 'More Participation, More Democracy?' in Beetham, David (ed.) *Defining and Measuring Democracy*, London/Thousand Oaks/New Delhi: 44-62.

Plattner, Marc F./Diamond, Larry (2007) 'Editorial', *Journal of Democracy* 4: 3.

Powell, G. Bingham Jr. (2005) 'The Chain of Responsiveness' in Diamond, Larry/Morlino, Leonardo (eds.) *Assessing the Quality of Democracy*, Baltimore: 3-18.

Pridham, Geoffrey/Lewis, Paul (eds.) (1996) Stabilizing fragile Democracies. Comparing new party systems in southern and eastern Europe, London/New York.

Pridham/Lewis (1996) 'Introduction: Stabilising fragile democracies and party system development' in Pridham, Geoffrey/Lewis, Paul (eds.) *Stabilizing fragile Democracies. Comparing new party systems in southern and eastern Europe*, London/New York: 1-23.

Randall, Vicky/Svasand, Lars (2002) 'Party Institutionalization in New Democracies', *Party Politics* 1: 5-29.

Ramonaite, Aine (2006) 'The Development of the Lithuanian Party System: From Stability to Perturbation' in Jungerstam-Mulders, Susanne (ed.) *Post-Communist EU Member States. Parties and Party Systems*, Aldershot: 69-91.

Rose, Richard (2007) 'Learning to Support New Regimes in Europe', *Journal of Democracy* 3: 111-126.

Rose, Richard/Munro, Neil/White, Stephen (2001) 'Voting in a Floating Party System: the 1999 Duma Election', *Europe-Asia Studies* 3: 419-43.

Rupnik, Jacques (2007) 'From Democracy Fatigue to Populist Backlash', *Journal of Democracy* 4: 17-26.
Schmitter, Philippe C. (2001) 'Parties are not what they once were' in Larry Diamond/Gunther, Richard (eds.) *Political Parties and Democracy*, Baltimore/London: 67-89.
Schmitter, Philippe C./Karl, Terry Lynn (1996) 'What Democracy Is ... and Is Not' in Diamond, Larry/Plattner, Marc F. (eds.) *The Global Resurgence of Democracy*, Baltimore/London: 49-63.
Segert, Dieter (2008) 'Parteiendemokratie in der Krise. Gründe und Grundlagen in Ostmitteleuropa', *Osteuropa* 1: 49-63.
Segert, Dieter (1997) 'Parteien und Parteiensysteme in der Konsolidierung der Demokratien Osteuropas' in Merkel, Wolfgang/Sandschneider, Eberhard (eds.) *Systemwechsel 3. Parteien im Transformationsprozeß*, Opladen: 57-101.
Segert, Dieter/Machos, Csilla (eds.) (1995) *Parteien in Osteuropa: Kontext und Akteure*, Opladen.
Segert, Dieter/Stöss, Richard/Niedermayer, Oskar (eds.) (1996) *Parteiensysteme in postkommunistischen Gesellschaften Osteuropas*, Opladen.
Siaroff, Alan (2000) Comparative Party Systems. An Analysis of Parliamentarian Elections since 1945, New York/London.
Sikk, Allan (2005) 'How unstable? Volatility and the genuinely new parties in Eastern Europe', *European Journal of Political Research* 3: 391-412.
Tavits, Margit (2008) 'On the linkage between electoral volatility and party system instability in Central Eastern Europe', *European Journal of Political Research* 5: 537-56.
Tiemann, Guido (2006) Wahlsysteme, Parteiensystem und politische Repräsentation in Osteuropa, Wiesbaden.
Tóka, Gábor (1998) 'Party Appeals and Voter Loyalty in New Democracies', *Political Studies* 3: 589-610.
Tóka, Gábor (1997) 'Political Parties in East Central Europe' in Diamond, Larry/Plattner, Marc F./ Chu, Yun-han/Tien, Hung-mao (eds.) *Consolidating the Third Wave Democracies. Themes and Perspectives*, Baltimore/London: 93-135.
Ware, Alan (1996) Political Parties and Party Systems, Oxford.
Webb, Paul (2005) 'Political parties and democracy: The ambigious crisis', *Democratization* 5: 633-650.
Webb, Paul/White, Stephen (2007a) 'Conceptualizing the Institutionalization and Performance of Political Parties in New Democracies', in Webb, Paul/ White, Stephen (eds.) *Party Politics in New Democracies*, Oxford: 1-21.
Webb, Paul/White, Stephen (2007b) 'Political Parties in New Democracies: Trajectories of Development and Implications for Democracy' in Webb, Paul/White, Stephen (eds.) *Party Politics in New Democracies*, Oxford: 345-371.
Webb, Paul/White, Stephen (eds.) (2007) *Party Politics in New Democracies*, Oxford.
Wolinetz, Steven (2004) 'Party Systems and Party Systems Types' in Katz, Richard S./Crotty, William (eds.) *Handbook of Party Politics*, London et al.: 51-63.

Internet sources

Eurobarometer 64. http://ec.europa.eu/public_opinion/archives/eb/eb64/eb64_en.htm
Eurobarometer 66. http://ec.europa.eu/public_opinion/archives/eb/eb66/eb66_en.htm
Eurobarometer 68. http://ec.europa.eu/public_opinion/archives/eb/eb68/eb68_en.htm.
Eurobarometer 70. http://ec.europa.eu/public_opinion/archives/eb/eb70/eb70_full_annex.pdf
Eurobarometer 72. http://ec.europa.eu/public_opinion/archives/eb/eb72/eb72_vol1_fr.pdf
European Union Candidate Countries Barometer (CCEB)
    2001.2: http://ec.europa.eu/public_opinion/archives/cceb/2001/cceb20011_en.pdf
    2002.2: http://ec.europa.eu/public_opinion/archives/cceb/2002/cceb_2002_en.pdf
    2003.2: http://ec.europa.eu/public_opinion/archives/cceb/2003/cceb2003.4_full_report.pdf
    2004.1: http://ec.europa.eu/public_opinion/archives/eb/eb61/eb61_en.pdf .
Nations in Transit, Methodology; http://www.freedomhouse.org/images/File/nit/2010/NIT-2010-Methodology.pdf
Nations in Transit, 2005 report; http://www.freedomhouse.org/template.cfm?page=42&year=2005
Nations in Transit, 2010 report; http://www.freedomhouse.org/images/File/nit/2010/NIT-2010-Tables-final.pdf
http://volitve.gov.si/dz2000/en/enindex.htm
http://www.dz-rs.si/index.php?id=69
http://www.parlament.hu/angol/append/factions_sum.htm
http://www.parlament.hu/cgi-bin/insurl?angol/factions.htm#_Toc214874307
http://www.parlament.hu/internet/plsql/ogy_fotit.fotit_frak_cikl?p_fejlec=I&p_stilus=nyito.css
http://www.psp.cz/cgi-bin/eng/sqw/fsnem.sqw
http://www.psp.cz/cgi-bin/eng/sqw/fsnem.sqw?zvo=1
http://www.riigikogu.ee/index.php?id=34618
http://www.riigikogu.ee/index.php?id=35324
http://www.saeima.lv/deputati_eng/1deputati_frakcijas.html
http://www3.lrs.lt/pls/inter/w5_show?p_r=3074&p_k=2
http://www3.lrs.lt/pls/inter/w5_show?p_r=6111&p_k=2
World Bank Governance Indicators; http://info.worldbank.org/governance/wgi/sc_country.asp

ARTICLE

Do Party Systems Make Democracy Work?
A Comparative Test of Party-system Characteristics and Democratization in Francophone Africa

Matthias Basedau and Alexander Stroh

Abstract According to the functionalist argument, party systems that show moderate fragmentation, high institutionalization and rather low polarization are more conducive to democracy than others. This hypothesis is systematically tested in four country cases in Francophone West Africa that share many historical, social and economic characteristics but differ in their level of democratization, thus providing an at least approximate most-similar-systems design that is best suited to isolating the impact of party-system characteristics. The employment of pertinent and innovative indicators for the three dimensions of party systems reveals that the central hypothesis must be rejected. At best, four indicators confirm the assumptions, while 13 show no relationship and five show inverse findings. The case with the most favourable fragmentation and institutionalization values, Niger, has in between experienced a substantial decline in democracy. The paper concludes that the link between party systems and democracy is, at least in Africa, less simple and straightforward than the literature suggests.

1. Introduction[1]

It seems to be conventional wisdom that political parties and party systems are indispensable to democracy (Lipset 2000). 'Modern democracy is party democracy' (Katz 1980: p. 1). In particular, certain features of political parties and party systems – such as moderate fragmentation and a high degree of institutionalization – are said to improve

---

1 The research for this article was funded by the Deutsche Forschungsgemeinschaft (German Research Foundation) and would have been impossible without our partners: Institut de recherche empirique en économie politique (IREEP, Benin), Centre pour la gouvernance démocratique (CGD, Burkina Faso), Groupe de recherche en économie appliquée et téchnique (GREAT, Mali), Institut National de la Statistique (INS, Niger), and Laboratoire d'études et de recherches sur les dynamiques sociales et le développement local (LASDEL, Niger). We would like to thank all participants at the 2008 annual meeting of DVPW's study group on democracy in Hamburg for their comments on an earlier version of this paper. The article is dedicated to the memory of Grégoire Kpekpede, IREEP, who passed away in 2009.

the functionality of the party system, thereby contributing to the establishment and consolidation of a democratic political system (Huntington 1968: pp. 397-433; Sartori 1976; Diamond 1999; Karvonen and Anckar 2002).[2] However, this claim has remained largely untested with regard to Africa. Theoretically, one school of thought denies that parties and other formal institutions have a substantial impact on democratic quality in Africa at all (e.g., Chabal and Daloz 1999: p. 151). Other scholars deeply doubt that African political parties have the capacity to contribute to democratization. However, their usual reproach that parties are purely power vehicles for individual politicians suggests that the parties' functional deficits will put democratization at risk (Monga 1999; Manning 2005; Randall 2005; most explicitly Sandbrook 1996). In contrast, two empirical studies (Kuenzi and Lambright 2005; Basedau 2007) have found that party systems' characteristics indeed matter for democracy in Africa. Despite affirmative results overall, however, these studies have tested relatively few characteristics.

Generally, this paper engages in a systematic empirical test of the functionalist argument that certain characteristics are more conducive to democracy than others. Thus, it brings in the following neglected aspects. First, it assesses the features of African party systems and their impact on democratic quality. Second, it particularly operationalizes an under-researched dimension of party system research: non-ideological polarization.

As an 'empirical testing ground' this study chooses four country cases in Francophone West Africa with different levels (and dynamics) of democratization and with many historical, social and economic characteristics in common, thus providing an at least approximate most-similar-systems design that is best suited to isolating the impact of party-system characteristics.

The paper proceeds as follows: The first section outlines the theoretical framework of the study. We then move to the comparative design and operationalization of the key variables. The results comprise both individual country cases and a pronounced comparative perspective. Finally, we draw theoretical conclusions and discuss challenges for future research.

2. Theoretical Framework: A Functionalist Argument

Before discussing the theoretical argument, we have to distinguish between political parties and party systems (Randall and Svåsand 2002, pp. 6-7; Basedau 2007). It must be stressed that a party system is more than just the sum of the political parties in a given country. A system is about the relative size of and the relations between its elements. The nature of the relations between the parties and the stability of interaction between them are what makes several parties work as a system. Moreover, the party system has to be conceptualized as a subsystem of the political system. More precisely,

---

2 Linz and Stepan (1996) as well as Merkel (1999b: pp. 145-146) underline the importance of functional political parties for democratic consolidation. Bendel and Grotz (2001), Emminghaus (2003) and Erdmann (2004) also acknowledge the utility of the functional approach for Africa. However, they show more reservation about direct links between structural features and the functionality of the party system.

the party system is characterized by its intermediate position between society (the population and interest and civil society groups) on the one hand and state and government on the other hand.

The link between the nature of the party system and democracy can be derived from a functionalist argument. Given their intermediate position, political parties and party systems mainly have to fulfil two functions[3] in a democratic political system: *inclusion*, which is crucial to democratic participation, and *efficiency*, which is a precondition to stabilizing any kind of regime. Efficiency can be conceptualized as a *democratic* function when efficient control by the government (or the ruling party/parties) is ensured. These functions cannot both be maximized at the same time since broader inclusion tends to challenge efficiency (cf. Grotz 2000, p. 31; Basedau 2007).

Since the functional performance as such is difficult to measure directly, the functional argument must be connected to descriptive characteristics of party systems that can be empirically captured through indicators that allow for cross-national comparison. The debate has identified three main characteristics (Sartori 1976; Nohlen 2004):

According to Sartori's classic work of 1976, party systems can be described by their level of *fragmentation* (that is, the number and relative size of relevant parties) and *polarization* (that is, ideological distance). Moreover, as studies on parties and party systems in Latin America and Eastern Europe have shown, a further central characteristic of party systems is their level of *institutionalization* (Mainwaring and Scully 1995; Bendel 1996). An institutionalized party system includes more than the 'mass parties' Sartori demanded for his 'structured party systems'. In an abstract sense, the notion of institutionalization is about the 'systemness' of the party system, its constituent elements (that is, the parties), and the party system's relations to society and the political system as a whole.[4]

However, there are various concepts of institutionalization. Differences can be identified with regard to the number of characteristics, the application to either the party or the party system level, the intra-system perspective versus the external relations of the system, and the integration of elements that can be conceptualized as being part of polarization (see Randall and Svåsand 2002; Bendel and Grotz 2001; Nohlen 2004, p. 69; Mainwaring and Scully 1995, pp. 4-5). Hence, some conceptual ambiguities remain. It is still unclear how many characteristics should be part of the concept and how the constituent elements are related to each other.

---

3 Several functions are discussed (e.g., Erdmann 2004; Diamond and Gunther 2001; Sartori 2005), but at the end of the day these can be reduced to two (Basedau 2007).

4 It might be argued that due to unstable patterns of interaction or the marginalized role of political parties in many African countries, though there are parties, there is no party system in the strict sense. Of course, the degree of 'systemness' of interparty interaction differs from country to country. Sometimes, we observe emerging party systems rather than consolidated or institutionalized systems (cf. Lindberg 2007). However, we generally utilize a practical approach that uses the term 'system' relatively independently of the degree of 'systemness' or the closely related notion of institutionalization. Our approach only excludes cases without elections and hence enables us to treat the degree of 'systemness'/institutionalization as an independent variable for the democratic quality of regimes.

Despite these manifold and sometimes contradictory definitions, we believe that institutionalization encompasses two main features. Institutionalized party systems should enjoy both stability and legitimacy (Basedau and Stroh 2008). Stability means that all relevant political parties enjoy strong and stable roots in society, have high levels of bureaucratic organization and cohesion (low or moderate factionalism), and a sufficiently competitive and participatory mechanism for electing leaders. Also, the party system should display low volatility between consecutive elections and stable patterns of competition (low level of floor crossing, low 'death and birth rate' for political parties). Legitimacy means that the party system should be accepted as and actually be the key decision-making forum in the political arena as a whole, being paramount to potential veto actors such as the military or powerful individuals ('big men' or 'political entrepreneurs').

Table 1: The Functionalist Link between Party-system Characteristics and Democracy

Characteristics	Link to functions	Favourable constellation
Fragmentation	F is procedurally efficient if the number of actors is limited and democratically efficient if there are at least two important actors (of which one is an opposition force). F is inclusive if the relevant number of interest groups in a society is met.	Moderate level of F supports democracy.[5]
Institutionalization (stability & legitimacy)	I is inclusive if the party system enjoys legitimacy with a great share of the population (and key political actors). I is efficient if the party system is stable.	High level of I supports democracy.
Polarization (ideology)	P_i is inclusive if the relevant conflicts in society are represented but competition does not exclude cooperation. P_i is efficient if majorities are possible, but alternatives are presented.	Moderate level of P_i with centripetal competition supports democracy.
Polarization (behaviour)	P_b is inclusive if cooperation is possible between all relevant political forces and if there is no boycott or significant extra-parliamentary opposition. P_b is procedurally efficient if cooperation is easily possible within a (minimal) governing majority and democratically efficient if talks with opposing forces are possible.	Low to moderate level of P_b with a majority which is able to make decisions supports democracy.
↓ Independent Variables	──────────── *functional link* ────────────▶	↑ Dependent Variable: Democratic quality of regimes (status & dynamics)

Source: Authors' compilation.

---

[5] What moderate means depends on a society's degree of interest homogeneity. (In the parliamentary arena, alliances and groups might be more important than the real number of parties, at least if they show a certain stability. The ability to cooperate certainly depends on the level of polarization.)

A third characteristic of party systems has been widely neglected in party research on Africa: the dimension of *polarization*. In the Sartorian sense, polarization is in the first place about the ideological distances between the relevant parties and the respective dynamics (centripetal vs. centrifugal). Though it can be argued that ideological differences are not relevant in the African context (van de Walle 2003, see below), polarization has a behavioural dimension which is principally independent from ideology. Inter-party relations can be characterized by cooperation *or* confrontation.

These three key characteristics can easily be related to the functions of inclusion and efficiency as discussed above (for an overview see Table 1):

As for *fragmentation*, the classical assumption is that a two-party system or a moderate multiparty system are favourable to forming governments and thus to permitting efficiency, whereas high fragmentation tends to hinder stable government (Hermens 1958; Karvonen 1993; Diamond 1999; as cited in Karvonen and Anckar 2002, p. 14; see also Sandbrook 1996; Bratton and van de Walle 1997, p. 251). Very low fragmentation, that is, the dominance of one party, may render decision making easier but can give way to authoritarian practices because government is not substantially checked and challenged by opposition parties which are politically willing and institutionally empowered to control the government in an effective manner. Moreover, high fragmentation is said to increase ideological polarization (Sartori 1976; Sani and Sartori 1983; Karvonen and Anckar 2002). The negative effects of fragmentation should not be overrated (Bendel and Grotz 2001, p. 71); however, it remains obvious that law making is easier and more transparent if the number of actors is limited.

Regarding *polarization*, moderate ideological differences between the political parties help secure real programmatic alternatives, which should correspond to various existing societal conflicts (Sartori 1976; Nohlen 2004, pp. 376-377; Sandbrook 1996). In terms of behavioural polarization, cooperation instead of confrontation in the party system is highly favourable for policy decision-making, implementation and acceptance (Bendel and Grotz 2001, p. 79). A low level of polarization is in the first place procedurally efficient, but it becomes *democratically* efficient when a spirit of cooperation includes the possibility of talks and negotiations with opposition forces.

Finally, a high level of *institutionalization* tends to be favourable to democratic development because it contributes to both efficiency and inclusion (see Mainwaring and Scully 1995; Bendel and Grotz 2001; Lindberg 2007): stability (low volatility, cohesion, high numbers of organizations) clearly favours efficiency, while legitimacy (acceptance by the population and key political actors, strong roots of the individual parties in society) fosters inclusion. These functions may interact: relatively strong organizational structures and cohesion as well as low volatility and stable interparty competition patterns help establish a party system that enjoys acceptance and the real position of an undisputed main forum in the political decision-making process.

Some authors argue that dysfunctional party systems are less of a problem as long as functional equivalents emerge. Civil society organizations are commonly mentioned as pertinent examples (Schmitter 1999; Randall and Svåsand 2002). This is a good argument against too much pessimism if party systems fail. However, we simply argue that a well-performing party system can do without functional equivalents, which certainly have their own shortcomings, as is precisely known in the case of civil society organizations (see e.g., Warren 2000).

A study of the link between party-system characteristics – which form the independent variables in this paper – also requires a clear-cut notion or concept of the dependent variable: the level of democracy. The core concept used here is based on Robert A. Dahl's classic notion of 'polyarchy' (Dahl 1971, 1998). A polyarchy is a political system that is characterized by high levels of competition and participation in the political system. A profound criticism of Dahl's and similar concepts questions whether the idea of liberal democracy can be applied to Africa. In fact, there is no convincing argument for using a different concept given that – inter alia – the respective discussion (see Ake 1996; Basedau 2003) has failed to prove that liberal democracy is incompatible with African culture (Bratton et al. 2005).[6]

Narrower criticism of the concept of polyarchy focuses among other things on the need for the rule of law and exclusive decision-making power on the part of elected officials (see Merkel 1999a; Schmitter and Karl 1991). This problem can be minimized by using the Freedom House (FH) and Bertelsmann Transformation Index (BTI) ratings as a starting point for operationalization, where these aspects are included.

Finally, it should be noted that several scholars, mostly area specialists, argue that political parties do not have a significant impact on democratization levels and dynamics in Africa. Either informal institutions are the bodies that count (Chabal and Daloz 1999) or parties are generally too weak in terms of institutionalization or vis-à-vis strong presidents (Monga 1999). We generally do not deny the validity of such hypotheses. Evidently, however, not all African countries have equal levels of democratic quality. We believe that party-system characteristics must be included in explaining these differences right from the outset. In fact, such hypotheses do not make the case against an empirical test of party system functions but rather require it.

Having clarified our key concepts and our main theoretical argument, we come to our central hypothesis, which reads as follows: *Party systems characterized by moderate fragmentation, relatively high institutionalization and low behavioural and moderate ideological polarization are favourable to the democratic quality of regimes.* By implication, party systems characterized by divergent features should contribute to the destabilization of democratic achievements.

3. Comparative Design

As already partly conceded in the previous section, we are well aware that party-system characteristics are not the sole determinants or preconditions of democracy in Africa (and elsewhere). Probably, various intervening variables besides party-system characteristics also affect democratic development. Such conditions (not only in Africa) include

---

6 To make matters worse, 'African democracy' has often been misused as a pretext to legitimize tyranny. When we ultimately keep in mind that there are no ratings available that are based on different concepts and cover the whole continent, there is no credible alternative to a liberal concept of democracy in this study.

socio-economic development; the presence of abundant natural resources; structural adjustment reforms; the level and dynamics of interethnic relations (or social conflict in general); the overall institutional set-up, including informal institutions; elite behaviour and good governance; the role of the military; and external factors (Basedau 2003; Berg-Schlosser 2008).

It is clearly beyond the scope of this paper to engage in a full-scale test of all these variables. The goal of this paper is primarily to investigate the direct link between the party system and the level of democratization. However, the possible impact of other conditions should be treated seriously. Hence, we have tried to select the cases under investigation carefully, holding the surrounding conditions as constant as possible. The sample of four countries under investigation – Benin, Burkina Faso, Mali and Niger – does not match the strict requirements of a most-similar-systems design (cf. Sartori 1994), but it does come fairly close to it. The four cases share a wide range of socio-economic, historical and political similarities. As former French colonies that became independent in 1960, they all lapsed into authoritarianism after independence, which resulted in single-party regimes. Moreover, the military played a key role in politics until the democratization processes that began in the early 1990s led to the institutionalization of multiparty politics. In socio-economic terms all four countries belong to the poorest nations on earth, ranking at the very bottom of the Human Development Index. Consequently, they have had to accept structural reforms and have been struggling with them since their introduction. Finally, all the countries are culturally fairly diverse, particularly in terms of ethnicity.

Yet, despite these numerous similarities, the level of democratization in the four countries differs substantially. While Benin and Mali are among the few showcases of successful democratization – rated 'free' by Freedom House and also leading in the BTI ratings for Central and West Africa – Burkina Faso and Niger have not managed to achieve high levels of democratization. Burkina Faso remains under the tight grip of President Blaise Compaoré and his dominant ruling party. Niger experienced a setback in 1996 but was again considered 'partly free' by Freedom House in 2007. While all the other countries have relatively stable democracy ratings over the period of investigation (see table 2), Niger has witnessed a fairly substantial decline in democratic quality recently. In 2009 President Mamadou Tandja refused to observe his two-term limit as president and dissolved both parliament and the constitutional court, which had ruled his actions unconstitutional (cf. Robert and Caspers 2010).[7] A contested referendum that allowed Tandja to stay for three more years in office was held in August of the same year. In October 2009 legislative elections were held, and the president's party won an

---

7 Technically, these developments took place after the end of the period of investigation. However, we exploit this latest development in addition to the more formal comparison because it fits perfectly with the overall topic of the special issue. The democratic quality of the other three regimes has remained stable. Thus, they constitute suitable cases for evaluating whether this stability is linked to a lack of (un)favourable features in the respective party systems. Shortly after this article had been accepted for publication, Niger saw a military coup which ousted Tandja and, eventually, brought the country back to democratic procedures in early 2011. Thus, very recently, Niger returned to a positive trend of democratization.

absolute majority. The major opposition parties had boycotted both the referendum and the elections.

All the aforementioned similarities between the countries are unable to explain the differences in the level of democracy. Hence, if we can find the expected differences in the party-system characteristics, according to our central hypothesis there is at least some reason to believe that party-system characteristics matter for democracy in the countries under investigation. In the general logic of comparison we expect the more democratic countries – Benin and Mali – to show moderate fragmentation, higher institutionalization and low to moderate polarization while the less democratic countries – Burkina Faso and Niger – should display less favourable characteristics. A perfect match would exist if the differences not only systematically distinguished the subgroups but also showed the same ranking for both democracy and party-system characteristics. Up to the year 2008, the order of democracy values was: 1st, Benin; 2nd, Mali; 3rd, Niger; 4th, Burkina Faso (see Table 2 and Annex 2). As regards the dynamics of democratization, Niger, as the sole case with a substantial regression towards autocracy, should have worse characteristics than all other countries. Concerning the remaining cases, we have to distinguish the fairly stable 'free' countries from Burkina Faso's hybrid regime. We must expect that the cases with more advanced democratic achievements do not show party system features predicting the decline of democracy while Burkina Faso's party system does not indicate values strongly suggesting democratic improvement.

Table 2: Recent Democracy Assessments and Trends for the Selected Cases

	Freedom House*				BTI**			
Year of reference	2005	2007	2009	Trend	Early 2005	Early 2007	Early 2009	Trend
Benin	2/2	2/2	2/2	→	7.60	7.90	7.70	→
Mali	2/2	2/2	2/3	→	7.35	7.25	7.15	→
Niger	3/3	3/3	5/4	↓	6.53	6.43	6.25	→
Burkina Faso	5/3	5/3	5/3	→	6.12	6.25	5.77	→

* political rights/civil liberties; ** status index democracy (deviations below 0.5 are regarded as within statistical tolerance); → relatively stable ratings; ↓ downward trend
Source: Authors' compilation based on Freedom House (www.freedomhouse.org) and BTI (www.bertelsmann-transformation-index.de) data.

However, conditions beyond the similarities shared by the four countries may be important. Thus, these surrounding conditions should be kept in the back of our minds. If the characteristics of the party system do not match the expected functional impact, we must conclude either that the theoretical assumptions about the relation between characteristics and functions are wrong or that the impact of other intervening variables is stronger than the effect of the party system.

4. Operationalization of Party-system Characteristics

In the empirical literature on party systems, many different measures of fragmentation have been employed; some have been used to measure institutionalization. Polarization has remained widely untested (Basedau 2007). In order to capture the multifaceted nature of all three characteristics and to check for robustness, we have opted to use a larger number of measures for each of the three characteristics. Another general principle has been to mix qualitative and quantitative measures. Quantitative measures allow for precise use in mathematical operations but – due to the lack of data – often lack validity vis-à-vis the theoretical concepts. Qualitative measures are closer to the concepts but tend to be subject to unreliable assessments by individuals. We believe that only the combination of the two makes optimal use of their advantages and minimize their weaknesses. Finally, this study is in the favourable position of being able to draw on the results of a study on political parties in Francophone Africa which collected valuable data, both in qualitative and quantitative terms, including the results of four representative survey polls on political parties in the four countries under investigation (Benin, Burkina, Mali and Niger).[8]

The operationalizations are shown in Table 2 (for more detailed information and sources, see Annex 1). Nevertheless, some brief comments on their selection are in order:

For *fragmentation* we have used the well-established indices Effective Number of Electoral Parties (ENEP) and Effective Number of Legislative Parties (ENLP), following Laakso and Taagepera (1979), which – though not flawless (Erdmann and Basedau 2008, see below) – can capture the relative size of political parties. Less sophisticated measures include the Absolute Number of Legislative Parties (ANLP) as well as the seat shares of the largest and second-largest party in parliament. Particularly the latter may measure whether there is a substantial opposition party that can check the biggest one. Given the criticism of quantitative measures, especially of ENEP and ENLP (Sartori 1991; Bogaards 2004), we also employ a pronounced qualitative measure: the 'intelligent counting' measure by Sartori (2005 [1976]), which distinguishes party systems according to the number of relevant parties present. Roughly speaking, the number of relevant parties is determined by the number of parties necessary for an absolute majority or those with blackmail potential. Taking into account a number of consecutive elections, one relevant party results in a dominant-party system, two parties in a two-party system, three to five in limited pluralism, and more than five in an atomized or pulverized party system.

For *institutionalization* we have distinguished between the measures for stability and legitimacy. Stability has been measured through the well-known volatility index

---

8 These were conducted in cooperation with local partners (see above) and comprised around 1,000 respondents each. For further details see Basedau/Stroh (2011).

(Pedersen 1979) and the seat share of new parties,[9] with both capturing electoral and parliamentary fluctuation. We have also calculated the average age of parties in the parliamentary arena, weighted according to their seat share in order not to overestimate old but small parties (cf. Basedau 2007). Legitimacy has been measured through voter turnout. However, we have used the share of the population estimates in the respective election years and not the share of the registered voters. Countries employ different registration procedures; thus, official turnouts are not really comparable (cf. Nohlen et al. 1999). The vote share for independent candidates (cf. Özbudun 1981) may be another good measure of the legitimacy of the party system because a high share may show that people prefer independents to political party members, thus demonstrating a rather low level of legitimacy of the party system among the population. For popular perception we have also been able to use our GIGA survey poll. We have grouped a number of pertinent questions regarding the respondents' perceptions of political parties together in a party-system legitimacy index[10]. Low values indicate that people have little respect for political parties in their country.

Because *polarization* is the party-system characteristic that is widely neglected in party research (see above), we have decided to use a wide range of innovative indicators, totalling 11. As was the case with institutionalization, it was necessary for this last party-system characteristic to look at two subsets of indicators. *Ideological polarization* has been measured using three indicators. For the ideological distance of voters we have made use of two questions from our representative survey poll. The first asked which party the respondents would vote for if elections were to be held soon. The second then asked them classical questions on the role of the state in various areas such as reduction of crime, provision of housing for the needy, retail of commodities, etc., assuming that this might distinguish voters in a classical Left–Right fashion. Moreover, we asked the respondents about ideological differences between the parties in three political subfields (democracy and human rights, economy, health and education). Since African politics rarely follow entrenched ideological lines, we have also assessed qualitatively whether single issues separate the political parties in the respective countries (importance: low, medium, high) using knowledge from extensive field research.

---

9 This is different from Lindberg, who employs the number of new parties without reference to their relative importance in parliament (Lindberg 2007). This can be misleading if many very small but politically marginal new parties gain seats in parliament.

10 The party-system legitimacy index combines answers to seven questions touching upon six indicators. All these questions include answer options that express attitudes or actions which imply that the respondent recognizes the legitimacy of the party system in general. Respective index points were allocated to the answer options. The indicators include trust in political parties, perception of the parties' capability to solve problems, general satisfaction with parties, consent to public financing of parties, personal identification with a party, and electoral participation. Finally, we divided the average number of points by the possible maximum of 12 to get a standardized legitimacy perception index whose values vary between 0 (no legitimacy) and 1 (full legitimacy). The exact phrasing of questions, answer options and coding values are available from the authors upon request.

For *behavioural polarization* we have employed some of the measures of the prevalence of 'electoral boycotts', 'electoral violence' and 'losers' acceptance of election results' already used by one of the authors (Basedau 2007), but we have also made use of two pertinent questions from the GIGA survey poll: 'Do you think it is easy to live in a neighbourhood which has different political attitudes?' and 'Do you think that parties should cooperate more or less?' Further indicators dealt with the relations between parties in coalitions and governments. General relations have been captured through the question of whether or not, or to what extent, all combinations of coalitions have been tried since 1990, with an 'anything goes' answer indicating a low level of polarization. If we observe inclusive government – for instance, an oversized coalition – this would also point to low polarization. A final question dealt with the internal politics of coalitions and their endurance. Frequent break-ups of course indicate a rather higher level of polarization.

The values of the indicators have to be measured according to the theoretical assumptions, that is, vis-à-vis the levels of democratization in the countries under investigation. We have already noted above that we have used two common operationalizations of the levels of democracy, namely, the ratings of Freedom House and the Bertelsmann Transformation Index (BTI). Using both measures allows for the ranking of the countries and for determining whether these assumptions match with the expected order in the indicators of the party-system characteristics.

Finally, it seems useful to specify how the abstract expectations formulated above relate to definite benchmarks for indicator values. The following list of characteristics/indicators (Table 3) shows which values are expected to have a positive impact on democracy according to our theoretical assumptions. In a second step, indicator values may be dichotomized according to whether or not they match the expectation. One caveat seems important at this point. When operating with abstract static values, it is a particular challenge to set the cut-off point that is to be used in order to classify all other indicators according to our assumptions (fits/misfits). This is why the perception indicators are simply sorted by values ranked in line with the assumed tendency (set in italics in the list).

5. Results

5.1 Country Cases

The following sections on the four country cases briefly describe the three main characteristics of their party systems (fragmentation, institutionalization, polarization) and assess whether these are in line with the theoretical expectations vis-à-vis their levels of democratization (Benin and Mali: democratic regimes; Niger and Burkina Faso: hybrid regimes). The country-specific analysis starts with the most democratic country according to Freedom House and BTI and then moves on to the second best, second worst and worst country in this respect (that is, Benin, Mali, Niger and Burkina Faso).

5.1.1 Benin

Benin is certainly an example of a highly fragmented party system that, according to Sartori, can be labelled as 'atomized'. The values for fragmentation indicators even underestimate the real number of parties involved since the electoral law allows lists with various parties and thus obstructs an exact identification of individual parties' votes and seats. Hence, the effective and absolute numbers as well as seat shares are not actually those of individual parties, but rather of party lists that combine different numbers of parties.[11]

We are aware of the fact that this leads to some minor inaccuracies since, for instance, a recent decrease in the ENLP is mostly due to a common (loose) list of three major parties and a common list of several dozen very small but formally independent parties which support the incumbent head of state, President Boni Yayi.[12] However, the general assessment of the party-system characteristics as regards fragmentation would not change by sophisticatedly eradicating these shortcomings. An atomized party system remains atomized even if more parties join the concert.[13]

Regarding institutionalization, Benin's party system enjoys neither stability nor substantial legitimacy among the Beninese people. Only a minority of today's political parties were established in the early days of the democratic renewal at the beginning of the 1990s. So far, parties have frequently emerged and disappeared. As a consequence, electoral volatility and parliamentary fluctuation rates are high. The GIGA survey results paint a poor picture of the people's confidence in the party system. Thus, our legitimacy perception index remains fairly low. However, the relatively high average turnout (27.9 per cent of the total estimated population) is an important sign of general consent to multiparty competition and, thus, of the general legitimacy of the party system as a central arena of politics.

While neither fragmentation nor institutionalization in the Beninese party system matches the theoretical assumptions, this might be different in terms of polarization, though not in terms of ideological polarization. Party supporters are very close to each other; even across oft-promulgated cleavages such as northern parties vs. southern parties or government vs. opposition the perception of policy differences is very low. There are no major issues which durably structured party competition between 1991 and 2008. Rather, the more serious confrontations on issues occur between civil society and government. Political parties rarely get involved.

---

11 Within-list cooperation varies between close and looser, which is difficult to include systematically in the assessment. Consequently, we have decided to work with official party lists only.

12 The purely strategic alliance of established parties included Mouvement Africain pour la Démocratie et le Progrès (MADEP), Parti Social-Démocrate (PSD), and Renaissance du Bénin (RB). It has been named Alliance pour la Démocratie et le Développement (ADD). The president's alliance member parties are largely unknown and therefore much more dependent on the umbrella of the Forces Cauris pour un Bénin Emergent (FCBE) party list, which is not a registered party itself.

13 This makes it more astonishing that the absolute number of party lists in parliament remained constant although the previously mentioned big alliances squeezed the ENLP.

Table 3: Party-system Characteristics and Operationalizations

Characteristic	Indicator	Positive impact on democracy expected if:
Fragmentation	Effective number of electoral parties (ENEP)	Moderate (2-5)
	Effective number of legislative parties (ENLP)	Moderate (2-5) and close to ENEP
	Absolute number of legislative Parties (ANLP)	Moderate (2-5)
	Seat share 1st party	Moderate (30-60)
	Seat share 2nd party	Close to 1st (Δ max. 10)
	Sartori's 'intelligent counting'	Two-party or ltd. pluralism
Institutionalization	Volatility (Δ % last/second last election)	Low
	Fluctuation (% new legislative parties)	Low
	Average age of parties	At least as old as multiparty period
	Turnout	High (>25)
	% Independents	Low
	Legitimacy of Parties Index (LPI)	High; at least, the higher the more democratic
Polarization (ideology and issues)	*Voters' ideological distance*	Moderate
	Perception of ideological differences	Moderate
	Importance of single issues	Moderate
Polarization (behaviour)	*More cooperation needed*	Moderate (closer to 0.5)
	Political neighbourhood	Low; at least, the lower the more democratic
	Boycotts	None or few
	Electoral violence	None or a few isolated incidents
	Losers' acceptance	Immediately
	Interparty cooperation	All major combinations realized, no explicit exclusions
	Inclusive government	Oversized coalitions (more than minimal majorities)
	Intra-gov. cooperation	No or rare coalition break-ups

For further details see Annex 1 and main text; italics indicate that values can only be tested against levels of democratization through cross-country comparison.
Source: Authors' compilation.

However, this rather low behavioural polarization might be favourable for democracy: The electoral behaviour of parties and their supporters in Benin is generally moderate with a positive tendency. The only significant boycott emerged from the presidential election in 2001, when the main opposition forces withdrew from the second round over alleged manipulation in favour of the incumbent, President Kérékou, during the first ballot. However, a significant total boycott never emerged and electoral violence remained minor; losing parties usually accept the results within a reasonable time span, some after rather ritual protests. The moderate will of party officials was demonstrated after the 2007 polls, when minor clashes occurred between supporters of the Parti du Renouveau Démocratique (PRD) and the Forces Cauris pour un Bénin Emergent (FCBE). Party representatives immediately called on their supporters to accept the results and calm down.

Interparty cooperation is very volatile and fluid. At least since the retirement of President Kérékou, no form of cooperation has been excluded. Former government parties have become electoral allies of Kérékou's severest opposition. The PRD even joined Kérékou's government although its party president had been sentenced to death by the dictatorial regime. Opposition forces are frequently included in the government for opportunistic reasons. Oversized government coalitions are common. The volatile, though not aggressive, behaviour of parties causes frequent coalition break-ups. However, such break-ups usually have no severe consequences for government due to the informal character of coalitions and due to the fact that a party which leaves government often sustain split-offs. The renegade factions form their own party, and remain in or rejoin the government.[14]

All in all, the Beninese party system is far from a 'best system' vis-à-vis the theoretical expectations. The level of fragmentation is too high, institutionalization is too low, and programmatic differences are virtually absent. It is only the low level of behavioural polarization that is in line with the hypothesis.

5.1.2 Mali

The Malian party system's level of fragmentation has changed substantially since the introduction of multiparty politics in 1991. The first two legislative elections in 1992 and 1997 saw the emergence of the Alliance pour la Démocratie au Mali (ADEMA) as a dominant party able to secure large absolute majorities, especially – due to an opposition boycott – in 1997. Following internal leadership struggles, ADEMA lost its absolute majority in the 2002 elections. Two big electoral alliances and a third one emerged, resulting in a high level of fragmentation with over five effective legislative parties.

The numerous splits the bigger Malian parties had been suffering from continued into the 2007 elections, certainly indicating the Malian party system's fairly weak level of institutionalization. Splits became so common to almost all parties that a repertoire of Malian political parties compiled by an international agency committed to party promotion included a special category for splits (NIMD 2004). In organizational terms, Malian parties do far from well, but they certainly show higher organizational levels than their counterparts in Benin. This is at least partly due to legal provisions that require the existence of offices in the capital, among other requirements (which are, however, often not adhered to), in order for the parties to receive state funding. The legitimacy of the party

---

14 An ideal typical case was the formation of the PRD-Nouvelle Génération party, headed by Kamarou Fassassi after his original party, PRD, left government in 1998. Inversely, some FCBE member and ally parties broke away quite a short time after the 2007 parliamentary election and formed a renegade group called G13 since they felt underserved within the government.

system is extremely low, as particularly illustrated by the low voter turnouts[15] and the deplorable values in the party-system legitimacy index. A certain anti-party stance in the political culture as a whole may be demonstrated by the fact that Amadou Toumani Touré ('ATT') – the second president in the multiparty period – formed an all-party coalition called the 'grand consensus' that resulted in the virtual absence of opposition parties for approximately three years after the 2002 elections. Only months before the 2007 elections, the second-biggest party, the Rassemblement du Peuple Malien (RPM), declared itself an official opposition party.

Generally, no constellation of alliances has been impossible, including what local interview partners call *'alliances contre nature'*.[16] After high levels of polarization in terms of inter-partisan behaviour in the mid 1990s – the 1997 elections were particularly marred by electoral boycotts and massive electoral violence – the Malian party system has in recent years demonstrated a low level of behavioural polarization, which might be the biggest asset in terms of democracy. Less favourable seems to be the lack of ideological and programmatic differences in the Malian party system. Even single issues rarely distinguish the parties.[17]

Summing up the findings, the Malian party system does not match the theoretical expectations of democratic functionality. Fragmentation was too low before 2002 and now seems too high. Institutionalization may justify calling it fairly 'chaotic', and programmatic differences are widely absent to virtually non-existent. It is only the low level of behavioural polarization that is in line with the hypothesis.

5.1.3 Niger

Notwithstanding a number of splits in the major parties that already existed at the beginning of the multiparty period, the Nigerien party system is moderately fragmented (around 4 ELP). At least, this applied until the contested 2009 legislative elections, which could not be considered in the systematic comparison of data. It was only during the undemocratic post-coup period from 1996 to 1999 – and after the 2009 elections – that one party held an absolute majority. It is also the period 1996–1999 and the moderate number of splits that account for the shortcomings in the stability of the party system. Otherwise, the Nigerien party system is surprisingly stable. Between 1993 and 2009 three major parties – the Mouvement National pour la Société de Développement (MNSD), the Convention Démocratique et Sociale (CDS) and the Parti Nigérien pour la Démocratie et le Socialisme (PNDS) – dominated party politics. The political parties' organizational level is hardly comparable to that of their Western counterparts, but the quality of offices, programmes and other features outperforms all the other cases exam-

---

15 These are not, however, as drastic as the official figures – related to the number of registered voters – seem to indicate. Voters are frequently registered both in the capital and in the rural villages they descend from. Registration rolls are often poorly updated, and deceased voters stay on the lists.
16 That is, parties formed as spin-offs of other parties form coalitions with their 'mother' parties.
17 The peace agreement with the Tuareg rebels in 2006, to which the government rushed after rebel attacks in May 2006, was denounced by the RPM as being too conciliatory and a reward for taking up arms.

ined here. All indicators more or less point to moderate levels of institutionalization, in terms of both stability and legitimacy. The level of polarization is apparently higher. Regarding ideological distances and the importance of single issues, Niger shows low levels of ideological distance between voters, but single issues – such as austerity measures (*'la vie chère'*), the treatment of opposition journalists, and the Tuareg crisis – have played a role in distinguishing government and opposition parties.

As regards the behavioural dimension of polarization, we find a certain tendency not to accept election results (at least initially). However, all combinations between the major parties – including alliances between parties and their spin-offs – have been tried. Yet, the coalition between the MNSD and the CDS and a number of smaller parties was fairly stable between 1999 and 2009. This explains why coalition break-ups are rare. However, the splitting of the CDS-PNDS coalition in 1994 was the beginning of an awkward *cohabitation* between then president Mahamane Ousmane and opposition premier Hama Amadou. It resulted in institutional deadlock and finally a military coup in 1996 that marked the end of the III Republic (and the first democratic experiment).

To summarize, the characteristics of the Nigerien party system do not match the theoretical assumptions. The moderate fragmentation and better levels of institutionalization would be typical, rather, of a more democratic case, and not the hybrid regime we find in Niger. The relatively high level of polarization is perhaps more in line with theoretical assumptions, particularly with regard to the substantial decline in democratic quality when President Tandja decided not to observe his two-term limit as president and dissolved both parliament and the constitutional court. Yet the general level of polarization does not really distinguish the case from the more (stable and) democratic cases.

5.1.4 Burkina Faso

The fragmentation of the party system in Burkina Faso seems to be moderate – at least according to the ENEP and ELEP. This may exemplify why Sartori's 'intelligent counting' is a more adequate measure for characterizing the nature of the fragmentation of the party system. In fact, the Burkinabè system has been dominated by the ruling Congrès pour la Démocratie et le Progrès (CDP) since the introduction of multiparty politics. The CDP is surrounded by a fairly large number of small parties, maybe representing one of the showcases of what some scholars have described as typical of African party systems: a combination of a dominant party plus a fragmented field of competitors (Fomunyoh 2001; van de Walle 2003).

In terms of institutionalization, an initial finding is that Burkina Faso's party system is relatively stable. Volatility and parliamentary fluctuation are still very moderate, though institutional amendments have established incentives for greater change. The average party age is above expectations; that is, the values are greater than the length of time since the beginning of the multiparty period.[18] All in all, the party system's legiti-

---

18 Some major parties have to fear generational change. For instance, the late Joseph Ki-Zerbo's – a historian with a worldwide reputation – Parti pour la Démocratie et le Progrès / Parti Socialiste (PDP/PS) virtually

macy is at least fairly average, if not above average when seen from a larger comparative perspective. This is probably not true of the turnout rates, which appear very high at first glance but prove to be much lower in reality.[19]

As for the ideological or programmatic dimension of polarization, the results reveal that the ideological distance of supporter groups is relatively high compared to all other cases under review. However, programmatic declarations and government policies, respectively, do not correspond to the supporter attitudes. Supporters of the leftist Sankarist movement UNIR/MS favour more freedom for the private market, while supporters of government party CDP, which implements the rather neo-liberal policy demands of the IMF and other donors, prefer stronger state intervention in the economy.[20] Single-issue confrontations confirm the citizens' perceptions. Several single issues, such as the country's policy towards the Ivory Coast and the rising cost of living, particularly separate the CDP from radical opposition parties. The most important and long-standing issue has been the assassination of investigative journalist and regime critic Norbert Zongo in 1998. The opposition parties have been pushing for a new trial as they suspect high-ranking state officials who were not prosecuted of being involved in his death. The ruling party sees no need to reopen the case.

Regarding the behavioural dimension of polarization, different indicators point to different levels. Higher levels may be indicated by the relatively high (though decreasing) number of boycotts and electoral violence (though isolated incidents only), and by government–opposition relations in general: tension and mistrust mark the relationship between government and the radical opposition.

To some extent, the party-system characteristics in Burkina Faso match the lower level of democratization in the country. A dominant party and a weak opposition are not ideal for democracy. Also, the somewhat higher levels of polarization may also be in line with the hypothesis. This is possibly less true for institutionalization. Though institutionalization is certainly not very high by absolute standards, it at least outperforms the democratic cases of the sample.

---

collapsed at the 2007 polls, some months after the honoured leader's death. In this case, generational change has been realized by strengthening a party that proposes younger protagonists while representing similar leftist oppositional interests, namely, the Union pour la Renaissance / Mouvement Sankariste (UNIR/MS).

19 Even though officially declared turnouts were relatively high over the years, more objective measurements reveal less impressive results. The average turnout as a share of the estimated total population is 15.6. An optimistic assessment would double this share to receive an approximate turnout of the population of full age. Such an optimistic estimation deviates from official parliamentary turnouts by 3.3 (1997) to 38.1 (2002) percentage points, or 18.5 percentage points on average.

20 Apparently, a confrontation between government and opposition is behind this difference. The CDP appears virtually as a state party, something which might stimulate its supporters to have trust in government and state action. UNIR/MS is a leading party of the so-called radical opposition, something which might incite its supporters to be more sceptical of all competencies given to the CDP-dominated state.

5.2 Comparative Analysis

When testing from a comparative perspective whether or not the more democratic cases also show the theoretically expected values in party-system characteristics, the results turn out to be fairly contrary to expectations. Out of six indicators for *fragmentation*, none shows the expected perfect link to the level of democratization measured through both FH and the BTI. Only the share of seats for second parties – our proxy for effective opposition – distinguishes the best democratic case Benin from the other three. Three indicators (ENLP, ANLP, seat share of the largest party) display no connection at all, while two further measures show unexpected relationships. The number of effective electoral parties (ENEP) shows an inverse relationship: more (effective) electoral parties are to be found in the more democratic countries. The same result is returned for the indicator 'Sartori's intelligent counting', which suggests that not moderately fragmented but rather more fragmented countries have better chances of successful democratization. The stable regime quality of Benin and Mali counters the assumption that highly fragmented party systems contribute to the regression of democracy.

A similar picture emerges when we look at the measures for *institutionalization*. Three indicators (volatility, fluctuation, number of independents) are clearly not systematically connected to the level of democratization. Voter turnout distinguishes the democratic top performer Benin from all the others. Again, two indicators yield inverse results. Both the average party age and the legitimacy of the political parties (as perceived by the population) are lower in the democratic success stories, while our hybrid regimes apparently have better-institutionalized party systems in this respect. In fact, low institutionalization does not contribute to a decline in democracy while stronger institutionalization neither supports the further democratization of hybrid regimes nor prevents further regression towards autocracy (see Niger).

The general pattern of the results reappears with the measures of *polarization*. No systematic relationship whatsoever emerges with seven out of 11 indicators (voters' distance, perception of differences, living in neighbourhoods with different political attitudes, electoral violence, boycotts, losers' acceptance, and inclusive government). An expected link is returned for a public attitude: in non-democratic countries people have a stronger feeling that more cooperation between parties is needed. The indicator for interparty cooperation distinguishes Burkina Faso from all other cases. Political parties there exclude particular coalitions, which may point to the institutionalization of a hybrid regime. Moreover, the decline in a formerly very inclusive cooperation pattern in Niger could have contributed to the recent autocratic regression in Niger.

Two measures show relationships contrary to expectations. Apparently, countries in which single issues play a certain role (Burkina Faso, Niger) are less democratic than those where this is not the case (Benin, Mali). Finally and possibly somewhat surprisingly in theoretical terms, infrequent break-ups of government coalitions are connected to less democracy while fluid coalition politics are apparently typical of the democratic cases.

Summing up the results on the level of democratization, all in all, the hypothesis is rejected. Out of 23 indicators, only one matches the theoretical expectation ('more cooperation needed'). In three cases we have weak affirmative tendencies (that is, the best case outperforms the rest), and in one case (part of) the hypothesis might be modified. However, in 13 cases no relationship could be detected, and in five cases there are inverse relationships that are more likely than the original assumptions (see Table 4).

Table 4: Summary of Results

Characteristics	Indicator	Relation to level of democratization (FH, BTI) according to hypothesis	Remarks
Fragmentation	ENEP	Inverse	Higher ENEP linked to democracy
	ENLP	No	
	ANLP	No	
	Seat share 1st party	No	
	Seat share 2nd party	(Yes)	Most democratic case has best value
	Sartori's intelligent counting	Modified	Both democratic cases are more pluralist
Institutionalization	Volatility (electoral)	No	
	Fluctuation (new legislative parties)	No	
	Average age	Inverse	Democratic cases have younger parties
	Turnout	(Yes)	Most democratic case has best turnout
	Share of independents	No	
	Legitimacy of Parties Index (LPI)	Inverse	Democratic cases have parties with less legitimacy
Polarization	Voters' distance	No	
	Perception of differences	No	
	Single issues	Inverse	Single issues play less important role in democratic cases
	More cooperation needed	Yes	
	Political neighbourhood	No	
	Electoral boycotts	No	
	Electoral violence	No	
	Losers' acceptance	No	
	Interparty cooperation	(Yes)	Least democratic case has worst value
	Inclusive government	No	
	Intra-gov. cooperation	Inverse	In democratic cases breakups more common

For further details see annexes and main text; parentheses indicate limited confirmation (see remarks). Source: Authors' compilation.

In looking at the dynamics of democratization, we expect that Niger should display the worst values given its dramatic decline in democratic quality after 2007 (beyond the period of investigation). Comparing party systems as a whole, Niger's party system does not match with its recent political turbulences. Possibly it demonstrates the theoretically more democracy-compatible features, except for polarization, particularly vis-à-vis the democratic cases. Altogether, we find that eight indicators distinguish Niger from the other cases (see Annex 2). Most convincingly, four polarization indicators provide explanatory value: No country shows a lower ideological distance of voters. 'Losers' acceptance' displays the worst value, in terms of both level and dynamics. Inclusive government, common to all other cases, is 'rare'. Of course, agency appears to be the main cause of the decline of democracy in Niger. However, a party system in which behavioural polarization has been fairly high may have been a fertile ground for this development while stable moderate fragmentation and advanced institutionalization could not obstruct Tandja's anti-democratic actions.

6. Conclusion

According to the functionalist argument, party systems that show moderate fragmentation, high institutionalization and rather low polarization are conducive to democracy. Testing pertinent indicators for these three dimensions in four comparable Francophone African countries reveals that this hypothesis must be rejected or, at least, modified. At best, four indicators confirm the assumptions, while 13 show no relationship and five show inverse findings. In principle, the following possible conclusions deserve discussion:

The first conclusion would be that party-system characteristics do not matter at all for democracy, as suggested by some area specialists for Africa. While this seems plausible if we assume a very strong connection between party systems and democracy in the hypothesized sense, some relationships, including a number of inverse links, instead support the idea that party-system characteristics do have a certain influence on democratization. But this influence is not as strong as generally suggested by functionalists and works through other causal mechanisms. In particular, high fragmentation and low institutionalization are apparently less harmful to democracy than commonly assumed, both in the literature and in the public discourse in African countries themselves.

Methodological considerations in the narrow sense may lead to the conclusion that other operationalizations for dependent and independent variables (time periods, aggregations), other party-system characteristics (such as ethnicization), and larger samples would return stronger effects of party-system characteristics on democratic stability, progress and decline. While other operationalizations seem to be a less convincing source of the weak relationships – testing the dynamics and disaggregated measures of democracy did not produce substantially different results[21] – other party-system characteristics deserve a brief discussion.

Some authors have suggested that ethnic polarization in the party system may be a key factor in explaining the failure of democracy (Carey 2002, p. 69). However, other authors argue that, under particular conditions, the representation of ethnic groups can be helpful in democratic development through the function of inclusion (Creevey et al. 2005 on Benin; Chandra 2005 on India; Kuenzi and Lambright 2005). Moreover, this paper's authors have found that, in the four cases discussed here, there is no systematic link between the ethnicization of the party system and democratic quality.[22] The need for a larger sample, however, should be taken seriously. It is possible that a larger sample would reveal probabilistic relationships. A four-case comparison is extremely sensitive to outliers. One exception will easily destroy relationships, and it has already been argued that Benin and Mali are exceptions in terms of their party systems' democratic compatibility (Basedau 2007).

Related to this, a possible conclusion refers to the context. We have already conceded that other variables may count, despite our efforts to hold important surrounding conditions constant. For instance, the role of the military after the (re)introduction of multi-party politics may help explain the diverging trajectories of democracy. In Benin the role of the military has constantly decreased, while in Mali the military was crucial to kick-starting the democratic transition in 1991. In contrast, in Niger the armed forces have played a more ambiguous role, ending the first democratic experiment in 1996 but initiating a new period in 1999. In Burkina the military remains one of the power pillars of President Compaoré, who himself emerged from the ranks of those military officers who overthrew former regime leaders several times. Moreover, party-system characteristics may impact democracy in conjunction with contextual variables. They could also have different impacts in different regime types (analogy: socio-economic development, cf. Przeworski et al. 2000; Berg-Schlosser 2008).

Further efforts in the field are necessary. However, we have little reason to believe that the link between party systems and democracy is as simple and straightforward as the functionalist literature has suggested. This is not to say that our findings suggest a total neglect of party-system characteristics. At the least, there is initial evidence of the pro-democratic effects of pluralism and moderate behavioural polarization in the party system.

---

21 Different subindices of the BTI (stateness, political participation, rule of law, stability of democratic institutions, political and social integration) and FH (civil liberties, political rights) were tested with no substantially different results. It may be further noted that the BTI category 'political and social integration' includes the functionality of the party system, thus producing endogeneity problems. The lack of systematic links for this category further supports the idea that the link is weak.

22 Benin (most democratic) is by far the most ethnicized party system, and Burkina Faso (least democratic) the least ethnicized. However, even the inverse relationship does not work. The second-best democratic case Mali is less ethnicized than the second-worst case Niger (Basedau and Stroh 2011).

Bibliography

Ake, Claude (1996) *Democracy and Development in Africa*, Washington.
Basedau, Matthias (2003) Erfolgsbedingungen von Demokratie im subsaharischen Afrika. Opladen.
Basedau, Matthias (2007) 'Do Party Systems Matter for Democracy?' in Basedau, Matthias/Erdmann, Gero/Mehler, Andreas (eds.) *Votes, Money and Violence. Political Parties and Elections in Africa*, Uppsala, 105-143.
Basedau, Matthias/Stroh, Alexander (2008) 'Measuring Party Institutionalization in Developing Countries: A New Research Instrument Applied to 28 African Political Parties', *German Institute of Global and Area Studies* Working Papers 69, Hamburg.
Basedau, Matthias/Stroh, Alexander (2011) 'How Ethnic are African Parties Really) Evidence from Foue Francophone Cases', International Political Science Review, online first..
Bendel, Petra (1996) Parteiensysteme in Zentralamerika. Erklärungsfaktoren und Typologien, Opladen.
Bendel, Petra/Grotz, Florian (2001) 'Parteiensysteme und Demokratisierung. Junge Demokratien in Afrika, Asien und Lateinamerika im Vergleich', *Nord-Süd-Aktuell* 1: 70-80.
Berg-Schlosser, Dirk (2008) 'Determinants of Democratic Successes and Failures in Africa', *European Journal of Political Research* 3: 269-306.
Bogaards, Matthijs (2004) 'Counting Parties and Identifying Dominant Party Systems in Africa', *European Journal of Political Research* 2: 173-197.
Bratton, Michael/Mattes, Robert/Gyimah-Boadi, Emmanuel (2005) *Public Opinion, Democracy, and Market Reform in Africa*, New York.
Bratton, Michael/van de Walle, Nicolas (1997) Democratic Experiments in Africa: Regime Transitions in Comparative Perspective, Cambridge.
Carey, Sabine C. (2002) 'A Comparative Analysis of Political Parties in Kenya, Zambia and the Democratic Republic of Congo', *Democratization* 3: 53-71.
Chabal, Patrick/Daloz, Jean-Pascal (1999) *Africa Works. Disorder as Political Instrument*. Oxford.
Chandra, Kanchan (2005) 'Ethnic Parties and Democratic Stability', *Perspectives on Politics* 2: 235-252.
Creevey, Lucy/Ngomo, Paul/Vengroff, Richard (2005) 'Party Politics and Different Paths to Democratic Transitions. A Comparison of Benin and Senegal', *Party Politics* 4: 471-493.
Dahl, Robert A. (1971) *Polyarchy. Participation and Opposition*, New Haven/London.
Dahl, Robert A. (1998) *On Democracy*, New Haven/ London.
Diamond, Larry (1999) Developing Democracy. Toward Consolidation, Baltimore.
Diamond, Larry/Gunther, Richard (eds.) (2001) *Political Parties and Democracy*, Baltimore.
Emminghaus, Christoph (2003) Politische Parteien im Demokratisierungsprozess. Struktur und Funktion afrikanischer Parteiensysteme, Opladen.
Erdmann, Gero (2004) 'Party Research: Western European Bias and the 'African Labyrinth'', *Democratization* 3: 63-87.
Erdmann, Gero/Basedau, Matthias (2008) 'Party Systems in Africa: Problems of Categorizing and Explaining Political Party Systems', *Journal of Contemporary African Studies* 3: 241-258.
Fomunyoh, Christopher (2001) 'Francophone Africa in Flux. Democratization in Fits and Starts', *Journal of Democracy* 3: 36-50.
Grotz, Florian (2000) Politische Institutionen und post-sozialistische Parteiensysteme in Ostmitteleuropa, Opladen.
Hermens, Ferndinand A. (1958) *The Representative Republic*, Notre Dame.

Huntington, Samuel (1968) *Political Order in Changing Societies*, New Haven.
Karvonen, Lauri (1993) Fragmentation and Consensus. Political Organization and the Interwar Crisis in Europe, Boulder.
Karvonen, Lauri/Anckar, Carsten (2002) 'Party Systems and Democratization: A Comparative Study of the Third World', *Democratization* 3: 11-29.
Katz, Richard S. (1980) A Theory of Parties and Electoral Systems, Baltimore.
Kuenzi, Michelle/Lambright, Gina (2005) 'Party Systems and Democratic Consolidation in Africa's Electoral Regimes', *Party Politics* 4: 423-446.
Laakso, Markku/Taagepera, Rein (1979) 'Effective Number of Parties: A Measure with Applications to West Europe', *Comparative Political Studies* 1: 3-27.
Lindberg, Staffan (2007) 'Institutionalization of party systems? Stability and fluidity among legislative parties in Africa's democracies', *Government and Opposition* 2: 215-241.
Linz, Juan J./Stepan, Alfred (1996) 'Toward Consolidated Democracies', *Journal of Democracy* 2: 14-33.
Lipset, Seymour M. (2000) 'The Indispensability of Political Parties', *Journal of Democracy* 1: 48-55.
Mainwaring, Scott/Scully, Timothy (1995) 'Introduction: Party Systems in Latin America' in Mainwaring, Scott/ Scully, Timothy (eds.) *Building Democratic Institutions: Party Systems in Latin America*, Stanford: 1-34.
Manning, Carrie (2005) 'Assessing African Party Systems After the Third Wave', *Party Politics* 6: 707-727.
Merkel, Wolfgang (1999a) 'Defekte Demokratien' in Merkel, Wolfgang/Busch, Andreas (eds.) *Demokratie in Ost und West*, Frankfurt/Main: 361-381.
Merkel, Wolfgang (1999b) *Systemtransformation*, Opladen.
Monga, Celestin (1999) 'Eight problems with African politics', in Diamond, Lary/Plattner, Marc F. (eds.) *Democratization in Africa*, Baltimore: 48-62.
NIMD (2004) *Repertoire des partis politiques au Mali*, Netherlands Institute for Multiparty Democracy [NIMD].
Nohlen, Dieter (2004) *Wahlrecht und Parteiensystem*, Opalden.
Nohlen, Dieter/Krennerich, Michael/Thibaut, Bernhard (eds.) (1999) *Elections in Africa. A Data Handbook*, Oxford.
Özbudun, Ergun (1981) 'The Turkish Party System: Institutionalization, Polarization, and Fragmentation', *Middle Eastern Studies* 2: 228-240.
Pedersen, Mogens N (1979) 'The Dynamics of European Party Systems: Changing Patterns of Electoral Volatility', *European Journal of Political Research* 1: 1-26.
Przeworski, Adam/Alvarez, Michael/Cheibub, José Antonio/Limongi, Fernando (2000) *Democracy and Development. Political Institutions and Well-Being in the World, 1950-1990*. Cambridge.
Randall, Vicky (2005) 'Political Parties and Social Structure in the Developing World' in Katz, Richard S./Crotty, William (eds.) *Handbook of Party Politics*, London: 387-395.
Randall, Vicky/Svåsand, Lars (2002) 'Introduction: The Contribution of Parties to Democracy and Democratic Consolidation', *Democratization* 3: 1-10.
Robert, David/Caspers, Anja (2010) 'Rückschlag für die Demokratie in Niger. "Ziviler Staatsstreich" bringt absolute Macht für Präsident Tandja', *KAS Auslandsinformationen* 1: 74-88.
Sandbrook, Richard (1996) 'Transitions without consolidation: democratization in six African cases', *Third World Quarterly* 1: 69-87.

Sani, Giacomo/Sartori, Giovanni (1983) 'Polarization, Fragmentation and Competition in Western Democracies' in Daalder, Hans/Mair, Peter (eds.) *Western European Party Systems*, Berverly Hills: 307-340.

Sartori, Giovanni (1976) Parties and Party Systems: A Framework for Analysis, Cambridge.

Sartori, Giovanni (1991) 'Comparing and Miscomparing', *Journal of Theoretical Politics* 3: 243-257.

Sartori, Giovanni (1994) 'Compare Why and How. Comparing, Miscomparing and the Comparative Method' in Dogan, Mattei/Kazancigil, Ali (eds.) *Comparing Nations: Concepts, Strategies, Substance*, Oxford: 14-34.

Sartori, Giovanni (2005) 'Party Types, Organisations and Functions', *West European Politics* 1: 5-32.

Sartori, Giovanni (2005) [1976] *Parties and Party Systems*, Colchester.

Schmitter, Philippe C. (1999) 'Critical Reflections on the "Functions" of Political Parties and their Performance in Neo-Democracies', in Merkel, Wolfgang/Busch, Andreas (eds.) *Demokartie in Ost und West*, Frankfurt/Main: 475-495.

Schmitter, Philippe C./Karl, Terry L. (1991) 'What Democracy is... and is not', *Journal of Democracy* 3: 75-88.

van de Walle, Nicolas (2003) 'Presidentialism and Clientelism in Africa's Emerging Party Systems', *Journal of Modern African Studies* 2: 297-321.

Warren, Mark E. (2000) *Democracy and Association*, Princeton.

Annex

Annex 1: Operationalization of Party System Characteristics

Characteristics	Measure	Time reference	Source
Fragmentation			
	Effective Number of Electoral Parties (ENEP)	Average all elections since 1990	Elections data (various)
	Effective Number of Legislative Parties (ENLP)	Ditto	Elections data (various)
	Absolute Number of Legislative Parties (ANLP)	Ditto	Elections data (various)
	Seat share of largest legislative party	Ditto	Elections data (various)
	Seat share of 2nd-largest legislative party in parliament	Ditto	Elections data (various)
	Sartori's intelligent counting (dominant, two-party…)	Last three elections	Authors' estimations
Institutionalization			
a. Stability	Volatility (Pedersen)	Average of changes of all elections since 1990	Elections data (various)
	Fluctuation: Seat share of new parties	Average all elections since 1990	Elections data (various)
	Average age of legislative parties (weighted according to seat share)	Ditto	Elections data (various), founding dates (Szaikowski 2003, various)
b. Legitimacy	Turnout (voters to population est.)	Ditto	Elections data (various), UNDP estimations
	Vote share independents	Ditto	Elections data (various)
	Party system legitimacy index	2006	GIGA survey
Polarization			
a. Ideological	Importance of contested single issues	Last 10 years	Authors' estimations
	Voters' ideological distance	2006	GIGA survey
	Perceptions of partisan ideological differences	2006	GIGA survey
b. Behavioural	'more cooperation needed' Population desires more interpartisan cooperation	2006	GIGA survey
	Possibility of living in neighbourhood with different political attitude	2006	GIGA survey
	Electoral boycotts	All elections since 1990	Lindberg 2006 (completed by GIGA)
	Losers' acceptance of electoral results	All elections since 1990	Lindberg 2006 (completed by GIGA)
	Electoral violence	All elections since 1990	Lindberg 2006 (completed by GIGA)
	Quality of inter-party cooperation	Since 1990	Authors' compilation of coalition data (various)
	Inclusive government	Since 1990	Authors' compilation of coalition data (various)
	Intra-government cooperation	Since 1990	Authors' compilation of coalition data (various)

Annex 2: Detailed Summary of Results

Indikator	Positive impact on democracy expected, if:	Benin			Mali			Niger			Burkina			Affirms expectation? (indicator useful)	
FHI 2007		2/2		steady	2/2		steady	3/3		steady	5/3		steady	STATUS	TREND
BTI 2008		7,90		steady	7,25		steady	6,43		steady	6,25		steady		
Dimension 1: Fragmentation															
ENEP	moderate (2-5)	9,7	0	osci. 0	5,3	0	incr. 0	4,1	1	steady 1	3,1	1	osci. 1	inverse	inverse
ENLP	moderate (2-5) and close to ELNP	6,1	0	decr. 1	3,2	1	incr. 0	3,5	1	rather steady	2,1	1	osci. 1	no	no
ANLP	moderate (2-5)	14,0	0	steady 0	11,3	0	incr. 0	7,8	0	steady 0	10,0	0	incr. 0	no	no
seat share 1st	moderate (30-60)	23,7	0	osci. 1	55,9	1	decr. 1	45,7	1	osci. 1	70,3	0	osci. 0	no	no
seat share 2nd	close to 1st (max 10)	14,8	1	steady 1	16,9	0	osci. 0	21,2	0	osci. 0	11,1	0	osci. 0	(yes)	(yes)
Sartori	twoparty or ltd pluralism	atomised	0	steady 0	ltd pluralism	1	incr. 0	ltd pluralism	1	steady 1	pre-dominant	0	steady 0	modified: the more plural...	no
Dimension 2: Institutionalization															
volatility	low	30,8	0	incr. 0	38,4	0	osci. 0	36,7	0	decr. 1	20,2	0	steady 0	no	no
fluctuation	low	29,5	0	osci. 0	29,0	0	osci. 0	45,0	0	osci. 0	13,2	1	osci. 0	no	no
average age	at least as old as multipartyism	-2,8	0	decr. 0	-0,6	0	decr. 0	1,6	1	steady 1	5,95	1	steady 1	inverse	inverse
turnout	high (>25)	27,9	1	steady 1	12,0	0	steady 0	17,1	0	steady 0	15,6	0	steady 0	(yes)	no
independents	low	0	1	steady 1	13,2	0	n/a	0	1	steady 1	0	1	steady 1	no	n/a
LPI	high, at least the higher the more democratic	0,396	4	n/a	0,452	3	n/a	0,497	2	n/a	0,513	1	n/a	inverse	n/a
Dimension 3a: Polarization (ideology and issues)															
voters distance	moderate	0,057	2	n/a	0,122	3	n/a	0,049	1	n/a	0,151	4	n/a	no	n/a
perception of differences	moderate	0,195	4	n/a	0,363	1	n/a	0,353	2	n/a	0,343	3	n/a	no	n/a
importance of single issues	moderate	low	0	steady 0	low		incr.	moderate		steady	moderate	1	steady 1	inverse	(inverse)

Dimension 3b: Polarization (behaviour)

Indicator									
more cooperation needed (closer to 0.5)	0.690 *2*	n/a	0.650 *1*	n/a	0.700 *3*	n/a	0.754 *4*	n/a	yes	n/a
political neighbourhood low, at least the lower the more democratic	0.492 *1*	n/a	0.563 *4*	n/a	0.546 *3*	n/a	0.525 *2*	n/a	no	n/a
boycotts none or few	a few 1	decr. 1	some 0 or major	decr. 1	a few 1	decr. 1	some 0	rather decr. 1	no	no
electoral violence none or a few isolated incidents	a few isolated 1 incidents	steady 1	isolated 0 or massive	decr. 1	isolated 0 incidents	osci. 0	isolated 0 incidents	osci. 0	no	yes
losers acceptance immediately	usually yes 1	incr. 1	reluctant 0	incr. 1	reluctant 0 or not	incr. 1	usually 1 yes	incr. 1	no	no
inter-party cooperation all major combinations realized, no explicit exclusions	yes 1	incr. 1	yes 1	steady 1	yes 1	decr. 0	no 0	steady 0	(yes)	yes
inclusive government oversized coalitions (more than minimal majorities)	common 1	osci. 0	common 1	steady 1	rare 0	incr. 1	common 1	steady 1	no	no
intra-govt. cooperation no or rare coalition break-ups	common 0	osci. 0	common 0	steady 0	rare 1	decr. 1	rare 1	decr. 1	inverse	inverse

Notes: incr. = increasing trend, decr. = decreasing, osci. = oscillating; numbers behind indicator or trend values: if binary, 1 = as expected, 0 = not expected; if in italics, rank order.

Source: Authors' compilation. Further details omitted due to limited space. All detailed data are available with the authors upon request.

ARTICLE

Elections, Democratic Regression and Transitions to Autocracy: Lessons from Russia and Venezuela

Rolf Frankenberger and Patricia Graf

Abstract Russia and Venezuela have both attempted to close (and to a great degree have achieved the closure of) their respective political systems by circumventing or even eliminating democratic standards. Interestingly, elections are both targets of de-democratization and a central means of de-democratization. To assess the role of elections in processes of democratic regression, we discuss their quality and functions in different systemic contexts. The case of Venezuela illustrates that elections can be used to legitimize undemocratic leadership styles like governing by decree. The Russian case is a perfect illustration of authoritarian assurance of power and electoral seismography. Analysing Venezuela and Russia, we want to show that the correlation between electoral conditions and functions and regime type is less stable than proclaimed, and that in part we can find democratic functions of elections in non-democratic circumstances and that serve non-democratic means. We argue that it is precisely these "democratic islands" of elections that help smooth transitions to autocracy.

Elections, Democratic Regression and Transitions to Autocracy: Lessons from Russia and Venezuela[*]

Russia and Venezuela belong to a group of at least regionally important states that, according to Freedom House, face a serious decline in the status of (already limited) freedom. From the 1999 Freedom House Freedom in the World Survey[1] to that of 2009, Venezuela's ranking declined from a 2.5 ("free") to a 4.5 ("partly free"), and Russia declined from a 4 ("partly free") to a 5.5 ("not free")[2]. The processes which led to these

---

[*] We thank all those participants of the 2008 Annual Meeting of the AK Demokratieforschung for their helpful comments. Special thanks go to Juan Albarracin and Andreas Boeckh for critically revising our paper and to Marianne Kneuer and Gero Erdmann for their helpful comments during the revision process.

[1] http://www.freedomhouse.org/template.cfm?page=439, rev. 2011-05-16. For more detailed overviews, compare Boeckh 2003; Barrios et al. 2003; Zeuske 2007; Fortescue 2006; Stykow 2006; Azarova 2008.

[2] http://www.freedomhouse.org/uploads/fiw10/FIW_2010_Tables_and_Graphs.pdf, rev.2010-06-23. For further reading see FN 1

fall-offs in freedom seem to be more open and radical in Russia under Vladimir Putin and Dmitrij Medvedev than in Hugo Chávez' Venezuela, but both illustrate an analogous process over time. From an optimistic point of view these would be called "democratic regressions", meaning qualitative regressions of democratic institutions and processes, assuming that there still are democratic flowers that could again grow if fertilized. Instead, we argue that what can be observed in Russia and Venezuela are not regressions but transitions, in this case transitions to autocracy. This argument is rooted in basic assumptions of functional-structuralist theories. Talcott Parsons argues that the transformation of social and political systems "requires organizational changes through recombinations of the factors of effectiveness, development of new agencies, procurement of personnel, new norms, and even changes in bases of legitimation" (Parsons 1963: 255). Almond argues that "when one variable in a system changes in its magnitude or quality, the others are subjected to strains and are transformed, and the system changes its pattern of performance; or the dysfunctional component is disciplined by regulatory mechanisms, and the equilibrium of the system is reestablished" (Almond 1965: 185).Thus, changing the right variables can lead to substantial changes in systemic quality and performance. Both countries have attempted to close (and to a great degree have achieved the closure of) their respective political systems by circumventing or even eliminating democratic standards, e.g. through the centralization of power, the restructuring of federalism, the devaluation of political parties and the rise of informal institutions as neo-patrimonial or clientelist structures.

But in fact, the most visible and critical targets of this process of democratic regression in both countries are national, regional and local elections. Elections are considered to be the core element of different research approaches in comparative politics. They are used as democratic root concepts by researchers on "defective democracy" (Merkel 2004) but are also core characteristics of concepts like "competitive authoritarianism" (Levitsky and Way 2002) and "electoral authoritarianism" (Schedler 2002, 2006). These and other approaches dealing with old and new forms of authoritarianism face the problem that elections are important and meaningful institutions in these political systems, even though the ruling elites might primarily be concerned with manipulating these elections to generate a favourable outcome for themselves (Schedler 2002). This leads to the main ambition of this article: Whereas elections are usually considered to be core elements of democratic rule (Schumpeter 1987; Merkel 2004) and one of the most important institutions for transitions to democracy, we argue that elections also are crucial for transitions to autocracy. The role of elections in semi-competitive and non-competitive systems has already been explored by Guy Hermet (1978) and many others. But what role do elections play in the transitional process? Our central hypothesis is that elections are a crucial means to gradually steer and to even smooth transition to autocracy, as they are the Archimedian Point for transitions in the above-outlined sense for changing political systems. To outline the conditions under which elections serve for system closure, we chose the cases of Venezuela and Russia because over the past ten years the Freedom House ratings of both countries have seen a decline and both countries have held regular elections in this period. Interestingly, both cases were used in several studies referring to the role of oil- and gas-rents (Bugueño Droguett and Placencia Rodríguez 2008), the "imitation" of democracy (Krastev 2006), presidentialism and populism (Medvedev 2004) and an expansive "regional" foreign policy (Harks and Müller 2007). Besides these factors, the two countries' systems can be regarded as quite different from one another with regard to regional context, country size, geo-strategic importance and political culture. First, we will discuss functions of elections in different systemic contexts, synthesizing the theoretical frameworks of Dieter Nohlen (2000) and Guy Hermet (1978). We will use (1) this analytical framework in combination with (2) a brief overview on the developments of the electoral arenas in both countries to (3) assess the role and functions of elections in the respective political systems and analyse the function of elections in autocratic transitions.

Functions of elections in different types of political systems

Ideally, three types of systemic contexts of elections can be distinguished: competitive, semi-competitive and non-competitive.[3] With regards to the functions, the recruitment of political personnel is regarded as a core function of elections. In addition, controlling the exercise of office of elected political personnel is a function attributed to elections (Hermet 1978: 13). Almond and Powell amend the recruitment function with a participatory function. According to their argumentation, the influence of the electorate on interest aggregation and policy-making can be secured by elections (Almond and Powell 1996: 52). Dieter Nohlen (2000) develops a more sophisticated description of functions. He distinguishes a double legitimization function of elections. Like Hermet he accentuates that elections legitimize incumbents. And if elections are held regularly and are conducted correctly, the belief in the legitimacy of the political system or diffuse support (Easton) for the political system as a whole will rise, and the belief in the legitimacy of a political process that is structured by elections will be vitalized.

---

3 Whereas elections and democracy are closely linked in general linguistic usage, some scholars, such as Dieter Nohlen (2000: 24), point to their thoroughly undemocratic history: Elections were held in contemporary democracies before universal suffrage was implemented. Elections are not per se democratic and, first and foremost, are a technique to form a corporate body or to delegate power to a leader (Nohlen 2000: 24).

Functions of elections in different types of political systems

Functions of elections	Type of political system		
	Competitive	Semi-competitive	Non-competitive
Legitimization of incumbents	X	X	
Legitimization of the political system	X	X	X
Structuration of political process	X		X
Stabilization of existing power structures		X	
Participation of the public	X		
Partial integration and visualization of opposition forces		X	
Education: socialization of voter to directed participation			X
Control of political process	X		
Political seismography: feedback on the electorate's support		X	X
Communication: Elections as means for government to transmit orders and cues to society			X
Recruitment	X		
Actualization of legitimate traditions of recruiting political leaders		X	
Internal hygiene: sanction political rivals			X

Source: own compilation based on Hermet 1978; Nohlen 2000.

But what functions do elections have, if this instrument is not embedded in the liberal elements mentioned above, but nevertheless make a constitutive contribution to a political system? Nohlen defines *semi-competitive elections* as temporarily limited situations in which competing beliefs can neither be integrated productively nor suppressed. Although elections do not seriously serve as a means to bring about a change of government, they do fulfil an outer-directed legitimization function, as they simulate democratic circumstances for an international audience[4] (Nohlen 2000: 36). Three single functions for semi-competitive elections can be derived from that analysis: first, legitimization of current conditions to ease internal tensions and to gain external reputation; second, partial integration and visualization of opposition forces; and third, the adaption

---

4 According to Nohlen there is no such inner-directed effect, as the opposition is well aware of the political limitations it has to face and frequently opposes the regimes' claims for legitimacy (Nohlen 2000: 36).

and stabilization of existing power structures/structures of domination to secure the political system (Nohlen 2000: 36). Again, a double legitimization function is important. As elections are held, legitimate traditions of recruiting political leaders are actualized even though this function is performed by other, maybe informal, institutions as the real recruitment process takes place behind closed doors. Furthermore, as elections structure the political process, they suggest a "same procedure as every year". We suggest that in semi-competitive circumstances, elections have another important function that should be integrated into the catalogue of functions: They serve as a *political seismograph*, as they give a feedback on the electorate's support of the non-democratic regime and its rules, e.g. through extremely low voter turnout. This function is closely linked with the communication function Guy Hermet articulated. Because in authoritarian systems with controlled media and widely demobilized and supervised societies, political elites tend to alienate themselves from the general population, they need some instruments to stay tuned to the wishes and interests of the population. Electoral seismography transfers this need into a functional logic. In the end, elections link government and people despite massive electoral manipulation by testing and capturing the electorate's willingness to systematically accept decisions of the government. Far from being interactive and competitive, elections are transformed into a detector that is adjusted to the special framework of an authoritarian regime[5].

Contrary to semi-competitive elections, elections under non-competitive conditions (exclusive electoral systems or façade electoral systems) lack any liberal aspects of integrating the diverse interests and any means of control (Nohlen 2000: 35). Guy Hermet (1978: 13–17) identifies four categories of functions, three of which refer to the relations between the government and the governed, and one referring to the governing "circles": 1. The *communication function* refers to the "occasion for the transmission of orders, explanations and cues from the government to the population. They give also the opportunity to recruit intermediaries – or scapegoats – acting on behalf of those in power" (Hermet 1978: 14); 2. The *educational function* points to the socialization of voters to directed participation. The possibility to vote creates the illusion that the electorate "ought to have the ability to influence their rulers [and ...] at the same time hides real inequalities of power through nominal equality at the ballot box" (Hermet 1978: 14). Elections are thus a manifestation of the existing order; 3. The *legitimization* function is of national and international importance for non-competitive regimes, as elections are a sign of good governance to the international community and at the same time are important internal resources of political integration, as "they become a sort of national festival the meaning of which has not yet been lost in the mist of time" (Hermet 1978: 16); 4. The *function of internal hygiene/sanitation* means that elections can serve to help elites sanction rivals in their own elite group, end conflicts between political

---

5 Authoritarian regimes are characterized more or less by public manipulation, propaganda, control and regulation of public interests. Opinion polls in authoritarian regimes face the problem of social desirability to a larger extent and as an effect all results are systematically distorted. This in turn implies that opinion polls are less credible sources for the interests and opinions of the electorate than they are in democracies, even if they are conducted by independent research institutes.

factions, and/or weaken the influences of societal veto players, such as religious or other traditional forces. Elections also may *"delineate* the conditions of future compromise" (Hermet 1978: 16) as positions and/or candidates are evaluated by the voters. And, in fact, elections can be used to "rejuvenate political elites, and/or weaken groups or individuals by conveniently isolating them" (Hermet 1978: 17). And finally, according to Przeworski (1992), less radical opponents can be attracted by the promise of regime change.

The aforementioned electoral conditions and functions of elections are usually associated with the corresponding regime types. Analysing Venezuela and Russia, we want to show that the correlation between electoral conditions and functions and regime type is less stable than often proclaimed in literature and that in part we can find democratic functions of elections in non-democratic circumstances and serving non-democratic means. We argue that it is precisely these "democratic islands" of elections that help to smooth transition to autocracy.

Core developments in the electoral arenas of Russia and Venezuela

As the functions of elections are closely linked to the respective systemic frameworks in which they are embedded, the core developments in the electoral arenas of both countries will be briefly described before going deeper into the analysis of their functions.

In Russia, elections are subject to ongoing institutional engineering. Institutional frameworks of presidential, parliamentary and local elections, as well as party law and regulations, were changed several times since the new millennium began[6]: (1) the change of the voting system from parallel voting to party-list voting with proportional representation for the Duma elections, that prevents independent candidates and candidates of smaller parties from gaining seats via direct mandates; (2) the accentuation of party registration and registration of candidates for the presidential election, that affects regional and local parties as well as independent candidates without the backing of an "electoral machine"; (3) the rise of the threshold for eligibility from 5 to 7 per cent, minimizing the chances of smaller opposition parties like Yabloko and the Union of Rightist Forces to be eligible; (4) the abolition of a minimum voter turnout in federal elections, which enables candidates to be elected despite massive abstentions from the ballots; (5) On the regional level, the direct elections of governors were abolished and now governors are appointed by the president and confirmed by the regional legislature; (6) Even though the multiparty system is anchored in Article 13 of the Russian Constitution, it is transformed into a directed party system with limited pluralism by repeatedly transformed party law and electoral law. All reforms seem to be perfectly designed

---

6 For election results and regulations, see http://www.cikrf.ru, rev. 2011-05-16, the site of the Central Election Commission of the Russian Federation. For an explanation of electoral systems of state Duma and presidential elections in Russia, see http://www.russiavotes.org, rev. 2011-05-16, run by the Centre for the Study of Public Policy, University of Aberdeen and Levada Centre Moscow. For an assessment, see also Nussberger and Marenkov 2007: 2–5; Sakwa 2008: 160–169.

to control the party landscape and to privilege big parties (Azarova 2008: 243–252; Buhbe and Makarenko 2007: 280–284)[7]. Some authors argue that the substantially favourable treatment of big parties leads to a one-party system with ornaments. Thomas Remington remarks that Vladimir Putin has established an "authoritarian dominant party regime" that can be characterized as follows: "In such a regime, the party and the state are closely intertwined. The party uses its access to state resources and policies to win commanding victories in regional and national legislative elections. In return, for their assured path to office, the elected legislators of the party guarantee the president assured passage of any legislation he proposes. In Russia, United Russia plays this role". (Remington 2008: 214)[8]; (7) Institutional arrangements for presidential elections were changed. The possibility to refuse candidate registration because of "extremist activities", as well as the tightened standards of eligibility and of candidate registration, further damage the supply dimension. According to enforced law, parties represented in the actual Duma do have the right to nominate a candidate by party resolution. As access to the Duma is restricted (see above), this further privileges loyal parties and candidates. Parties without seats in the Duma can also nominate a candidate, but need to collect 2,000,000 signatures out of which at most 50,000 can stem from one federal subject. This regulation hinders regional parties from nominating a candidate. Independent candidates need to present a group of supporters of at least 500 persons and 2,000,000 signatures within 20 days of the announcement of the election date. The results of the past election show that only the candidate who has the administrative and financial resources of the state at his disposal (and therefore the support of the incumbent candidate) has a real chance to win an election[9].

Besides these institutional changes in electoral and party law, some social and political developments influence the electoral arena. First, federal elections experienced several disturbances of power exertion by the electorate[10] and results in several regions are

---

[7] The party law implemented in June 2001 and amended in 2004 comprises a massive tightening of party registration conditions. To register a party, 50,000 members are necessary with at least 500 members in each regional branch of the party.

[8] This argumentation is backed up by the dominant position of United Russia not only on the national level (with 64.3% of the votes in the 2007 Duma elections, i.e. 315 out of 450 seats) but also by its leading role in nearly all federal subjects.The reforms of electoral and party law led to a concentration of the party system with four important parties remaining: the presidential party United Russia, Fair Russia as a artificial and systemic opposition party, the right-wing Liberal Democratic Party (LDPR) of Vladimir Zhirinovsky (that often votes in line with the president) and the Communist Party of the Russian Federation (CPRF) as a more or less compliant, membership- and programme-based opposition force. Splinter parties as well as democratic opposition parties like Yabloko and the Union of Right Forces were marginalized.

[9] Both Vladimir Putin in 2000 (52.94% of the votes and a turnout of 68.64%) and Dmitrij Medvedev in 2008 (70.28% and a turnout of 68.8%) defeated their opponents clearly in the first round. This may be due to the excessively used state resources and a privileged access to the media as well due to the etatist subject culture and the diverse measures of influence and voter fraud (or, at least rumors about fraud that were spread frequently and proved sometimes).

[10] See for example http://www.laender-analysen.de/russland/pdf/Russlandanalysen152.pdf, rev. 2011-05-16

self-explanatory. There is a striking discrepancy between regional electoral data and electoral data from the urban centres, with the latter in part being far below the country average and probably reflecting the real ratios of voter turnouts and electoral results of parties[11]. Second, personalization and centralization of power within the so called "vertical of power" produce an environment of non-accountability; as Lilia Shevtsova puts it: "The leader is formally placed on a pedestal as the sole legitimate player. He is the mono-subject on the Russian political scene and the only one who has all the means and instruments and levers of power. At the same time he has to shirk responsibility in order to survive. He would otherwise be answerable for every failure of his bureaucracy from top to bottom" (2007: 52). Third, most of the national print media and television stations are either owned or controlled by the state, or at least promote official positions and opinions. The population does not have substantial access to different and independent sources of information.

Furthermore, free expression seems to be seriously in danger in Russia, as exemplified by the government's attacks on voices of opposition (as evidenced by the murders of journalist Anna Politkovskaya and human rights activist Natalja Estemirova), its passing of a 2007 law on extremism (Schroeder 2007), its pressuring of NGOs and activists[12], and its attempts to influence voters.

And last but not least, the integrity of office holders and institutions can be considered as not existing, as Transparency International ranks Russia 147th in the 2008 corruption perceptions index (CPI)[13] and Freedom House considers corruption to be a serious problem in the 2008 country report: "Corruption in the government and business world is pervasive"[14].

In Venezuela developments in the electoral arena are less dramatic at first glance, as President Hugo Chávez was voted into office in three fair elections. And since Chávez took office, one parliamentary and several local elections were free and fair[15]. Nevertheless Hugo Chávez is often blamed for supposedly having interrupted the long tradition of democratic elections in Venezuela (Kornblith 2007). Looking at the history of the Venezuelan electoral system and the praxis of elections, this allegation has to be revised, as until 1989 electoral choice was limited[16]. Chávez has not broken a tradition of

---

11 Duma elections 2007: Voter Turnout (Percentage of United Russia): Chechnya 99.46%, (99.36%) Ingushetia 98.35% (98.72%), Kabardino-Balkaria 96.68% (96.12%), Dagestan 91.74% (89.23%); Moscow City 55.12% (53.95%), St. Petersburg 52.47% (51.47%). Source: http://www.cikrf.ru/eng/elect_duma/protocol_data/index.jsp, rev. 2009-08-04

12 http://www.hrw.org/sites/default/files/reports/russia0609webwcover.pdf, rev. 2009-07-28

13 http://www.transparency.org/policy_research/surveys_indices/cpi/2008, rev. 2011-05-16

14 http://www.freedomhouse.org/inc/content/pubs/fiw/inc_country_detail.cfm?year=2008&country=7475&pf; rev. 2009-07-28

15 The software used in the 2005 parliamentary elections for electronic voting was not safe and the electoral council recalled the voting machines (Zilla and Pfütze 2005: 2)

16 In 1978, the quinquennial-combined conducting of national and local elections was ruled out (Ellner 1993: 5). In 1989 direct elections of the governors and mayors were implemented. This strengthened the candidates'

democratic elections; rather, he is continuing the very special Venezuelan electoral tradition in a much more subtle way, as the institutional changes show: (1) One main pattern is the strengthening of plebiscitarian elements within elections and referenda, the latter of which is a new phenomenon of electoral processes in Venezuela[17]. Referenda are processed by the Federal Election Commission and counted as elections, and referenda are accompanied by intense electoral campaigns. The legitimacy of Hugo Chávez derives from, among other things, his good performance in electoral processes and referenda. (2) An independent electoral organ is one of the most important institutions for the control of elections (Diamond and Morlino 2004: 25). But the Venezuelan electoral board has been provisional since 1999, as it was not appointed according to the rules outlined in the Venezuelan Constitution. Although members of the board should not be members of any political party, in fact all current members are Chávistas (McCoy and Myers 2004: 281) [18]. (3) Political parties are marginalized, as they do not have constitutional status and state funding for them was abolished[19]. By monitoring internal elections, the state directly controls political parties (Article 293, Paragraphs 6 and 8). In addition, the organized will of civil society is threatened by artificial and state-run intermediary organizations (Rösch and Röder 2004: 202), for example the Fuerza Bolivariana de Mujeres and the Fuerza Bolivariana de Trabajadores, with the former supporting the public education sector and the latter aiming to replace the labour union CTV. (4) Electoral law was amended several times and limits free competition. In 1997, personalized proportional representation was adopted into Venezuelan electoral law. This included the nominal attribution of mandates, with an equivalence of deputies and votes and a frequent redefinition of the size of constituencies. This law is still enforced, but was amended in 2001. Since then, all public representatives have been elected in a dual electoral system with 40% of them elected via national party lists and 60% via uninominal constituencies. This system can be misused, as the last parliamentary elections illustrate – the pro-Chávez movements organized a labour division: As the Movimiento Quinta República ran solely for list votes, the other movements formed a coali-

---

positions and they were able to prevail over candidates that were preferred by the national party rulers (Hellinger 2003: 33).

17 Although the 1997 electoral law included referenda (Kestler 2008: 587), this instrument became much more important with the constitutional reform of 1999. In Article 71 facultative and obligatory referenda as well as decisive and consultative ones are envisioned as the "fifth constitutional power". De facto, consultative referenda that normally need the approval of the parliament are treated as decisive referenda (Brewer Carías 2001: 123).

18 Opinion polls asking for the perception of the Electoral council CNE show a clear polarization of society. About one half of the population each trusted and mistrusted the work of the CNE. Itemized by party identification, the results show that 78.4% of the regime supporters trust the work of CNE whereas 88.7% of those opposing the regime show mistrust (Kornblith 2007: 18).

19 The role of state funding of parties is heavily discussed in political science. In Russia state funding is a central mechanism of controlling parties, as private funding is limited. In Venezuela the abolishment of state funding especially weakened the opposition parties AD and COPEI, as they had been accustomed to receiving state funding.

tion called the "Union of Election Winners" that ran exclusively for direct mandates (Nohlen 2007: 252, 260; Friebe 2006). This was a way to avoid the regulations for impending mandates. To guarantee this double strategy, the movements appealed for vote-splitting in their electoral campaigns.

In addition, some other social and political developments affect the electoral arena: (1) There is a lack of checks and balances due to the parliament being dominated by Chávistas. The reason for this solid majority is the boycott of opposition parties. Even though only 10% of registered candidates and 18 out of 355 lists withdrew from 2005 parliamentary elections, this had a massive effect, as the candidates and lists of the most important opposition parties, (social democrats AD (Acción Democrática), Christian social COPEI (Comité de Organización Política Electoral Independiente), PJ (Primero Justicia) and PRVZL (Proyecto Venezuela)) were among them (Zilla and Pfütze 2005: 2). (2) Abstention rates are extremely high in Venezuelan elections. A closer look at elections after 1998 reveals that the municipal elections in 2000 and 2005 and the parliamentary elections in 2005 were especially affected. As the former may have been caused by the close link of national and municipal elections, the latter can be explained as an effect of the opposition boycotting the election, thus preventing many voters from voting against the politics and policies of Hugo Chávez (Zilla and Pfütze 2005: 2). (3) The militarization of state bureaucracies in Venezuela seriously affects elections, as the following four examples illustrate: First, the candidacy of military staff for public office (Ottaway 2003; Kornblith 2007) may threaten the free formation of preferences of the electorate. Second, active members of the military received "key positions at all levels of public administration" and retired military officers "serve as ministers in the presidential cabinet" (Trinkunas 2000: 105) Third, armed forces were ordered to control and supervise electoral processes[20]. And fourth, due to Chávez' "Plan Bolívar 2000", the armed forces played an important role in the renovation of infrastructure and the distribution of basic goods among the population. (4) In 2004, the revocatorio, a referendum on whether Chávez should leave office or not was held Personal data of the people having signed for the conduct of the referendum were published in the so called "lista Tascón". On the basis of the voter data, it was possible to exclude people from social programs or public service that were suspected of being against Chávez (Welsch and Briceno 2008; Kornblith 2007); (5) The media in Venezuela are self-censoring and tendentious (Petkoff 2005: 118). But the state, too, violates the freedom of the press[21] verbally and through the law, e.g. through Article 148 of the criminal code, which imposes prison sentences on the defamation of any official[22]. The accusation of treason against the voter union "Súmate" on the basis of receiving American donations the eviction order against the head of the Venezuelan Human Rights Watch office, because

---

20 According to the Plan República, servicemen supervised the security of the ballots and the voting booths in the 2006 presidential elections. This was harshly criticized by the opposition (Hidalgo 2006: 6).
21 See http://www.hrw.org/sites/default/files/reports/venezuela0908web.pdf, rev. 2011-05-16, for detailed information.
22 Criminal code, Gazette No. 494, Article 148, http://cianz.org.ve/archivos/LeyesyReglamentos/ LEYES-PENALES/CODIG%20OPENAL.pdf, rev. 2011-05-16

theypublished bulletins critical of the state'shuman rights policies (*El Tiempo*, 19 September 2008), and the tightening of entry, departure and visa regulations for journalists and scientists[23] further constrain freedom of expression and freedom of the press.

Functions of elections in Russia and Venezuela

What are the functions of elections in Russia and Venezuela, countries that have experienced serious changes in both institutional and socio-political spheres?

According to some experts, elections in Russia are held for two reasons. First, because elections have a long tradition, and second, because the regime can afford to hold elections because to a large extent the candidates preferred by the ruling elites are elected[24].

Especially presidential elections can be considered manifestations of trust and faith and thus have a strong *legitimatory function*, while they do not have it for political parties. This also is reflected in manifold opinion polls regarding the role of political institutions. Frequently, the president is named as the most important institution, whereas parliament (Duma and Federation Council) and especially political parties have extremely low reputations and are perceived as powerless and of no real relevance in the political game.[25] Looking at attempts to legitimize the status quo of power to ease political tensions which are typical for semi-competitive elections, the question of whether contemporary Russian government still needs such strategies arises. All statements of politicians, including those of Vladimir Putin, alluding to Russian sovereign democracy, the dictatorship of law and other topics, point in this direction. Although being able to buy legitimacy by distributing rents derived from the control over gargantuan oil and gas reserves, it can be observed, that even powerful presidents, be they named Putin or Medvedev, are in need of a legitimate electoral cushion and a clear mandate to be able to remain in power and to silence rivaling elites. In Venezuela, the double legitimization function is limited Elections legitimize the incumbent, especially Hugo Chávez. But it is interesting that first and foremost the referenda serve this function, as Chávez uses referenda as plebiscites on his person:[26] Therefore Venezuela mirrors Russia in that it is first and foremost the president that gains legitimacy in the electoral process. As in Russia, in Venezuela the reputations of all political parties have been destroyed for several reasons. With the erosion of Punto Fijo, several anti-party lobbies gained power (Levine 2002). This phenomenon became very obvious in the election campaign of 1998, as the election was dominated by independent candidates who relied only on movements –

---

23 This information is based on personal and scientific exchanges with Venezuelan political scientists and thus is not verifiable.

24 The following argumentation and information is partly based on expert interviews conducted in October 2008 in Moscow.

25 http://wciom.com/novosti/reitingi/reiting-federalnykh-gosudarstvennykh-institutov.html, rev. 2009-03-13.

26 Positive results produce direct legitimacy whereas negative results lead neither to a substantial loss of legitimacy nor to formal consequences, except for a revocation referendum.

pure election clubs such as the movement IRENE, founded by the former beauty queen Irene Sáez. New parties like MVR that were founded at the beginning of the Bolivarian republic are more like social movements than parties and are built as platforms for the articulation of movements and personalities that support Chávez[27].

The second function, the *legitimization* of the political system, can be found in Venezuela, even though it shows the characteristics of semi-competitive elections in the sense of a manifestation of the existing order that allows citizens to participate by voting. This function is destabilized by the oppositions' boycott and other elements that reduce the integrity of the elections (armed forces to secure elections, publication of the "lista Tascón", deficient voting machines, twin tactics of the Movimiento Quinta República (MVR)).

An important function of elections in Russia is the function of structuration. Elections formally structure, ritualize and divide the political process into periods. Thus the *education function* of non-competitive elections exists in Russia. While political interests in civil society are demobilized, citizens are educated to participate in a ritualized way that follows the traditions of the Soviet era.

In Venezuela the *structuration function* of elections as a method of peaceful conflict settlement undergoes a bizarre transformation. Elections polarize opinions and highlight the illegitimacy of competing interests. In the case of Venezuela, we therefore can find the educational function of elections, just as we can in Russia, but with a different shape: In Venezuela elections are a clear moral game that "help" citizens to decide between good and evil. Therefore elections in Venezuela are a strong means to transmit ideologies. Electoral campaigns with their permanent usage of media offer the possibilities for both the government and the opposition to address the population with regulations, ordinances, explanations and details. Government usually takes the chance to rant about the devil that is the USA or to name the friends of Venezuela, from Bolivia to Cuba, from Russia to Iran, or to praise the socialist project[28]. We therefore find Hermet's *communication function* to a greater extent in Venezuela than in Russia.

An interesting difference between Russia and Venezuela is that in Venezuela elections interrupt rather than strengthen the structure of the political process. Short-term referenda and delayed or cancelled elections ensure that elections are not the same every year.

---

27 The MVR was founded by Hugo Chávez in 1994 after his release from prison and is the successor of the former Revolutionary Bolivarian Movement 200 (MBR-200, Movimiento Revolucionario Bolivariano). The ideologies, interests and hopes of these actors were partially of divergent natures (López Maya 2002: 115). The leftist MVR dominated the Patriotic Pole, a coalition of several, smaller left-wing parties and the supportive base of Chávez. McCoy compares the MVR with the party Acción Democrática during the Trienio, representing the part of society that had not been included into the system of Punto Fijo (McCoy 2004: 285). Molina characterizes the MVR as "personalistic and highly unstable" with "strong antisystem orientations" (Molina 2004: 166, 167).

28 The role of the *internal hygiene function* should be analysed urgently, as the barely differentiated structure of the MVR and the lack of prominent party politicians besides Chávez point to this function.

An important function of competitive elections is the *recruitment function*. In Russia, political elites are usually recruited out of cadres, and personal connections are more important than elections. The *recruitment function* thus is not fulfilled as political elites are usually recruited out of cadres and old boys' networks, a fact illustrated by the cases of many office holders and even presidential candidates such as Putin and Medvedev, who were both presented as candidates by their predecessors. Central positions are often appointed or at least proposed by the president.

In the Venezuelan case the *recruitment function* is performed to some extend. Even today, the systemic framework for elections in Venezuela enables political opposition to have a certain impact. A centralized elitist network of the Russian kind cannot be found in Venezuela, and the rise of Hugo Chávez has shown that also the former elite of Punto Fijo could not operate on the basis of such a network. In Russia, unlike in Venezuela, informal politics and institutions work efficiently, and eventually there will be no real chance for the opposition. On the contrary, in Venezuela legitimacy is not yet bought through the manipulation of elections. If the opposition engages wholeheartedly in preparing for the next parliamentary elections it could have a chance to defeat Chávez. But the weakness of the opposition and the annulment of the prohibition of re-election mean that a change in power has not yet happened. Thus the *control function* is not fulfilled as the opposition boycotts elections, and Chávez uses a rather decree-based style of governing. Also, there is no programmatic competition, as opposition parties as well as governing parties are characterized by programmatic vacuousness and political competition solely concerns the distribution of economic resources.

The influence of the Russian parliament is often minimized. Conflicts are usually settled in committees that are not legitimized (or are indirectly legitimized) by elections. In addition, institutions without any electoral control or legitimacy – like the presidential administration and other advisory institutions – become the informal arenas where decisions are made that should normally be made by elected representatives in the legislature or in the executive branch. Thus, these institutions do not reflect the will of and are not subject to *control* by the electorate. In fact, an electoral power shift is unthinkable in contemporary Russia for several reasons: Opposition forces are fragmented and their political positions are weakened by laws and regulations, informal measures, and limited access to the media. There is no programmatic political competition in electoral campaigns. For example, Vladimir Putin and Dmitrij Medvedev repeatedly refused to take part in candidate debates and roundtables. And the only major programmatic point in the campaign for the 2007 Duma elections was the support of the president or alternatively the designated prime minister. Anyway, this support was good enough to gain a satisfactory majority, as was predicted by all opinion polls in advance of the elections[29].
Representation of the electorate's interests and opinions is also problematic. On the institutional side, especially the abolition of direct mandates and the reforms of party law led to an exclusion of regional and local interests in the Duma and an affiliation of formerly independent candidates with United Russia. The re-composition of the Federal Council (second chamber of parliament) in the course of the federal reforms and the

---

29 See for example www.russiavotes.org/duma/duma_vote_preferences.php, rev. 2011-05-16.

partial dependence of governors on the president further reduced the representation of manifold regional interests in the centre of power. Looking at political programmes, another problem with representation arises, as political programmes do play a minor role in elections, especially for the "party of power", United Russia, that supports the President. Thus, programmatic alternatives either do not exist or are marginalized by electoral reforms.

In Venezuela the *representation* of the interests and opinions of at least a part of the population seems to be fulfilled The extension of social welfare has led to electoral gains for Chávez despite the real necessity of these programs. Direct democratic elements fulfil the function of representation.

As in Venezuela, in Russia the *integration* of social pluralism and formation of a politically powerful common interest is reduced, but in a very different manner. In Russia we can find the incorporation of vast parts of the political landscape into the vertical of power. As no noteworthy or strongly limited and regulated political pluralism exists, the *integration function* becomes obsolete. Also, electoral campaigns and elections with a lack of programmatic competition and independent media neither create political consciousness nor do they raise awareness for political problems. In Venezuela we find the integration of parts of the society. The examination of the *integration function* paints an ambivalent picture. On the one side, the population is much more well integrated into the political process through elections and referenda, and political consciousness in society is much higher than it was before 1978, as political problems are now explained and discussed in electoral campaigns. On the other side, these positive effects are destroyed by the polarization of the political process, by the limitation of political alternatives, and by Chávez' decree-based governing. In fact, Chávez has mobilized huge parts of the electorate, as the figures of recent voter turnouts illustrate.

In Russia *mobilization* of the electorate is incorporated to promote social values, political goals, programmes and interests represented by the president and the party of power. Despite some attempts to ideologize power, e.g. through the pro-Putin *Nashi* movement, the population is demobilized (Silitski 2009: 42). Demobilizing the population is a typical characteristic of authoritarian political regimes (Linz 2000: 159). The work of NGOs is obstructed by law reforms and the attempt to incorporate them into the so-called Public Chamber; opposition and political movements suffer from the 2007 law on extremism and bans on demonstrations, and parties are retarded by tightened party law. These effects are aggravated by censored media coverage and restrictions on public political commitment beyond the wishes of those in power.

Looking at elections in Russia, a barely discussed but more or less obvious function of elections comes to mind, that which we call *electoral seismography*. The fact that in Russia electoral outcomes do not differ too much from opinion poll results seems to be an effect of electoral engineering rather than of an adequate representation of truth, as results are balanced on the federal level, where for example high – somewhat suspiciously high – percentages for United Russia in the 2007 Duma elections balanced the comparably "low" ones in the urban centres (Petrov 2007). I order to keep track of with public opinion that is at best only partly reflected by the media and opinion polls, the Russian regime depends on elections as a seismograph. The electoral results and voter turnouts of urban centres like St. Petersburg and Moscow[30] can be taken as quite precise indicators of public opinion and of support of the regime's policies and policy outcomes, as well as of the popularity of politicians. With the option "against all" on the ballots, the political system had a detector at its disposal that captured the numbers of politically active citizens who were dissatisfied with the regime but not willing to retreat into the privatism of non-voting. Using this data along with voter turnout numbers, the Russian government has been able to draw precise conclusions on the critical mass of systemic discontent. Apparently without any force the 'against-all' option was abolished on the advice of a research team that found out that this option didn't exist in any other electoral system. Although there seem to be rational calculations of the political expenses of referenda in Venezuela, the seismograph function seems to be rather underdeveloped. For example, recent modernizations and reforms do not take into account the decisions of the latest referendum.

To sum up, elections in Russia have a non-competitive character and some central functions of elections, especially the *representation* and *legitimization* functions, are reinterpreted in an authoritarian sense. With the abolition of the option "against all", elections are threatened with the loss of one of their central functions (apart of the legitimization and education functions) and tend to become dysfunctional for the existing regime. Thus further institutional engineering in the electoral field is likely to occur in order to readjust electoral functions to the needs of the regime and to further contribute to authoritarian stabilization. Compared to Russia's, Venezuela's case is more ambivalent. Functions of competitive, semi-competitive and non-competitive elections can be found. The functions of competitive elections are found to some extent in Venezuela, but are transformed widely by other functions that switch off the original ones. Incumbents are legitimized but barely controlled by elections. The population can participate through elections and referenda but constantly has to fear sanctions from the military apparatus or being excluded from public welfare programs (Welsch and Briceno 2008). In addition, the voice of the electorate is frequently undermined by the rule of decree. Despite all these facts, the legitimacy of the political system is supported by elections, and political parties and movements are obliged to take part in elections, whereas the true exertion of power moves taking place behind closed doors. Elections additionally fulfil functions that are usually found in semi-competitive elections. As the reaction of Hugo Chávez to the electoral boycott illustrates, elections are used to make opposition visible and to partly integrate it in the system. Opposition forces serve as "bad guys" who contrast the glory of Hugo Chávez with their own programmatic shortcomings. And the existence of an opposition in elections would simulate the control function of elections if the opposition weren't so weak. Elections therefore are an important instrument in securing power in Venezuela (Kornblith 2007: 113). But this instrument is played in an authoritarian context as the transformation of political structures, the populist leading style, and a weak opposition substantially reduce the characteristic insecu-

---

30 Duma elections 2007: Voter Turnout (Percentage of United Russia): Moscow City 55.12% (53.95%), St. Petersburg 52.47% (51.47%). Source: http://www.cikrf.ru/eng/elect_duma/protocol_data/index.jsp; rev. 2009-08-04

rity of pluralistic competition. This is nothing new in Venezuela. Hugo Chávez continues the tradition of the Punto Fijo by reducing political insecurity and competition by implementing a stability pact. This tradition was only once interrupted by a short period of decentralization when the mass parties faced serious political competition.

Functions of elections in a comparative perspective: an outlook

The cases of Russia and Venezuela illustrate the role of elections in processes of de-democratization and transitions to autocracy. In both cases, elections are neither a democratic technique (Schumpeter 1987: 248) nor do they constitute a democratic threshold against authoritarian developments. Quite to the contrary, in both countries elections are used to implement and/or stabilize authoritarian rule. The case of Venezuela shows that elections can be used to implement a process of de-democratization, as they can be used to legitimize undemocratic leadership styles like governing by decree; to circumvent parliamentary or plebiscitarian decisions; and to implement more or less undemocratic laws and orders. In Russia, too, elections serve to centralize power and personalize leadership. In both cases these functions are based on a tradition of centralization of power and delegative practices. Interestingly, in the Venezuelan case, these traditions have long been ignored. This might be because this tradition of centralizing power clashes with another one, the long tradition of democratic recruitment of officials. Even today, the systemic framework for elections in Venezuela enables the political opposition to have a certain impact. Contrary to that, the case of Russia is a perfect illustration of authoritarian assurance of power by elections and electoral engineering.

These differences in the extent of electoral engineering and regime closure show that as there are many different ways of transition to autocracy, there are correspondingly many different ways elections can support these transitions. In Russia we mainly find functions of semi- and non-competitive elections. Contrary to this, in Venezuela we find functions of competitive elections existing side by side with functions of non-competitive elections. It has therefore been shown that in the Venezuelan case the correlation between electoral conditions and functions and regime type is less stable. The mixture of electoral functions enables a smooth, even hidden process of de-democratization to occur. Furthermore the result of this process is less clear than in the Russian case, as in the Venezuelan case the regime type has to be regarded as being in the grey zone between authoritarianism and democracy. Why do we have these different electoral patterns in Venezuela and Russia? Is it due to the electoral system or electoral traditions that a quicker, more extensive transformation is not possible in Venezuela? Or is it due to informal institutions, namely the dense elitist network, that recruitment of political personnel takes place completely behind the scenes? The comparison of electoral functions in Russia and Venezuela points at several interdependent factors and systemic context variables that influence the functions and phenomenology of elections in non-democratic regimes: socio-economic development and the type of state revenues; political culture; informal institutions and practices; degree and type of centralization and personalization of power and leadership; functionality of formal institution and institutional checks and balances; and, last but not least, the structure and freedom of the media. Depending on the combination and characteristics of these variables, political systems with different functional logics emerge. Our study strongly suggests that especially different values of the variables' "political culture" and "informal institutions" influence the authoritarian power of elections. Thus further research should concentrate on these variables in order to shed light not only on processes of transitions to autocracy and authoritarian consolidation, but also on new concepts of typologizing political systems along their characteristic functional logics.

"I'm convinced that this visit will give a boost to our collaboration and relations between Russia and Venezuela [...,] which is one of our most important partners in Latin America"[31], Russian President Dmitrij Medvedev said during a meeting with Venezuelan President Hugo Chávez in November 2008, when both were signing a nuclear energy deal in Caracas. Besides the intensified cooperation in the energy and military sectors, Hugo Chávez seems to take the old bonmot "to learn from Russia is to learn to triumph" seriously and made elections the most important tool to restructure Venezuelan polity and policies. But he did much more than just copying the Russian prototype of de-democratization: He developed his own style of transition to autocracy, perfectly adapted to Venezuelan political culture and institutional tradition with elections serving as both a last hope for a democratic turn and a crucial stabilization factor of autocratic rule.

Literature

Almond, Gabriel A. (1965) 'A developmental Approach to Political Systems', *World Politics* 2: 183-214.
Almond, Gabriel/Powell, Bingham (eds.) (1996) *Comparative Politics Today. A world view*, New York.
Almond, Gabriel/Verba, Sydney (1963) The Civic Culture. Political Attitudes and Democracy in Five Nations, Princeton.
Azarova, Aitalina (2008) 'Formal Institutions and Informal Politics in Russia' in Meyer, Gerd (ed.) *Formal Institutions and Informal Politics in Central and Eastern Europe*, Opladen: 233-266.
Beck, Martin/Boeckh, Andreas/Pawelka, Peter (1997) 'Staat, Markt und Rente in der Sozialwissenschaftlichen Diskussion' in Boeckh, Andreas/Pawelka, Peter (eds.) *Staat, Markt und Rente in der internationalen Politik,* Opladen: 232-256.
Boeckh, Andreas/ Siedlaczek, Magdalena (2006) 'Venezuela nach 8 Jahren Hugo Chávez: Versuch einer Bilanz', Presentation transcript, in http://www.politikwissenschaft-lateinamerika. de/downloads/VenezuelaBoeckhSiedlaczek.pdf.
Boeckh, Andreas/Graf, Patricia (2005) 'Der Comandante in seinem Labyrinth' in Boeckh, Andreas (ed.) *Venezuela. Die Bolivarische Republik,* Bad Honnef: 81-105.
Boeckh, Andreas/Pawelka, Peter (eds.) (1997) *Staat, Markt und Rente in der internationalen Politik,* Opladen.

---

31 http://www.france24.com/en/20081127-medvedev-chavez-sign-nuclear-show-defiance-against-us-russia-venezuela, rev. 2008-12-04.

Boeckh, Andreas (2003) 'The Painful Transition of a Rentier State: Globalization and Neopopulist Regression in Venezuela' in Beck, Martin/ Barrios, Harald/ Boeckh, Andreas/Segbers, Klaus (eds.) *Resistance to Globalization. Political Struggle and Cultural Resilience in the Middle East, Russia, and Latin America*, Berlin/London/New York: 142-157.

Brewer Carías, Allan-Randolph (2001) Golpe de Estado y proceso constituyente en Venezuela, Mexico City.

Brownlee, Jason (2007) Authoritarianism in an Age of Democratization, Cambridge.

Bugueno Droguett, Rodrigo/Placencia Rodriguez, Raul (2008) 'Hugo Chávez y Vladimir Putin hidrocarburos, regimenes autoritarios y diplomacia energetica', *Lateinamerika Analysen* 19: 143-176

Buhbe, Matthes/Makarenko, Boris (2007) 'Das Mehrparteiensystem im neuen Russland' in Buhbe, Matthes/Gorzka, Gabriele (eds.) *Russland heute. Rezentralisierung des Staates unter Putin*, Wiesbaden: 273-292.

Collier, David/Levitsky, Steven (1997) 'Democracy with adjectives. Conceptual Innovation in Comparative Research', *World Politics* 3: 430-451.

Dahl, Robert A. (1971) Polyarchy. Participation and Opposition, New Haven.

Dauderstädt, Michael/Schildberg, Arne (eds.) (2006) *Dead Ends of Transition. Rentier economics and protectorates*, Frankfurt/Main.

Diamond, Larry/Morlino, Leonardo (2004) 'The Quality of Democracy. An Overview', *Journal of Democracy* 4: 20-31.

Eckstein, Harry (1975) 'Case Study and Theory in Political Science' in Greenstein, Fred I./Polsby, Nelson W. (eds) *Strategies of Inquiry. Handbook of Political Science Volume 7*, Reading/Mass.: 79-138.

Ellner, Steve/Hellinger, Daniel (eds.) (2003) *Venezuelan Politics in the Chávez Era. Class, Polarization, and Conflict*, Boulder.

Ellner, Steve (1993) 'The Deepening of Democracy in a Crisis Setting: Political Reform and the Electoral Process in Venezuela', *Journal of Interamerican Studies and World Affairs* 4: 1-42.

Erdmann, Gero/Engel, Ulf (2006) 'Neopatrimonialism Revisited - Beyond a Catch-All Concept', *GIGA* Working Paper 16, Hamburg.

Fortescue, Stephen (2006) Russia's Oil Barons and Metal Magnates. Oligarchs and the State in Tranistion, Basingstoke.

Friebe, Anne (2006) '100 Prozent für die Revolution bei 25 Prozent Wahlbeteiligung', *Lateinamerika Nachrichten* 379, in http://www.lateinamerikanachrichten.de/index.php?/artikel/757.html.

Gandhi, Jennifer/Przeworski, Adam (2007)' Authoritarian Institutions and the survival of Autocrats', *Comparative Political Studies* 11: 1279–1301.

Gil Yepes, José Antonio (2004) 'Public Opinion, Political Socialization, and Regime Stabilization', in McCoy, Jennifer/Myers, David (eds.) *The Unraveling of representative Democracy in Venezuela*, Baltimore: 231-262.

N.N. (2007) 'Chavez kann Venezuela per Dekret regieren', *Handelsblatt* January 09, 2007.

Harks, Enno/Müller, Friedemann (2007) *Petrostaaten. Außenpolitik im Zeichen von Öl*, Baden-Baden.

Hellinger, Daniel (2003) 'The Breakdown of Puntofijismo and the Rise of Chavismo' in Ellner, Steve/Hellinger, Daniel (eds.) *Venezuelan Politics in the Chávez Era. Class, Polarization, and Conflict*, Boulder: 27-54.

Helmke, Gretchen/Levitsky, Steven (eds.) (2006) Informal institutions and democracy. Lessons from Latin America, Baltimore.

Hermet, Guy (1978) 'State-controlled elections: a Framework' in Hermet, Guy/Rose, Richard/Rouquié, Alain (eds.) *Elections without Choice*, London: 1-18.
Hidalgo, Manuel (2008) '"Por ahí no, mi Comandante": freno en el referéndum al Socialismo del Siglo XXI', *Análisis del Real Instituto Elcano* (ARI) 3, Madrid.
Kestler, Thomas (2008) 'Das politische System Venezuelas' in Stüwe, Klaus/Rinke, Stefan (eds.) *Die politischen Systeme in Nord- und Lateinamerika*, Wiesbaden: 581-600.
Kornblith, Miriam (2007) 'Venezuela: calidad de las elecciones y calidad de la democracia', *América latina hoy: Revista de ciencias sociales* 45: 109–124.
Krastev, Ivan (2006) 'Democracy's "Doubles"', *Journal of Democracy* 2: 52-62.
Ledeneva, Alena (2006) How Russia really works. The informal Practices that shaped post-soviet politics and business, Ithaca.
Levine, Daniel H. (2002) 'The Decline and Fall of Democracy in Venezuela', *Bulletin of Latin American Research* 2: 248-269.
Levitsky, Steven/Way, Lucan A. (2002) 'Elections without Democracy. The Rise of competitive Authoritarianism', *Journal of Democracy* 2: 51-65.
Linz, Juan A. (2000) Totalitarian and Authoritarian Regimes, Boulder.
López Maya, Margarita (2002) 'Partidos de Vocación Popular en la Recomposición del Sistema Político Venezolano. Fortalezas y Debilidades', *Rev. Venez. de Econ. y Ciencias Sociales* 1: 109–131.
McCoy, Jennifer (2004) 'From Representative to Participatory Democracy', in McCoy, Jennifer/Myers, David (eds.) *The Unraveling of Representative Democracy in Venezuela*, Baltimore: 152–178.
McCoy, Jennifer/Myers, David (eds.) (2004) The Unraveling of Representative Democracy in Venezuela, Baltimore.
Medvedev, Sergei (2004) ' Putin's Second Republic: Russian Scenarios', *Internationale Politik und Gesellschaft* 1.
Merkel, Wolfgang (2004) ‚Embedded and Defective Democracies', *Democratization* 5: 33-58.
Molina, José (2004) 'The Unraveling of Venezuela's Party System' in McCoy, Jennifer/Myers, David (eds.) *The Unraveling of Representative Democracy in Venezuela*, Baltimore: 152-178.
Mommer, Bernhard (2003) 'Subversive Oil' in Ellner, Steve/Hellinger, Daniel (eds.) *Venezuelan Politics in the Chávez Era. Class, Polarization, and Conflict*, Boulder: 131-146.
Nohlen, Dieter (2000) *Wahlrecht und Parteiensystem*, Opladen.
Nohlen, Dieter (2007) *Wahlrecht und Parteiensystem*, Opladen.
Nussberger, Angelika/Marenkov, Dmitry (2007) 'Wahlgesetz als Steuerungsmechanismus: Zu den neuen rechtlichen Grundlagen der Duma-Wahlen im Dezember 2007', *Russlandanalysen* 146: 2-5.
Ottaway, Marina (2003) Democracy Challenged. The Rise of Semi-Authoritarianism, Washington D.C.
Parsons, Talcott (1963) 'On the Concept of Political Power', *Proceedings of the American Philosophical Society* 3: 232-262.
Petkoff, Theodoro (2005) 'Chávez und die Medien' in Sevilla, Rafael (ed.) *Venezuela. Die bolivarische Republik*, Bad Honnef: 113-122.
Petrov, Nikolai (2007) 'The Consequences of the State Duma Elections for Russia's Electoral System', *Russian Analytical Digest* 32: 5-8.
Pleines, Heiko (2008) Reformblockaden in der Wirtschaftspolitik, Wiesbaden.

Przeworski, Adam (1992) 'The Games of Transition' in Mainwaring, Scott (ed.) *Issues in Democratic Consolidation. The new south American Democracies in Comparative Perspective*, Notre Dame: 105-152.

Puddington, Arch (2008) 'Is the Tide turning? The 2007 Freedom House Survey', *Journal of Democracy* 2: 61-78.

Remington, Thomas F. (2008) 'Patronage and Power: Russia's Dominant Party Regime', *Politische Vierteljahresschrift* 2: 213-228.

Rösch, Michael/Röder, Jörg (2004) 'Abgesang auf eine weitere enttäuschte Hoffnung - Der Niedergang der bolivarianischen Republik' in Kurtenbach, Sabine (ed.) *Die Andenregion - Neuer Krisenbogen in Lateinamerika*, Frankfurt/Main: 189-208.

Sakwa, Richard (2008) *Russian Politics and Society*, London/New York.

Schedler, Andreas (ed.) (2006) Electoral Authoritarianism: The Dynamics of unfree competition, Boulder.

Schedler, Andreas (2002) 'The Menu of Manipulation. Elections without Democracy', *Journal of Democracy* 2: 36–50.

Schroeder, Friedrich-Christian (2007) ‚Die Russischen Strafvorschriften gegen Extremismus', *Russlandanalysen* 149: 14-16.

Schumpeter, Joseph A. (1987) [1950] *Kapitalismus, Sozialismus und Demokratie*, Tübingen.

Shevtsova, Lilia (2007) Russia - Lost in Transition. The Yeltsin and Putin Legacies, Washington D.C.

Silitski, Vitali (2009) 'Reading Russia. Tools of Autocracy', *Journal of Democracy* 2: 42-46.

Stykow, Petra (2006) Staat und Wirtschaft in Russland. Interessenvermittlung zwischen Korruption und Konzertierung, Wiesbaden.

Trinkunas, Harold A. (2000) 'Crafting Civilian Control in Emerging Democracies: Argentina and Venezuela', *Journal of Interamerican Studies and World Affairs* 3: 77-109.

Way, Lucan A. (2005) 'Authoritarian State Building and the Sources of Regime Competitiveness in the Fourth Wave. The Case of Belarus, Moldova, Russia, and Ukraine', *World Politics* 2: 231–261.

Welsch, Friedrich/Briceno, Héctor (2008) 'Populistische Milieus in der politischen Kultur Venezuelas' in Graf, Particia/Stehnken, Thomas (eds.) *Lateinamerika. Politik, Wirtschaft und Gesellschaft*, Baden-Baden: 193-202.

Weyland, Kurt (1999) 'Populism in the Age of Neoliberalism', in Conniff, Michael L. (ed.) *Populism in Latin America*, London: 172-190.

Zeuske, Michael (2007) *Kleine Geschichte Venezuelas*, München.

Zilla, Claudia/Pfütze, Luise (2005) 'Venezuela nach den Parlamentswahlen Zwischen interner politischer Polarisierung und regionalem Führungsanspruch', *Stiftung Wissenschaft Politik - Aktuell* 61, Berlin.

ARTICLE

Wilted Roses and Tulips: The Regression of Democratic Rule in Kyrgyzstan and Georgia

Christoph H. Stefes and Jenniver Sehring[1]

Abstract In the mid 1990s Georgia and Kyrgyzstan were beacons of hope for democratic transition in the former Soviet Union as they witnessed economic and political liberalization in the wake of the collapse of communist rule. Yet towards the end of the decade these hopes were dashed, when early democratic gains gave way to increasing authoritarianism. When the so-called coloured revolutions swept away the semi-authoritarian governments in Georgia and Kyrgyzstan in 2003 and 2005, respectively, the hope returned that the path towards democracy would now be cleared. Yet once again disillusionment sunk in; the new rulers have frequently relied on the same non-democratic means as their predecessors to stay in office. Combining insights from the studies of Stephen Fish as well as Steve Levitsky and Lucan Way, we argue that super-presidentialism, a weakly organized and fragmented opposition, and the adverse impact of authoritarian neighbours have stood in the way of democratization in these two countries. Nevertheless, today's Georgia is in a better position than Kyrgyzstan to cement democratic rule due to strong Western leverage.

1. Introduction

The countries of the former Soviet Union (FSU), minus the Baltic states, form the only region in the world where political rights and civil liberties have witnessed a steady decline since 2001 (Freedom House 2009a). Yet after popular uprisings that toppled semi-authoritarian governments, Georgia and Kyrgyzstan initially appeared to be promising cases for reversing authoritarian developments in the region. Following Georgia's Rose Revolution (November 2003) and Kyrgyzstan's Tulip Revolution (March 2005), the incoming governments promised democratic reforms. This paper does not attempt to explain these popular uprisings, as numerous studies have already addressed this puzzle (e.g., Beissinger 2007; Bunce and Wolchik 2006; McFaul 2005; Way 2008). Instead, we

---

[1] The authors thank Julie George, Kim Johnson and the three anonymous reviewers for their insightful comments. The paper was completed in May 2010 and can therefore only cover the events up to this date.

will take stock of the political developments in both countries since their 'revolutions'.² Thus far, this topic has received scant scholarly attention (e.g., Hale 2006; Laverty 2008; Tudoroiu 2007). The findings are sobering. Half a decade after the revolutions, authoritarianism is still entrenched in both countries. In fact, while Kyrgyzstan initially had a democratic window shortly after the Tulip Revolution, Georgia's new leadership immediately moved away from its proclaimed democratic agenda. In recent years, the outlook for a democratic Georgia has brightened somewhat, while yet another popular uprising toppled Kyrgyzstan's authoritarian regime in April 2010. At this point it is too early to tell whether Kyrgyzstan will be able to use this second chance to initiate a democratic turnaround or whether the country will go through another cycle of unstable authoritarian rule.

We argue that super-presidentialism and the corresponding near-absence of horizontal accountability as well as weak vertical accountability due to feeble civil societies and opposition parties are the main causes of democratic regression in both countries. In Kyrgyzstan the weakness of civil society is compounded by the fact that powerful authoritarian neighbours offset Western influence. In contrast, Georgia's exposure to Western leverage is considerably stronger, especially since the Russia-Georgia War in 2008. While Western countries, especially the United States, initially ignored the new Georgian president's authoritarian streak, since 2008 the West has been somewhat less forgiving.

The first section of this paper outlines its theoretical framework. In the next section we summarize the political developments in both countries since independence. The third section applies the theoretical framework to explain political developments since the revolutions. In the fourth section we compare Georgia and Kyrgyzstan with two other countries that experienced the ouster of semi-authoritarian regimes in the wake of popular uprisings. This comparison provides further empirical support for the argument advanced in this paper. The paper concludes with a set of policy recommendations.

2. Theoretical Framework

The regression of democracy is often explained by pointing towards the lack of a civic culture (Almond and Verba 1963, Inglehart and Welzel 2005), economic inequality (Arat 1991), low levels of economic development (Przeworski and Limongi 1997), ideological polarization (Sartori 1976), etc. Yet as Stephen Fish convincingly shows, for post-communist countries, 'most of the "usual" causes do not readily explain democratic erosion' (Fish 2001, p. 65). Instead, Fish argues that three factors are the major culprits in bringing about authoritarianism in post-communist countries. First, the seeds of democratic erosion can often be found in constitutions that concentrate power in the

---

2 We adopt the widely used term 'revolution' in this paper as shorthand for the events in 2003 and 2005. However, it is clear that the popular uprisings have not brought about any fundamental political, social and/or economic changes in these two countries. For a further discussion of the term revolution in the context of the popular upheavals in four post-communist countries, see Charles Fairbanks (2007).

presidency. Super-presidentialism weakens institutional checks and balances, allowing the president to usurp power through formal and informal, legal and illegal means. The concentration of power in the presidency encourages the political and economic elite to rally around the holder of this office. As Henry Hale explains, 'This is because of the great power a patronal president has to influence the fates of these stakeholders, be it actively (through repression or rewards for loyalty) or passively (through overlooking corruption charges or ignoring pleas for resource transfers)' (Hale 2006, p. 312). While super-presidentialism is neither a necessary nor a sufficient condition for democratic erosion, Fish demonstrates that in post-communist countries, super-presidentialism has usually set in motion the establishment of authoritarian regimes.

Super-presidential regimes are often created in the immediate aftermath of major political shifts that catapult new leaders into power. Ironically, the intention thereby is to bolster democracy 'against entrenched forces of the old regime' (Fish 2001, p. 70). These new regimes are characterized by (a) an inflated presidential apparatus that overshadows any other state agency in size, resources, and expertise; (b) expansive presidential authority to rule by decree and to control the state budget; (c) a judiciary whose members' tenure depends largely on the goodwill of the president; (d) a parliament whose legislative authority and power to control the executive branch are sharply circumscribed; and (e) 'provisions that make impeachment of the president extremely difficult' (Fish 2001, p. 69).

In a corresponding study Fish (2006) emphasizes the crucial role of parliaments for democratic development. Parliaments fail to curtail presidential abuses of power if the constitution does not entitle them to conduct independent investigations of the chief executive, appoint the prime minister and individual ministers, vote against the prime minister and his cabinet and/or a proposed budget without fear of being dissolved by the executive branch, and pass (almost) veto-proof legislation (Fish 2006, p. 8). Moreover, weak parliaments stifle the development of political parties, as super-presidential regimes encourage personalist and informal politics. As 'parties are the main vehicles for structuring political competition and for linking the people and their elected officials', a weak parliament bodes ill for the development of democratic institutions (Fish 2006, p. 13).

The importance of political parties – and especially opposition parties – is echoed in Fish's second variable, 'the condition of political oppositions to chief executives' (Fish 2001, p. 72). A political opposition not organized into coherent and well-organized parties further compounds the malady of weak parliaments and super-presidents. Without a viable political alternative, citizens are less prone to protest and more likely to become apathetic. Finally, Fish argues that even in the absence of strong *domestic* checks and balances, prospective dictators might be reluctant to abuse their power when they depend on the support of *foreign* governments that are unwilling to tolerate blatant authoritarian rule. On the other hand, presidents might be less hesitant to violate constitutional rights and procedures if they can count on an external patron that is less keen on protecting and developing democracy inside and outside its own borders (Fish 2001, p. 73ff). Steven Levitsky and Lucan Way (2005) develop this point further. While Fish seems to emphasize what Levitsky and Way call 'Western leverage', they argue that 'Western linkage' is a more important pro-democratic force: 'mechanisms of leverage

[...] were by themselves rarely sufficient to democratize post-Cold War autocracies. Rather the more subtle and diffuse effects of linkage contributed more consistently to democratization' (Levitsky and Way 2005, p. 21).

The authors define Western leverage 'as authoritarian governments' vulnerability to external democratizing pressure' (Levitsky and Way 2005, p. 21). This vulnerability varies considerably from country to country. Economically and/or militarily powerful states depend less on the West and are therefore less susceptible to Western diplomatic and economic pressure, military intervention and political conditionality. Moreover, the West might be less willing to employ these means if a country is of strategic importance to the West. Finally, and in line with Fish's thesis, the existence of a powerful external patron that bolsters authoritarian leaders can offset Western leverage (Levitsky and Way 2005, p. 21-22). Yet even if countries are exposed to democratizing pressure, without strong social, economic and political ties to the West, the consequences of Western leverage might be disappointing. Where linkage is weak, autocrats and would-be autocrats might assume – often accurately – that Western countries will settle for a democratic façade. On the other hand, 'where linkage is extensive, it creates multiple pressure points – from investors to technocrats to voters – that few autocrats can afford to ignore' (Levitsky and Way 2005, p. 25).

The last point goes beyond the role of political parties, addressing the importance of civil society more generally. Larry Diamond (1994, p. 221) defines civil society as 'The realm of organized social life that is open, voluntary, self-generating, at least partially self-supporting, autonomous from the state, and bound by a legal order or a set of shared collective rules'. These societal organizations often serve as watchdogs, detecting government abuses, communicating this knowledge to the public and/or organizing the masses to force governments to change course. Ultimately, executive heads are restrained not only by formal constitutional provisions (horizontal accountability) but also by pressure from below (vertical accountability). Governments that have come to power in the wake of popular uprisings are undoubtedly aware of the power of the masses.

In short, super-presidential regimes are prone to slide towards authoritarian rule, especially if the opposition is weak and democratic pressure from abroad is absent. Under these circumstances, even democratically elected presidents might be willing to abuse their vast resources to stay in office, enrich themselves and/or pursue their political agendas. The presidents of Georgia (Zviad Gamsakhurdia, Eduard Shevardnadze and Mikhail Saakashvili) and Kyrgyzstan (Askar Akaev and Kurmanbek Bakiev) have undoubtedly found this temptation irresistible as well. However, not all have been willing or able to abuse their positions to the same degree. As the cases of Saakashvili and Bakiev demonstrate, this difference can be explained by taking the variables discussed above into account.

3. From 'Feckless Pluralism' to 'Dominant Power Politics': Georgia and Kyrgyzstan since Independence

In a seminal article, Thomas Carothers identifies two forms of regimes 'stuck' somewhere between democratic and authoritarian rule (Carothers 2002). The one regime type is characterized by 'feckless pluralism', the other by 'dominant power politics'; the former largely corresponds to a regime that most scholars would call semi-democratic, the latter more closely resembles a semi-authoritarian form of government. In feckless pluralist regimes, elections are relatively free and fair, giving the opposition a chance to drive the incumbents out of office. However, 'democracy remains shallow and troubled, [as] political participation, though broad at election time, extends little beyond voting' (Carothers 2002, p. 10). Citizens do not trust the political class and do not expect much from it. The state is fragmented, weak and ineffective.

In the presence of dominant power politics, however, regimes rarely meet democratic standards. Although elections are not stolen outright, the political space is so narrow that the competition is not fair, depriving the opposition of any real chance to drive the incumbents from office. The latter thereby rely heavily on state resources – that is, 'money, jobs, public information (via state media), and police power' (Carothers 2002, p. 12) – to consolidate their rule. Moreover, unlike the case in feckless pluralist regimes, the judiciary is not independent but toes the government's line. Horizontal accountability is therefore sharply reduced. Since their independence in 1991, both Georgia and Kyrgyzstan have moved steadily from feckless pluralism to dominant power politics. While this process had already begun under President Shevardnadze in Georgia and Akaev in Kyrgyzstan, it significantly accelerated in Georgia immediately following the Rose Revolution and in Kyrgyzstan about two years after the Tulip Revolution.

From Independence to Revolution

Georgia declared independence in April 1991. Its independence movement scored overwhelming victories in the parliamentary and presidential elections of 1990 and 1991. Yet its leader, Zviad Gamsakhurdia, 'a long-time nationalist and anti-Soviet dissident' (Hesli 2007, 346), showed little tolerance for the opposition and the country's ethnic minorities once he was in power. His authoritarian leadership and national chauvinism soon caused a short civil war, which led to his ouster. In addition, ethnic minorities in South Ossetia and Abkhazia fought successful secessionist wars against the Georgian majority. In the wake of these wars, Georgia's state and economy collapsed (Stefes 2006, Chap. 2). To save the country from state failure, Gamsakhurdia's successor, Eduard Shevardnadze, was forced to engage in a delicate political balancing act. The former first secretary of Georgia's Communist Party thereby relied on former colleagues from the Soviet *nomenklatura* to run the state apparatus but simultaneously brought young reformers into his government to mollify the West and secure foreign aid and loans. This awkward coalition was institutionalized in the presidential party, the Citizen's Union of Georgia (CUG) (Fuller 1998). In 1995 a new constitution created a presidential republic. In the successive parliamentary and presidential elections, the CUG and Shevardnadze won by wide margins.

The next five years saw spurts of political liberalization. Western aid and loans combined with market reforms initially resulted in solid economic growth rates. Yet the Soviet legacy of endemic corruption reversed early economic gains and caused a rapidly widening gap between rich and poor, sparking small-scale uprisings throughout the country (Stefes 2006, Chap. 5). By the early years of this century, the differences between the reformers and the old (corrupt) guard in the government had become insurmountable. In 2001 a leading reformer, Mikhail Saakashvili, deserted the government ranks and founded the National Movement (NM). Other reformers soon followed him, turning the upcoming 2003 parliamentary elections into a rallying point for the opposition.

Unlike Georgia, Kyrgyzstan experienced a far less traumatic transition from Soviet rule, despite early conflicts between various regional cliques as well as between the Kyrgyz majority and the Uzbek minority. Initially, the government under President Akaev promoted a liberal agenda. A multiparty system evolved and a relatively vibrant civil society and a pluralistic media emerged with the support of international institutions. Despite some shortcomings, the parliamentary and presidential elections in 1995 came close to meeting democratic standards. At the time, Kyrgyzstan was considered a success story for post-Soviet transitions towards democracy and a market economy (Juraev 2008, p. 256; Spector 2004, p. 19).

Yet these early achievements in building democratic institutions were reversed in the second part of the 1990s. National referenda were the most common means of undermining formal democratic institutions, especially those targeting the powers of the parliament and subordinating the judiciary to the president (Huskey 2002; Von Gumppenberg 2004). A dubious interpretation of the constitution allowed Akaev to run for a third presidential term in 2000. The presidential and parliamentary elections that year did not meet OSCE standards for democratic elections. The government increasingly cracked down on critical media outlets. By the early years of this century, independent TV channels had ceased to operate (Juraev 2008, p. 256). In January 2003 a new constitution was adopted, further consolidating presidential power (Beyer 2006; Tolipov 2006).

Simultaneous to this gradual regression of democracy through formal constitutional changes, informal political practices increasingly undermined democratic institutions. For instance, Akaev used informal pacts and bribery to muzzle the parliament. He also relied on trumped up criminal charges to dispose of regime critics. For instance, Akaev's main rival in the presidential elections, the former prime minister Felix Kulov, was arrested on corruption charges and sentenced to seven years in prison (Lewis 2008, p. 125f; Tolipov 2006, p. 67). As was the case in Georgia, bribery and extortion became widespread in the political sphere. Using patronage, Akaev attempted to balance the interests of different regional networks. However, he was increasingly perceived as favouring his own clique of relatives and followers from the northern part of the country (Collins 2002; Spector 2004).

The so-called Aksy Event in March 2002 heralded the end of Akaev's rule. Hundreds of protestors gathered in Aksy (southern Kyrgyzstan) to protest the arrest of a prominent parliamentarian from the region. The protests turned violent, and the police shot six protesters. It was the first time that security forces had shot at and killed peaceful protestors (Radnitz 2005; Sehring 2005). These events triggered a serious political crisis, and demands for Akaev's resignation became louder.

The Rose and Tulip Revolutions

In both countries the opposition was able to capitalize on increasing authoritarianism, corruption and socio-economic hardship. Rigged elections eventually served as the trigger for mass protests that led to the overthrow of Shevardnadze and Akaev. Yet the revolutions unfolded in distinct ways. While a somewhat united opposition with popular appeal and a clear reform agenda spearheaded the popular uprising in the Georgian capital, the revolution in Kyrgyzstan had its origins in the rural areas of the South, and popular uprisings were initially localized and largely uncoordinated. Only when protestors marched towards the capital did an identifiable opposition leadership emerge. It is also noteworthy that the Kyrgyz opposition mobilized only a small fraction of the population in comparison to the genuine mass mobilization in Georgia.

While elections in Georgia had been falsified before, it was only in 2003 that Georgians engaged in mass demonstrations of up to 100,000 protestors as a result. The general mood had summarily turned against Shevardnadze's regime, and Saakashvili's NM, together with other opposition parties, offered real political alternatives for the first time (Mitchell 2009). When official results showed the opposition trailing, despite the fact that independent exit polls predicted a majority for the opposition, people took to the streets, demanding a rerun of the elections and Shevardnadze's resignation. After days of protests, Shevardnadze resigned, paving the way for new elections. Saakashvili won the presidential elections with more than 96 per cent of the vote, and his party, which had merged with another major opposition party shortly before the elections, won the parliamentary elections by a landslide as well. The National Movement, renamed the United National Movement (UNM) after the merger, became the dominant party in the Georgian parliament.

In Kyrgyzstan, the parliamentary elections of February 2005 were held in accordance with the new electoral system, which had been changed from a proportional system to a single-member district system with a reduced number of parliamentary seats. Stiff competition therefore ensued, and local strongmen were often the most promising candidates (Lewis 2008, p. 133f). The first protests arose two weeks prior to the elections when the Central Election Commission failed to register some opposition candidates. After the elections and by-elections, which did not meet OSCE standards, protests continued, especially in Kyrgyzstan's South, where protestors seized government buildings. The opposition demanded Akaev's resignation and a rerun of the parliamentary elections. The protesters eventually marched to Bishkek, where they joined the capital's opposition. On 24 March roughly 10,000 protestors reached the presidential residence and seized the building without facing any meaningful resistance from the security guards. President Akaev was forced to flee the country.

Former prime minister Bakiev was appointed interim president, even though he had never been a central figure of the opposition movement. His rise to the top of the opposition party has indeed remained somewhat obscure (Pannier 2009a). After his release from prison, Kulov also joined the ranks of the incoming government. As Kulov represented northern interests and Bakiev the interests of Kyrgyzstan's South, there were fears of growing tensions. The two therefore agreed to form an alliance with Bakiev as presidential candidate and Kulov as designated prime minister. Bakiev won the subsequent election with almost 90 per cent of the votes, and Kulov became prime minister.

The Aftermath

Most analysts predicted that Saakashvili's victory would give Georgia a chance to defeat systemic corruption and reverse the ominous slide towards authoritarianism that had started during Shevardnadze's second presidential term (Fairbanks 2004; King 2004; Wertsch 2005). Saakashvili initially made good on his promises. His fight against corruption was determined and largely successful. Economic liberalization further reduced the opportunities for corruption and provided a boost to the economy. The successive increase in economic activity in the legal market caused state revenues to quadruple within a short time (Stefes 2006, p. 168). Saakashvili also forced the resignation of Aslan Abashidze, who had ruled the country's south-western province of Adjara like a personal fiefdom in clear defiance of the central government. Shortly after taking control of Adjara, the Saakashvili government successfully negotiated the closure of the last remaining Russian bases in Georgia. With Abashidze's defeat and the expulsion of Russian troops, Saakashvili made an important step towards the restoration of Georgia's territorial integrity, a top priority on his political agenda.

However, an utter disregard for democratic norms accompanied Saakashvili's laudable attempts to reverse state disintegration. In the first year of his presidency, Georgia moved from a presidential to a 'hyperpresidential' system (Fairbanks 2004). In its fight against corruption, the government frequently violated the rule of law. Moreover, media freedom came under attack (Areshidze 2007, Chap. 10–13; Mitchell 2009, Chap. 5). In November 2007 security forces dispelled mass protests with excessive use of force. Saakashvili subsequently declared a state of emergency, which allowed him to take the last independent TV station off the air. Snap presidential and parliamentary elections in January and May 2008 revealed a heavily skewed playing field. Saakashvili won the presidential elections in the first round (this time, however, with just 53 per cent of the votes), and his party took more than two-thirds of the parliamentary seats (albeit with slightly less than 60 per cent of the votes). Shortly after the elections, Russia provoked Georgia into launching a military assault on South Ossetia; this culminated in an all-out war, which the Georgian side quickly lost. The August War provided the opposition with a welcome opportunity to organize another round of mass protests, though these fizzled out – without the intervention of security forces however (George and Stefes 2006).

In Kyrgyzstan the first two years after the Tulip Revolution were chaotic and marred by violence and government paralysis. The departure of Akaev and his followers allowed for the redistribution of the country's major economic assets. The ensuing rivalry between various (legal and illegal) business groups became increasingly violent as the state apparatus was unable to enforce the law. Criminal groups also accessed formal political structures. In 2005/06 several contract killings of parliamentary deputies who were alleged mafia leaders shook the country (Graubner and Wolters 2007). In response to the president's feebleness, disappointed allies of Bakiev began to join the opposition.

While a fledgling state and the increasing criminalization of the political and economic spheres generally do not bode well for democratic reforms, the deadlock between the supporters of President Bakiev and Prime Minister Kulov also meant that neither side was able to consolidate its power. This power vacuum provided political space, allowing civil society to recover, political participation to increase, and freedom of speech to flourish. OSCE observers assessed the presidential elections in June 2005 more positively than they had previous ones. In 2006 former Bakiev allies formed an opposition alliance that organized several protests and led to some government concessions (Lewis 2008, p. 153). As of 2007, however, Bakiev consistently took steps to cement his rule. He set up his own presidential party, which won a vast majority of the parliamentary seats in December 2007 amidst allegations of massive electoral fraud (Juraev 2008). The government put pressure on opposition leaders, journalists and NGO representatives (Bertelsmann Transformation Index 2008). In July 2009 Bakiev was re-elected despite widespread dissatisfaction with his corrupt government.

Despite the president's attempts to cement power, the Bakiev regime collapsed in April 2010 amidst a popular uprising that in many ways resembled the Tulip Revolution. As before, popular protests emerged in response to socio-economic hardship and government corruption, and as in 2005, the protests emerged spontaneously without a clearly discernible leadership. This time, however, the security forces did not hesitate to use deadly force to repel the protestors. More than one hundred people died in the violent clashes between protestors and the riot police. Bakiev eventually followed the example of his predecessor and resigned.

The following figure, which summarizes Freedom House's Freedom in the World (FW) index, illustrates the political developments in Georgia and Kyrgyzstan. The addition of ratings for Uzbekistan, one of the most repressive dictatorships in the region, and Estonia, a former Soviet country that has consolidated liberal democracy, puts the political developments in these two countries into perspective.

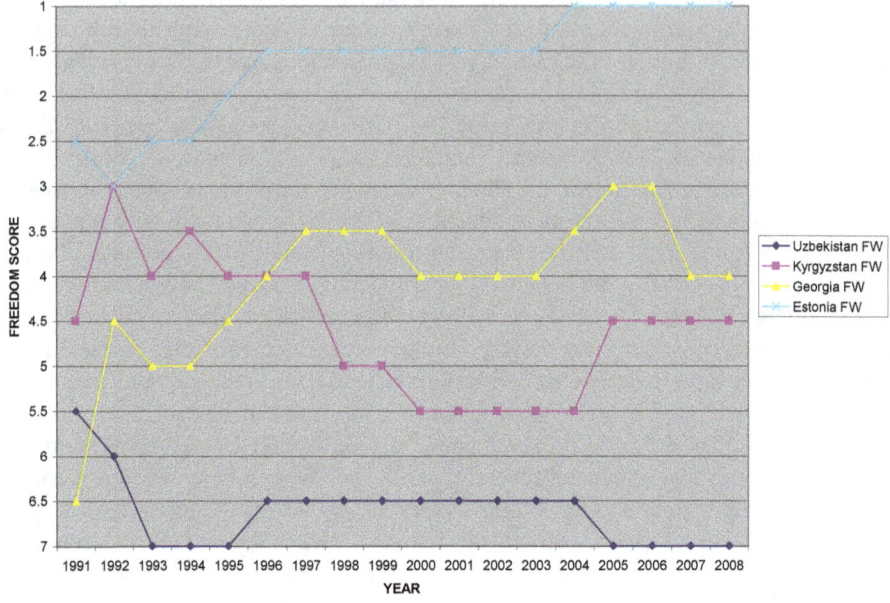

Source: Freedom House (n.d.), Freedom House (2009a); 'Freedom Score': combined scores (1: free; 7: not free); 'Year': years covered (not publication year).

Figure 1: Political Developments in Selected Post-Soviet Countries (Freedom in the World)

Several scholars have criticized Freedom House's methodology, pointing to the flawed validity and reliability of the FW index (Bollen 1993; Munck 2009). The shortcomings concerning the reliability of the index become especially apparent when the FW scores are compared with the Nations in Transit (NT) scores for Georgia and Kyrgyzstan. Although the data is collected by the same organization and follows largely the same methodology, even a cursory analysis reveals a stark discrepancy between the Nations in Transit index and the FW index; the two diverge sharply in their evaluations of political developments in Georgia and Kyrgyzstan. Namely, FW arrives at a more sanguine assessment of the post-revolutionary developments than does NT. While NT sees few democratic improvements in Georgia following the Rose Revolution, FW notes an increase in freedom until 2007 (followed by a return to pre-revolution levels). The same holds true for Kyrgyzstan. Here, FW notes continuing improvements from after the Tulip Revolution until today, while NT observes no improvements until 2007 and a decline in freedom after 2007. Finally, for 2008, FW considers both countries semi-authoritarian (partially free, non-electoral regimes), while NT differentiates between the two, labelling Kyrgyzstan a 'consolidated authoritarian regime' and Georgia a 'transitional government or hybrid regime'.

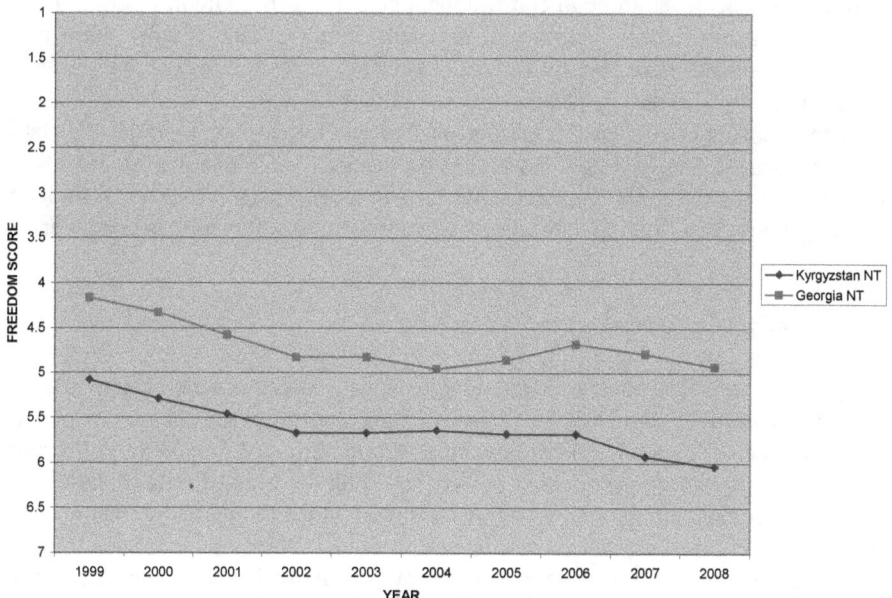

Source: Freedom House (2009b); 'Year': years covered (not publication year).

Figure 2: Political Developments in Georgia and Kyrgyzstan (Nations in Transit)

By taking into account the increasing centralization of power in the presidency, the increasing abuse of state resources for political purposes, the frequent violations of the rule of law, widespread vote rigging, and the shrinking space for critical voices and organized opposition, NT more accurately reflects the reality of both countries move from feckless pluralism to dominant power politics. Unlike FW, NT appears unimpressed by Saakashvili's democratic rhetoric. Moreover, NT correctly identifies 2007 as a decisive year for political developments in Kyrgyzstan – that is, towards less freedom, something that goes unnoticed by FW. Finally, while calling Georgia 'a transitional government' might seem optimistic, NT correctly labels Kyrgyzstan an 'authoritarian regime'. Based on this assessment, the following questions arise. Why did Georgia begin to move towards semi-authoritarianism immediately after the Rose Revolution? Why did the same thing happen in Kyrgyzstan but with a two-year delay? Finally, what makes the Georgian regime less authoritarian than its Kyrgyz counterpart?

4. Post-revolution Blues: Explaining the Regression of Democracy

The regression of democracy in the wake of both the Georgian and Kyrgyz revolutions had its origins in the concentration of power in the head of state and the corresponding subordination of parliament and judiciary to the presidency. This amassment of executive power was achieved through constitutional changes (especially in Georgia) as well as informal means such as patronage (especially in Kyrgyzstan). After these power grabs, the presidents were able to use state resources to repress opposition parties and stifle civil society. The Kyrgyz leadership was initially able to rely on Russia's political and economic support. When this support waned and turned into hostility, the Bakiev regime collapsed. The Georgian leadership benefited from Western governments that turned a blind eye on creeping authoritarianism. This complicity has changed somewhat since the August War, forcing the Georgian government to soften its grip on power.

From Presidential to Super-presidential Systems

Taking advantage of his popularity and a large majority in parliament, the newly elected President Saakashvili pushed through far-reaching constitutional changes within less than three weeks of taking office, obviating any opportunity for public deliberation. These changes enhanced presidential powers, entitling the head of state to dissolve the parliament (for example, in the event that legislators failed to approve a state budget in three successive votes) and to keep a prime minister and cabinet in place even if they do not enjoy parliamentary support (for example, by dissolving the parliament and appointing a prime minister by decree) (EurasiaNet 2004). After further amendments, the president also gained the power to appoint and dismiss the justice, interior, and defence ministers without the prime minster's approval. Since Saakashvili is also the unrivalled leader of the ruling party, the legislative body has turned into a rubber stamp. As Lincoln Mitchell observes, 'The UNM members in parliament are loyal to the president as many were hand picked by him to be on the party list for the 2004 and 2008 elections. As a result, there is little opposition in parliament' (Mitchell 2009, p. 92).

Presidential control over the judiciary branch has also expanded. The president is empowered to appoint and dismiss all judges based on the recommendation of Georgia's Supreme Council of Justice (half of whose members the president appoints). Armed with these legal mechanisms, the executive branch has frequently disregarded judicial independence, using the threat of disciplinary measures to keep judges in line. Saakashvili has personally meddled in trials, putting prosecutors and judges under pressure (Anjaparidze 2005). As Charles Fairbanks (2004, p. 118) concludes, 'Shevardnadze's "superpresidential" constitution is now Saakashvili's "hyperpresidential" constitution'. Surprisingly, the creation of a 'hyperpresidential' system initially encountered little resistance. The situation of the Georgian state and economy was so dire that most citizens agreed that strong leadership was needed. While under Shevardnadze the Georgian state was too weak to impose dictatorial rule, Saakashvili has been able to rely on a disciplined and loyal state apparatus (Cheterian 2008, p. 703). Since Saakashvili sees himself as a state- and nation-builder first, and as a democrat only second, the emergence of dominant power politics was probably inevitable (Mitchell 2009, Chap. 4; Transitions Online 2007).

In Kyrgyzstan, the creation of a super-presidential system following the Tulip Revolution was delayed. Unlike Saakashvili, Bakiev did not enjoy widespread popularity, nor could he initially rely on a strong presidential party. Instead, his presidency depended on a fragile alliance between various political groupings from the country's North and South. In the first two years, Bakiev faced a recalcitrant opposition consisting of regional strongmen who vocally demanded a transfer of power from the presidency to the parliament. After a week of mass protests in November 2006, Bakiev finally gave in and signed a new constitution that curtailed presidential authority and strengthened the parliament. However, what appeared to be a fatal defeat for Bakiev's government and 'another manifestation of Kyrgyzstan's move towards a democratic state with high rates of civic engagement' (Marat 2006) turned out to be the last throes of a doomed opposition.

In December 2006 the parliament passed constitutional amendments, returning several powers to Bakiev. The Supreme Court struck down both texts. In response, Bakiev submitted a new draft, which was approved by the public in a national referendum in October. There was little time to debate the constitution. Moreover, widespread vote rigging secured a large majority in favour of the new constitution, which gave the president direct control over the security and law-enforcement structures and empowered him to appoint the defence and security ministers. The president was given the power to dissolve the parliament, while parliament could impeach the president only with 80 per cent of the votes (Marat 2007). In addition, the new constitution reintroduced a proportional system. This new electoral system undermined the power of local and regional strongmen, who had previously bought their seats in parliament by bribing voters in single-member districts. By introducing a 5 per cent threshold and a clause that required parties to garner at least 0.5 per cent of votes in every administrative region in order to enter parliament, the constitution undercut smaller parties.

Shortly before the referendum, Bakiev had announced the creation of a new, pro-presidential bloc, Ak Zhol. One day after the referendum, Bakiev dissolved the parliament and called for snap elections in December 2007. Ak Zhol soon attracted smaller parties which did not expect to gain seats. Relatives of the president, state officials, and members of the economic elite who anticipated a landslide victory for Bakiev's party also joined. In fact, Ak Zhol won 71 of 90 seats, with the remaining seats being allocated between two moderate opposition parties. Yet the main opposition party, Ata Meken, was denied any parliamentary representation because it had allegedly failed to pass the 0.5 per cent threshold in one region. The OSCE observer mission deemed the elections neither free nor fair, as administrative resources and vote rigging were used on a massive scale to secure Ak Zhol's victory (OSCE/ODHIR 2008).

In short, Bakiev was able to break the deadlock with the parliament and consolidate his rule through two swift moves, the passing of a new constitution and the securing of an overwhelming victory for his newly founded party. In effect, the president had worn down the opposition after more than two years of street protests and government paralysis that had left the public longing for a strong leader (Sershen 2007). Bakiev promptly took advantage of his new powers by appointing close relatives and loyal followers to key government positions, especially in the security apparatus. Moreover, his control over the ruling party reduced the parliament to an institution whose main task was 'to rubber stamp decisions emanating from the president's office' (ICG 2008, p. 6). In control of the security structures and the country's economic resources, Bakiev subsequently embarked on a campaign to neutralize any challenges to his regime.

Fading Opposition

From the beginning, Saakashvili made no secret of his contempt for critique and the political opposition, perceiving critiques 'either as personal challenges or as evidence of disloyalty' (Hesli 2007, p. 363). Saakashvili is part of a small Western-oriented and often Western-educated elite that has come to power with the declared goal of eliminating the remnants of the Soviet past and modernizing the country. There has been little concern for ordinary citizens' needs, and no patience for alternative political agendas (Cheterian 2008). Several civil society leaders published an open letter in 2004, lamenting that 'intolerance towards people with different opinions [was] being planted in Georgian politics' because the government was accusing critics of being traitors and enemies of the nation (Zakareishvili et al. 2004).

The government's hostile rhetoric has been accompanied by concerted government efforts to marginalize opposition parties by depriving them of financial resources and equal access to the media. In the aftermath of the Rose Revolution, several parties, including the CUG, dissolved or merged with the UNM. Of the remaining opposition parties, only two passed the 7 per cent threshold in the 2004 elections (the Industrialist and New Rights parties). In 2005 two other parties, the Republican Party and the Conservative Party, founded by former allies of Saakashvili, emerged. All of them have faced an uneven playing field.

Saakashvili's war against corruption has proceeded with utter disregard for the rule of law. What initially appeared to be the result of overzealous law enforcement officers in fact served a political purpose. It was an effort to fill state (and allegedly UNM) coffers by shaking down business people and former officials. These accused individuals were tortured during pre-trial detention and only released (without a trial) after paying hefty 'fines' to the state. The campaign sent a signal to other officials and entrepreneurs that their well-being depended on their continuing loyalty to the new government (Areshidze 2007, p. 211; Muskhelishvili and Jorjoliani 2009, p. 693-94). With its coffers filled, the UNM has easily outspent the opposition in every election since 2004.

Saakashvili was well aware that his approval ratings also depended heavily on positive media coverage. Tying the business elite to his government has made it easier for his government to control the airwaves. Government-friendly entrepreneurs have taken over TV and radio stations from owners who were pressured to sell their assets. Other stations have had their licenses revoked, and direct pressure on critical journalists has resulted in self-censorship. Finally, the government has sharply restricted access to information for critical media outlets (Areshidze 2007, p. 250; Fuller 2010, p. 221; Mitchell 2009, p. 92). Since the Rose Revolution, Freedom House has continuously downgraded Georgia in its Freedom of the Press report. The country is currently ranked on 128th out of 195 countries (Freedom House 2010). The opposition has accordingly been denied fair media coverage. Finally, the government has utilized administrative resources during electoral campaigns. For instance, election observers have reported that the government has exerted pressure on state officials to vote for Saakashvili and the UNM (Fuller 2010, p. 219).

Under these circumstances, it is not surprising that opposition parties have fared badly in local and national elections. In the 2008 parliamentary election, three opposition parties won only one-fifth of the seats. Yet the weakness of the opposition is not just a function of government repression. The opposition parties have also failed to widen their electoral base. The Republicans, for instance, recruit voters mainly from Tbilisi's small intellectual elite, and the Conservative Party lacks a popular leader. Moreover, the opposition parties rarely agree on a common strategy to counter the government. While some prefer boycotts and mass protests, others engage in a constructive dialogue (Areshidze 2007, p. 285-88; George and Stefes 2008, p. 346; Fuller 2010, p. 215f). Saakashvili has therefore largely succeeded in consolidating single-party rule.

Given the obvious government crackdown on dissent, it is somewhat surprising that Georgia's NGOs have largely remained silent. Before the Rose Revolution, Georgian civil society was considered vibrant, not least due to massive injections of European and American democracy aid. Several authors have highlighted the crucial role of civil society in bringing down the Shevardnadze regime (Laverty 2008; McFaul 2005; Mitchell 2004). However, other scholars arrive at a more sobering conclusion (Tudoroiu 2007; Wheatley 2010). First, Georgia's NGOs are only weakly rooted in the general population and their leaders see themselves as an avant-garde that would lead the country towards a better future with little respect for dissenting views. As two Georgian analysts argue, 'the NGOs did not promote "freedom of speech for everybody"; instead they promoted "freedom of speech for those who promote freedom of speech"' (Muskhelishvili and Jorjoliani 2009, p. 689).

After the Rose Revolution, numerous NGO leaders joined government ranks or took seats in the parliament, weakening the organizational base of Georgia's civil society. As parliamentarians and ministers, they have maintained the same uncompromising positions. For instance, Giga Bokeria (formerly with the Liberty Institute, now a leading UNM parliamentarian) openly supported unlawful arrests on corruption charges as the 'government's main weapon' (quoted in Cheterian 2008, p. 704). UNM members have meanwhile infiltrated numerous NGOs, taking leading positions in organizations that range from student clubs to professional associations (Muskhelishvili and Jorjoliani 2009, p. 696). While some NGOs have nevertheless maintained their critical stance towards the government, they receive little media coverage.

Following his power grab at the end of 2007, Kyrgyzstan's president relied on tactics similar to those of Saakashvili's – albeit with a stronger dose of outright repression. While Bakiev initially pledged to complete the political and economic reforms that his predecessor had begun in the early 1990s, he soon revoked these promises. As his advisers argued, 'The liberal democratic model has failed […]; the Russian model of limited democracy, a marginalised opposition and strong presidential power is far better suited to the country at this stage in its development' (ICG 2008, p. 1). Even more than his Georgian colleague, Bakiev thereby relied on the security apparatus as well as the army and tax police, whose top officials, often relatives or loyal followers of the president, are directly subordinated to him. The security apparatus was employed in the appropriation of economic assets, notably the key industries that were formerly owned by the Akaev family. This takeover did not run into any legal problems, as the president controlled the appointment and removal of all judges, including Supreme Court judges, through his hold over parliament (Marat 2009a; Saidazimova 2008).

Being in command of the country's key economic assets, courts, and security structures allowed Bakiev to build a powerful and highly centralized patronage system. Any larger business depended on the government's blessing for its survival. 'Pressure on the private sector [thereby] serves both to enrich the president's allies and ensure that his enemies' war coffers remain empty' (ICG 2008, p. 10). Indeed, without access to business donations, the political opposition was unable to run effective campaigns. Moreover, the opposition had little to no access to independent media outlets. Threatened with libel suits, physical intimidation, and the tax police, media owners and journalists decided either to renounce their critical stance or to leave the country altogether. In 2009, for instance, four journalists were severely beaten and two were killed. In the Freedom of the Press index, Kyrgyzstan ranked in the bottom quarter of the survey, 158th out of 195 countries (Freedom House 2010). In addition, the government relied on direct means of intimidation. '[O]pposition leaders are persecuted with the help of ingenious techniques. Their relatives are threatened with administrative and criminal charges, while opposition leaders themselves fear their physical removal' (Marat 2009b).

In short, political repression decimated the political opposition in Kyrgyzstan. However, some analysts argue that the opposition itself was at least partly to blame for its weakness. Opposition leaders underestimated Bakiev's determination to drive them out of parliament and government. They were unable to build a unified bloc and execute a common strategy (Pannier 2009b). In addition, opposition leaders were timid because they could easily be blackmailed. 'The opposition's unimpressive performance was in part due to its intimate relationship with the country's political leadership [...] Many have grown rich on their access to power and are now afraid to lose everything by being too energetic in opposition.' (ICG 2008, p. 7) The 2009 presidential elections exposed the opposition's weakness: Bakiev won in a landslide despite growing socio-economic problems, widespread rumours about government corruption and nepotism, and rolling blackouts.

Until 2010 Kyrgyzstan's civil society therefore seemed to be no match for Bakiev's authoritarian regime. Several instances of physical assaults on NGO leaders left the community scared and apathetic.[3] To understand how a largely unorganized mass was nevertheless able to remove the president, it is helpful to recall Eric McGlinchey's insightful study of Central Asian protest movements. As McGlinchey (2009, p. 125) argues, 'strategies of protest are learned and though they may develop in one institutional environment they persist even when the coercive capacity of authoritarian regimes increases or decreases'. In other words, the presence of a protest culture can compensate

---

3 Personal conversation with Erica Marat, Nonresident Research Fellow with the Central Asia-Caucasus Institute & Silk Road Studies Program Joint Center (13 March 2010).

for the absence of strong opposition organizations due to government repression. However, under these conditions it is difficult for any government to restore political order. In fact, Kyrgyzstan's interim government under the leadership of Bakiev's former foreign minister Roza Otunbayeva is struggling with an anarchical and criminalized political environment. It is therefore likely that Kyrgyzstan (as well as Georgia) is 'prone to go through cycles of societal upheavals and extra-electoral replacements of governments, followed by a new round of political protests that destabilize the political regime' (Wooden and Stefes 2009, p. 254).

The Role of Foreign Actors

As Levitsky and Way (2005) argue, international linkage, and to lesser degree leverage, might deter would-be dictators from establishing authoritarian regimes. To estimate the degree of linkage, the following measures might serve as proxies: the BTI International Cooperation Index, which captures what Levitsky and Way call 'geopolitical linkage'; the amount of money that the US government has spent on democracy assistance (Levitsky and Way's 'transnational civil society linkage'); combined imports and exports and foreign direct investment as percentage of GDP ('economic linkage'); net migration and workers' remittances ('social linkage'); and Internet users per 100 people ('communication linkage').[4]

Without going into much detail, the numbers show that among the Soviet successor states (excluding the three Baltic states) Georgia and Kyrgyzstan rank in the middle for almost every measure. The exceptions are US democracy aid, with Armenia being the only country that has received more democracy aid per capita than Georgia and Kyrgyzstan, and Internet users per 100 people, with Kyrgyzstan in third place (after Ukraine and Moldova). When compared to countries in other regions, except in sub-Saharan Africa, Georgia and Kyrgyzstan rank considerably lower. Levitsky and Way are therefore correct when they consider Georgia – and by extension, Kyrgyzstan – low-linkage countries (Levitsky and Way 2005, p. 30f). Following their argument, international linkage was arguably too weak to check the authoritarian streaks of Saakashvili and Bakiev.

Yet Georgia and Kyrgyzstan vary considerably regarding Western leverage, with the former being more vulnerable than the latter. Both countries are small as well as economically and militarily weak. Western leverage should therefore be high in both cases. This leverage is somewhat offset by the economic importance of Georgia, which is a transit country for Caspian oil, as well as the military importance of Kyrgyzstan, which hosts a US airbase that is critical for operations in Afghanistan. In order to maintain their interests in both countries, Western countries should therefore be less inclined to be overly critical of the Georgian and Kyrgyz governments. The crucial difference, however, is the availability of a foreign patron that could replace Western military, political and economic support. Uzbekistan, Kazakhstan and especially Russia have

---

4 Sources: Bertelsmann Transformation Index (2008); U.S. Department of State (2010); World Bank (2010).

played this role for Kyrgyzstan at least until now, while Saakashvili's government has no alternative to Western support. The Western-oriented foreign policy agenda of the Georgian government should further increase Western leverage.

In Kyrgyzstan, President Akaev relied to a significant degree on Western support. The newly independent Kyrgyzstan became a member of several international organizations and introduced liberal economic reforms before most other former Soviet republics, thus receiving Western aid and loans in return. However, as Martha Brill Olcott (2005) argues, Western support for Kyrgyzstan was miniscule and had little effect. The economy only slowly recovered from the post-communist slump, and the living conditions of most Kyrgyz deteriorated sharply. Kyrgyzstan nevertheless turned out to be a staunch supporter of the US war against terror, allowing the US military to build an airbase adjacent to Bishkek's international airport.

Under Akaev's successor, Kyrgyzstan increasingly turned towards its regional neighbours and Russia, which had criticized Akaev for his pro-Western foreign policy agenda. Bakiev asked Russia repeatedly for political and economic support. In an attempt to drive back Western influence in Kyrgyzstan, Russia initially provided this support, strengthening its military and diplomatic ties through bilateral and multilateral agreements (Blagov 2006). In addition to Russia's growing leverage, the linkages between the two countries also deserve mention. The dominance of Russian media programs in Kyrgyzstan drove anti-Western sentiments while promoting Russia and its model of 'managed democracy' (Marat 2009a; Marat 2010). The importance of Russia's influence became apparent when Russia withdrew its support of Bakiev, allegedly due to Kyrgyzstan's return to a more pro-American foreign policy. Just weeks before the anti-government uprising, Russia's media coverage of Bakiev turned from overly benign to outright hostile, accusing the Kyrgyz president of corruption and authoritarianism. The Russian leadership also failed to condemn the uprising and offered no support for the embattled president. Russia apparently pulls the strings in its 'near abroad' (Kramer 2010; Pan 2010).

In contrast, the Western footprint in Central Asia is diminishing. Western countries are remote and lack strong ties in the region. Nor can Kyrgyzstan, as an Asian country, be baited with eventual EU membership. Moreover, Bakiev skilfully used the US airbase to silence Washington. As his government repeatedly threatened to close this base, the US government not only agreed to increase payments to the Kyrgyz government, but also decreased spending on democracy assistance in the country. US criticism of the falsified presidential election in 2009 was limited as well (Kalandadze and Orenstein 2009, p. 1411; Marat 2009a; Transitions Online 2006).

The Georgian government's foreign policy agenda could hardly be more different. While Shevardnadze at least attempted to achieve a semblance of good neighbourly relations with Russia, Saakashvili has pursued a rabid pro-Western course, making NATO and EU membership his declared foreign policy goals. Western countries have reacted positively, increasing their diplomatic, economic and military ties with Georgia and thereby arousing an outright belligerent reaction from Russia, whose foreign policy agenda has become increasingly aggressive since 2000. The tensions peaked in August 2008 when the two countries fought a weeklong war over Georgia's two breakaway regions, South Ossetia and Abkhazia. Georgia lost the war and is now completely dependent on Western support for its political and economic survival.

Given these circumstances, Western leverage has undoubtedly increased since the Rose Revolution. Yet Europe and especially the US have not used their predominant position in Georgia to press for democratic reforms – at least not until recently. Western countries largely refrained from criticizing the constitutional changes in 2004, and Western condemnation of the violent crackdown on peaceful protesters in 2007 and the undemocratic elections in 2008 was muted. In fact, the US government under George W. Bush repeatedly praised Georgia as a 'beacon of democracy' in the region, thereby undercutting the political opposition, which lamented Saakashvili's authoritarian streak (Muskhelishvili and Jorjoliani 2009, p. 684). Moreover, international support for the development of civil society, media and opposition parties has been sharply reduced since the Rose Revolution. Instead, money has been directed towards reforming state and government structures (Mitchell 2009, p. 129).

How can this Western restraint be explained? First, some Western governments might have naively assumed that the Rose Revolution was not the potential beginning but rather the endpoint of a democratic process. Second, President Bush had no interest in pointing out democratic shortcomings, as Georgia served as the poster child for his administration's campaign of spreading democracy throughout the world. Finally, the Saakashvili government was the most pro-Western government the Bush administration could have hoped for. As a member of an American NGO that operated in Georgia revealed, 'We were told many times [by the US government] to fully support the new regime and not point out the shortcomings of the new government' (cited in: Mitchell 2009, p. 130). Yet occasional demands from European governments and organizations have been fruitful in compelling Saakashvili to concede space to the opposition. For instance, as a result of European pressure the Georgian government agreed to lower the electoral threshold from 7 to 5 per cent in 2008 (Mitchell 2009, p. 96). And under the watchful eyes of Western diplomats, Saakashvili refrained from using violence to disperse the opposition demonstrations following the August War. Instead, he reached out to the opposition and offered positions in public institutions (George and Stefes 2008, p. 347).

In the end, the legitimacy of Saakashvili's government stands and falls with his promise to integrate Georgia into the Western community. While democracy has never been Saakashvili's priority, it has been an 'identity marker of becoming part of the West', as Vicken Cheterian argues. 'In this sense, democracy was an *external* attribute, a self-declared ideology that aligned Georgia with the West, rather than a certain political practice concerning the organization not of the political sphere through competitive elections, and other *internal* attributes of democratic performance' (Cheterian 2008, p. 695). Yet without the Western stamp of approval, Saakashvili's legitimacy would evaporate. This is especially true after the loss of Abkhazia and South Ossetia, which was a major setback for Saakashvili in terms of his most important goal, the restoration of territorial integrity. The looming threat of Western disengagement has arguably restrained Saakashvili's authoritarian tendency (as has sporadic diplomatic pressure).

5. Beyond Georgia and Kyrgyzstan: Ukraine and Serbia in Comparison

How does Fish's argument hold up when we compare Kyrgyzstan and Georgia to the other two countries in which popular uprisings forced the abdication of semi-authoritarian governments? In 2000, mass protests led to the toppling of President Slobodan Milosevic and his government. In 2004, hundreds of thousands of protestors prevented President Leonid Kuchma from handpicking his successor. As in Georgia and Kyrgyzstan, falsified elections served as triggers for the anti-regime protests. Yet the aftermath of the revolutions in Serbia and Ukraine were different. In Ukraine, the victory of the camp that stood behind the Orange Revolution was never complete, and the camp itself broke apart shortly after President Victor Yushchenko took office. As a result, three equally powerful political parties vied for power: Yushchenko's Our Ukraine party, Yulia Tymoshenko's bloc, and the party of Yushchenko's challenger in the presidential elections, Victor Yanukovych (Party of Regions). All sides jealously made sure that no group would appropriate state resources to gain an unfair political advantage. This task was made easier by constitutional amendments passed in 2006 which transferred power from the president to the parliament (for example, the right to name the prime minister). In fact, international observers have rated every parliamentary and presidential election since the Orange Revolution as free and relatively fair (Freedom House 2009b).

In Serbia the two parties that succeeded Milosevic's Socialist Party in 2000 – President Vojislav Kostunica's Democratic Party of Serbia and Prime Minister Zoran Djindjic's Democratic Party – engaged in a fierce competition that exemplified the country's division into nationalist and pro-Western blocs. While this competition slowed down necessary reforms, it also prevented either side from marginalizing the other side by unfair means. Serbia's nascent democratic structures even survived the state of emergency that was declared after Djindjic's murder in 2003. In 2006 a new constitution that significantly increased the protection of political rights and civil liberties was passed.

In both Serbia and Ukraine, political rivalry has often translated into a stalemate. Moreover, the revolutions have not eliminated corruption and organized crime. Nevertheless, constitutional checks-and-balances that have been reinforced through the balance of power among the various political groups have prevented any group from (re-)establishing authoritarian rule, as the following figure demonstrates.

While the freedom scores for Serbia and Ukraine increased notably after their revolutions, the opposite is true for Georgia and Kyrgyzstan. The contrast would be even starker if the ratings for corruption and judicial framework and independence were excluded (Freedom House 2009b). Yet the poor ratings for these two areas are not the result of government repression. They are an expression of the prevalent legacy of socialist rule – that is, systemic corruption (Stefes 2006). In short, the cases of Serbia and Ukraine clearly reinforce the argument that super-presidentialism is the main culprit of authoritarian developments in the post-communist countries.

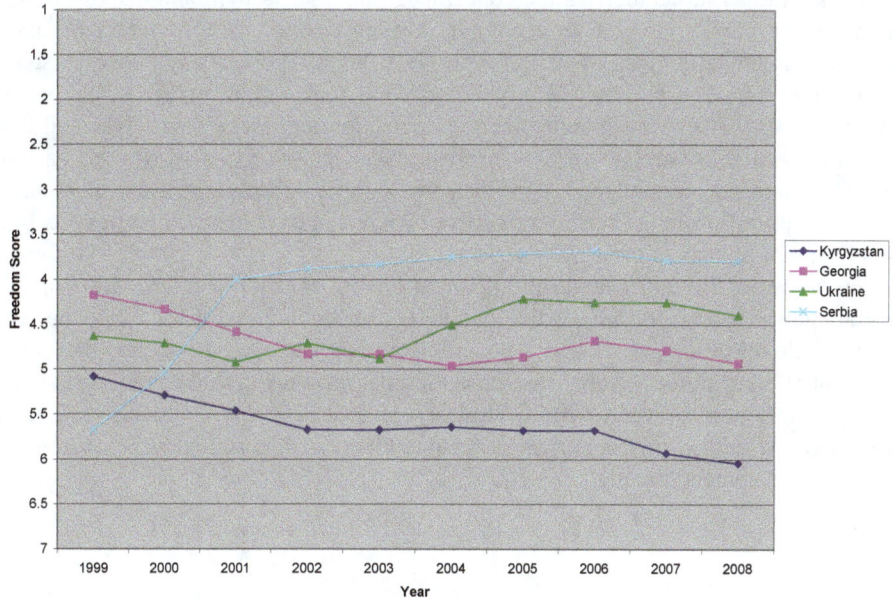

Source: Freedom House (2009b); 'Year': years covered (not publication year).

Figure 3: Coloured Revolutions and Their Aftermaths in Comparison

6. Conclusion

As the cases of Georgia and Kyrgyzstan suggest, the creation of a super-presidential system greatly facilitates the move towards dominant power politics. With the amassment of power in the presidency and the related diminution of legislative and judicial checks, state resources in the two countries have been appropriated for political purposes, and the protection of civil rights and political liberties has suffered. For instance, independent courts could have stopped Saakashvili's unlawful campaign against allegedly corrupt officials and business owners. The Kyrgyz case is even more telling in this regard, as government repression increased notably only after the introduction of a new constitution in 2007. Super-presidentialism is also necessary to create and maintain a regimented patronage system. For without the credible threat of using the courts and the tax police against potential dissenters, the continuing loyalty of the business and political elite is uncertain.

The circumstances and the motives under which the super-presidential systems were founded differed somewhat. While Saakashvili seized the opportunity that his popularity brought immediately after the Rose Revolution, Bakiev had to bide his time until the opposition let down its guard. These two and a half years were a period of uncertainty in which a more democratic Kyrgyzstan could have emerged as a solution to the political deadlock. And as far as motives are concerned, while Saakashvili and his government might indeed pursue the goal of eventually turning Georgia into a modern European country, Bakiev's motives were certainly less noble. Either way, once a superpresidential regime was established, both presidents took full advantage of the powers invested in their offices to marginalize the opposition and make themselves and their parties unassailable. Strong Western leverage over Georgia explains why Saakashvili has relied less on outright repression than his Kyrgyz colleague. On the other hand, domestic opposition in the form of assertive NGOs and/or opposition parties has been largely absent in both countries.

For the West, this study holds an important lesson: constitutional changes that concentrate power in any executive office should be stopped in their tracks. While the West had too little influence over Bakiev's government to prevent the introduction of a superpresidential constitution in 2007, the constitutional changes in 2004 in Georgia could have probably been prevented if the West had reacted promptly and decisively. If the West had not missed this opportunity, today's Georgia might already be on track in consolidating democratic rule.

References

Abdrakhmanova, Ainagul (2009) 'Doubts about Kyrgyz Political Reform Plan', *IWPR's Reporting Central Asia* September 28, 2009, in http://www.iwpr.net/index.php?apc_state=hen&s=o&o=p=rca&l=EN&s=f&o=355955 [accessed on May 24, 2010].
Almond, Gabriel A./Verba, Sidney (1963) The Civic Culture: Political Attitudes and Democracy in Five Nations, Princeton.
Anjaparidze, Zaal (2005) 'Judges Allege that Saakashvili's Team Is Purging Georgia's Judicial Bench', *Eurasia Daily Monitor* December 8, 2005, in http://www.jamestown.org/single/?no_cache=1&tx_ttnews[tt_news]=31193 [accessed on May 24, 2009].
Arat, Zehra F. (1991) Democracy and Human Rights in Developing Countries, Boulder.
Areshidze, Irakly (2007) *Democracy and Autocracy in Eurasia*, East Lansing.
Beissinger, Mark R. (2007) 'Structure and Example in Modular Political Phenomena: The Diffusion of Bulldozer/Rose/Orange/Tulip Revolutions', *Perspectives on Politics* 2: 259-276.
Bertelsmann Transformation Index (2008) *Country Report Kyrgyzstan*, Gütersloh.
Beyer, Judith (2006) 'Rhetoric of 'Transformation': The Case of the Kyrgyz Constitutional Reform' in Berg, Andrea/Kreikemeyer, Anna (eds.) *Realities of Transformation. Democratization Policicies in Central Asia Revisited*, Baden-Baden: 43–62.
Blagov, Sergei (2006) 'Moscow Beefs Up Security Ties with Kyrgyzstan', *Eurasia Daily Monitor* October 13, 2006, in http://www.jamestown.org/single/?no_cache=1&tx_ttnews[tt_news]=32131 [accessed on May 24, 2010).
Bollen, Kenneth (1993) 'Liberal Democracy: Validity and Method Factors in Cross-National Measures', *American Journal of Political Science* 4: 1207-1230.
Bunce, Valerie J./Wolchik Sharon L. (2006) 'Favorable Conditions and Electoral Revolutions', *Journal of Democracy* 4: 5-18.
Carothers, Thomas (2002) 'The End of the Transition Paradigm', *Journal of Democracy* 1: 5-21.
Cheterian, Vicken (2008) 'Georgia's Rose Revolution: Change or Repetition? Tension between State-Building and Modernization Projects', *Nationalities Papers* 4: 689-710.

Collins, Kathleen (2002) 'Clans, Pacts and Politics in Central Asia', *Journal of Democracy* 3: 137-152.
Diamond, Larry (1999) Developing Democracy: Toward Consolidation, Baltimore.
EurasiaNet (2004) 'Saakashvili Opponents in Georgia Say President is Using Anti-Democratic Methods to Advance', in *Eurasianet.org* March 1, 2004, in http://www.eurasianet.org/departments/insight/articles/eav030104.shtml [accessed on March 24, 2009].
Fairbanks, Charles H. Jr. (2004) 'Georgia's Rose Revolution', *Journal of Democracy* 2: 110-24.
Fairbanks, Charles H. Jr. (2007) 'Revolution Reconsidered', *Journal of Democracy* 1: 42-57.
Fish, M. Steven (2001) 'The Dynamics of Democratic Erosion' in Anderson, Richard/Fish, M. Steven/Hanson, Stephen E./Roeder, Philip G. (eds.) *Postcommunism and the Theory of Democracy*, Princeton: 54-95.
Fish, M. Steven (2006) 'Stronger Legislatures, Stronger Democracies', *Journal of Democracy* 1: 5-19.
Freedom House. 'Freedom in the World. Country Ratings and Status, FIW 1973-2009', http://www.freedomhouse.org/uploads/fiw09/CompHistData/FIW_AllScores_Countries.xls [accessed on May 25, 2010].
Freedom House. (2009a). 'Freedom in the World 2009'. http://www.freedomhouse.org/template.cfm?page=445 [accessed on May 02, 2009].
Freedom House. 2009b. 'Nations in Transit 2009. Nations in Transit 2009 Tables'. http://www.freedomhouse.org/uploads/nit/2009/Tables-WEB.pdf [accessed on May 25, 2010].
Freedom House. 2010. 'Freedom of the Press'. http://www.freedomhouse.org/template.cfm?page=16 [accessed on May 23, 2010].
Fuller, Liz (1998) 'The Sorcerer's Apprentices' Apprentice', *Radio Free Europe/ Radio Liberty* September 2, 1998, in http://www.soros.org [accessed on September 03, 1998].
Fuller, Elizabeth (2010) 'Nations in Transit 2009: Georgia' in Freedom House (ed.) *Nations In Transit,* Washington.
George, Julie A./Stefes, Christoph H. (2008) 'The Fate of Georgian Democracy', *Current History* 711: 344-347.
Graubner, Cornelius/Wolters, Alexander (2007) 'Kirgisischer Feldversuch Demokratie', *Osteuropa* 8-9: 195–206.
Hale, Henry E. (2006) 'Democracy or autocracy on the march? The colored revolutions as normal dynamics of patronal presidentialism', *Communist and Post-Communist Studies* 3: 305-329.
Hesli, Vicki L. (2007) Governments and Politics in Russia and the Post-Soviet Region, Boston.
Huskey, Eugene (2002) 'An economy of authoritarianism? Askar Akaev and presidential leadership in Kyrgyzstan' in Cummings, Sally (ed.) *Power and Change in Central Asia*, New York: 74-96.
International Crisis Group (ICG) (2008) 'Kyrgyzstan: A Deceptive Calm', *Asia Briefing No. 79* August 14, 2008, in http://www.crisisgroup.org/home/index.cfm?id=5627 [accessed on May 25, 2010].
Inglehart, Ronald F./Welzel, Christian (2005) *Modernization, Cultural Change, and Democracy.* Cambridge.
Juraev, Shairbek (2008) 'Kyrgyz democracy? The tulip Revolution and beyond', *Central Asian Survey* 3-4: 253–264.
Kalandadze, Katya/Orenstein, Mitchell A. (2009) 'Electoral Protests and Democratization. Beyond the Color Revolutions', *Comparative Political Studies* 11: 1403-1425.
King, Charles (2004) 'A Rose among Thorns: Georgia Makes Good', *Foreign Affairs* 2: 1-6.

Kramer, Andrew E. (2010) 'Before Kyrgyz Uprising, Dose of Russian Soft Power', *New York Times* April 18, 2010, in http://www.nytimes.com/2010/04/19/world/asia/19kyrgyz.html [accessed on May 7, 2010].

Laverty, Nicklaus (2008) 'The Problem of Lasting Change: Civil Society and the Colored Revolutions in Georgia and Ukraine', *Demokratizatsiya* 2: 143 – 162.

Levitsky, Steven/Way, Lucan (2005) 'International Linkage and Democratization', *Journal of Democracy* 3: 20-34.

Lewis, David (2008) The Temptations of Tyranny in Central Asia, New York.

Marat, Erica (2006) 'Opposition Celebrates as New Constitution Adopted in Kyrgyzstan', *Eurasia Daily Monitor* November 9, 2006, in http://www.jamestown.org/single/?no_cache=1&tx_ttnews[tt_news]=32214 [accessed on March 25, 2010].

Mart, Erica (2007) 'Kyrgyzstan Constitutional Referendum Set for October 21', *Eurasia Daily Monitor* October 9, 2007, in http://www.jamestown.org/single/?no_cache=1&tx_ttnews[tt_news]=33062 [accessed on March 25, 2010].

Marat, Erica (2009a) 'Another Opposition Leader Escapes the Bakiyev Regime', *Eurasia Daily Monitor* September 17, 2009, in http://www.jamestown.org/single/?no_cache=1&tx_ttnews[tt_news]=35508 [accessed on March 25, 2010].

Marat, Erica (2009b) 'Bakiyev Promises Reform and Persecutes Opposition', *Eurasia Daily Monitor* September 10, 2009, in http://www.jamestown.org/single/?no_cache=1&tx_ttnews[tt_news]=35474 [accessed on March 25, 2010].

Marat, Erica (2010) 'Nations in Transit 2009: Kyrgyzstan' in Freedom House (ed.) *Nations In Transit,* Washington.

McFaul, Michael (2005) 'Transitions from Postcommunism', *Journal of Democracy* 3: 5-19.

McGlinchey, Eric (2009) 'Central Asian Protests Movements: Social Forces or State Resources?' in Wooden, Amanda E./Stefes, Christoph H. (eds.) *The Politics of Transition in Central Asia and the Caucasus. Enduring Legacies and Emerging Challenges,* London: 124-138.

McMann, Kelly M (2004) 'The Civic Realm in Kyrgyzstan: Soviet Economic Legacies and Activists' Expectations' in Jones Luong, Pauline (ed.) *The Transformation of Central Asia. States and Societies from Soviet Rule to Independence*, Ithaca: 213-245.

Mitchell, Lincoln (2004) 'Georgia's Rose Revolution', *Current History* 675: 342-48.

Mitchell, Lincoln (2009) Uncertain Democracy: U.S. Foreign Policy and Georgia's Rose Revolution, Philadelphia.

Munck, Gerardo L. (2009) Measuring Democracy. A Bridge Between Scholarship and Politics, Baltimore.

Muskhelishvili, Marina/Jorjoliani, Gia (2009) 'Georgia's ongoing struggle for a better future continued: democracy promotion through civil society development', *Democratization* 4: 682-708.

Olcott, Martha Brill (2005) *Central Asia's Second Chance*, Washington, D. C.

OSCE/ODHIR (2008) 'OSCE/ODIHR Election Observation Mission Final Report: Kyrgyz Republic, Pre-term Parliamentary Elections' April 24, 2008, in http://www.osce.org/documents/odihr/2008/04/30844_en.pdf [accessed on March 21, 2010].

Pan, Philip P. (2010) 'Russia is said to have fueled unrest in Kyrgyzstan', *Washington Post* April 12, 2010, in http://www.washingtonpost.com/wp-dyn/content/article/2010/04/11/AR2010041103827.html [accessed on May 7, 2010].

Pannier, Bruce (2009a) 'Interview with Radio Free Europe/Radio Liberty: "Was Kyrgyz President Bakiev Ever a Democrat?"', *Radio Free Europe/Radio Liberty* July 24, 2009, in http://www.rferl.org/content/Was_Kyrgyz_President_Bakiev_Ever_A_Democrat/1784761.html [accessed on March 16, 2010].

Pannier, Bruce (2009b) 'A Primer on Kyrgyzstan's Presidential Election', *Radio Free Europe/Radio Liberty* July 22, 2009, in http://www.rferl.org/content/A_Primer_On_Kyrgyzstans_Presidential_Election/1782995.html [accessed on March 23, 2010].

Pétric, Boris-Mathieu (2005) 'Post-Soviet Kyrgyzstan or the birth of a globalized protectorate', *Central Asian Survey* 3: 319-322.

Przeworski, Adam/Limongi, Fernando (1997) 'Modernization: Theories and Facts', *World Politics* 2: 155-83.

Radnitz, Scott (2005) 'Networks, localism and mobilization in Aksy, Kyrgyzstan', *Central Asian Survey* 4: 405-424.

Saidazimova, Gulnoza (2008) 'Three Years ON, Kyrgyz President Taken to Task for Rampant Nepotism', *Radio Free Europe/Radio Liberty* July 10, 2008, in http://www.rferl.org/content/Three_Years_On_Kyrgyz_President_Taken_To_Task_For_Nepotism_/1182894.html [accessed on March 23, 2010].

Sartori, Giovanni (1976) Parties and Party Systems: a Framework for Analysis, Cambridge.

Sehring, Jenniver (2005) 'Ein Strauß aus Mohn und Tulpen. Die ‚Revolution' in Kirgistan verdient ihren Namen nicht', *iz3w* 287: 10-14.

Sershen, Daniel (2007) 'Kyrgyzstan: A New Bout of Constitutional Wrangling Begins', *Eurasianet.org* September 26, 2007, in http://www.eurasianet.org/departments/insight/articles/eav092607.shtml [accessed on March 16, 2010].

Spector, Regine (2004) 'The Transformation of Askar Akaev, President of Kyrgyzstan', BPS Working Paper Series, Berkeley: University of California, in http://iseees.berkeley.edu/sites/default/files/u4/bps_/publications_/2004_02-spec.pdf [accessed on March 25, 2010].

Stefes, Christoph H. (2006) Understanding Post-Soviet Transitions: Corruption, Collusion and Clientelism, New York.

Tolipov, Farkhod (2006) 'Power, Nation-Building, and Legacy - A Comparative Analysis of Central Asian Leadership' in Berg, Andrea/Kreikemeyer, Anna (eds.) *Realities of Transformation. Democratization Policies in Central Asia Revisited*, Baden-Baden: 63–79.

Transitions Online (2006) 'Krygyzstan: Democracy Lite', September 12, 2006, in http://www.tol.org/client/article/17504-democracy-lite.html [accessed on June 12, 2009].

Tudoroiu, Theodor (2007) 'Rose, Orange, and Tulip: The failed post-Soviet revolutions', *Communist and Post-Communist Studies* 3: 315-342.

U.S. Department of State (2010) 'U.S. Government Assistance to and Cooperative Activities with Eurasia', in http://www.state.gov/p/eur/rls/rpt/c10250.htm [accessed on March 25, 2010].

Von Gumppenberg, Marie-Carin (2004) 'Kirgistan' in von Gumppenberg, Marie-Carin/Steinbach, Udo (eds.) *Zentralasien. Geschichte - Wirtschaft - Politik. Ein Lexikon*, München: 153-162.

Way, Lucan (2008) 'The Real Causes of the Colored Revolutions', *Journal of Democracy* 3: 55-69.

Wertsch, James V. (2005) 'Georgia as a Laboratory for Democracy', *Demokratizatsiya* 4: 519-35.

Wheatley, Jonathan (2010) 'Civil Society in the Caucasus: Myth and Reality', *Caucasus Analytical Digest* January 22, 2010: 2-6, in http://georgien.boell-net.de/downloads/CaucasusAnalyticalDigest12.pdf [accessed on March 25, 2010].

Wooden, Amanda E./Stefes, Christoph H. (2009) 'Multivaried and Interacting Paths of Change in Central Eurasia' in Wooden, Amanda E./Stefes, Christoph H. (eds.) *The Politics of Transition in Central Asia and the Caucasus. Enduring Legacies and Emerging Challenges*, London: 249-263.

World Bank (2010) 'World Development Indicators', in http://ddp-ext.worldbank.org/ext/DDPQQ/member.do?method=getMembers&userid=1&queryId=135 [accessed on March 25, 2010].

Zakareishvili, Paata et al. (2004) 'To His Excellency, the President of Georgia, Mr. Mikheil Saakashvili. Reprinted', *Civil.ge* October 18, 2004, in http://www.civil.ge/eng/article.php?id=8100 [accessed on March 24 2010].

ARTICLE

Democratic Survival or Autocratic Revival in Interwar Europe
A Comparative Examination of Structural Explanations

Svend-Erik Skaaning

Abstract At the beginning of the interwar period, almost all European countries had introduced democratic rights. But at the end, more than half were under outright autocratic rule. Using csQCA, this article tests five structural explanations of why democracies either survived or did not gain a foothold. The results show that early state-building was a necessary condition for democratic survival. In the case of the predominant path to democratic stability, this factor was combined with weak landlords and a subordination of religious interests to political authority. Furthermore, the findings indicate that strong landlords and the absence of a liberal hegemony were prerequisites for establishing or continuing autocratic rule. In conjunction with late state-building or a strong, independent religious leadership, these factors made up two paths that applied to all democratic reversals but one. As regards lessons from history, the study suggests that deficient state-building and 'strongmen', such as powerful agrarian and religious elites, impede the construction, stabilization and deepening of democracy in today's developing countries.

1. Introduction

In the wake of the third wave of democratization (cf. Huntington 1991), optimism about the realization of a democratic world flourished. Especially after the fall of Communism in East-Central and Eastern Europe, it was difficult not to be affected by the hopefulness that characterized friends of democracy in the 1990s. However, such hopes and expectations should always be confronted with a critical look at the realities. Tellingly, a similar euphoria on behalf of democratic regimes had occurred once before. In the aftermath of World War I (henceforth WWI), Europe was, by and large, populated by democratic regimes. They were either (reformed) continuations of pre-war regimes or constructed in the countries emerging from the breakdown of the German, Austrian-Hungarian, Russian and Ottoman empires (Aarebrot and Berglund 1995: 211).

But twenty years later, at the outbreak of World War II, many democracies in Southern, Central and Eastern Europe had been replaced by different kinds of autocratic rule, such as fascism and personal dictatorship (Bermeo 2003: 21). This history of democratic regression and the uncertain stability of today's fledgling democracies raise two central research questions: First, what conditions determined whether European countries were democracies or autocracies at the end of the interwar period? Second, what – if anything – do the European interwar experiences tell us about the fate of contemporary regime changes? Understanding the democratic successes and failures of the past is an interesting topic in itself, but increased knowledge of it might also help us understand the present. To quote Seymour M. Lipset (1983: 16), in the situation of 'a major crisis, it is likely that national politics will vary along lines that stem from the past, much as they did during the 1930s.'

Attempting to answer these questions, I take advantage of the fact that Europe between 1919 and 1939 provides what Valerie Bunce (2003: 169) has called an ideal laboratory for comparative inquiry. For several reasons, a comparative examination of regime developments in this setting is particularly appealing. First, the cases show an interesting mix of socio-economic, political and cultural characteristics; some are shared by most countries, and others only by a few. Second, the period is clearly demarcated by the world wars, which sets it apart from earlier and later developments through essential changes in the internal and external political landscapes. Third, the number of cases is large enough to facilitate systematic comparisons. Last but not least, virtually all countries besides Hungary and Russia could initially be categorized as minimally democratic, while democracies only endured to the end of the period in 13 out of the 29 cases (cf. Berg-Schlosser and De Meur 1994: 253; Berg-Schlosser and Mitchell 2000: 1).

Previous comparative studies on democratic survival and breakdown in interwar Europe have provided valuable findings (e.g., Berg-Schlosser and Mitchell 2002; Bermeo 1997; 2003; Ertman 1998; Luebbert 1991; Stephens 1989). The present study attempts to contribute to their generalizations through a unique combination of analytical features. First, this study includes all 29 European countries in the period. Second, it uses a configurational comparative method (csQCA) well suited to handle the theoretical propositions in question through a systematic reduction of complexity. Third, the explanatory model represents a novel integration of structural factors that have been developed to account for regime outcomes in the interlude between WWI and WWII.

Based on this research design, I find strong support for the proposition that early state-building was a necessary condition for democratic survival. In the case of the predominant path to democratic stability, this factor was combined with weak landlords and a subordination of religious interests to political authority. Only Ireland, Great Britain and Czechoslovakia followed different routes to democratic stability. Furthermore, the analysis indicates that strong landlords and the absence of a liberal hegemony were prerequisites for the (re-)establishment of autocratic rule. In conjunction with late state-building or a strong, independent religious leadership, these factors made up two paths that applied to all democratic reversals but one (Germany). As regards lessons from history, the study underlines that deficient state-building and 'strongmen' such as powerful agrarian and religious elites, elements found in many present-day developing countries, constitute serious obstacles to the construction, stabilization and deepening of democracy.

In the first section of the following discussion, I summarize a number of prominent hypotheses about interwar regime development and operationalize five structural variables related to them: strength of the agricultural elite, modernization level, pre-war liberal hegemony, state-building tradition, and the strength and autonomy of political authority vis-à-vis religious leadership. In the second section, I employ a crisp-set qualitative comparative analysis (csQCA) to analyse the relationship between the explanatory variables and democratic survival and decay in interwar Europe. In light of the results, I go on to discuss the prospects for new democracies in the contemporary era.

2. Hypotheses and Measurement

Many explanatory factors have been advanced to account for political regime outcomes in interwar Europe. It does not serve any purpose to present, and even less to test, an exhaustive list of hypotheses found in the literature. Instead, I emphasize some of the most prominent accounts with an explicitly comparative outlook and a structural focus. The selection of explanatory factors for the general model is facilitated by the fact that, given these restrictions, systematic studies and theories 'of the special structural roots of fascism, authoritarianism, and democracy have remained relatively rare' (Berg-Schlosser and De Meur 1994: 254).

Among these studies, we have Barrington Moore's (1991[1966]) classic, *Social Origins of Dictatorship and Democracy*. Moore's core claim is that there have been three main historical routes from preindustrial societies to modernity, that is, democratic, fascist and communist routes, as illustrated by European examples from Great Britain and France, Germany, and Russia, respectively. His account is rather complex and not very strict (cf. Skocpol 1973); however, he accentuates the fact that the relationship between the landed upper classes and the peasants and the bourgeoisie is of utmost importance. In short, Moore suggests that both of the undemocratic routes depend on the presence of a strong labour-repressive gentry, while a strong bourgeois 'impulse' is associated with democracy – recall Moore's (1991[1966]: 418) notorious dictum: 'No bourgeoisie, no democracy'.

In a test of Moore's theoretical framework on a wider group of Western European cases, John Stephens (1989: 1070; cf. Rueschemeyer et al. 1992: ch. 4) has summarized his findings in this way:

> ... the agrarian class relations and patterns of state-class alliances of the nineteenth and early twentieth centuries were necessary though not sufficient causes of the breakdown of democracy in interwar Europe. The existence of a large landed class changed the alliance options for other classes in both the late nineteenth century and in the twenties and thirties and as a consequence changed the political outcomes.

This statement (H1) asserts that had the countries experiencing democratic breakdowns not had a politically powerful landed elite (and the resultant state-class relations), autocratic rule would not have triumphed (Rueshemeyer et al. 1992: 147). The similarity of Stephens' and Moore's conclusions is evident; they both agree that labour-intensive and labour-repressive agriculture under the direction of large landowners impedes democratic stability (cf. Kitschelt 1992: 1029).

To operationalize their main argument, I use a data set compiled by Svante Ersson (1995). Inspired by Stephens' work, he has constructed a variable (AG1) that reflects whether or not a country was characterized by the absence (1) or presence (0) of a significant landed upper class engaged in labour-repressive agriculture. It is indispensable, however, to qualify his coding in one respect. Ersson assigns Albania a score of 1, which indicates weak landlords. In contrast, the historical accounts tend to agree that the landed aristocracy (and the clan leaders) constituted the power elite in pre-communist Albanian society and was an essential pillar for the installation of Zogu's autocratic rule (Vickers 1999: 118; Fischer 2007: 46; Rotschild 1974: 361-363). Tellingly, Pollo and Puto (1981: 189) write that, 'Zogu and his clique relied mainly on the support of the great landowners in their fights against the democratic opposition.'

Next to the strength of the landlords, two other factors included in the subsequent analysis have also been inspired by the seminal work of a 'grand old man' in political science, viz. Stein Rokkan's (1975) conceptual map of Europe. Frank Aarebrot and Sten Berglund (1995) are sympathetic to Rokkan's attempt to link crisis in state- and nation-building processes to democratic demise or survival. But they revise his framework in two significant ways. First, they expand the geographical scope to include the countries of East-Central and Eastern Europe. Second, they reconsider and simplify the two major dimensions of his map and end up with an 'East-West axis based on the strength of city networks and political centre formation, and a North-South axis based on the integration of state and church – strong in the Protestant North and weak in the Catholic South' (Aarebrot and Berglund, 1995: 212; cf. Rokkan and Urwin, 1983: 30).

As regards the first dimension, Aarebrot and Berglund (1995: 217) distinguish between countries with a historical tradition of state-building and those without much such experience at the outset of WWI. In their framework, all the Western and Central European countries had been exposed to state-building. In contrast, the Russian and Ottoman historical empires, and the countries devolving from them in the late nineteenth and early twentieth century, had experienced much more limited state-building efforts. The first group shared a Charlemagne heritage and was influenced by Roman law, feudalism, state formation and early national awakening. The second group shared a Byzantine heritage and lacked all these features, meaning that, for example, ethnicity and clientelism played a much more significant role than in the rest of Europe (Aarebrot and Berglund, 1995: 217).

Aarebrot and Berglund (1995: 217) also dichotomize the second dimension, which covers the strength and autonomy of political authority vis-à-vis religious leadership. Their emphasis is on a strong and independent religious leadership that could influence regime outcomes through the platform it created for legitimizing counter-movements to democracy. Religious interests were isolated from political rule or constituted a subordinate, more or less integrated part of the state apparatus in Protestant and substantially secularized states. This separation had not taken place in most of the Catholic, Orthodox and Muslim countries, where secularization within the regime was not achieved at the outset of the interwar era.

Based on these distinctions, Aarebrot and Berglund (1995: 218) claim that the prospects for democracy were intimately linked to the formation and autonomy of states. Consequently, they expect a strong link between unsuccessful state- and nation-building and the rise of undemocratic regimes. In support of their argument, they draw on Max Weber's (1964[1922]) thoughts about the twin bases for rational political rule (*Herrschaft*), that is, the consolidation of state authority through the monopoly on the legitimate use of violence and the relative autonomy of the bureaucracy. Generally speaking, the hypothesis (H2) states that the Charlemagne heritage (early state-building) and the isolation of religious interests from political rule (Protestant and/or secularized) were individually necessary and jointly sufficient conditions for democratic survival. Furthermore, the absence of just one of these features was sufficient for an autocratic regime (H3) to emerge. To operationalize the two conditions, I employ Aarebrot and Berglund's own (dichotomous) coding, meaning that countries with early state-building (1) are distinguished from those that did not have this feature (0). Moreover, I distinguish between countries with a strong and autonomous religious leadership (0) and those without (1).

Modernization theory is undisputedly the best known and most often cited account for regime developments, both in general and concerning the period in focus. Lipset advanced this perspective in his classic article, 'Some Social Requisites of Democracy', stating that socio-economic development has a significant impact on the political regime form. In Lipset's words (1959: 56), 'the more well-to-do a nation, the greater the chances that it will sustain democracy' (H4). If the title of his article is taken literally, modernization is regarded as a necessary condition for democracy. However, as Goertz and Starr have emphasized (2003: 5-6), Lipset's discussion of the relationship – including the sentence just quoted – actually makes more sense as a sufficiency hypothesis. I use the most commonly used wealth indicator, that is, gross domestic product per capita, to measure this variable.[1]

The final explanation to be examined has been suggested by Gregory Luebbert (1987; 1991). According to him, the destiny of democracies was determined by the political legacy of the political and economic crisis of the 1920s and 1930s and the urban-rural coalition formed in reaction to this crisis. As regards the political legacy, the most important aspect is whether or not liberal ideas and parties were hegemonic before WWI. A liberal hegemony was established in industrialized countries when the middle classes 'were not politically divided by antagonisms within them rooted in religious, regional, linguistic and urban-rural differences' (Luebbert 1991: 7). In these cases, liberals could make concessions allowing them to ally with the emerging workers' movement and parties.

According to Luebbert (1991: 8), democratic stability between the two world wars was secured in those countries by broad working-class acceptance of the liberal order

---

[1] The data refer to 1913 and are based on Angus Maddison's compilation of historical statistics: http://www.ggdc.net/maddison/. I use a threshold of $2400, placed in a theoretically convincing natural gap in the distribution, to separate relatively rich countries (1) from the rest (0) as csQCA can only handle dichotomized variables.

and 'the formation of center-right coalitions of middle-class consolidation that left socialist parties isolated and ineffective and to the organizational incoherence of the trade unions'. Put differently, he considers pre-war liberal hegemony to be a sufficient condition for democratic survival (H5). Luebbert himself counts Great Britain, France and Switzerland among the countries with a hegemonic liberal legacy. These countries – including Ireland, which was under British rule before it declared its independence in 1919 – are assigned the score of 1, while all others are scored 0.

The explanatory variables linked to the propositions outlined above are combined in a comprehensive model to evaluate their individual and/or joint connection to the outcome in question. The model thus includes five conditions: weak agrarian elite, early state-building, Protestant/secularized, rich, and liberal hegemony. As should be clear from the scoring procedures above, I expect high values (presence) for the explanatory variables to be positively related to democratic survival. Regarding the outcome, that is, democratic survival (1) or not (0) around 1938, my scoring of the cases relies on the overviews provided by Bermeo (1997: 2) and Berglund and Aarebrot (1995: 215).

3. Empirical Analysis

The next analytical step is to confront the hypotheses with empirical evidence. But the novelty of the method used to examine the variables calls for a few words on its logic. With his introduction of the configurational method, csQCA, to the social sciences, Charles Ragin (1987) attempted to narrow the gap between quantitative (variable-oriented) and qualitative (case-oriented) research. Like case-oriented approaches, this method treats cases as wholes, meaning that the different aspects of a case are defined in relation to each other. However, it also shares the variable-oriented techniques' broad understanding of social phenomena – and embraces their ability to achieve systematic complexity reduction. Since csQCA is based on set theoretical reasoning (Boolean algebra), it is a useful tool if one wants to test the necessity and/or sufficiency of conditions and if one expects multiple conjunctural causations.[2] This feature is highly relevant for the present study as at least four hypotheses, and arguably all, have a deterministic rather than probabilistic character expressed in terms of necessity and sufficiency. Moreover, the medium-N and the fact that the available data (with the exception of the modernization variable) are dichotomous also justify the employment of csQCA.

For readers not familiar with this method, upper-case letters designate the presence of a condition and lower-case letters its absence. Regarding the Boolean operators, * means logical *and*, whereas + means logical *or*. As the required dichotomization of the conditions is already in place, the information needed to construct a truth table has been provided.[3] This is accomplished by regrouping all identical cases, in terms of their

---

[2] For introductions to the logic and procedures of csQCA, see Ragin (1987), Schneider and Wagemann (2007), Caramani (2008), and Rihoux (2008).

[3] In the analysis, I try to follow the standards of good practice suggested by Wagemann and Schneider (2008).

scores on the conditions, into a single configuration. The result is shown in Table 1, where eleven different configurations cover the 29 cases.

Table 1: Truth Table Representation of the Data

	Survival of democracy (DEMO)	Weak agrarian elite (WEAGR)	State-building (STATE)	Protestant/ secularized (AUTO)	Rich (RICH)	Liberal hegemony (LIBHEG)
France, Switzerland	1	1	1	1	1	1
Belgium, Denmark, Luxembourg, Netherlands, Norway, Sweden	1	1	1	1	1	0
United Kingdom	1	0	1	1	1	1
Ireland	1	0	1	0	1	1
Finland, Iceland	1	1	1	1	0	0
Czechoslovakia	1	0	1	1	0	0
Germany	0	0	1	1	1	0
Austria, Italy	0	0	1	0	1	0
Hungary, Portugal, Spain	0	0	1	0	0	0
Estonia, Latvia, USSR	0	0	0	1	0	0
Albania, Bulgaria, Greece, Lithuania, Poland, Romania, Yugoslavia	0	0	0	0	0	0

The grouping of cases makes good theoretical sense. For example, the same configuration covers the Scandinavian and Benelux countries, whereas another covers Poland, Lithuania and the Balkan countries. Moreover, there are no contradictions, that is, no cases have identical conditions but different outcomes. Since contradictions would normally occur – given the number of cases and variables – if relevant explanatory variables had been omitted (Marx 2006), this finding supports the specification of the integrated model. In comparison, Berg-Schlosser and De Meur (1994) reached the opposite conclusion in their evaluation of studies on the conditions of democracy in interwar Europe (including those of Lipset, Luebbert and Stephens). Also using csQCA, they showed that all the major structural theories tested – when examined separately – were ridden with contradictions.

Berg-Schlosser and De Meur were mainly occupied with uncovering sufficient paths to democratic survival, even though the presence of contradictions does not undermine the possibility that one or more of them are necessary. However, the information provided in this study's truth table suffices to identify any necessary conditions. In this case, the truth table reveals that early state-building (STATE) is present in all of the configurations linked to a positive outcome, a pattern indicating that this condition was necessary for democracy to survive. No further conditions appear to have been necessary for democracy. On the other hand, a closer look at the evidence supports the assertion that both strong landlords and the absence of liberal hegemony were necessary for a democratic breakdown.

Given the contradiction-free truth table, the identification of necessary conditions is followed by a search for sufficient paths in the form of combinations of conditions. The csQCA software[4] carries out a systematic reduction of empirical complexity by employing the so-called minimization rule. The rule says that if two Boolean expressions (configurations) differ in only one causal condition but produce the same outcome, the causal condition distinguishing the two expressions is irrelevant and can be removed to create simpler, combined expressions (Ragin 1987: 93; Rihoux 2008: 35-36).

If we first focus on cases showing a positive outcome (democratic survival), early state-building may constitute a prerequisite, but the results underline the fact that this condition in itself was not sufficient to secure democratic victory. It had to be combined either with the simultaneous presence of a weak agrarian elite, political autonomy, and wealth – in the cases of Benelux, Scandinavia, France and Switzerland – *or* with political autonomy and the absence of wealth and pre-war liberal hegemony; *or* with wealth, a liberal hegemony, and strong landlords. All cases are accounted for by only one path, and the first shows the highest unique coverage with 62 per cent of the cases. In formal terms, the paths explicitly connected to democratic endurance are as follows:

$$\text{WEAGR*AUTO*RICH}_{(Belgium, Denmark, Luxembourg, Netherlands, Norway, Sweden+France, Switzerland)} \ (62\%) \ +$$

$$\text{STATE*} \begin{cases} \text{AUTO*rich*libheg}_{(Czechoslovakia+Finland, Iceland)} \ (23\%) \ + \\ \text{weagr*RICH*LIBHEG}_{(Ireland+United Kingdom)} \ (15\%) \end{cases}$$

As indicated by the many terms in the expressions, the results are still somewhat complex and, moreover, the direction of some of the explanatory factors is counter-intuitive. This could be a consequence of limited empirical diversity – a circumstance that often restricts the achievement of parsimonious results if we do not rely on simplifying assumptions. In the next analytical step, I have therefore allowed the software to make use of 'easy counterfactuals', that is, empirically unobserved configurations (combinations of attributes) that do not disagree with the empirical evidence and the theoretically expected 'direction' of the individual conditions (Ragin 2008: Ch. 9), thereby achieving a more parsimonious result:

---

4 To run the analyses, I employed the freeware fs/QCA 2.0 (www.fsqca.com) and TOSMANA 1.3 (www.tosmana.net) provided by Charles Ragin et al. and Lasse Cronqvist, respectively.

STATE* { WEAGR*AUTO$_{(Belgium,Denmark,Luxembourg,Netherlands,Norway,Sweden+France,Switzerland+Finland,Iceland)}$ (46%) +

AUTO*rich$_{(Czechoslovakia+Finland,Iceland)}$ (8%) +

RICH*LIBHEG$_{(Ireland+United Kingdom+France,Switzerland)}$ (15%)

Translating the formalized solution into ordinary language, the results signify that the most common path to democratic survival was to combine early state-building with weak landlords and political autonomy from religious leadership. Countries showing a conjunction of early state-building and *either* autonomous political authority and low socio-economic development *or* high socio-economic development and a liberal hegemony make up alternative paths.[5]

Before addressing the correspondence of these results with the five hypotheses, the results of an equivalent analysis of routes towards democratic reversal is needed. The reason is that due to limited empirical diversity, we cannot assume causal symmetry between the results associated with positive and negative outcomes. Concerning the necessary conditions, this supplementary analysis shows that the lack of hegemonic liberal rule before WWI is a feature all the autocracies share; this also applies to the presence of a powerful landed upper class. The employment of the minimization rule produces the following solution formula:

STATE*RICH$_{(Austria,Italy+Germany)}$ (19%) +

weagr*libheg* { auto*rich^6 $_{(Albania, Bulgaria,Greece,Lithuania,Poland,Romania,Yugoslavia+Hungary,Portugal,Spain)}$ (19%) +

state*rich$_{(Albania, Bulgaria,Greece,Lithuania,Poland,Romania,Yugoslavia+Estonia,Latvia,USSR)}$ (19%)

We see that almost all terms in the expressions show the expected direction, as demonstrated by the dominance of lower-case letters. Quite a few of the cases are covered by two paths linked to the same configuration, that is, structurally unprivileged countries as Bulgaria, Greece, Lithuania, Poland, Romania and Yugoslavia. The expression covering Austria, Italy and Germany constitutes a flagrant exception to the expectations as these three countries were rather socio-economically developed and had well-established states. On the other hand, they were also characterized by significant agrarian elites and the lack of a strong liberal tradition.

Allowing for the inclusion of easy counterfactuals in the reduction procedure provides a somewhat more parsimonious result:

---

5 Since the cases of France, Switzerland, Finland and Iceland are all covered by two expressions, the results are characterized by some degree of explanatory overdetermination, which explains why the values of partitioned coverage of the individual paths (shown in parentheses) do not total 100.

weagr*libheg* { RICH$_{(Austria,Italy+Germany)}$ (6%) +

auto$_{(Austria,Italy+Hungary,Portugal,Spain+Albania,Bulgaria,Greece,Lithuania,Poland,Romania,Yugoslavia)}$ (19%) +

state$_{(Albania,Bulgaria,Greece,Lithuania,Poland,Romania,Yugoslavia+Estonia,Latvia,USSR)}$ (19%) +

A strong gentry, and the absence of pre-war liberal hegemony in conjunction with *either* a consolidated state *or* political autonomy from religion, now constitute the two pathways with the highest partitioned coverage. In contrast, the combination of the two necessary conditions and high socio-economic development only contributes with unique coverage of one case, namely Germany.

Now, how do the findings relate to the hypotheses derived from the literature? H1 suggested that a powerful class of landholders was a necessary condition for democratic breakdown. The analysis corroborates this claim, and thus Moore's and Stephens' conclusion remains strong when tested for all European cases rather than for just a selection. Notice, furthermore, that they were also right in arguing that the presence of strong landlords was not a sufficient condition for autocratic victory.

H2 and H3, however, are not supported to the same degree. Based on Berglund and Aarebrot's work, the propositions stated that early state-building and religious subordination to political authority were necessary and jointly sufficient conditions for democratic survival, and that the absence of one of them was sufficient for democratic reversal. In contrast to the relationship predicted by Aarebrot and Berglund's framework, neither the lack of successful state-building nor the presence of a strong and religious leadership were sufficient for democratic collapse.[6] Moreover, the results also disprove the proposition that the mixture of a viable state and Protestantism/secularism was a sufficient safeguard against autocracy. On the other hand, successful experiences with state formation indeed turned out to be a prerequisite for democratic stability. This finding is in line with Nancy Bermeo's (1997: 19) observation that states with a sound institutional basis for providing civic order had an advantage when it came to the management of the economic crisis in the interwar period. Consequently, 'One of the reasons that virtually none of the older democracies in Europe collapsed was because their states had had the time to develop more effective institutions for facilitating civic order'.

Bermeo (1997: 15-16) also points out that systematic comparisons show how a harsh economic crisis was neither a sufficient nor necessary cause of democratic breakdown. The evidence leads her to reject the 'scarcity-madness connection'. But her analysis does not take into account the potential impact of the absolute level of socio-economic development stated in H4. Nevertheless, the results of this study do not point to wealth as a highly crucial factor as it was neither necessary nor sufficient in itself. To be fair, the proposition is often understood to be expressed in probabilistic terms, thereby implying that csQCA may not be the best method to apply. Therefore, I have carried out a discriminant analysis to examine whether the independent variables are useful predic-

---

6 At least if the conclusion is only grounded on theoretically and empirically informed (plausible) assumptions about unobserved variation.

tors of the dependent variable, that is, democracy or autocracy. In this way, we can also get a general impression of the results when a method based on a different set of assumptions is employed. The supplementary analysis (see Appendix 1) indicates that wealth (still) does not make a significant contribution, contrary to all the other explanatory variables. Thus, the conclusion derived from the principal findings is supported – or at least not rejected.

As regards the last hypothesis, H5, the findings do not confirm Luebbert's claim that a pre-war liberal hegemony was sufficient to reject autocracy. The formalized results reveal that this condition does not constitute a separate expression as it is combined with early state-building and wealth in the path covering France, Switzerland, Great Britain and Ireland. However, Luebbert probably assumed that these additional criteria were in place. Given the principal focus on Western Europe (cf. Luebbert 1991: 258-262), these criteria merely worked as scope conditions for his study. The hypothesis thus 'survives' if we take this qualification into consideration. What is more, the mirror image of the hypothesis finds support since the absence of liberal hegemony, prior to WWI, was a necessary condition for the collapse of democracies.

Will History Repeat Itself in a Third 'Reverse' Wave?

Freedom in the world, as measured by Freedom House standards and procedures, has now been in decline for the last five years (2006-2010). This trend of setbacks and resilience has actually made Arch Puddington (2008; 2009), Freedom House's director of research, pose an interesting question: Is the tide turning? In addressing this challenging question, I do not attempt to carry out another systematic empirical analysis. Rather, I discuss contemporary regime developments in the light of the findings from the historical analysis since knowledge about the consolidation of first-wave democracies could yield lessons for countries included in the third wave of democratization (Huntington 1991: 270). More particularly, the discussion addresses the issue of 'stateness' in fledgling democracies.

Among the vast studies on the consolidation of third-wave democracies, Juan Linz and Alfred Stepan's (1996) *Problems of Democratic Transition and Consolidation* stands out as one of the most acknowledged. When Stepan was asked what he thought was the book's main contribution, he answered, 'The idea that democracy is impossible without a "usable state"' (Munck and Snyder 2007: 422; cf. Linz and Stepan 1996: 7, 16-37). However, Linz and Stepan are not the only ones to have emphasized that stateness is a prerequisite for democracy – something that has just been shown to apply to interwar Europe. A few years before them, Rueschemeyer et al. (1992: 67) made the general theoretical point that 'Where the consolidation of [the] authority of the state is seriously in question, where it is challenged by armed conflict and where its reach is uncertain, democratic forms of rule are impossible'.

Recently, Francis Fukuyama (2004; 2005) has also emphasized the imperative of state-building, making a plea for a 'stateness first' approach to democracy promotion because, basically, you need a state before you can have democracy and economic development. However, according to Rose and Chin (2001), most countries in the third wave of democratization have democratized in a backwards manner: they have introduced competitive elections before establishing basic institutions of a modern state, and the outcome has been – at best – incomplete democracies. Bratton and Chang (2006), who focus exclusively on sub-Saharan Africa, have shown that new democracies emerge only in the context of relatively effective states.

This is bad news because weak and failed states exist in many developing and transformation countries. No less than 33 out of the 125 countries covered by the *Bertelsmann Transformation Index 2008* even have severe defects (scores of five or lower) in terms of at least one of the defining attributes of a modern national state: monopoly on the use of force, agreement about citizenship, and basic administrative structures.[7] These numbers indicate that a low degree of stateness was not just a problem in interwar Europe but continues to be a significant burden to democratic consolidation.

What is more, for several reasons this situation will most likely not improve much. First, after WWII there has been a noteworthy international agreement about the fixity of borders. Second, and consequently, contemporary wars have a different nature, with no external threat of annihilation in the form of violent state death, whereas domestic wars that tend to disintegrate states are widespread. Third, state-building is hampered by the availability of revenues from foreign aid and natural resources such as oil and minerals (Jackson and Rosberg 1982; Krasner 2005; Sørensen 2001; Tilly 1992: ch. 7). Fourth, the pre-colonial and post-colonial political cultures and structures of authority in many third world countries do not overlap neatly. This mismatch accounts for low levels of state legitimacy and, consequently, state capacity (Englebert 2000).

To be fair, the Asian 'tigers' have succeeded in establishing rather consolidated and well-functioning states (cf. Evans 1995; Doner et al. 2005), so the task is not impossible. Compared to most post-Soviet and post-Yugoslavian countries, the nation- and state-building processes in East-Central Europe under communist rule were rather successful. Importantly, the communist experience also put an end to large landowners and the political influence of religious leaders – the two other factors that constituted the dominant pathway to autocratic revival in Europe in the period from 1919 to 1939. Hence, in the light of history, these changes have increased the prospects for enduring democracy in this region. The influence of the European Union, a democracy-endorsing organization that emerged in the aftermath of WWII without any previous equivalent in European history (and the world for that matter), reinforces this expectation (cf. Vachudova 2005).

Some countries in Latin America, for example, Chile and Uruguay, and in South East Asia, for example, South Korea and Taiwan, also show high levels of stateness. However, the general picture is that the authority of the state is frequently undermined by local 'strongmen', such as *caciques, effendis, caudillos*, landlords, kulak-type rich peasants, moneylenders, and chiefs, who maintain alternative – and fundamentally undemocratic – organizational structures and garner the obedience of the population (Migdal

---

7 Indicating the number of countries placed in a 'risk zone', a relaxation of the criterion for severe defects with just one point (to six) would add another 43 to the group.

1988). In addition, it is more the rule rather than the exception that the state apparatus in developing countries is ridden with neo-patrimonial practices (e.g., Bratton and van de Walle 1997; Kitschelt and Wilkinson 2007). This means that even if a democratic breakthrough has been – or will be – achieved at the central level, the political autonomy and effectiveness of the state remain weak and the stabilization and deepening of democracy face a major barrier.

One cannot expect this problem to be counterbalanced by the kind of liberal political culture that characterized a number of European countries in the nineteenth and early twentieth centuries. A decades-long liberal hegemony seems to have been the product of circumstances that are improbable outside Western Europe and the British settler colonies (Australia, Canada, New Zealand and the USA). Even if free and fair elections have been established in countries without a strong democratic tradition, politics there tend to be personalized and populist rather than ideologically structured and mediated by party organizations rooted in a vibrant civil society (Mainwaring 1998).

On the other hand, the end of the Cold War struggle between the two superpowers introduced a new world order characterized by a liberal hegemony, at least partially, on the international scene (Levitsky and Way 2002: 61). First world countries (and organizations) have used both carrot and stick to promote democracy, and the efforts have not been without success (Burnell 2000). Nonetheless, it is more the rule than the exception that democracy assistance has a lower priority than economic and political interests such as a stable oil supply and the fight against terrorism. It is also less likely that positive and negative incentives offered by external powers have a deeper and more lasting impact than internally led changes (Welzel 2009); they even risk provoking the domestic elite and ordinary citizens into taken undemocratic countermeasures.

The current zeitgeist (democracy as the only legitimate form of rule) and conditionality imposed by the OECD countries mean that 'autocratization' is in most cases not an abrupt process, and that countries tend to slide into – or remain – minimalist democracy or soft 'electoral' authoritarianism rather than 'closed' authoritarianism (cf. Schedler 2002). That said, however, this could change, just as it did in interwar Europe, in the wake of economic crisis, the demise of liberalism, and the rise of counter-models exemplified by totalitarian ideologies and their respective 'frontrunner' regimes in Italy and Russia.

Conclusion

At the beginning of the interwar period, almost all European countries had (re)introduced the formal rights associated with democratic regimes. But at the end of this period, more than half, 16 out of 29, were under outright autocratic rule. In this study, five prominent hypotheses sharing two basic features have been identified and tested; these hypotheses have been elaborated to account for the different regime trajectories in interwar Europe and have focused on structural conditions.

Referring to the diversity of experiences and the multiplicity of theories, Huntington (1991: 38) has suggested the following five propositions concerning the causes of democratization: (1) no single factor is sufficient to explain the development of democracy in all countries or in a single country; (2) no single factor is necessary to the development of democracy in all countries; (3) democratization in each country is the result of a combination of causes; (4) the combination of causes producing democracy varies from country to country; (5) the combination of causes generally responsible for one wave of democratization differs from that responsible for other waves.[8] Notice that these statements only concern transitions to democracy and not democratic stability, which is the issue addressed in this article. Nonetheless, I use them as an outline to structure the summary of my findings.

As regards the question of sufficiency, none of the conditions found were sufficient for democratic stability or reversal in interwar Europe. Thus, Luebbert claim that a liberal hegemony before WWI in itself guaranteed democratic survival in this period was not sustained as it rested on assumptions about some of the other examined variables. However, the findings have indicated that the absence of such liberal hegemony was a necessary condition for the installation of autocratic regimes. This also applies to labor-repressive agriculture under the direction of large landowners (cf. Moore and Stephens), while a relatively high degree of stateness was necessary for democratic endurance (cf. Aarebrot and Berglund). In sum, the factors examined were strongly associated with the outcome in question, although in different ways than proposed in the hypotheses.

Logically, then, the paths to democratic survival and autocratic revival were characterized by combined conditions. The conjunction of early state-building, weak landlords and political autonomy covered no less than two-thirds of the survivor cases. Furthermore, covering all cases but one, the dominant pathways to autocratic victory emerged through a mixture of a lack of a liberal tradition, strong landlords, and either a weak state or a strong religious leadership. Thus, even though more routes to the outcomes existed, they not particular to individual cases as the countries tended to cluster into just a few.

The world of today's fledgling democracies is significantly different from the context of interwar Europe. Hence, identical causes of regime (in)stability should not be expected across time. However, the discussion has demonstrated that the issue of stateness is still of critical importance in the contemporary era, and that democracy does not gain a strong foothold in the presence of autonomous and undemocratic elite groups. As only few countries can rely on a liberal political culture, the absence of appealing alternatives to democracy in the form of counter-ideologies and counter-regimes appears crucial. Otherwise, a significant third wave of democratic reversal could take off.

As always, debates on the topics addressed in this study are still to be had. The inclusion of 29 cases and several explanatory variables in the present study cannot but leave more detailed aspects of the strategies of core political actors unexplored.[9] Accordingly,

---

8 Notice that these propositions only concern transitions to democracy and not democratic stability (consolidation), which is the issue addressed in this article.

9 For comparative actor-based analyses of regime developments in interwar Europe, see Linz (1978), Zimmermann and Saalfeld (1988), and Cappoccia (2001).

the obvious research agenda emerging from this study is a stringent theoretical integration of the most significant factors and an elaboration of the causal mechanisms linking the conditions to the outcomes.

Appendix A: Results of Discriminant Analysis

This appendix presents the results of a particular variant of statistical analysis, namely, a discriminant analysis. This secondary analysis of the structural explanations is carried out to investigate whether different and/or theoretically meaningful conclusions emerge from this kind of test. Generally, a multi-methods approach is warranted, for the following reason:

> If the area under investigation is best described by a general linear, additive logic, then conventional statistics ... is probably the most appropriate methodological tool, and if it is characterized by complex causality and sufficient and/or necessary explanations, the QCA methods have a strong standing because of their ability to handle set-theoretical propositions. ... In general it depends on the character of the phenomena under consideration whether it is more rewarding to see them as complementary or competitive alternatives. As we cannot determine the character of social phenomena a priori, we have to apply methods based on different assumptions and subsequently evaluate the plausibility of their respective results based on theoretical and substantial insight. (Skaaning cited in Rihoux and Ragin 2008: 172)

Among the statistical methods developed especially to handle a dichotomized dependent variable, we find logistic regression. But, as a rule of thumb, this technique based on maximum likelihood demands a case number over 200, and an attempt to employ it for the present research agenda did not generate any valuable results. In contrast, a discriminant analysis proved to be a more viable option.

Using the latter method, the variance accounted for by the model, including all five explanatory factors, is no less than 83 per cent. The results strongly indicate that the independent variables are useful for predicting membership in the two groups defined by the dependent variable (democracy versus autocracy) as the cross-validated classification accuracy – that is, based on the function derived from all cases other than the case in question – is significantly higher than the accuracy obtainable by chance alone. More concretely, the cross-validated classification only misclassified the cases of Czechoslovakia, Germany and Ireland. Among the independent variables, only GDP per capita does not achieve statistical significance. Finally, the net effects of the independent variables indicate their explanatory weights, suggesting that the relative importance of a weak landed elite and a liberal hegemony was somewhat higher than early state-building and Protestantism/secularism.

Table 2: Results from Discriminant Analysis

	Survival of democracy (Discriminant Analysis)
Constant	-2.395
Weak agrarian elite	2.777*** (0.812)
Early state-building	1.382** (0.515)
Protestant/secularized	1.195** (0.456)
Rich (GDP/cap.)	0.000 (-0.144)
Liberal hegemony	2.207*** (0.707)
Fit (1- Wilks' Lambda)	0.83
N	29

Note: Unstandardized function coefficients are reported with standardized function coefficients in parentheses – both refer to an analysis in which all independent variables are entered together. However, the significance levels refer to an application of the stepwise method. *significant at the 0.1 level; **significant at the 0.05 level; ***significant at the 0.01 level (one-tailed).

List of References

Aarebrot, Frank/Berglund, Sten (1995) 'Statehood, Secularization, Cooptation: Explaining Democratic Survival in Inter-War Europe – Stein Rokkan's Conceptual Map Revisited', *Historical Social Research* 2: 210-225.

Berg-Schlosser, Dirk/De Meur Gisèle (1994) 'Conditions of Democracy in Interwar Europe: A Boolean Test of Major Hypotheses', *Comparative Politics* 3): 253-279.

Berg-Schlosser, Dirk/Mitchell, Jeremy (2000) 'Introduction' in Berg-Schlosser, Dirk/Mitchell, Jeremy (eds.) *Conditions of Democracy in Europe, 1919-1939: Systematic Case Studies*, London: 1-39.

Berg-Schlosser, Dirk/Mitchell, Jeremy (eds.) (2002) Authoritarianism and Democracy in Europe, 1919-1939: Comparative Analyses, London.

Bermeo, Nancy (1997) 'Getting Mad or Going Mad? Citizens, Scarcity and the Breakdown of Democracy in Interwar Europe', *Center for the Study of Democracy* Working Paper 97-06.

Bermeo, Nancy (2003) Ordinary People in Extraordinary Times: The Citizenry and the Breakdown of Democracy, Princeton.

Bratton, Michael/van de Walle, Nicolas (1997) *Democratic Experiments in Africa*, Cambridge.

Bratton, Michael/Chang, Eric C. (2006) 'State Building and Democratization in Sub-Saharan Africa', *Comparative Political Studies* 9: 1059-1083.
Bunce, Valerie (2003) 'Rethinking Recent Democratization: Lessons from the Postcommunist Experience', *World Politics* 2: 167-192.
Burnell, Peter (ed.) (2000) Democracy Assistance: International Cooperation for Democratization, London.
Cappocia, Giovanni (2001) 'Defending Democracy: Reactions to Political Extremism in Inter-war Europe', *European Journal of Political Research* 4: 431-460.
Caramani, Daniele (2008) Introduction to the Comparative Method With Boolean Algebra, London.
Doner, Richard F./Ritchie, Bryan K./Slater, Dan (2005) 'Systemic Vulnerability and the Origins of Developmental States: Northeast and Southeast Asia in Comparative Perspective', *International Organization* 2: 327-361.
Englebert, Pierre (2000) 'Pro-Colonial Institutions, Post-Colonial States, and Economic Development in Tropical Africa', *Political Research Quarterly* 1: 1-20.
Ersson, Svante (1995) 'Revisiting Rokkan: On the Determinants of the Rise of Democracy in Europe', *Historical Social Research* 2: 161-187.
Ertman, Thomas (1998) 'Democracy and Dictatorship in Interwar Western Europe Revisited', *World Politics* 3: 475-505.
Evans, Peter (1995) Embedded Autonomy: States and Industrial Transformation, Princeton.
Fischer, Bernd J. (2007) 'King Zog, Albania's Interwar Dictator' in Fischer, Bernd J. (ed.) *Balkan Strongmen*, London: 19-50.
Fukuyama, Francis (2004) 'The Imperative of State-Building', *Journal of Democracy* 29: 17-31.
Fukuyama, Francis (2005) '"Stateness" First', *Journal of Democracy* 1: 84-88.
Goertz, Gary/Starr, Harvey (2003) 'Introduction: Necessary Condition Logics, Research Design, and Theory' in Goertz, Gary/Starr, Harvey (eds.) *Necessary Conditions: Theory, Methodology, and Applications*, Lanham: 1-24.
Huntington, Samuel P. (1991) The Third Wave: Democratization in the Late Twentieth Century, Norman.
Jackson, Robert H./Rosberg, Carl G. (1982) 'Why Africa's Weak States Persist: The Empirical and the Juridical in Statehood', *World Politics* 1: 1-24.
Kitschelt, Herbert (1992) 'Political Regime Change: Structure or Process-driven Explanations?', *American Political Science Review* 4: 1028-1034.
Kitschelt, Herbert/Wilkinson, Steven (2007) Patrons, Clients, and Policies: Patterns of Democratic Accountability and Political Competition, Cambridge.
Krasner, Stephen (2005) 'The Case for Shared Sovereignty', *Journal of Democracy* 1: 69-83.
Levitsky, Steven/Way, Lucan (2002) 'The Rise of Competitive Authoritarianism', *Journal of Democracy* 2: 51-65.
Linz, Juan J. (1978) Crisis, Breakdown, and Reequilibration, Baltimore.
Linz, Juan J./Stepan, Alfred (1996) Problems of Democratic Transition and Consolidation: Southern Europe, South America, and Post-Communist Europe, Baltimore.
Lipset, Seymour M (1959) 'Some Social Requisites of Democracy', *American Political Science Review* 1: 69-105.
Lipset, Seymour M. (1983) 'Radicalism of Reformism: The Sources of Working-class Politics', *American Political Science Review* 1: 1-19.
Luebbert, Gregory (1987) 'Social Foundations of Political Order in Interwar Europe', *World Politics* 4: 449-478.

Luebbert, Gregory (1991) Liberalism, Fascism or Social Democracy: Social Classes and the Political Origins of Regimes in Interwar Europe, Oxford.
Mainwaring, Scott (1998) 'Party Systems in the Third Wave', *Journal of Democracy* 3: 67-81.
Marx, Axel (2006) 'Towards More Robust Model Specification in QCA: Results from a Methodological Experiment', *COMPASS Working Paper* 2006-43.
Migdal, Joel (1988) *Strong Societies and Weak States*, Princeton.
Moore, Barrington (1991)[1966] *Social Origins of Dictatorship and Democracy*, Houndmills.
Munck, Gerardo/Snyder, Richard (2007) *Passion, Craft, and Method in Comparative Politics*, Baltimore.
Pollo, Stefanaq/Puto, Arben (1981) *The History of Albania*, London.
Puddington, Arch (2008) 'Is the Tide Turning?', *Journal of Democracy* 2: 61-73.
Puddington, Arch (2009) 'Freedom in the World 2009: Setbacks and Resilience', in http://www.freedomhouse.org/uploads/fiw09/FIW09_OverviewEssay_Final.pdf [accessed on March 27, 09].
Ragin, Charles (1987) The Comparative Method: Moving Beyond Qualitative and Quantitative Strategies, Berkeley.
Ragin, Charles (2008) Redesigning Social Inquiry: Fuzzy Sets and Beyond, Princeton.
Rihoux, Benoit (2008) 'Crisp-Set Qualitative Comparative Analysis (csQCA)' in Rihoux, Benoit/Ragin, Charles (eds.) *Configurational Comparative Methods*, London: 33-68.
Rihoux, Benoit/Ragin, Charles (2008) 'Conclusions – The Way(s) Ahead' in Rihoux, Benoit/Ragin, Charles (eds.) *Configurational Comparative Methods*, London: 167-178.
Rokkan, Stein (1975) 'Dimensions of State Formation and Nation-Building: A Possible Paradigm for Research on Variations within Europe' in Tilly, Charles (ed.) *The Formation of National States in Europe*, Princeton: 562-600.
Rokkan, Stein/Urwin, Derek (1983) Economy, Territory, Identity: Politics of Western European Peripheries, London.
Rose, Richard/Shin, Doh Chull (2001) 'Democratization Backwards: The Problem of Third-Wave Democracies', *British Journal of Political Science* 2: 331-354.
Rothschild, Joseph (1974) East Central Europe between the Two World Wars, Seattle.
Rueschemeyer, Dietrich/Stephens, John/Huber Stephens, Evelyne (1992) *Capitalist Development and Democracy*, Cambridge.
Schedler, Andreas (2002) 'The Menu of Manipulation', *Journal of Democracy* 2: 36-50.
Schneider, Carsten/Wagemann, Claudius (2007) Qualitative Comparative Analysis and Fuzzy Sets: Ein Lehrbuch für Anwender, und jene die es werden wollen, Opladen.
Skocpol, Theda (1973) 'A Critical Review of Barrington Moore's Social Origins of Dictatorship and Democracy', *Politics and Society* 1: 1-34.
Stephens, John (1989) 'Democratic Transition and Breakdown in Western Europe, 1870-1939: A Test of the Moore Thesis', *American Journal of Sociology* 5: 1019-1076.
Sørensen, Georg (2001) 'War and State-Making: Why Doesn't It Work in the Third World', *Security Dialogue* 3: 341-354.
Tilly, Charles (1992) Coercion, Capital, and European States, AD 990-1992, Cambridge.
Vachudova, Milada (2005) Europe Undivided: Democracy, Leverage and Integration After Communism, Oxford.
Vickers, Miranda (1999) *The Albanians: A Modern History*, New York.
Wagemann, Claudius/Schneider, Carsten (2008) 'Standards of Good Practice in Qualitative Comparative Analysis (QCA) and Fuzzy Sets', COMPASSS Working Paper 2007-51.
Weber, Max 1964[1922] *Wirtschaft und Gesellschaft*, Köln.

Welzel, Christian (2009) 'Theories of Democratization' in Haerpfer, Christian/Bernhagen, Patrick/ Inglehart, Ronald/ Welzel, Christian (eds.) *Democratization*, Oxford: 74-91.

Zimmermann, Ekkart/Saalfeld, Thomas (1988) 'Economic and Political Reactions to the World Economic Crisis of the 1930s in Six European Countries', *International Studies Quarterly* 3: 305-334.

Neu im Programm Politikwissenschaft

Blanke, Bernhard / Nullmeier, Frank / Reichard, Christoph / Wewer, Göttrik (Hrsg.)
Handbuch zur Verwaltungsreform
4., akt. u. erg. Aufl. 2011. XXI, 616 S. Br.
EUR 49,95
ISBN 978-3-531-17546-1

Das Handbuch liefert einen Beitrag zur Einordnung unterschiedlicher Konzepte und Orientierung für die Umsetzung der Verwaltungsreform. In 66 Beiträgen werden vielfältige Ansätze der Verwaltungsreform vorgestellt, ihr Entstehungszusammenhang erläutert, praktische Anwendungsfelder beschrieben und Entwicklungsperspektiven untersucht. Die Beiträge stammen von renommierten WissenschaftlerInnen und erfahrenen PraktikerInnen. Themenblöcke: Staat und Verwaltung, Reform- und Managementkonzepte, Steuerung und Organisation, Personal, Finanzen, Ergebnisse und Wirkungen, Erfahrungen und Perspektiven.

Boeckh, Jürgen / Huster, Ernst-Ulrich / Benz, Benjamin
Sozialpolitik in Deutschland
Eine systematische Einführung
3., grundl. überarb. u. erw. Aufl. 2011.
491 S. Br. EUR 22,95
ISBN 978-3-531-16669-8

Der Band führt systematisch in das breite Spektrum von Geschichte, Strukturen, Problemlagen, Lösungswegen und die europäischen Zusammenhänge von Sozialpolitik in Deutschland sowie in die Theorie des Sozialstaates ein. Der besseren Verständlichkeit dienen ausführliche geschichtliche Dokumente und aktuelle Daten zur sozialen Entwicklung bzw. zur Sozialpolitik. Gibt es Grenzen des Sozialstaates? Diesen sucht sich der Band im geschichtlichen Rückgriff auf die Weimarer Republik systematisch und sozialräumlich zu nähern.

Dingwerth, Klaus / Blauberger, Michael / Schneider, Christian
Postnationale Demokratie
Eine Einführung am Beispiel von EU, WTO und UNO
2011. 236 S. (Grundwissen Politik) Br.
EUR 24,95
ISBN 978-3-531-17490-7

Internationale Organisationen stehen im Zentrum der Diskussion über das „Demokratiedefizit" internationaler Politik. Während politische Entscheidungen zunehmend auf internationaler Ebene getroffen werden, zweifeln Kritiker immer wieder an der Legitimation dieser Entscheidungen. Das Buch führt ein in die Diskussion über demokratisches Regieren „jenseits des Staates", es stellt die Funktionsweise von EU, WTO und UNO vor und diskutiert, inwieweit das Regieren in diesen Organisationen demokratischen Grundsätzen genügt bzw. wie sich Demokratiedefizite beheben lassen.

Erhältlich im Buchhandel oder beim Verlag.
Änderungen vorbehalten. Stand: Juli 2011.

www.vs-verlag.de

VS VERLAG

Abraham-Lincoln-Straße 46
65189 Wiesbaden
tel +49 (0)6221.345 - 4301
fax +49 (0)6221.345 - 4229

Elemente der Politik

Hrsg. von Bernhard Frevel / Klaus Schubert / Suzanne S. Schüttemeyer / Hans-Georg Ehrhart

Blum, Sonja / Schubert, Klaus
Politikfeldanalyse
2., akt. Aufl. 2011. 198 S. Br. EUR 16,95
ISBN 978-3-531-17276-7

Dehling, Jochen / Schubert, Klaus
Ökonomische Theorien der Politik
2011. 178 S. Br. EUR 16,95
ISBN 978-3-531-17113-5

Dobner, Petra
Neue Soziale Frage und Sozialpolitik
2007. 158 S. Br. EUR 12,90
ISBN 978-3-531-15241-7

Frantz, Christiane / Martens, Kerstin
Nichtregierungsorganisationen (NGOs)
2006. 159 S. Br. EUR 14,90
ISBN 978-3-531-15191-5

Frevel, Bernhard
Demokratie
Entwicklung – Gestaltung – Problematisierung
2., überarb. Aufl. 2009. 177 S. Br. EUR 12,90
ISBN 978-3-531-16402-1

Fuchs, Max
Kulturpolitik
2007. 133 S. Br. EUR 14,90
ISBN 978-3-531-15448-0

Jahn, Detlef
Vergleichende Politikwissenschaft
2011. 124 S. Br. EUR 12,95
ISBN 978-3-531-15209-7

Jaschke, Hans-Gerd
Politischer Extremismus
2006. 147 S. Br. EUR 14,95
ISBN 978-3-531-14747-5

Johannsen, Margret
Der Nahost-Konflikt
2., akt. Aufl. 2009. 167 S. Br. EUR 16,95
ISBN 978-3-531-16690-2

Kevenhörster, Paul / Boom, Dirk van den
Entwicklungspolitik
2009. 112 S. Br. EUR 12,90
ISBN 978-3-531-15239-4

Kost, Andreas
Direkte Demokratie
2008. 116 S. Br. EUR 12,90
ISBN 978-3-531-15190-8

Meyer, Thomas
Sozialismus
2008. 153 S. Br. EUR 12,90
ISBN 978-3-531-15445-9

Schmitz, Sven-Uwe
Konservativismus
2009. 170 S. Br. EUR 16,90
ISBN 978-3-531-15303-2

Erhältlich im Buchhandel oder beim Verlag.
Änderungen vorbehalten. Stand: Juli 2011.

www.vs-verlag.de

VS VERLAG

Abraham-Lincoln-Straße 46
65189 Wiesbaden
tel +49 (0)6221.345 - 4301
fax +49 (0)6221.345 - 4229

GPSR Compliance

The European Union's (EU) General Product Safety Regulation (GPSR) is a set of rules that requires consumer products to be safe and our obligations to ensure this.

If you have any concerns about our products, you can contact us on

ProductSafety@springernature.com

In case Publisher is established outside the EU, the EU authorized representative is:

Springer Nature Customer Service Center GmbH
Europaplatz 3
69115 Heidelberg, Germany

www.ingramcontent.com/pod-product-compliance
Lightning Source LLC
LaVergne TN
LVHW010339260326
834688LV00036B/780